P9-BBT-372

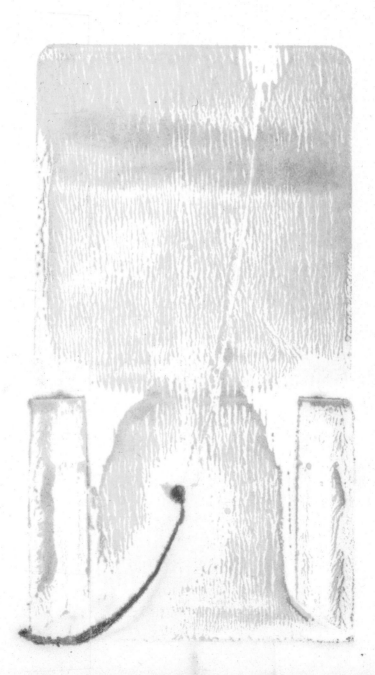

How to Father

How to Father

Dr. Fitzhugh Dodson

Edited by Jeanne Harris

With a Foreword by
Richard A. Gardner, M.D.

Cartoons by
Al Lowenheim

Nash Publishing, Los Angeles

Library of Congress Catalog Card Number: 73-83527
International Standard Book Number: 0-8402-1301-8

Published simultaneously in the United States and Canada
by Nash Publishing Corporation, 9255 Sunset Boulevard,
Los Angeles, California 90069

Printed in the United States of America

First Printing

To my children,
Robin, Randy and Rusty,
who taught me a great deal
about how to father.

Acknowledgments

To these people, my special thanks:

As with my first book, *How to Parent,* I am again impressed that any book is the product of the thought and work of many people. I want to express my special thanks to those persons who have contributed in one way or another to the writing of this book.

I am grateful to the thousands of psychologists and behavioral scientists throughout the world who have studied children and their parents and upon whose experimental and clinical research I have drawn in this book. In particular, I owe a great debt of gratitude to Dr. Arnold Gesell, Dr. Frances Ilg, Dr. Louise Bates Ames, and their associates for their classical developmental studies of children.

I am aware that Dr. Gesell's studies have been criticized as being based on a relatively small sample of middle-class children in and around New Haven, Connecticut. His critics point out that it is difficult to generalize to rural children in Mississippi or ghetto children in Harlem on the basis of the Gesell studies.

While there are aspects of the development of children in other social classes and other regions of the country which are quite different from the findings of the Gesell studies, there are other ways in which the age profiles derived from Gesell's careful and meticulous observations fit quite adequately other children from quite different backgrounds. For example, I found I could predict reasonably accurately from Gesell's studies of the four-year-old what four-year-old black children in California Head Start classes were like. The point is that the Gesell studies represent years of painstaking empirical work, and we would be infinitely poorer in our knowledge of children's growth and development without them.

I have found the studies to be of inestimable help in my clinical work with children and parents, and it will be obvious to the attentive reader that I have drawn heavily upon them. However, at the same time I have tried to bring them up to date by indicating how much more sophisticated today's children have become since the time the Gesell studies were done.

I am grateful also to the children and their parents who have taught me a great deal in the course of my twenty years of clinical practice. However, as I have already expressed in my dedication, I have probably learned the most about how to father from my own three children: Robin, Randy, and Rusty.

Three people have been especially helpful to me in the writing of this book. First and foremost, Jeanne Harris, my editor, who as an expert in changing twenty-six-word sentences into seventeen-word sentences, has earned the gratitude of every reader. Second, Richard Gardner, M.D., who not only wrote the foreword but aided me enormously by a careful reading of the manuscript and thought-provoking discussions with me. Third, Al Lowenheim, who illustrated the book, because he has expressed so delightfully in cartoon form what I have said in written form.

I also want to express my sincere gratitude to all who have enabled the original rough manuscript to grow into the completed book. To Lee Morris, for service above and beyond the proverbial call of duty as my secretary; to Bill McLaughlin, Jim Burns, M.D., and Scott Putnam, who read the original manuscript and made helpful suggestions; to Carol McMullen and Harold Guttormsen, who helped with the annotated bibliography of children's books in Appendix C; to Miriam Sherman, who gave generously of her time and expertise in the preparation of the listing of children's records in Appendix D; to Ron Gagliardi for aiding in the creation of the cartoon ideas for the book.

Finally, to Sylvia Cross, my executive editor at Nash Publishing, who has helped me at various times, according to my needs, as editor, Dutch Uncle, and quasi-therapist, my sincere thanks.

I am profoundly grateful to all of these people. Without them I would not have written this book.

Fitzhugh Dodson
Redondo Beach, California
Spring 1973

Contents

Foreword

We are living at a time when, more than ever before in recent generations, the father's vital role in the child-rearing process is beginning to be valued. Not only have women been denied opportunities in the traditionally male realms, but men as well have been taught to believe that too much involvement in the upbringing of their children is somehow unmanly and likely to compromise their masculinity.

Although much progress is being made toward giving women their due in the extradomestic realm, there has been less emphasis on changes in the male role that will be necessary if men are to fulfill themselves in the domestic area. This book, so far as I know the first written specifically for the child-rearing father (almost unconsciously, many writers of such manuals have composed them with the mother in mind), is meant to fill a vacuum that has existed too long and that should long ago have been filled.

Dr. Dodson well appreciates that parents, regardless of their sex, are not born with an inner knowledge of how to raise a child. Puberty brings with it only the capacity to *bear* a child, not the knowledge of how to rear it.

In our society, little girls, through emulation of their mothers, learn far more about child rearing than little boys. Thus the need for a book like this to compensate for this unfortunate defect in the little boy's educational experience. Hopefully, in future generations in which fathers will take a more active role in raising their children, there will be less of a need for such supplementary instruction. It is hard for me to imagine a time, however, when no extra education will be necessary; for parental identification alone cannot fully provide the child with all the information he will need when his or her own time comes to assume a parental role.

Dr. Dodson correctly points out in addition, that valuable as instruction may be, it must be used in combination with the basic love of the parents for their child (moments of resentment and frustration notwithstanding) if he is to thrive. The book cannot replace love; but it can do much toward helping a loving father raise his children so that they may become better functioning adults.

Although this book was written primarily for the married father, Dr. Dodson appreciates as well the immensely important role of the mother. Although she is not often specifically mentioned here, she is very much present—contributing vitally to the child's upbringing. Divorced and widowed fathers who have been left with the full responsibility of child raising will also find this book to be rich in the information it provides about normal development. A parent may feel ill equipped to decide whether to attempt to alter a particular behavioral manifestation unless he knows whether or not it is normal behavior for most children. Most readers will be reassured that the usual development of a child is characteristically filled with periods of irrationality, unpredictability, inappropriate hostility, and primitive behavior—often of the most bizarre form.

But Dr. Dodson goes further than just reassuring the father that the child's irrationality is to be expected and that much of it must be tolerated and lived through. He explains the underlying *rationality* of the child's seeming irrationality, and then makes specific suggestions based on this understanding. I have found this to be a most valuable and useful aspect of the book.

Throughout, Dr. Dodson emphasizes the importance of sympathetic understanding of the child's inner thoughts and feelings: the importance of trying to put oneself in the child's position and of seeing things from his vantage point and trying to help the child verbalize his reactions. Such parental empathy is essential to the child's healthy psychological development. Dr. Dodson understands as well that mere encouragement of the child to express his feelings— valuable as that is—may not be enough. Often the child has to be encouraged to *do* something with the expressed feelings—something that will bring about some alteration or alleviation of the problem that may have engendered the unpleasant suppressed feelings in the first place.

This is not merely a theoretical book. It is filled with illustrative material from Dr. Dodson's own life, his family, and his extensive clinical experience. His anecdotal material is presented in a warm and open fashion that enhances the book's readability. A discussion of adolescent behavior—especially regarding sexual activity and involvement with drugs—is particularly good and, without question, most timely.

Dr. Dodson's views on a host of other aspects of child rearing are worthy of the father's serious consideration. I was especially impressed with his discussions of "spoiling," the difference between spanking and beating, the importance of the nursery-school experience, the so-called "latency period," the vital experience of time alone together, noncensorship of television viewing, and his "natural-consequences" principle of discipline.

I know of no book on raising a child with such extensive and useful appendices. Parents, teachers, guidance counselors, therapists and anyone else involved with children will find a wealth of valuable information here regarding books, records, and toys for children of all ages.

I end this discussion, however, with a warning. There is so much information in this book that the father may find it somewhat overwhelming; he may feel guilty and that he is neglecting his child if he doesn't do most, if not all, the things described here. This is not, I am sure, Dr. Dodson's intent. Rather, he would like his reader to know that there is much here that can be of interest and of use to him, and that the best thing a father can do is to read its pages, and then relax and enjoy his children. He would like the father to use what he has learned in this book, naturally, in the normal course of his relationship with his children. He would like the father's attitude to be: "It's good to have read it, and it's good to know it's there when I'll be needing it again."

Richard A. Gardner, M.D.
Associate in Child Psychiatry
College of Physicians and Surgeons
Columbia University
New York City

Preface

I have written this book for several different groups of people: First, for married fathers; this is the general psychological point of view of the book. But divorced fathers, for whom there is a special chapter in the book, are not neglected. They, no less than married fathers, need to know the psychological stages of a child's development.

Even though the book is written from the father's point of view, mothers should find it helpful too. My earlier book, *How to Parent*, was written mainly from the mother's point of view and concentrated on the first five years of life. Although this book, like *How to Parent*, also starts with the child at birth, it concentrates on the psychological stages of development from age six through age twenty-one. If you are the mother of a seven-year-old, for example, you, no less than your husband, need to have valid information about this stage of development.

Since there is such a generation gap today between parents and their teen-agers, I have devoted a great deal of space to early and late adolescence. Both mothers and fathers need to know this material.

I have up-dated the five-part appendix of *How to Parent,* and taken it up to adolescence, as well as including new books, toys, and records in the preschool years that have come out since *How to Parent* was published.

So please do not think of this book as being directed only to the married father. Married fathers, divorced fathers, married mothers, divorced mothers—I wrote it for all of you. I hope you find it helpful.

If you want to address questions, criticisms, or comments to me, I will welcome them. Please write to me c/o my publisher, Nash Publishing Company, 9255 Sunset Blvd., Los Angeles, California, 90069.

How to Father

1
Fathering

My first experience of fathering occurred many years before I actually became a father.

It was as a counselor at a boy's summer camp in West Virginia that I first coped with the management of young children. My responsibilities included ten active, energetic, rambunctious boys between the 'ages of five and seven. No previous experience or training had prepared me for this kind of fathering.

I knew nothing about child psychology. Given a test and asked to describe the difference between a five- and a six- and a seven-year-old boy, I would have flunked miserably. The psychological methods of effective child discipline were as remote from me as the surface of the planet Mars.

The only intelligent thing I did for the first few weeks of camp was to take the boys on a long, long hike every afternoon. The fresh air and vigorous exercise always insured that they would be tired and go to sleep promptly at night!

A few weeks of feeling completely inadequate sent me scurrying over to the library at West Virginia University. Frantically I began reading books on child psychology. This was extraordinarily helpful in enabling me to understand the behavior of the boys and how to deal with it.

Unfortunately, most new parents know as little about children as I did when I worked as a camp counselor. My clinical impression is that both mothers and fathers start out equally ignorant about babies and small children. Mothers eventually learn something about them by sheer trial and error. Fathers are not even that fortunate.

And that's where the tragedy lies.

Fatherhood was meant to be a deeply satisfying experience. Few things are more rewarding emotionally than the delight a man gets from satisfactorily guiding his children from birth through their various stages of development until they are off on their own.

But a child is a complex being. Approximately ten billion brain cells are stored inside the head of a child. This is an infinitely more complex assemblage of units than is to be found in the most intricate high-speed computer.

How can a father possibly find much joy and emotional satisfaction in guiding this complex human being from infancy to adulthood if nobody gives him any instructions? Society does not train men for fatherhood before they become fathers. Nor do they get on-the-job training afterwards.

In these rapidly changing times it is much more difficult for a father to define and fulfill his role.

Contrast the role of the father twenty-five years ago with the role of today's father. Twenty-five years ago masculine and feminine behavior and the roles of father and mother were quite clear-cut. Today, masculine and feminine social behavior and the family roles of mother and father are undergoing a tremendous shift. No one can yet predict what final form these roles will take when they become stabilized. The Women's Liberation movement is merely one indication of the vast upheaval that is going on in our society.

Twenty-five years ago fathers prepared their sons for an adult life which was similar to their own. Due to the fantastic rapidity with which our culture is changing, this is no longer true.

Scientists who study social change tell us that of the 100 children you see playing in an elementary-school playground, 50 will eventually work at jobs which do not even exist today! Fathers can no longer prepare their children for an adult life similar to their own because society will have changed too much by the time their youngsters grow up.

One simple example of culture change is grade-school homework. Twenty-five years ago a father had little difficulty in helping his children with their homework. Schools still taught the same basic concepts that he had learned. The school curriculum, like the culture, remained fairly constant. But due to the "information explosion," the rapid rate at which we are acquiring new knowledge about our world, today's school curricula are in a process of constant change. We have "new math" and "new English" and "new sciences." And these are only the first of the "new" subjects that will be taught in our school curriculum. Today's father may need to go to school for a parent's course in new math before he can help his sixth grader with his homework!

Guiding a teen-age boy or girl through adolescence is much harder today than it was twenty-five years ago. At that time, father and mother were still respected as authorities, as were school teachers, administrators, policemen, and elected officials. Teen-agers today are skeptical of age as a qualification for authority. Their cry is: "Don't trust anyone over 30." So today's father needs a better basis for relating to his teen-agers than simply being older.

Present-day teen-agers are exposed to potential dangers which simply did not exist before. Probably the chief problem is drugs. Fathers must recognize the fact that teen-age sons or daughters are exposed every day to the contemporary drug culture. They must teach children to confront a bewildering variety of new experiences that future decades will hold.

Fulfilling your role as a father in these troubled times is no easy task—particularly without any training!

Of course, you can go at your job the way many fathers do, simply by trial and error. But there are better ways, and that's what this book is all about.

No one is born a good father. To be a good father is a matter of patience, study, and love. But it is also a matter of *information!* It's important to learn everything you can about two basic subjects: child psychology and teaching methods.

Every father, whether he is aware of it or not, functions as a child psychologist. He must understand the psychology of his children in order to guide them wisely. If he doesn't know the vast psychological difference between a three- and a four-year-old, how can he possibly discipline the two ages in an intelligent fashion?

Information about teaching methods is vital because parents are the most important teachers children have. Before your child ever sets foot in school, you and your wife are his first teachers. Even after school begins he will still learn the most important and lasting "lessons" of his life at home.

A great deal of information about child psychology and successful teaching methods has accumulated through scientific research. A good father needs a working knowledge of this information.

This book will obviously not increase the love you have for your child. If you didn't love your child, you would not be bothering to read these words. But we need to distinguish between love of a child, and information which enables you lovingly to guide your youngster.

This is a good place to stop and say a few words about parental guilt. Too many books on child raising have the effect of making parents feel guilty about whether or not they are doing or not doing the things they read about. I certainly don't want this book to have that effect on you. But if you are the father of a three-year-old or a seven-year-old or a thirteen-year-old, and you read this book, you might end up saying to yourself, "I guess I really goofed when Ronnie was younger. I handled him this way and the book says I should have handled him differently." Then you may start feeling at fault and blaming yourself.

I hope you won't do that. Feeling guilty is not something that makes you into a better parent. No parent deserves blame. All of us need to take the attitude that we are doing the best we can in raising our children. Considering the fact that most of us have absolutely no training in parenting, I think we do a remarkably good job!

The way we learn anything new—from playing bridge to flying an airplane or playing golf—is by first making mistakes, literally thousands of mistakes, and by learning from them. You don't feel guilty because you can't play golf like the pro at the club after your third lesson. In the same way, you needn't feel guilty that you have to learn to be a good parent by first making mistakes. I have certainly made thousands of mistakes in raising my three children. One of the reasons I've written this book is so that you can at least avoid making some of my mistakes!

I have tried to cram the book (and the five-part appendix) with

suggestions for the many many things you can do with your children, things that will enrich and deepen the relationship between you, and enable you to get more joy out of being a father. The reason I included so many activities is to give you a wide range of choices. Some activities will appeal to one father, others to another. But no one father could possibly do all of the things I have mentioned in this book, so please don't feel guilty that you can't! And, remember! Being a good father is determined by the quality rather than the quantity of time you spend with your children.

In *How to Father* we will follow a hypothetical child in his development from infancy through adolescence, describing how you can guide him at each stage of psychological development. Since the behavior of boys and girls is quite different at various stages, we will take each in turn and explore your role as a father in the development of each sex.

For the sake of clarity, I will describe developmental changes in only one child. (However, from time to time, I will talk about brothers and sisters and the effects they have on each other and the family.) If you happen to be the father of four or five children you will need to make the appropriate adjustments in your mind as you read!

When describing the psychological growth and development of our hypothetical child, it would be cumbersome to keep writing "he-or-she-whichever-the-case-may-be." So for convenience, I'm going to refer to the child as "he." If you have a little girl, you can mentally read "she" in the appropriate places.

FATHERS GET PREGNANT, TOO!

Fatherhood actually begins when your wife first determines that she is pregnant. She will go through numerous physiological changes in the nine months prior to the birth of your baby. These physiological changes trigger drastic psychological changes in her as well. She may become moody, or irrational, or suddenly demanding. She may burst into tears over what seems to you nothing at all. Her behavior may confuse and bewilder you. It is important for you to realize that *all these things are quite normal for a pregnant woman.*

In the same way that you need to make allowances for psychological changes in your wife during her monthly period, you need to make allowances for psychological changes during pregnancy. Don't expect her behavior to be the same as when she is not pregnant.

Understanding these psychological changes is especially important to those men whose wives become pregnant a few months after they are married. Sometimes a new husband, confronted with the bewildering psychological behavior of his pregnant wife, thinks to himself: "Is this what it's like to be married? If so, forget it!" He does not realize that since his mate became pregnant so soon he has had little opportunity to find out how she is going to act psychologically as a wife. All he sees is her psychological behavior as a *pregnant* wife.

Try to be tolerant and understanding of any psychological quirks your wife exhibits during her pregnancy. It will mean a great deal to her if you are able to listen to her troubles and woes during that time.

Before discussing your role as a father in the first stage of your baby's development, two other points need to be made: First, although this book will give you information about the psychological aspects of fatherhood, there is also the practical mechanics of parenthood, such as how to hold a baby and change a diaper. If you have never been a father before, you need to learn these important details, from demonstrations and role playing. For the practical mechanics of parenthood enroll in a Red Cross class for expectant parents.

Second, there are some aspects of parenthood that can be handled equally well by either a mother or a father. For instance, if a baby is bottle fed it makes little difference whether he is fed by his mother or his father. There is no "male" or "female" way of bottle feeding a baby. Either parent may perform this task, depending on which one has the available time.

My earlier book, *How to Parent,* covered the period of parenthood during the first five years of a child's life. Much of what was written applied to both mothers and fathers. Rather than repeat material from *How to Parent,* I will occasionally refer to sections of that book to illustrate a point.

But there are other aspects of being a parent where the feminine role of the mother is different from the masculine role of the father. The two sexes are not interchangeable. A growing child needs a model for feminine behavior and a model for masculine behavior. *One parent cannot possibly play both roles.* Some aspects of father-

"I HAVE TO KEEP TELLING MYSELF THAT THIS IS *NORMAL FOR* A *PREGNANT WOMAN.*"

hood are interchangeable with similar aspects of motherhood. But certain phases are unique to the father and only he can play this part of the parental role. If he fails to fulfill this role, his wife cannot take over and do the job no matter how good a mother she is.

Now let's turn to the first stage of the psychological development of your child and your role in it: the stage of infancy.

2
Infancy

"Congratulations, Mr. Jones, it's a girl!"

Fatherhood is going to have a different meaning for each man who hears these words. One will feel great when he gets the news; another will worry, wondering if he will be able to do a good job as a father. One man will like children and will have had a good deal of experience with them; another will not particularly care for children and will intend to spend little time with them. For one father the birth of this baby will be something he and his wife have been planning and looking forward to for several years; for another, the pregnancy was an accident which he and his wife have reluctantly accepted.

The reactions of a man to the news that he will become a father for the first time are determined by his own childhood experiences and his relationship with his father and mother. Not only is the meaning of fatherhood different for each man, but for each some of this meaning is conscious and some unconscious. In other words, you may not be fully aware of some of your reactions to the news of your impending fatherhood. Therefore I want to emphasize a quite typical reaction.

When mother and child come home from the hospital things are radically different from before. Previously, the husband enjoyed 100 percent of his wife's love and attention. Now he finds her spending much of her time on the new arrival. Suddenly, in his unconscious mind, it is as if he were no longer a husband to his wife nor father to his child. Instead, his feelings are projected back to his own childhood. His wife is now his mother and the new baby is a younger brother or sister. He is unaware of these feelings, of course; they take place in his unconscious.

Unaware as he may be, these feelings produce changes in the father's behavior. Instead of relating to his new baby in the role of a father, he unconsciously considers him a rival. He criticizes his wife for spending too much time with the baby, and they begin to quarrel over trifles. His bewildered wife wonders what has suddenly gone wrong with their marriage.

A young lawyer, whose first child was a girl, had been happily married for several years before the arrival of the baby. But after she was born his marriage became quite stormy, and the couple came to me for counseling. One of the things the lawyer learned was that the birth of his little girl had triggered in his unconscious mind deeply repressed angry feelings about the birth of his younger sister. He hated his sister because he felt his parents preferred her to him. As he began to understand this through counseling, he was able to relate to his little girl as she really was, and not as a stand-in (or substitute figure) for the sister of his own childhood.

So if you are annoyed by the attention your wife pays to your baby, or if you find it difficult to get really interested in your child, consider the possibility that the birth of your baby could have triggered off in your unconscious the feelings that you had at the birth of a brother or sister during your own childhood. These feelings are almost universally held and hidden, because they are not acceptable to the adults whose love you need.

Many fathers also shy away from children when they are young because deep down they feel it isn't masculine to hold a little baby. This is not a true feeling, of course. A man should feel fully at ease with a young baby. In fact, the man most sure of himself is most likely to hold and play with a tiny baby without feeling self-conscious.

"HOWARD HASN'T QUITE ADJUSTED TO DIAPER CHANGING YET"

A father may feel inadequate around an infant and shy away; but feelings of inadequacy when dealing with something new are normal, and most fathers know very little about young babies. We all feel inadequate when doing something physically for the first time such as riding a bike, playing the piano, or hitting a golf ball. Holding a newborn baby is no exception. Inadequate and awkward at first, we quickly learn how to hold the baby more easily and comfortably.

Avoid the mistake so many fathers make. Don't wait until your child is older before you get involved with him. Do it as soon as he is born. You simply cannot develop strong feelings for a child with whom you have never had close physical contact—a child you have never held in your arms or fed or given a bath.

"Getting involved" means learning to do the variety of everyday things such as feeding, changing diapers, giving a bath, etc.

Now hold on, father, don't get your back up! This doesn't mean you should take over as soon as you get home from work and act as a substitute full-time mother. But, at times, you should include in your day doing these simple things with your baby.

It will not take long, especially at first, since new babies spend most of their time sleeping. But these experiences will matter tremendously to *you* in developing a close emotional relationship. Don't postpone your fatherhood until the baby is older and has learned to walk or talk. Start right in with the tiny tyke. Pick him up. You won't hurt him. Feed him. Talk to him. Hold him. Play with him.

It is important for you to start your relationship with your child early, *because the first five years of his life are the most important ones.*

By six years his basic personality structure has been formed, and this determines, to a large extent, what kind of an adolescence he will have, how successful he will be in his adult life, what kind of a woman he will marry, and how happy and lasting that marriage will be.

Not only are the first five years crucial for a child's emotional growth; they are critical for his intellectual growth as well. Children develop approximately 50 percent of their intelligence by age four, another 30 percent by age eight, and the remaining 20 percent by age 17.

I have said that the first five years are the most important. Now I will go one step further and emphasize that *the first year of life,* the stage of infancy, is the *most important* of the first five years.

Why is that? Because the most important factor in forming your child's basic personality structure is his self-concept. And the most important part of his self-concept is formed as an infant.

His self-concept is the mental map a child has of himself. His mental map determines whether he is self-confident or has self-doubt, whether he is outgoing or withdrawn, whether he asserts himself or hangs back in fear. Your child's self-concept is like a pair of colored eyeglasses through which he looks at the world.

Your child's self-concept is the single most important thing to understand about him.

No child is born with a self-concept. He learns it from his mother and father, and, to a lesser extent, from brothers and sisters. He begins to learn as soon as he is born . . . in the stage of infancy.

The infancy stage continues until your child is able to walk, at which time the next stage of development begins. The stage of infancy covers approximately the first year of life. What does a child learn during this stage? He learns his basic outlook on life.

He is forming, from a baby's point of view, his philosophy of life, his basic feelings about what it means to be alive. He is learning either a basic sense of trust and happiness or a basic sense of distrust and unhappiness.

You need to help your baby form a basic sense of trust in himself and his environment. This is determined by the atmosphere you and your wife provide for him. Early environment creates the first lenses of those self-concept eyeglasses through which he sees the world. If your baby's basic needs are fulfilled, then he will develop a sense of trust and optimism and attain the maximum development of his potentialities.

BASIC EMOTIONAL NEEDS

Let's start with your baby's emotional needs. Many of an infant's emotional needs are also physical needs, such as: hunger satisfaction; warmth; sleep; urination and defecation; physical cuddling; a strong relationship with a mother and father.

1. *Hunger satisfaction* is probably the most important. Whether your wife is breast or bottle feeding your baby, plan to take over part of the time. If your wife is breast feeding, you can offer a supplementary bottle occasionally. If your wife is bottle feeding, you can give him the bottle as well as she.

You may feel awkward at first, holding, feeding, and burping him, but soon you will begin to relax and feel quite comfortable. There is nothing like holding your baby in your arms to develop strong feelings of love and affection as his father. One of the reasons many fathers do not develop deep feelings for their young children is that they have never once had the experience of feeding their babies.

I hope you and your wife decide to feed your baby on what is called self-demand rather than a schedule. To use self-demand feeding means that you are respecting your child's true individuality beginning at birth. Each baby is unique, with his own internal time clock for hunger. An external time clock, a schedule, is bound to be wrong. Not only is your baby different from all others, but even his own hunger will vary from day to day. Respect your child's individuality. Let him tell you by his crying when he wants to eat.

Your baby will then come to feel: "This world is a safe and satisfying place to live in, because when I let the world know I'm hungry I get fed. I know that everything will turn out all right for me and my world."

2. *Warmth.* We do not need to go into any detail here because almost all parents provide enough warmth to prevent their babies from being chilled.

3. *Sleep.* Your baby will take care of this himself. He will sleep as much as he needs and when he has enough he will wake up.

Unfortunately, your baby's sleeping patterns are absolutely independent of your adult patterns. Your sleep will be considerably disturbed during this stage of infancy. Some babies are easier on you than others. Some start sleeping through the night quite early. Others take many months before they sleep the whole night through.

Unless you are luckier than most parents, at times your baby will wake up crying in the middle of the night. It will not be due to hunger because he will refuse the bottle or breast. The crying may be due to colic or stomach distress, and even physical cuddling will not comfort him or stop his crying. He is crying his little head off and you and your wife want desperately for him to stop so you can get back to sleep.

At times like this, you discover that civilization is only a thin veneer covering a primitive and savage self. You may find yourself furious at your baby, feeling like shaking him or hitting him or yelling at him: "Shut up! Don't you know I've got to get back to sleep so I can feel halfway decent at work tomorrow?" Many parents feel guilty about having such feelings because nobody told them about these things ahead of time. Relax! Welcome to the club! It's perfectly normal to feel this way. Notice: I said *feel* this way. However, if you find yourself actually losing control and hitting your baby, then you need professional help. Even though it is certainly normal to feel frustrated and angry in such situations, you should be able to control your actions.

4. *Urination and defecation.* You will have no trouble with this need during the stage of infancy unless you make the mistake of trying to toilet train your baby during his first year of life. The neuromuscular development of a child's sphincter muscles is not usually mature enough for him to be toilet trained until he is about two years old. So wait until that time.

5. *Physical cuddling.* This is the way by which your baby knows that he is loved. He needs to feel love in a physical way: by being held, cuddled, rocked, talked to, and sung to.

Generally, when your baby cries he is hungry. But at other times he will cry because he is lonely and wants to be held. Always pay attention to your baby's crying, for it is his only language. An older child can tell you when he is lonely or frightened and needs companionship. But your baby can only tell you by crying.

Here I want to deal with something which seems to be a bugaboo for many parents: the fear that they will "spoil" the baby if they pay too much attention to him. Parents fear that too much attention to a baby will "spoil" him at a later age. Therefore they "ration" their attention.

This is utter nonsense. You cannot spoil an infant. Play with him as much as you want. Hug him and cuddle him as much as you want. Talk to him and sing to him as much as you want. You won't spoil him!

These things give your baby a deep and abiding feeling that he is loved and help him develop a strong and secure self-concept. The best thing for your baby during the stage of infancy is to have his basic needs gratified with as few frustrations as possible. His sense of selfhood is too tender and immature for him to be able to cope with many frustrations. There will be plenty of time for life to teach him about frustrations when he is older.

The concept of "spoiling" should never be applied to the stage of infancy. An eight-year-old child who always demands his own way, cries at the drop of a hat when he does not get it, is unable to take no for an answer to anything, and, in general, acts as if the world exists only to minister to his needs could in truth be considered "spoiled." Such behavior would be infantile for an eight-year-old. But don't forget: an infant *is* infantile! We should give our infants the right to be infantile, but require that our older children act with a maturity corresponding to their age and stage of development.

As I said before, one of the reasons babies need cuddling and physical contact is that it is only through these actions that a baby can tell he is loved. But the way a mother or a father cuddles or plays with a baby may be entirely different. For example, when my children were infants, singing "Rockabye Baby" just wasn't my bag! So I sang "The Erie Canal" and "Home on the Range" to them. To date, I haven't heard of any mothers singing those particular songs when cuddling their babies. So sing to your baby or play with him in your own unique way, doing whatever you feel comfortable doing. If enough fathers start enjoying their babies we may eventually lick the "taboo on gentleness" which many American males feel. Different feelings are appropriate to different occasions. At times, a male needs to be aggressive and tough; at other times he needs to be gentle. Playing with his baby may give a father the opportunity he needs to bring to the surface the repressed gentle side of himself.

6. *A strong relationship with father and mother.* Naturally, a baby's relationship will ordinarily be stronger with his mother since she spends more time with him. But your baby needs a strong relationship with you, his father, as well. The father who doesn't develop an emotional relationship with his child until the child is older, is robbing both of them of something very important. Of course, you don't say to yourself: "Today I'm going to develop a strong relationship with my baby!" But if you are doing the other things I mentioned previously (taking a turn at feeding your baby, playing with him, cuddling him, changing diapers, giving him a bath, etc.) you will inevitably be developing a strong emotional relationship between you.

BASIC INTELLECTUAL NEEDS

People used to believe that each child was born with a fixed amount of intelligence which developed as he grew older. Recent research indicates this is not true. We now know that each baby is born with his own maximum potential for intelligence. One child's maximum potential may be that of a genius. Another child's maximum potential may be that of an average person. But what newer research has shown is that *whether a child will reach his maximum potential intelligence depends to a great extent on how much sensory and intellectual stimulation he gets in the first five years of his life.*

As the father, you play an important role in giving your baby sensory and intellectual stimulation. For example: don't change his diapers or give him a bath in silence. Talk to him! Sing to him! Communicate with him! When he is a very young baby he will not respond overtly to you. Nevertheless, the stimulation is being registered in his brain. When you sing and talk to him and make funny noises for him and rock him and play with him you are giving him sensory stimulation which will promote his intellectual development. See Dr. Ira Gordon's book, *Baby Learning Through Baby Play* (Appendix E), which is a very helpful guide to parents in providing sensory stimulation for a baby. But don't let playing with him become a grim obligation. Keep it fun. Talk to him when you feel like it. Cuddle him when you want to. That way you will enjoy him and he will enjoy you.

As your baby gets older and is able to grasp things, give him objects he can safely handle, mouth, and chew on. (See Appendix A which describes toys for a baby at this stage). These objects can also be simple household materials such as plastic bottles and dishes, paper bags, kitchen utensils, or cellophane he can crumple. Since everything will go into his mouth, you must be careful that these objects are not small enough to choke him.

You can also obtain or build cradle gyms, mobiles, or other sensory stimulation toys that can be hung over his head in his crib or attached with stout cord to the crib where he can handle and manipulate them.

TEACHING YOUR BABY THROUGH PLAY

What does all of this sensory stimulation do? It makes your baby eager to learn more and more about the world in which he finds himself. It fosters an intellectual drive, at his infantile level, to explore and understand his environment. The French psychologist Piaget put it very well: "The more the child sees and hears, the more he wants to see and hear."

The more information you have about the stage of infancy, the more you will get out of your contact with your baby. Two books may be of particular help in giving you this information. One is my earlier book, *How to Parent.* The other is *Infant and Child in the Culture of Today* by Dr. Arnold Gesell and Dr. Frances Ilg. Both books start with the newborn baby and trace his gradual development through six years of age. Follow your baby's development by reading the appropriate sections of these books. His psychological development will become much more meaningful to you if you know the difference between a six-month baby and a nine-month baby. (And, let's face it, most fathers don't!)

By the time your baby is nine months old, enormous changes have taken place. At this age you can begin to play with him in ways which will aid him tremendously in his intellectual development. You can begin to teach him to label his environment.

This is very easy to do. Speak to your baby in single-word sentences which point out and identify features of his environment.

This "labeling game" is one you can play anywhere, anytime. Hand him a spoon and say "spoon." As you feed him some peaches, say, "peaches." When you give him a bath, splash the water a little and say, "water." When you see a car, point to it and say, "car."

At this stage of your baby's development he will only register internally what you are saying. At a considerably later stage of language development he will repeat the word. At a still later stage you can point to an object and he will say the word. But make no mistake about it: what he hears you say to him at nine months is definitely registered in his brain cells and is an important stimulus to his language development and intellectual growth.

Let me summarize this first stage of development: the stage of infancy.

What has your baby learned in this first year of life?

If he has been fed on demand when he was hungry, he learned that he can feel a basic sense of trust in his environment to meet his physical needs.

If he received cuddling from both mother and father he learned that he is loved in a meaningful way.

If both mother and father responded to his crying as urgent messages, he learned to trust his environment to respond to his needs.

If through numerous contacts he experienced a satisfying emotional relationship with both his mother and father, he will be prepared to make satisfying emotional relationships with other human beings he encounters throughout life.

If his mother and father have exposed him to sensory and intellectual stimulation, he found the world to be a fascinating and wonderful place rather than a bleak and dull prison.

If your baby experienced all these things by the end of his first year, then he has developed a good sense of basic trust and optimism about himself and his world. His sense of basic trust forms the first and most important lens in his self-concept eyeglasses. His sense of basic trust will give him the best possible foundation for his next stage of development: toddlerhood.

If you, as his father, have done the things I suggested, your baby will be no stranger to you as he begins to walk and enters this new stage. He will be someone you feel close to, someone about whom you have deep feelings. He is really *your baby*. And you are really his father. And that's the way things should be.

3
Toddlerhood

As soon as your child learns to walk, he is ready to leave the stage of infancy and enter the stage of toddlerhood. We can sum up this new stage in a single sentence. Toddlerhood is the age of exploration. No scientist will explore his environment more enthusiastically than your little tyke researching his home and backyard. He will become a particular authority on the underside of things.

Your role of father at this stage will be much easier than your wife's role as mother. She has to cope all day long with his enormous drive to explore, and her typical, plaintive cry will be: "He's into everything!" You should be able to deal with his exploration drive more easily, for you only have to manage it in small doses. And if you are not trying to do something else while you keep your eye on him (in other words, if you are free just to play with him or watch him while he plays with some of his favorite toys) then this is truly a delightful age.

If your child learned either basic trust or basic distrust during infancy, what is he learning in this new stage? In the age of exploration, he is learning either self-confidence or self-doubt.

He needs your help in mastering his developmental task of acquiring self-confidence.

Free to explore and research his environment, he will build his self-confidence. He will acquire the confidence to use both his large and small muscles; to walk and run and climb and jump; to play with cars and trucks, to play with dolls and stuffed animals; to play with sand and dirt and water; to play and socialize with you and his mother, to babble and try new sounds as his language develops, to play with books and have you and his mother read to him. If he is allowed and encouraged to do all these things freely in a stimulating environment, he will acquire feelings of confidence.

These feelings will form the second lens in his self-concept eyeglasses. He will think: "I am a worthwhile person. I can try new things I have never done before, and I can succeed. It's fun to try new things and have my mother and father approve of what I do."

Unfortunately, there are a number of homes in which this happy outcome does not take place. In these homes, the parents do not adapt the purely adult environment of the house to their toddler. They leave valuable vases or bric-a-brac in place and expect the toddler to adapt to their adult environment. They slap his hand and say "no-no" each time he touches some adult object, not realizing that they are undermining his self-confidence. They feed his self-doubt, and at the same time quench his curiosity about the world, his main motive for learning.

Treated this way, your toddler will begin to feel: "I'm a bad person. It's wrong for me to want to try new things or find out about my world. I want to touch and handle things, but my mother and father say no-no whenever I do. I guess all these feelings and impulses within me are bad, and I must be bad for having them."

I hope you choose to adapt your house and yard to your toddler during this stage, rather than force him to adapt himself to a completely adult environment. He should be able to explore your house and yard freely without running the risk of hurting himself or breaking an important article. So remove breakable objects or put them high enough so that they cannot possibly be reached. You can return them when your child is older and his impulse control is at a more mature level.

Not only does your toddler need a house from which breakable

"AH, THE GOOD OLD DAYS."

adult objects have been removed; he also needs a house which is *safe* for him to explore. It is your responsibility to protect him from potential dangers in your house. Safety experts estimate that 50 to 90 percent of all accidents which seriously injure or kill small children can be prevented if parents take proper precautions and "childproof" the house.

Three pages of detailed instructions on how to childproof a house are included in my previous book (*How to Parent,* pp. 56-58, hard-cover, and 77-80, paperback). I suggest you go over them carefully.

The English call the toddler a "runabout baby," and that is an apt description. He is able to run about, but he is still basically a baby in his judgment and discrimination. Therefore, you must keep an eagle eye on him. For example, don't take him to your garage workshop and then become so engrossed in a project that you forget about him and what he is doing. The next thing you know he might be pushing the "on" button of some power tool.

Let's suppose you have childproofed your house. You have re-moved the beautiful but breakable adult objects. Now you need to go one step further and bring into your house new objects, toys, and materials for play, which will stimulate your toddler's development and build his self-confidence.

Recommended toys for a toddler are listed in Appendix A, and I suggest you go over this carefully. Your toddler has enormous physical energy. He needs toys and playthings which give him a chance to work off this energy, and at the same time develop both his large and small muscles. Your toddler also needs you to play with him or supervise as he plays in the sandbox or climbs the playdome or slides down the slide. And your toddler will be delighted if you take him to the nearest park to play on the climbing equipment. This may sound as if the only thing you have to do is play with your toddler! But, realistically speaking, he can entertain himself if you have chores to do.

There is one particular way in which your toddler will have special need of you as a father. Mothers are usually protective as toddlers run and play and climb, and this is good. But some mothers also tend to be overprotective, which is not so good. For example, many mothers forbid their toddlers to climb on park benches or on certain pieces of climbing equipment in the playground.

I can recall when my oldest boy was eleven months old and he climbed to the top of a six-foot stepladder. My wife (who is usually not overprotective) stood by wringing her hands and worrying. I said: "Relax, dear, he's going to make it all right, and I'm here to catch him if he falls." Remember that no matter how good a mother she is, she has never been a little boy. It often takes a man really to understand the adventurous, aggressive nature of little guys.

This is one of the reasons, among many others, that a child needs both a father and a mother who are actively involved in guiding him to adulthood. In general, fathers tend to be more unaware of the accidents that can happen to young children. And mothers, although much more on guard against the possibility of an accident, tend to be overprotective. A child (especially a boy) raised by an overprotective mother and a father too absorbed in his work to spend much time with him, is going to suffer considerable loss of self-confidence.

Not only does your toddler need to develop self-confidence through vigorous play; he also needs to develop self-confidence in more intellectual types of play.

Books should be a definite part of his play materials now. To a child of this age a book is not yet a continuous story with a beginning and an end. It is basically something which has pictures of objects or people, and words that tell what they are. A book is a printed version of the "label the environment" game you have already been playing. Once you understand this, you can easily see that to a toddler, a toy catalog, a Blue Chip Stamp catalog, a Sears or Ward catalog, or an old picture magazine are all thought of as "books." Point to the object or person in the book or magazine or catalog and say the name aloud.

Two books will be particularly helpful in teaching your toddler to label his environment and thus increase his vocabulary and foster his language development. One is Richard Scarry's *Best Word Book Ever,* and the other is Dr. Seuss's *Cat In The Hat Dictionary.* Both books are terrific investments because they can be used throughout the preschool years. At first you will point to the picture and say the word. As your child matures he will be able to "find the fireman, find the farmer, find the tractor." Still later, when you point to the picture your child will say the word which describes that object or person.

At this age, the child also likes to listen to rhymes, in small doses. The Mother Goose rhymes are now quite appropriate. Personally, I like *Brian Wildsmith's Mother Goose* because Wildsmith's pictures are beautiful. I also like Richard Scarry's *Best Mother Goose Ever* because the pictures of the animals are so captivating for young children. Pick and choose carefully among the Mother Goose rhymes because some of them have outgrown their usefulness for today's children. A good selection read aloud to your child will help to stimulate his language development and to prepare him for liking poetry at an older age.

Toddlerhood is a good time to begin a bedtime ritual which includes reading to your youngster. Since mother is with the child during the day, it is appropriate for father to read the bedtime story.

It would be nice for parents if children had a built-in need to go to bed at the appropriate time. Unfortunately, they don't. Therefore, a pleasant and satisfying ritual which a child learns to take for granted makes it easier to get him to bed. Otherwise, bedtime to a child means he is banished to a dark room while the rest of the family is doing interesting things.

Begin the ritual about half an hour before bedtime by giving him a bath. Bathing not only gets him clean but offers pleasant and relaxing water play with his favorite plastic ships or water toys. Following his bath, Daddy reads a story or two, and then tucks him in and kisses him goodnight. (Mother will probably join in this part of the ritual also.) If this is begun during toddlerhood, it can continue until the youngster is seven or eight. This special time creates a warm and cosy relationship between the two of you which will be enormously important to your child. Incidentally, do not conclude that when your child learns to read that he is "beyond" being read to. Not at all. Having you read to him is not merely an intellectual game; it is a source of emotional support and comfort. He will let you know when he has outgrown it. But don't be surprised if it's not until he's nine or ten years old.

As the child gets older the reading period with Daddy will probably also be used for conversation and little intimate talks about various things. As he grows and develops, be alert to any signs that there is something on his mind he wants to discuss.

If you have several children, don't try to read to all of them at once. Ordinarily, this does not work out too well. Arrange to read to each child separately. Deep down, each child wishes he had no brothers and sisters and did not have to share mother and daddy. That's why reading to him alone is appreciated. His wish to have you all to himself is gratified at least for a little while. If you try to read to several children at once, they often bicker and fight because each one wishes the others were not there.

Reading is only one way of playing the "label the environment" game. You can do this anytime, anyplace. Point to objects or people and name them. This will do tremendous things for your child's language development.

There are two main aspects to language development: passive language (understanding what is said to him) and active language (talking). The passive-language phase will predominate in toddlerhood. But it will not be long before he will begin speaking in one-word sentences. By the time your toddler is eighteen months old he may have a vocabulary of from three or four to 100 words. The extensiveness of his vocabulary and richness of his language development will depend to a great extent on how much you talked and played with him in these early years.

DISCIPLINE FOR TODDLERS

When your child was a baby you didn't need to concern yourself with discipline. But now that he is up and walking, the subject inevitably comes up.

Let me clear up one fundamental misunderstanding about discipline right away. Many people think the words "discipline" and "punishment" mean essentially the same thing. Wrong! Punishment is something negative we do to our child as a result of some action of his. The "something negative" may range from a scolding or tongue-lashing to a spanking. Punishment is a very ineffective method of discipline, as I will point out in Chapter Five. For punishment, strangely enough, often has the effect of teaching the child to behave in exactly the opposite way from the way we want him to behave! Many parents use punishment simply because no one has ever taught them better ways of disciplining their children.

Discipline should be thought of as "teaching." It is related to the word "disciple." When we "discipline" a child we are trying to teach him to be a "disciple" of us, his parents.

All parents try to teach their children desirable types of behavior and to avoid undesirable behavior. That is essentially what we are doing when we discipline children. When we talk about discipline we mean a teaching process on the part of the parent and a learning process on the part of the child.

Psychological research has shown which teaching methods are successful with children and which are not.

However, observe an average set of parents attempting to discipline a toddler and you will find the teaching methods are very limited. Mostly they consist of telling the child what to do or stop doing, and then spanking him if he doesn't obey. I observed a family recently in an airport waiting room with a child who looked about eighteen months old. The father said, "Toby! Don't climb up on that seat! Toby! Do you want a spanking?" Once the father said these things, his repertoire of teaching methods appeared exhausted.

So let's take a look at the teaching methods which are successful with toddlers (and with older children, too).

First and most important is "environmental control." If you have the right kind of environment for a toddler, one adapted to his needs, you will not have to surround him with a thousand "no-no's." For example, when your toddler is enjoying a playground, are you constantly interrupting his play with no-no's? Of course not, because the environment is adapted to his needs. Why not adapt your house and backyard into a suitable environment for him? Then you eliminate the cause of many discipline problems. You are using "environmental control" to prevent discipline problems from arising.

Nevertheless, you cannot completely eliminate the need for no-no's in your house. There will still be things like fires in the fireplace and hot stoves and ovens. When you do say "no-no" to your child, don't make it vague or general. He will not know exactly what you want him to avoid. Be specific with your "no-no." Say "No—fire is hot" or "No—stove is hot, it will hurt Danny" or "Don't touch the knife; it's sharp—it will cut Danny."

The second method of discipline for a toddler is distraction. Here we can use one of the typical characteristics of this age child. A toddler has a short attention span and is highly distractible. When you see him about to do something he shouldn't or about to get into something you prefer he did not, it is a beautiful time to use distraction. Then you are like a magician who says to your child, "Look here, look here! See this wonderful terrific thing I have for you to do over here! (And come away from that light socket you were about to get into!)."

The third method of discipline is reinforcement or reward. We know a great deal about this because animal psychologists have done literally thousands of experiments using the method of reinforcement. For example, suppose you want to teach a dolphin to jump through a flaming hoop. You don't tell him to jump through the hoop. And you don't spank him when he doesn't get the message. You depend entirely on reinforcement.

We know from experiments with both animals and humans that

behavior which is reinforced or rewarded tends to be repeated. Once you understand that very basic principle then you know how to get a child to do the things you want and avoid doing things you don't want him to do.

Let's get back to our dolphin and the hoop. The dolphin is swimming around in his tank. A hoop is placed in the water. When he swims in the other direction nothing happens. But when he swims through the hoop, he is rewarded or reinforced with a fish. Before long, as soon as the hoop is put in the water the dolphin will swim through it to collect his reinforcement, a fish. When that behavior is anchored down pretty well, you raise the hoop out of the water. At first, nothing happens. The dolphin merely swims by underneath the hoop. But if he does that he gets no fish. Sooner or later, he jumps through the hoop and is then reinforced with a fish. Once that particular bit of behavior is pretty well established, the hoop is set on fire. The dolphin may not jump through it at first. But sooner or later he does and he is again reinforced with a fish.

The goal was to get the dolphin to behave in a certain way: to jump through a flaming hoop suspended out of the water. That behavior was learned not by threats or scoldings or spankings, but by reinforcing each step toward the ultimate goal.

Children, in this respect, are very similar. With dolphins the reinforcement is food. Children will also respond to food, but a much better (and less fattening) reinforcement is praise and love and attention from their mother and father.

The catch is that parents pay little attention to children when they are behaving well. They are not bothering us so we tend to ignore them. We do nothing to reinforce their good behavior. But when the child acts up, he gets immediate attention! Parents do not realize that to a child negative attention is better than no attention at all. So when parents give a child their negative attention they are unwittingly reinforcing undesirable behavior.

For example, a father has taken his four-year-old son to the hardware store with him. The boy is delighted to go. The father runs into a friend at the store and is soon deep in conversation. The little boy asks his father, in a pleasant, courteous tone of voice, to buy him a hammer and saw. The father, engrossed in his adult conversation, pays no attention. The boy asks a little more loudly. "Later, later," the father says, waving the boy off. Finally the boy stomps up and down, pulls at his father's pants, and whines in a loud, obnoxious voice: "I want a hammer and saw; I've got to have a hammer and saw!" Finally he gets attention. The father, of course, is completely unaware that he is encouraging his son to ask for things in a loud, whiny, and obnoxious way.

If parents pay attention to children only when they act obnoxious, they unwittingly reinforce this behavior. The remedy? Take the time to reinforce desirable behavior, instead of ignoring your children when they are behaving well. Reward your child with praise or a hug when he is behaving cooperatively, or working independently at something, or engaging in any type of behavior you consider desirable.

These three discipline methods should suffice for the stage of toddlerhood. Unfortunately, there is one teaching method which is heavily used by some parents during the toddlerhood stage: spanking. I say "unfortunately" because apart from a few very extraordinary occasions, there should be no need to spank a child under the age of two. If your toddler persists in doing something dangerous such as running across a street, you may have no alternative but to give him a swift whack on the bottom. But preferably you should be able to handle the behavior of your toddler by arranging a home environment without the need for thousands of "no-no's," by the method of distraction, by reinforcement of his positive behavior, and by physical restraint where necessary.

Spanking is for later ages. Even then parents should use spanking only as a last resort, because every time you spank your child you are teaching him to hate and fear you. Since these are negative emotions which tear down positive relationships, it is unwise to teach hate or fear any more than is absolutely necessary.

There are families where spanking is the chief discipline method used during toddlerhood. This leads to a poor relationship of the child with his mother and father. If you find that you are losing your patience and your temper so frequently with your toddler that you are spanking him a good deal of the time . . . then you probably need professional help to work out your own emotional problems.

SEX AND THE TODDLER

Now I want to take up what is a sensitive subject for many parents: sex.

"What!" you may say. "Surely a child at this age isn't thinking about sex!"

You are right. Ordinarily a child at the stage of toddlerhood is not thinking about sex. His sex organs to him are no different than his toes or ears. But the sad fact is that many parents *teach* a toddler to think about sex in a negative way. Parents teach him to regard his sex organs as something "dirty" and different from the other parts of his body. How can we avoid doing this?

First of all, teach your toddler the names of his sex organs and organs of elimination in the same way you teach him the names of other parts of his body. You should teach a toddler "penis" and "rectum" and "vagina" the same as you teach him "thumb" and "elbow" and "shoulder." If you do not teach him the names of his sex organs he will feel that there is something "bad" and "taboo" (but fascinating) about them.

Second, when a toddler is having his bath and playing with his ears, we don't make any particular fuss about it. If he plays with his toes, it doesn't raise our blood pressure. But if he discovers his penis and plays with it, what should you do? Exactly the same as when he was playing with his ears or toes: ignore it. To a toddler, his penis is no more inherently interesting than any other part of him. It is only when we react as though there is something bad or naughty about it that we teach him to become morbidly interested. We make his sex organs a "taboo" part of his body and teach him to associate them with shame and guilt. But our toddlers will only develop sex hang-ups if we teach them to.

Let me summarize this period of development and your relationship to your youngster at this stage.

This is the age of exploration. Your toddler is tirelessly exploring his physical environment of house and backyard. He is exploring what things he can do with his body, both with his large muscles and his small muscles. He is exploring by babbling and playing with sounds and words and speech patterns as his language develops. He is exploring by playing with books and having adults read to him, by playing with rhythms and sounds and listening to music.

If he is allowed to play and explore freely he will acquire feelings of confidence about himself. These feelings of self-confidence will form the second lens in his self-concept eyeglasses. But if he meets a constant stream of "no-no's" or spankings he will develop feelings of self-doubt, which will later be devastating to his initiative and drive as an adult.

You can help him to explore in these various ways when you are with him. In addition, you can be supportive of your wife as she encourages his exploration during the day. With a toddler in the house, your wife can make basically one of two choices: she can choose to have a spotless house and raise a toddler full of self-doubt; or she can choose to have a periodically littered house and raise a toddler full of self-confidence.

You can help her by realizing that her housekeeping is going to suffer with a toddler in the house. Don't come home and expect a perfectly kept house that looks as if only adults lived in it . . . not with an eager, active toddler around! If you're going to give your toddler the freedom to explore, it means you need to give your wife the right to keep a less than perfect house during this period of toddlerhood.

4.

First Adolescence (Ages Two to Three)

Toddlerhood is a delightful stage. A father can really enjoy being with a toddler and playing with him. The stage that follows is not such a delight. In fact, without an adequate understanding of this next stage and the reasons for it, a father could get pretty exasperated with the behavior of his child.

I call the next stage "first adolescence." There is a great similarity between this stage of development and the teen-age years (which I will call "second adolescence"). Perhaps a few words about "second adolescence" may help fathers understand "first adolescence" better.

The teen-age years are a transition between childhood and adulthood. Before he becomes a teen-ager a child has established a fairly good psychological equilibrium within himself and is reasonably pleasant to be around. But in order for him to become an adult he has to break up that equilibrium and those patterns of behavior which served him so well as a child. When he does, we are suddenly dealing with a different person: a teen-ager. And this teen-ager is rebellious, negativistic, and uncomfortable to relate to. He doesn't know what he wants, but he is clear about what he doesn't want. He doesn't want to do most of the things we want him to do! The only thing he apparently wants to do is negate our parental wishes and desires.

A teen-ager is seeking a sense of positive self-identity. But the first step toward a positive self-identity and sense of selfhood is a *negative* self-identity, a negation of the values and desires of his parents. The teen-age years are a transition period, with considerable storm and stress and emotional upheaval.

The father who doesn't understand the nature of the transition period of teen-agers, and the fact that *negative self-identity must precede positive self-identity,* is going to have a difficult time during this period. He will not understand that the breakup of the equilibrium of childhood behavior patterns is a positive step forward in the development of his teen-ager. He thinks that his child is going to the dogs and that he better crack down on him pretty severely. This, of course, will only make things worse.

The father of a two-year-old needs to understand that the year between two and three is a transition period very similar to the teen-ager years. "First adolescence" is a transition from babyhood (the toddler, you remember is a "runabout baby") to childhood. The first adolescent is as negative and rebellious as his teen-age counterpart. His favorite word is "no." Furthermore, he rarely knows what he wants. If you offer him milk, he wants a juice. If you offer him juice, he wants milk. He is Mr. Yes-and-No. He can be very, very exasperating to deal with. As his father, you can be thankful at times that you don't have to deal with him throughout the daytime hours as your wife does. And she may need a little sympathy and home-grown therapy from you after she has finished riding herd on him solidly for eight or nine grueling hours.

It is most important for you to recognize that the breakup of his delightful patterns of babyhood and the beginning of the negativistic phase of first adolescence are important as a positive step forward in his psychological growth. It would be much easier on parents if the development of children proceeded smoothly and evenly as they grew older. Unfortunately, it doesn't work out that way. In general, periods of psychological equilibrium in children are followed by periods of disequilibrium, particularly in the early years.

It is clear that the stage of first adolescence (approximately second to third birthday) is a stage of disequilibrium. Then comes the three-year-old, a stage of equilibrium, followed by the four-year-old, another stage of disequilibrium. If you want an easy way to remember these, the odd numbers (three and five) are years of equilibrium and the even numbers (two and four) are years of disequilibrium.

Remember that these stages do not correspond exactly to the age of your child; they are only rough approximations.

When your toddler, at around the age of two (or perhaps slightly earlier if he is precocious in his development), begins being negativistic and defiant then you know he has entered the stage of first adolescence.

What is your child learning at this stage of development? What lens of his self-concept eyeglasses will be added now? During the first-adolescence stage, your child is learning *self-identity* versus *social conformity.* (Incidentally, this is a younger age version of exactly the same developmental task he will go through much later in his teen-age years.)

Your child's developmental task for this age is to acquire a firm sense of selfhood, of who he is as a person. However, at the same time he must learn to conform to what society (mostly his parents, at this age) expects of him.

Basically there are two ways in which you can handle things incorrectly at this stage.

First, you can make far too many demands for control and conformity. Depending on how your child reacts to your excessive demands, he will either become a passive, timid child, or he will bitterly resist your excessive demands, and this whole stage will become an unhappy battleground.

On the other hand you may be reluctant to exercise adequate control with your child. When he demands something, you always give in and let him have it. When he refuses to obey the reasonable rules you set, you change the rules to suit him. Soon it becomes clear that your child is running the family and not you. This type of youngster does not learn any of the worthwhile lessons of conformity during this stage. He is going to have a difficult time later on in school when he finds that the teacher and the other children expect a reasonable amount of conformity to rules.

It certainly is difficult for a father to know what rules to set and how to enforce them with a child at this stage. The first adolescent swings back and forth from one extreme to the other. Much of the time he will proclaim "I'll do it myself!" Other times he will demand that you do it for him. Back and forth he goes, between his wish to be independent and his desire to hold on to his babyish dependence.

Perhaps the best advice I could give you when your child is going through this difficult stage is to be flexible in your rules and limits. It is a mistake to insist on one absolute set of rules for dressing, bathtime, or anything else for a child of this age. Rigid rules don't belong in this stage of development because it is filled so full of ambivalent feelings and urges.

I remember when my son Randy was at this stage. His older sister had just finished putting on a puppet play at school. The teacher was going to take her and the other children out for ice cream. She asked Randy if he wanted to come along. First he said "No." Then he said: "Wait a minute—yes, I'll go." As he started to get in the car he suddenly turned around and said, "No, I don't want any ice cream!" The teacher and the other children prepared to drive off. "Wait!" he screamed, "I'm coming too!" They opened the car door for him again. He hesitated: "No, I don't want to." By this time I had had it, so I said: "Randy, no more choices! I know you'd like some ice cream and you'll be disappointed if they go without you. So get in the car—you're going!" Over his furious cries of protest I bundled him into the car and sent him off with the others for ice cream.

That incident is typical of this stage of development, and the wise parent will learn to be flexible and roll with the punches. Don't get me wrong and think that it is not important for parents to have consistent rules and limits. It *is* important. And these consistent rules and limits can begin around the age of three and continue thereafter. But in this particular stage of development, temper your consistent rules with large doses of flexibility.

DISCIPLINE FOR THE FIRST ADOLESCENT

Several principles of discipline which we discussed in the last chapter will continue to be important in this stage of development and throughout childhood, that is, environmental control and reinforcement of behavior which you want the child to repeat. The principle of distraction (in a more sophisticated form) can still be used occasionally in this stage, but the first adolescent is nowhere near as distractible as the toddler. And after the stage of first adolescence the principle of distraction is of no further use.

But there is a new principle of discipline which should begin now. This new principle is: you must make a distinction between your child's *feelings* and your child's *actions*.

By "actions" I mean the outward behavior of a child, such as running across the street, hitting another child, grabbing away a toy or sharing a toy.

By "feelings" I mean internal emotions such as fear or anger or love or excitement.

Why is it important for you, as a father, to make this distinction between feelings and actions? Because a child can learn to control his actions, but *he cannot learn to control his feelings.* His feelings, like his thoughts, come into his mind unbidden; he isn't able to change or banish them at will.

This distinction between feelings and actions is an important principle to remember in disciplining your child all the way through his growth and development, up to and including adolescence.

For example, take the feeling of anger. A child cannot help feeling angry; he cannot control this feeling. What he *can* learn to control are actions which express this angry feeling in an antisocial way, such as hitting another child or throwing sand.

Your primary task as a father is to help him set reasonable limits to his actions. But what are reasonable limits for a child of two or two and a half? A careful reading of the sections on the two-year-old in *How to Parent* or Gesell and Ilg's *Infant and Child in the Culture of Today* will be particularly helpful. They give a more detailed picture of what a child at this age *is* capable and *not* capable of.

Unfortunately, most of us learn the hard way—on our first child! Since we have not had children before, we usually expect more mature behavior than he is capable of. Typically, when our first child is two we expect him to stick to limits and obey like a four-year-old. But he can't; he can only mind like a two-year-old! It is only after our firstborn has passed through the stage of first adolescence that we know what can reasonably be expected at this age. That's what we usually expect of our second child.

Begin by assuming that you are probably expecting your two-year-old to act as if he were a year or two older than his actual age. Try to relax your expectations a little.

Next, you might ask yourself, "What is the absolutely minimum amount of rules and no-no's that I need for my child at this age?"

There is no specific list of correct limits which all parents should set for their children. Families have different life-styles and different personalities. Some parents may be relatively easygoing, with only a few rules which they consider important; others may be stricter, with more limitations on their children's actions. The second group of parents would feel most uncomfortable if their children were to do some of the things the first parents allowed in their children.

Personally, I don't think it matters much what limits you set on your child's actions, as long as they are reasonable and *consistent*, and as long as you can justify these limits to yourself and your child. It helps if you and your wife generally agree on the limits you want to set—and you may count yourself lucky when you do.

By and large, I believe most parents are pretty sensible about the limitations they set on the actions of their children. But when we come to the feelings of children many parents handle things poorly.

In order to raise youngsters to be psychologically healthy, with a strong self-concept, parents need to allow children to express their feelings freely. Unfortunately, most parents do not.

Suppose a father takes his son to the park to play, and, when it's time to go home, his two and a half-year-old says, "No, I don' wanna go home—I hate you!" What will dad do? Chances are he will react with irritation and anger and say something like, "Don't you dare talk that way to me!"

Why is it a mistake not to allow a child to express his negative feelings, his feelings of anger? First of all, remember that, like adults, the little boy has no control over his angry *feelings;* they come into his mind without knocking and asking permission, and are there whether or not they are allowed. Only when a child is permitted to express his negative feelings without fear, and get them out of his system, can he also express positive feelings. Otherwise he will hold down all emotions for fear the negative disallowed ones will show. Feelings of love and affection cannot emerge until feelings of anger and hostility are vented.

If it's good to allow our children to express all feelings, negative as well as positive, why don't we parents allow our children to express their negative feelings? The reason probably lies in that when we were children ourselves, we were not allowed to express *our* negative feelings. And so we pass along these same psychological inhibitions to our own children.

It is good to inhibit our child's antisocial *actions* (hitting, throwing sand, stealing, etc.), but not his antisocial *feelings.* Very young children will tend to express their feelings freely until we parents make the mistake of teaching them not to. If we teach them to repress their feelings and drive them underground, all sorts of trouble will develop in many disguised ways.

Repressed feelings cause serious psychological problems. Adults with psychological problems learn through psychotherapy how to express their feelings adequately. When a man with an ulcer learns to express the feelings whose repression caused the ulcer, it disappears. Teach children to express their feelings adequately when they are young. This increases their chances for good mental health when they become adults.

Not only do children need to express their feelings in words, they need to know that their parents truly understand how they feel. How can you, as a father, demonstrate your understanding of your child's feelings?

Of course, you can try to do this by saying to him: "I know just how you feel. I felt that way when I was your age." But that's too easy, superficial, and not necessarily convincing. There is a better way of conveying your deep understanding of how he feels. This was first discovered many years ago by a psychologist named Dr. Carl Rogers. He called it "reflecting feelings."

THE FEEDBACK TECHNIQUE

Here's how it works. You show your child you really understand how he feels by putting his feelings into your own words and reflecting them back to him, like a mirror. In this early stage of development this is easy to do. To reflect his feelings, you can often use the very same words he used to express himself.

For example, your two-year-old comes up to you, crying: "Tommy (your four-year-old) threw sand at me!" You can reflect his feelings in his own words. With the appropriate tone of indignation in your voice, say, "Tommy threw sand at you!" Or you can say: "You're mad because Tommy threw sand at you"; or, "That really makes you angry because Tommy threw sand at you"; or, "You feel very angry inside because Tommy threw sand at you." You put his feelings in your own words and reflect them back to him. I call this the "feedback technique" because you are feeding back to your child his own feelings. You are showing him you understand how he feels.

And this technique has a built-in corrective factor. If you don't feed back your child's feelings accurately, he will usually tell you: "No, that's not how I feel!"

Notice that most parents do not use the feedback technique. Instead, they try to talk their child out of his negative feelings.

For example, a ten-year-old boy says to his father: "Gee, Dad, I've got a math test tomorrow and I'm really worried I'm going to flunk it." Typically, the father will respond something like this: "Now don't worry about it, son; I'm sure you'll pass it"; or, "Well, you've passed all your math tests this year, I'm certain you'll pass this one"; or, "Now let's not have that negative thinking, son; let's try to think positively about that old test!" The father means well, but it does not help the son one bit with his feelings of fear and worry about the test. Instead, the son will feel inside (but probably not say), "Golly, no sense talking to Dad about this; he just doesn't understand how I feel!"

But by using the feedback technique, the father could respond in this way to his son: "You really feel worried about this test, I see. Tell me why you're worried." The son would then explain why he was fearful of this test. The father could put the boy's apprehensions in his own words and feed them back to him. If he did this, the boy would think: "Gee, Dad really understands." And knowing that his father understood his fears and worries, the boy would feel he had a real ally. This tends to reduce his fears. *After* the father had fed back his boy's feelings of fear and worry, he could reassure him in some positive way. The positive reassurance coming *after* the feeding back of feelings of worry would now mean something to the boy.

I call this method the "feedback *technique*," but it is not merely a technique or gimmick. *It is actually a way of life.* At first it may seem awkward to you to go around feeding back the feelings of your children in his and your own words. But as you get more comfortable with it, you will see that it is really a *total psychological attitude.* It is a way of life in which you as a father learn to pay genuine attention to the feelings of your children and respect their right to have feelings and to express them.

This feedback technique is easy to understand but hard to put into practice. Why? Because we were probably not raised that way. I certainly wasn't. If we were not allowed to express our feelings when we were children, we will probably have difficulties allowing our children to express their feelings to us. Try to overcome this hurdle and experiment a bit with the feedback technique. Once you see that it really does help a great deal in handling children, you will be likely to use it more and more.

The use of the feedback technique is not an absolute guarantee of a good parent-child relationship, nor is it a universal method of handling all childhood problems. I do not want to leave you with the impression that allowing a child to express his feelings is the cure-all for all difficulties. It may be a very basic first step, but it is not the final answer.

For example, if your child comes home from school in tears because he was not invited to another child's birthday party, you can begin by feeding back his hurt and angry feelings. But then you need to do something about the situation that caused him to have the hurt and angry feelings. You might say to him: "I know how unhappy you are because Ronnie didn't invite you to his birthday party. But you and I can have a special little party here this Saturday morning instead. And maybe you can invite Jack and Philip." In other words, you have not merely utilized the feedback of your child's feelings, but you have taken positive action about the situation that caused those feelings. Your child now has double evidence that you care: you have genuinely listened to his feelings and, in addition, you have done something about the situation that caused them.

Of course, if your child's negative feelings are caused by your saying "no" to something he wants, the situation is different. If he wants another ice-cream cone and you say no and he bursts into angry tears, you can reflect his feelings, but to give him another ice-cream cone would be teaching him that by being angry and crying he can manipulate you and get you to change your mind. Giving in to his manipulation undermines the basic foundation of parental authority.

But if your child is shy, or fearful, or angry about some situation, then you need to help him deal in some realistic way with the situation causing him to feel shy, fearful, or angry. For example, if he is afraid to play with other children, you need to allow him to express his shy feelings and feed them back to him. But you also need to plan a slow, gently paced program of having one youngster at a time over to the house to play with him. You can reinforce that youngster's visit with a snack, as I will explain in the next chapter.

If he is angry because other children won't play with him since he is bossy and bullies them, then you need to point this out without

"I'D LOVE TO PLAY 18 HOLES
TODAY, PHIL, BUT I PROMISED MY
SON THAT I'D TAKE HIM FOR
A CRAWL IN THE BACK YARD."

lecturing or scolding him. "Jimmy, I wonder if the reason the other children don't like to play with you is because when they don't do what you want them to do, you throw sand at them and make them cry?"

Many parents make the mistake of trying to solve their children's problems in the ways I have suggested *before* they have given the child a chance to express his feelings, and before they have shown him they understand how he feels by using the feedback technique.

Let me summarize where we are at this point. I have said it is important for you as a father to make a distinction between your child's feelings and your child's actions. I have suggested that you set reasonable limits on your child's actions, but that you allow him to express the feelings he has inside him. I have described the feedback technique as a way of showing him you really understand how he feels. Now I want to use a concrete example from the stage of first adolescence to show how the distinction between feelings and actions works out in actual practice.

The following incident occurred several times when my oldest son was around the two-and-a-half-year level. I had taken him to the park where he was playing happily in the sand. Finally it was time to leave.

"No—I dowanna go." (Why should I expect him to want to go? After all, he's having a great time!)

I reflected his feelings: "I know you don't want to go because you're having a lot of fun playing in the sand."

"I'm not gonna go!"

"You're having so much fun you don't want to budge at all!" I reflected his feelings for a few more minutes. Finally, I picked him up bodily and carried him over to the car, kicking and yelling, with me reflecting his feelings all the way: "You're very mad at Daddy because you want to stay and play in the park and he's making you leave!"[1]

If I had allowed my son to coerce me into staying at the park longer, I would have taught him to refuse to submit to reasonable limits. I would not be helping him to incorporate within himself resonable standards of social conformity.

On the other hand, if I had refused to allow him to express himself, he would have repressed his feelings and thus negated his growing sense of self-esteem. By feeding his feelings back to him I was affirming his right to have feelings and express them.

TOILET TRAINING

This is the stage of development where toilet training belongs (in our culture at least). On the whole, your wife will be more involved than you in your child's toilet training, but you will play a role as well and should know the psychological principles behind it. Toilet training is basically a simple problem of teaching a new skill. Unfortunately, parents botch this relatively simple teaching job. For one thing, parents may not understand that toilet training is a complex learning task for a two-year-old. I spent eleven pages in my previous book, *How to Parent,* describing the details of how to train a child in bowel and bladder control, beginning when he is two years old. I suggest you take a look at pages 111-123. It is especially important for you to know that since toilet training is essentially teaching your child a new skill, punishment should play *no part* in it.

You reward or reinforce your child for his successes and ignore his failures. You give your child a hug or a kiss or say something like "good boy," or, "Daddy's proud of you."

LANGUAGE DEVELOPMENT

In discussing the stage of toddlerhood, I pointed out that there are two phases of language learning: passive language (understanding) and active language (talking). In toddlerhood, the passive-language phase predominates. But in first adolescence, the active language phase comes into its own.

As far as language is concerned, the second birthday is an important transition point. Your child still speaks in one-word sentences, but, increasingly, he is putting words together in more and more complex sentences. What was registered in his brain in the toddler stage will now begin to appear in speech.

Stop and think about it. Learning to speak a language is a fantastic intellectual accomplishment for so young a child. All over the world two-year-olds are learning to speak the language of the country in which they live, whether it is English, Japanese, Russian, Spanish, or Swedish. Any doubts about the intellectual abilities of a preschool child should be put to rest if we really stop to reflect on what it means that your two-year-old is learning to speak your language.

Your child's new language ability means a great deal to his intellec-

"MY PARENTS THINK I'M
AFRAID OF THE DARK... I'M NOT
THOUGH. I'M JUST TERRI-
FIED OF TURNING OFF LIGHTS."

tual development. Now he can conceptualize his world. He can reason with himself. He can project a simple future. He can play imaginatively. He can fantasize.

In the toddlerhood stage, your child spent a fantastic amount of time practicing motor skills such as climbing up and down stairs. With his new-found language abilities, you will find him spending enormous amounts of time practicing the use of words.

By all means continue to play "label the environment" with your first adolescent. In this stage of development he is what Dr. Gesell calls "word hungry." You will find him an enthusiastic participant in this word game.

At this age, your child will probably introduce you to a new variation of the "label the environment" game you have been playing with him. His new variation can be called the "question-asking" game.

Treat his questions with genuine respect. They are his attempts to find out about the world he lives in. He will ask questions about anything and everything. And the more intelligent he is the more questions he will ask.

Unfortunately, many mothers and fathers think of the questions of their two-year-old as nuisances. But when he asks you a question and you answer him, he is really an eager pupil in a class called The Wonder and Mystery of the World. You are his respected teacher. Treat your child and his questions with the genuine respect that his growing little intellect demands.

Ideally you should answer all your child's questions. By doing so, you help him develop his vocabulary, his reasoning power, his language skills, and his general intelligence. In reality, however, no flesh-and-blood father is up to answering the questions of a first adolescent all the time. Do the best you can. But don't hesitate to say at times: "No more questions. Daddy's tired!"

BOOKS AND THE FIRST ADOLESCENT

In the previous chapter I suggested you start a bedtime ritual of reading to your child during the stage of toddlerhood. At that stage "reading" was mostly using a single word to label a single picture. In first adolescence, reading really begins to flower. Now you can begin to read story books with a beginning, middle, and end.

4

First Adolescence 51

At this stage your child is fascinated by words and wordplay. He
will continue to love nursery rhymes for their rhythm and repetition
of sounds. At this age he enjoys repetition, such as is found in *The
Three Little Pigs* and *Chicken Little.* He likes to recognize what is
coming next in the story and chant it with you as you read. He loves
sounds of all sorts, particularly unusual or funny ones. When you
come across a sound in a book you are reading, ham it up a little and
go all out in making the sound.

Reading to a first adolescent should be a cooperative affair. Hold
the book so that he can see the pictures. Help him to read the details
of the pictures by asking him questions about the different people
and objects.

A child at this stage often has favorite books he wants you to read
to him day after day. He can get quite rigid about it. Sometimes it is
difficult to get him to listen to a new book.

Richard Scarry's *Best Word Book Ever* continues to be a splendid
book to use with a child of this age. And Richard Scarry has two
other books which are not only excellent for the first adolescent, but
can be used throughout the preschool years: *What Do People Do All
Day?* and *The Big Schoolhouse.* These are truly unique books which
pack an enormous amount of information in them for young children.

Now is a good time to begin getting acquainted with good children's books. A magnificent reference book of children's books,
from babyhood through adolescence, called *A Parent's Guide to
Children's Reading* by Dr. Nancy Larrick, is available in paperback. I
have used it extensively to get suggestions for books to read to my
three children.

In addition to reading to your child, you might like to become
really adventurous and try telling stories. If you've never done
anything like this before and feel somewhat inadequate . . . relax! At
this age your child will love your stories no matter how you tell
them.

One type he will enjoy is made up stories about a man remarkably
like yourself, and his adventures at work. You can also make up
stories about a child who is remarkably like your youngster.

When you're telling stories to a child at this age, really ham it up!
Put in lots of funny sounds and noises. Use a simple trick of the
public speaker: raise or lower your voice dramatically at times. Let
your child move the story along by asking him from time to time,
"And what do you think happened next?" Never fear—he will tell

you! And then you can incorporate what he tells you into the story: "That's right. Tommy did find a little puppy in the street, and he brought it home to his family."

I hope you will enjoy reading to your first adolescent and telling him stories because these things will pay big dividends both in his language development and in deepening the relationship between the two of you.

There are many other things you can do with your first adolescent, but I hesitate to spell them out in detail. Fathers vary enormously in what they enjoy, and you should *enjoy* the time you spend with your child. If you're playing in the sand pile with your child but having a miserable time because that's just not your cup of tea, then don't do it! Your child will sense your discomfort and will not gain much from the time you spend together.

First adolescents enjoy many things that fathers can do with them. They like to paint and crayon. They like to play in the sand. They like to be taken to a playground or a park. They like to go swimming and wading. They like to go for a drive. They like to be taken with you if you go to a hardware store: a trip that you might take for granted, but is high adventure for them. They like to go just for a leisurely walk down the street, where they can pick up rocks or pebbles or investigate ants in the grass. They like almost any kind of animal, and they love to go to the zoo.

There are many, many things that a first adolescent enjoys. Each father will have to discover by experience what activities he finds enjoyable with his youngster at this age.

Let me summarize this chapter by saying that you will no doubt find your first adolescent quite exasperating at times. This is why some educators have nicknamed this period the "terrible two's." But don't ever forget that the negative, rebellious, and abrasive quality of this stage is part of the positive thrust which is going to enable your child to achieve his self-identity.

It is quite ironic that fathers want their children to grow up to be strong and dynamic adults, but are not able to accept the very same qualities of personality when their child is two and a half! And nobody could accuse a first adolescent of being a Caspar Milquetoast. In his demands for instant gratification, his enthusiastic and total commitment to the world as he experiences it, his vigorous protests against restraint, and his hearty, sensuous enjoyment of life, he is nothing if not dynamic! And it is precisely this dynamic drive which

"MY FATHER TOOK ME TO
THE ZOO TODAY."

"I HOPE YOU DIDN'T LET
HIM MISBEHAVE—YOU KNOW HOW
FATHERS ARE."

is an important psychological resource for your child—not only at this stage, but at every later stage of his life. You do not want your youngster to lose this vigorous, dynamic quality of personality. You do not want to scare it out of him.

Your respect, as his father, for this dynamic quality of your first adolescent's personality will help him to add the special lens of healthy self-identity to his self-concept eyeglasses at this crucial stage of his development.

5
Fathers and Discipline

I want to pause in our coverage of the different stages of development to discuss a subject which is of great concern to parents: discipline. Some aspects of child discipline were mentioned in the last two chapters, but this chapter covers the basic principles that will be of use to you in disciplining your child until he reaches adolescence.

There is often a conflict between mothers and fathers about disciplining their children. Mothers complain that fathers are too strict, and fathers complain that mothers are too lenient (or the other way around). One of the reasons for the conflict and misunderstanding is that neither mothers nor fathers have given a great deal of thought to what exactly discipline is, or how to achieve their goals of child discipline.

One of the widespread misunderstandings about discipline is that it is synonymous with punishment. You can easily see that a father is thinking of discipline in this way when he says that "The trouble with kids nowadays is that they haven't had any discipline!" Punishment, instead of being synonymous with discipline, should be a very minor part of discipline, used only as a last-ditch technique when every other possible way has been tried and has failed. Punishment is only one of the means of enforcing discipline.

If discipline isn't punishment, what is it? Basically, to discipline a child consists of teaching a child to behave in ways that the parent considers to be desirable and to avoid behaving in ways he considers undesirable. Discipline is a teaching process on the part of the parent, and a learning process on the part of the child.

Since discipline is a teaching/learning process, immediate help is available to evaluate which methods are best for a parent to use. That help comes from literally thousands upon thousands of psychological experiments on how children learn. From these experiments we have discovered which teaching methods are successful in helping children learn, and which are unsuccessful. This is vital information for a parent to possess, but, unfortunately, most parents do not. They are in the unhappy position of a new first-grade teacher trying for the first time, at the beginning of the school year, to teach her class of children to read. Unfortunately, this hypothetical teacher has not had a single hour of instruction to learn which teaching methods she should use to accomplish her goal. It is this information that I want you to have. When disciplining your child, you are basically functioning as his teacher. You need information about teaching methods that will enable you to accomplish your job satisfactorily.

First, you need to be clear about the goal of discipline: its goal is not merely to get the child to "mind" immediately. This is a very narrow and stultifying view of your aims. If the goal of discipline were only to achieve the immediate result of having the child "mind," you would be presuming that someone will always be around to tell the child what to do and what not to do and to exact his obedience.

A father should, on the contrary, think in long-range terms about the goal of discipline. A father is starting with a newborn baby, a being who is basically a "delightful little savage," who wants what he wants when he wants it and, of course, has no notion of socially acceptable or socially unacceptable behavior. Father and mother take this young baby and guide him from infancy through adolescence. Patiently they teach him to behave in desirable ways and avoid behaving in undesirable ways, until the final goal of discipline is achieved. The final goal is for the child, now an adult, to be capable of *self-discipline:* of being self-motivated to behave in socially desirable ways and to avoid socially undesirable behavior. This is our goal: to start with an undisciplined baby, and teach him step by step, until, at the end of adolescence, he has become a self-disciplined and self-regulated adult. What are the teaching methods that enable a parent to achieve this goal?

First, the father (and the mother, too) must thoroughly understand the stages of the child's development from infancy through adolescence. He needs to know what children are capable and what they are not capable of learning at each stage of their growth. He needs to know what a child is like "typically" at each age and stage of development. I think it is safe to say that 99 percent of inexperienced parents do not know this. After all, why should they? Our schools do not teach much about children.

I think both mothers and fathers start out with approximately the same ignorance about what normal children are like at different ages. Mothers learn more what a normal three-year-old or a six-year-old or an eight-year-old are like simply because mothers are around children more. They learn what normal children are like by a sheer trial-and-error process of observation. Fathers are around children much less and hence, have less reasonable standards of what to expect from a normal child.

I stress this point because much of a father's problems with discipline stems from his unawareness that he is expecting his child to function at an impossible level of perfection at each age. He may be expecting behavior from a four-year-old that only a seven-year-old would be capable of, or expecting an eleven-year-old to behave as if he were fifteen.

For instance, suppose a father brought home a young pet monkey and left him in the living room to wander about freely. Suppose that the father expected the young monkey to sit quietly in a chair, not to jump and climb around or swing from lamps or knock over ashtrays and vases or pull books out of the shelves. The monkey, being normal, would be incapable of sitting quietly. The father would become increasingly frustrated that the monkey was not "minding" him.

Incredible, you say. No father would be so foolish as to expect that kind of "civilized" behavior from a monkey. And yet, every day, fathers all over the country are quite as unrealistic about the behavior they expect from their children.

A normal child is thoughtless and inconsiderate of other people in many ways. He thinks of himself first and of what he wants. His normal behavior is often irritating and annoying to adults. Frequently he is a poor loser and becomes angry and cries. He does not think to turn off lights or the TV set when he leaves a room to play somewhere else. He needs to be reminded to bring in his metal toys after he has finished playing with them in his sandbox. And so on and so on.

In other words, *children are not adults.* There is a vast emotional and intellectual gap between the world of childhood and the world of adulthood. Children are not interested in the same things as grown-ups. Children are not motivated to do many of the things that grown-ups do.

Adults forget what they were like at two or four or seven. Since we have been living in the world of adults for many years we unconsciously tend to expect our children to act as we do as adults, only on a smaller scale. This is unrealistic. One of my favorite cartoons shows a mother dragging a small child behind her and saying: "Oh, stop it, Timmy—you're acting just like a child!" Of course he is! Normal children act like normal children—they cannot act like adults in pint-size form. And a child should never be punished or scolded for simply acting like a normal child. To help you to visualize the behavior which actually can be expected from a normal child at each age and stage of development, I will begin with a thumbnail sketch of what you might discover when you observe a typical child of that age and stage of development. A general rule of thumb for fathers: you should probably assume that you are expecting more mature behavior out of your child at *every* age than he is capable of achieving.

For example, after a lecture I gave on the stages of development in the preschool child, one father came up to me and said: "I was so bothered by the way my four-year-old boy has been behaving lately I was seriously considering getting professional help for him. After your lecture tonight I've decided that he's just a normal, obnoxious four-year-old!"

Second, if you are to do a good job of teaching your child desirable behavior, you need to develop a positive relationship with him. The first thing every good teacher does is build an effective rapport and a good emotional relationship with his students. If the students hate and despise the teacher he is not going to be able to teach them much. It is the same with a father and his child. It doesn't take that much to maintain a good relationship with your child. There is no innate instinct in a child to love you or wish to obey you and respect you. You have to *build* a feeling of love and trust and respect by spending time with him. And this deep emotional relationship of love and acceptance has to be built in the early years or you won't be able effectively to teach your child in his later years.

A fifteen-year-old boy I had in therapy complained bitterly to me: "Now that I'm getting in trouble with drugs and other stuff my Dad is suddenly pulling the big pal routine on me, wanting to take me to ball games and stuff like that. Well, where was he when I wanted him to play with me and pay some attention to me all those other years? So I say the hell with him now!"

Take stock of the time you spend with your child. Each day and each week you need to spend some time with him in a one-to-one relationship where the two of you are just having a good time doing something together. When your son or daughter wants you to do something with him (or her) is your characteristic answer, "Daddy's busy now, I'll do that with you later" (and then later never comes)?

Analyze how your child sees you: Is 99 percent of your role one in which you are expecting something of him, reminding him to do something, scolding him to stop doing something, or getting after him for misbehaving? If so, you are not building a deep positive emotional relationship. He needs time with you when you are not demanding anything from him, time when the two of you are mutually enjoying yourselves. And he especially needs this time in the first five years of his life, because these are the years for building this kind of relationship with your child. Most abnormal rebellions of adolescents could have been prevented if the father had spent time building a deep and close relationship during the preschool years.

Third, fathers need to be firm with their children in the early years so that they know that father means what he says and will back it up. And, which cannot be overemphasized, the father's firmness should be in relation to the child's *actions*, not the child's feelings. A child cannot control his thoughts and his feelings, but he can control his actions (or if he is a very young child, he can *learn* to control his actions over a period of time). This is where fathers often get confused on the permissiveness/strictness issue. They wonder: "Am I being too strict or too permissive?" Permissiveness or strictness should only refer to a child's *actions*, never to a child's feelings.

You should permit children to express their feelings and, using the feedback technique I presented in the last chapter, you should let your child know you understand how he feels. However, never be permissive with your child in the sense of letting him do something of which you disapprove and that you know is not good for him to do. For example, you should not let him hit or kick another child, destroy property, skip school, steal things, con you into letting him have a chocolate sundae just before his dinner, or indulge in any type of action which is detrimental to him or socially unacceptable. You are certainly not doing your child a favor by being wishy-washy, so that he isn't ever really sure of how sure you are. What you permit your child to do should be geared to what is normal behavior for a child of his age and stage of development.

Having restated all that, let me go back to the main point I want to emphasize: It is important for you as a father to be firm in setting wise limits and boundaries for your child's actions at each behavioral stage. Limits and boundaries should be reasonable and based on what can normally be expected for his age. Then be firm in enforcing these limits and boundaries. By doing this you are helping your child establish his own inner controls of his antisocial impulses. If you are not firm in enforcing limits, you are making it that much harder for him to establish this inner control system; and a child who does not firmly establish an inner control in early childhood is going to become an adolescent who will have great difficulty saying "no" to drugs or other anti-social behavior during his difficult teen-age years.

Fourth, fathers should make use of the valuable information psychologists and educators have amassed through research, not only on how to teach children successfully, but on how to teach animals successfully. If that statement sounds a bit bizarre to you at first, consider this important fact. Children, particularly young and immature children, possess many psychological characteristics in common with animals such as dogs, cats, dolphins, and chimpanzees. Psychologists have learned many things about teaching children by experiments in training and teaching animals. Perhaps the most important teaching methods have been learned from what has been called "reinforcement psychology."

Reinforcement psychology has taught us that behavior which is rewarded is positively reinforced and tends to be repeated. You remember, in chapter three we talked about how an animal psychologist trained a dolphin in a sea aquarium to jump through a flaming hoop. The same basic psychological principles apply to fathers who want to teach their children desirable ways of behavior.

1. The teacher must reward and thus reinforce the desired behavior of the learner. For animals, the reinforcement is food. For children it is the love and attention and praise of the parent.

2. The teacher should reinforce whatever he wants the child to do, and pay no attention to what the child does that is undesirable. Of course, if the undesirable behavior involves the risk of hurting himself or other children or destroying property, the parent-teacher must intervene; he must use his common sense.

If your two-year-old is running out into a busy street, you obviously cannot ignore this undesirable behavior. You might have to hold him firmly with both hands and say: "No, Jimmy, no running into the street! That might hurt Jimmy." But I want to stress that it is *only* when your child is about to hurt himself or another child or destroy property that you should intervene. The rest of his undesirable behavior (dawdling, complaining, being thoughtless, etc.) should be ignored in the same way that the animal trainer ignores the behavior of the dolphin when it does *not* swim or jump through the hoop. The animal teacher concentrates on positive rewards for the behavior which he is trying to teach the dolphin, and pays no attention to the behavior which he is trying to teach the dolphin to avoid.

Unfortunately, most parents do exactly the opposite! They ignore their child when he is behaving as they want him to, thus giving no reinforcement to this desirable behavior! On the other hand, if the child acts up and behaves undesirably, the parent usually gives him his immediate attention, thus unwittingly rewarding the child for undesirable behavior!

Let me tell you a story on myself to illustrate the unwitting way in which we "teach" other people undesirable behavior. When I was away at college, and my younger sister was in high school, we corresponded back and forth. In one of her letters she sent a poem she had written and asked for my critical evaluation of it. I took her at her word and did just that. I analyzed the poem line by line and wrote her comments such as: "This is well put," "That's corny," "That's a cliché," "This is a good metaphor," and so on. What was the result? She has never written another poem from that day to this. Of course, I had no intention of "teaching" her *not* to write any more poetry. And yet that's exactly what I unwittingly did.

What would I have done had I been acquainted with the principles of reinforcement psychology at that time? I should have praised her for the good parts of the poem, and paid no attention to the not-so-good parts. This would have been quite genuine, for her poem had many good parts. Had I done this, I would have been reinforcing or rewarding her for writing poems and for the parts of her initial attempt which were good.

Many fathers make the same mistake inadvertently. Praise a child's first fumbling efforts to learn some desirable behavior, whether it is to take care of his room or to remember to feed the dog, rather than dish out both praise and reproof; you do not realize that you are discouraging the child from learning the very behavior you want him to learn. Even worse, a father may ignore a child's good behavior and only dish out reproof for his bad behavior—which discourages the child even more.

3. Reinforce every step your child takes in the direction of a worthwhile goal. Don't wait until he gets all the way to the goal before reinforcing him. The animal trainer did not wait for the dolphin to get to the final goal of jumping through the flaming hoop before reinforcing him with a fish. (If he had, he never would have been able to motivate the dolphin to get to that final goal!) In the same way, if you want your nine-year-old to keep his room clean, don't expect him to reach the 100 percent goal of room cleanliness you have in mind in one day. Instead, offer praise for each positive step he makes along the way until, over a period of time, the child achieves the goal of room cleanliness you had in mind (and do not expect adult standards of room cleanliness from a nine-year-old)!

4. In the early stages of training it is important to reinforce every desirable response of the child. Once the learning is well under way, the reinforcement may be spaced out.

5. Instead of punishment (scolding, lecturing, spanking), when you are trying to stop your child from doing something undesirable, use what psychologists call "extinction techniques." When a psychologist wants an animal to stop doing something he stops reinforcing the undesirable behavior. If he is rewarding a monkey with food for pressing a lever and he now wants the monkey to *stop,* he merely

ceases giving the food. Sooner or later, when the reinforcement stops, the animal will stop pressing the lever.

This is an ideal example of the use of extinction techniques in connection with a four-year-old who is starting to bring home four-letter words to shock his parents. Many parents do exactly the wrong thing at this point. They reinforce the child's use of these words by their shocked attention. Unconsciously, they teach him to continue using the words, since he gets such an emotional response from them. Instead, parents should ignore the four-letter words. Sooner or later, when the child discovers the words have no appreciable effect he will stop using them. You have "extinguished" his use of the words by refraining from reinforcing them.

Most parents are quite naive in their belief that if you want to get a child to stop doing something, all you have to do is to punish him for it and he will stop. Fathers, particularly, tend to believe that "all that kid needs is a good licking." If this naive belief were true, our prisons would not be so full of adult criminals, many of whom received a large number of "good lickin's" when they were children. No, paradoxically enough, parents often teach their child undesirable behavior by punishing him for that very behavior.

To the parental mind, punishment is a deterrent to undesirable behavior. But many children look upon punishment as a reward (even though a negative one) of the parent's attention. This does not mean that the child *consciously* thinks of it in this way. He does not get up in the morning and think to himself: "I'll see if I can get my parents to scold me and punish me today."

No; unconsciously the child is saying to himself: *"Negative attention is better than no attention at all."* One six-year-old boy I had in child therapy put it with astonishing candor: "My father doesn't usually pay much attention to me because he's too busy with his work, but when I act up, then he *has* to pay attention to me!"

So I hope you will get the naive belief out of your mind that punishment is the best way to prevent undesirable behavior. Instead, knowing that punishment often acts as a *paradoxical reward* for undesirable behavior, use extinction techniques. Let me repeat once again, in case some father is getting the wrong impression: This does *not* mean you ignore undesirable behavior which is dangerous to your child or to others or that will destroy property. You need to take *firm action* in these cases, but do not *punish*. If a child is hitting a playmate, hold his hands firmly, preventing him from hitting the other child, and say very emphatically: "You must not hit Doug. If you are mad at him, tell him you're mad, but you must not hit him."

Reinforcement methods of discipline with children have been derived mainly from experiments with various animals. But there are other teaching methods that are uniquely applicable to children, and cannot be used with dogs or dolphins or parakeets. A dog or a dolphin does not have a self-concept. But a child does. Remember, your ultimate goal in disciplining your child is to help him become a self-regulating person, who will be able to practice self-discipline. The extent to which he becomes self-regulating depends upon the strength of his self-concept. Therefore, all of the following methods of discipline have in common the goal of strengthening the self-concept of the child and enabling him to move toward the goal of self-regulation.

Using "environmental control" minimizes the need for other methods of discipline. This is especially true with young children. Parents who provide an interesting and stimulating environment in their home and backyard will be using environmental control to prevent problems.

Similarly, parents who take young children on a long automobile trip and expect them to sit quietly and watch the passing scenery are asking for discipline problems. But parents who provide games and puzzles and books, who stop frequently and give the children a chance to run around and let off some of their excess energy, are providing a wise environmental control that will help to prevent discipline problems.

Second, giving a child freedom to explore his environment and assume self-regulation helps to build a strong and positive self-concept. As soon as a child can feed himself, dress himself, turn on his own bath water, the parent should let him. It is undeniably faster to do these things for a small child than to let him do them. But it is much more beneficial to the growth of a strong self-concept if he does them himself.

Third, rely on the powerful force of unconscious imitation as an effective builder of a positive self-concept. Children are terrific imitators and because of this parents have a powerful teaching technique at their disposal. They can be living models of positive personality traits and good habits. Their children will learn from them by unconscious imitation. Understanding this concept should save needless coercive battles with your children. For example, if you and your wife use good table manners, your children will imitate you when they are old enough. Not at two years or four years, but when they are older. If you want to teach your child to respect the rights and feelings of others, you need to begin by respecting his rights and feelings, and not deal with him in a high-handed or tyrannical manner.

Fourth, treat the feelings of your child differently than you treat his actions; this will build a positive self-concept in your child. I have already discussed this in chapter four so I will not elaborate any further here, except to suggest a book you can read for a deeper understanding of its importance. *Play Therapy* by Dr. Virginia Axline, which is available in paperback (Ballantine Books), was written for child therapists rather than for parents. However, it is in clear and non-technical language and I recommend it to all parents. It is full of verbatim reports of what the child said and did and how the therapist responded to show he understood the child's feelings. The same principles of acceptance and reflection of the child's feelings which work in the play-therapy room also work in the home. You need to learn gradually how to gain skill in their use.

Fifth, allowing a child to learn by natural consequences also helps him to build a strong self-concept. This is a powerful tool which parents can use in teaching their children. Unfortunately, few parents use it. Here is how it works. If a child is called for dinner and comes twenty minutes late, his food will be cold when he eats. If a child does not do his homework at night, he will be marked down in school the next day. If a child dawdles and misses the school bus, he will have to walk and be late. If a child spends all of his fifty-cent allowance the day he gets it, he will have no more money to spend until the next week. All of these things deal with the natural consequences of a child's actions.

Usually, the natural consequences of his actions which are unpleasant are very powerful deterrents against repeating them. If parents step in and protect a child from the unpleasant natural consequences of his actions, the child loses the educational value of the experience. We are then teaching him that he can always depend upon us to protect him from unpleasant consequences of his own actions. This is bad for his self-concept, for it promotes infantilization rather than emotional growth and the ability to stand on his own two feet.

Sixth, at times we will have to use artificial unpleasant consequences, which we call "punishment." It would be very nice if we could rely entirely on the natural consequences of inadequate or undesirable behavior to discipline a child. Unfortunately, natural consequences will not always do the job, and as a last-ditch technique, we may be forced to resort to one of these three main types of "artificial consequences."

1. We can use social isolation by sending the child out of his social group or to his room.

If you use this, be sure to make the isolation open-ended rather than closed-ended. For example, if your four-year-old is behaving badly and disrupting the play of a group of children in the backyard, do *not* say to him: "Okay, Charley, you're behaving so badly you're going to have to play in your room for the rest of the afternoon!" This is "closed-ended isolation" and does nothing to motivate your child to behave better and *not* disrupt the group play. Instead, say: "Charley, I see that you're not able to play well with your friends right now. You keep pestering them and causing trouble. You'll have to go to your room and play by yourself for a little while. When you think you are able to play all right with the other children you may come and tell me."

The "time-out" technique is one valuable social isolation technique. In a time-out, a child is sent either to his room or to a neutral room such as a bathroom for a period of five minutes. This does not reinforce the undesirable behavior which has preceded the calling of the time-out, because the child does not get your attention, even your negative attention. All he gets to do is to spend five minutes in a boring place.

The "time-out" technique is particularly effective when two children are bickering or fighting. Send each of them to a dull and neutral environment, such as a bathroom, for the specified five minutes. Tell them: "You two aren't able to get along well with each other now, so you will each have to go to a separate bathroom and stay there for a time-out of five minutes. I'll call you when the five minutes are up." This time-out through social isolation gives each child a chance to cool down and be able to start a more positive relationship later.

Just knowing about the time-out procedure is in itself a great comfort to many parents, because now the parent has something simple and effective he can do which will immediately cope with bickering or fighting.

2. You can deprive your child of something important to him. If your child rides his bicycle where he is not supposed to, and there are no unpleasant natural consequences, then you may need to impose unpleasant artificial consequences. "George, you know the rule is you are not to ride your bike on Whizzer Boulevard because it is such a busy street with too much fast traffic. So I'm not going to let you ride your bike for the next two days. That will help to remind you to ride your bike only where you are allowed." In depriving a child of something important to him, fathers should be sure not to deprive the child of something for so long a time that the deprivation becomes, in effect, meaningless. For example, if you deprive your child of the right to ride his bicycle for three weeks, this is such a long time that it would not serve its purpose of helping your child to control his impulse to ride in forbidden territory. Instead, since the time interval is too long, your child would probably feel: "Three weeks sounds like a year! The heck with that noise; I'll sneak out and ride my bike anyway when Mom or Dad won't know about it."

3. You can spank your child.
Since the publication of my earlier book *How to Parent*, I have been amused and sometimes amazed at the reactions of people to my statement that it is impossible to raise children effectively, particularly aggressive, forceful boys, without spanking them. In *How to Parent*, I tried to make it clear that my reason for feeling it is all right for parents to spank children is not that spanking is of great value to the child, but that spanking is of great value to the parent.

If parents were 100 percent perfect people, they probably could raise their children without ever having to resort to spanking. But we parents are not such paragons of virtue. Spanking is a way to get irritated and angry feelings out of our system and clear the air so that both parent and child can start over again.

Although I devoted only two-and-a-half pages to spanking out of two solid chapters on discipline methods, you would have thought from the reactions of various TV talk-show interviewers that I believed spanking was the most important thing a parent could do to bring his child up right. This is 180 degrees off what I actually said in

How to Parent. Once more I want to make it clear that I regard spanking as a very, very, minor method of dealing with the problems of discipline. Other methods I have discussed in this chapter, such as reinforcing desirable behavior, the feedback technique for letting your child know you understand how he feels, the use of natural consequences for undesirable behavior, etc., are all a thousand percent more important and more successful than spanking. Moreover, I believe there should be no need whatsoever to spank a child before the age of two, and there should be relatively little occasion to spank a child after the age of eight or nine if you have used other sensible and effective methods of discipline.

Remember, the main motive for your child to learn to behave in desirable ways is because he loves you, his parent. But each time you spank your child you are teaching him not to love you, but to hate and fear you. So keep spankings down to an absolute minimum.

With all of those negative things about spanking made clear, let me try to tell you now what its positive values are. Some psychologists and psychiatrists have stated in print that a parent should *never* spank a child. I think this is unfortunate and unrealistic. It makes no allowance whatsoever for the parent as a fallible, human being. When you have had it up to the eyebrows with some particularly irritating behavior, it is much better psychologically for you to give your kid a few swift whacks on the bottom than to continue to seethe inside with no outlet for your angry feelings. This kind of fast-lick spanking lets your child know in no uncertain terms how angry you are, and it clears the air so that both you and he can start over. With the angry feelings out of your system you can once more feel positive toward your child. You can once again assume your rightful role of firm and loving parental authority.

If you are the kind of father who is able to control his child's undesirable behavior by physically removing him from the scene without ever spanking him—fine! If you are the kind of father who never loses his cool with his child and never swats him—terrific! More power to you! But I find that most fathers (myself included) are not able to be such reasonable and firm parents all the time.

But I want to make it clear that there is a world of difference between the "fast-lick" kind of spanking which relieves a parent's angry feelings, and a cruel and sadistic beating with a whip or stick or some other sort of weapon. This is a "beating" rather than a "spanking" and it fills a child with a deep hatred of the parent and an intense desire for revenge. A humiliating slap in the face or a

"I KNOW, DR. DODSON SAYS
IT HELPS *MY FATHER* BUT IT
SURE DOESN'T HELP *ME*."

spanking administered in front of his friends is also deeply resented by a child, and should be avoided.

Now let us consider the seventh basic method of discipline which helps to build a strong self-concept in a child and to move him along the road toward the goal of self-discipline. This is what Dr. Thomas Gordon calls the "no-lose" method of handling conflicts between parent and child.

Parent-child interaction inevitably involves conflict between what the child wants to do and what the parent wants him to do. Most parents tend to think of resolving the conflict in terms of someone winning and someone losing. When a conflict erupts between parent and child most parents are silently asking themselves: Shall I be strict here (the parent wins) or shall I be permissive (the child wins)?

Here is an example of a typical "parent-wins-child-loses" resolution of a conflict between a father and his twelve-year-old daughter:

Jane: 'Bye, I'm off to school.

Parent: Honey, it's raining and you don't have your raincoat on.

Jane: I don't need it.

Parent: You don't need it! You'll get wet and ruin your clothes or catch a cold.

Jane: It's not raining that hard.

Parent: It is, too.

Jane: Well I don't want to wear a raincoat. I hate to wear a raincoat.

Parent: You march right back to your room and get that raincoat! I will not let you go to school without your raincoat on a day like this.

Jane: But I don't like it. . . .

Parent: No "buts"—if you don't wear it your mother and I will have to ground you.

Jane: (angrily), All right, you win! I'll wear the stupid raincoat![1]

But in "parent-wins-child-loses" methods of resolving conflict, the parent pays a high price for winning. The child will have little or no motivation to carry out the solution to the conflict, since he was given no voice in making the decision. The child usually looks for ways to avoid carrying out the parent's decision. If he cannot get out of it, he usually goes through the motions, barely doing what is required and nothing more. In addition, the "parent-wins-child-loses" method causes the child to resent the parent, and offers no opportunity for the child to grow in self-discipline.

Here is the same basic raincoat scene, only this time the permissive parent gives in and the child wins:

Jane: 'Bye, I'm off to school.

Parent: Honey, it's raining and you don't have your raincoat on.

Jane: I don't need it.

Parent: You don't need it! You'll get wet and ruin your clothes or catch a cold.

Jane: It's not raining that hard.

Parent: It is, too.

Jane: Well I don't want to wear a raincoat. I hate to wear a raincoat.

Parent: I want you to.

Jane: I hate that raincoat. I won't wear it. If you make me wear it, I'll be mad at you.

Parent: Oh, I give up! Go on to school without your raincoat. I don't want to argue with you anymore—you win.[2]

A child who grows up in a family where the "child-wins-parent-loses" method of resolving conflicts is used predominantly, will lack inner controls on his impulses and will become very self-centered and demanding. Such children are often unmanageable and have great difficulties with other children. They are so used to getting their way with their parents they assume they should get their way with everyone. These children have difficulties in adjusting to the rules and regulations of school.

Some parents use predominantly the "parent-wins-child-loses" method of resolving conflict; others use mainly the "child-wins-parent-loses" method. Sometimes parents start out using one method and shift to the other, or vacillate between the two.

However, there is a better way of handling conflict which Dr. Gordon calls the "no-lose" method. In this method, when parent and child encounter a conflict situation, the parent asks the child to join him in a joint search for some solution *acceptable to both parties.* Both child and parent may offer possible solutions to the problem. After each person has come up with possible ideas to resolve the conflict, both parties critically evaluate the proposed solutions and eventually decide on a final solution acceptable to both. Neither party "loses." Here is the familiar raincoat problem, this time resolved with the "no-lose" method:

Jane: 'Bye, I'm off to school.

Parent: Honey, it's raining outside and you don't have your raincoat on.

Jane: I don't need it.

Parent: I think it's raining quite hard and I'm concerned that you'll ruin your clothes or get a cold.

Jane: Well, I don't want to wear my raincoat.

Parent: You sure sound like you definitely don't want to wear that raincoat.

Jane: That's right, I hate it.

Parent: You really hate your raincoat.

Jane: Yeah, it's plaid.

Parent: Something about plaid raincoats you hate. huh?

Jane: Yes, nobody at school wears plaid raincoats.

Parent: You don't want to be the only one wearing something different.

Jane: I sure don't. Everybody wears plain-colored raincoats—either white or blue or green.

Parent: I see. Well, we really have a conflict here. You don't want to wear your raincoat 'cause it's plaid, but I sure don't want to pay a cleaning bill, and I will not feel comfortable with you getting a cold. Can you think of a solution that we both could accept. How could we solve this so we're both happy?

Jane: (Pause.) Maybe I could borrow Mom's car coat today.

Parent: What does that look like? Is it plain-colored?

Jane: Yeah, it's white.

Parent: Think she'll let you wear it today?

Jane: I'll ask her. (Comes back in a few minutes with car coat on; sleeves are too long, but she rolls them back.) It's okay with Mom.

Parent: You're happy with that thing?

Jane: Sure, it's fine.

Parent: Well, I'm convinced it will keep you dry. So if you're happy with that solution, I am, too.

Jane: Well, so long.

Parent: So long. Have a good day at school.[3]

With this method, neither Jane nor her father "lost." A solution was found which satisfied the needs of both, and both could walk away from the problem-solving session feeling warm rather than hostile toward each other.

The "no-lose" method of resolving conflicts has many psychological advantages for both parents and children. The child is motivated to carry out the solution because he has participated in the
decision-making process leading to the solution; it has not been
imposed upon him by his parents. Furthermore, the use of the
"no-lose" method develops children's thinking skills. This method is
like a challenging puzzle in which both parent and child put their
heads together to figure out the answer to the puzzle.

The use of the "no-lose" method of resolving conflicts should
result in a reduction in hostility on the part of the child. When both
parent and child can agree on a solution, resentment and hostility are
much less likely to arise.

Finally, since it is a problem-solving process, the use of the
"no-lose" method often gets beyond the superficial or "presenting"
problem to the real problem which underlies it. For example, the
"raincoat problem" turned out to be caused by the child's fear of
being embarrassed by having to wear a *plaid* raincoat.

You can begin to use the "no-lose" method of solving conflicts
between parent and child when your child is five. If you use this
method consistently, beginning at age five, by the time your children
reach adolescence you will have set the stage for a very positive
method of working out the traditional conflicts between parents and
adolescents.

This concludes the seven most basic methods of strengthening
your child's self-concept and thus helping him along the road to
self-discipline. However, I also want to mention one unsuccessful
method which many fathers use with their children: lecturing. Some
of the lectures are short, one-sentence lectures; others are long-
winded, fifteen-minute dissertations. The subjects of the lectures
vary enormously, but one thing all the lectures of fathers have in
common: they do absolutely no good in motivating the child to
better behavior in the future. Most fathers do not realize this, of
course, or they would not rely so heavily on lectures as a method of
discipline.

The next time you feel tempted to lecture your child about
something, imagine yourself "lecturing" the dolphin on why he
should not swim aimlessly around in the tank but should swim over
and jump through the hoop as you want him to do. Your lectures
have about as much effect on the behavior of your child as they

"COME HERE, SON. YOU AND I SHOULD HAVE A LITTLE TALK ABOUT YOUR MESSY ROOM."

"SHALL I BRING A NOTEBOOK?"

would on the dolphin. So leave the lecture in the Museum of Ancient Parental Curiosities where it belongs.

These seven methods of discipline will work very adequately until the time your child becomes a teen-ager. Then they will have to be considerably modified. For example, praising behavior that you want your child to repeat generally works well up to adolescence. But since part of normal adolescent behavior is to rebel against parental authority, your teen-ager does *not* want to please you and earn your praise in the same way he did when he was younger.

For example: One evening my sixteen-year-old daughter came into the living room dressed for a date and looking quite lovely. Instead of saying nothing, my wife made the mistake of saying: "Robin, you look just wonderful in that dress!" Five minutes later Robin went back to her room. She reappeared shortly thereafter dressed for the date in her moldiest old shirt and her scruffiest pair of blue jeans! So, with a teen-ager we have to modify drastically our parental adage that behavior that is praised will tend to be repeated. Our teen-agers are motivated *not* to wear their hair in styles that please us, *not* to dress in ways that please us, *not* to listen to the type of music that pleases us. We will discuss the discipline methods appropriate to the teen-age years when we get to that part of our story. But up to the age of thirteen, these seven methods will work out well.

Before concluding this chapter, I would like to recommend that you read further in other books on the subject of discipline since it is crucial in raising a child successfully. I would suggest that you read chapters 8 and 9 of my book *How to Parent,* "Can You Teach a Dolphin to Type?" and "Discipline through Self-Regulation," and that you read both of Dr. Haim Ginnot's books, *Between Parent and Child* and *Between Parent and Teenager.* All three books are available in paperback. I also recommend that you read *Improving Your Child's Behavior* by Dr. Madeline Hunter and Dr. Paul Carlson, and Dr. Thomas Gordon's excellent book, *Parent Effectiveness Training.* If you read these five sources I think you will have an in-depth view of discipline which will help you to become a more effective father.

6
The Preschool Stage I (Ages Three to Five)

It will no doubt come as a delightful piece of news to parents that the next stage of your children's development, the preschool stage, is one which is vastly easier on a parent than the stage of first adolescence.

This period begins around the time of your child's third birthday and runs to his sixth birthday. In contrast to the previous developmental stages, your child is faced with not just one single developmental task at a time; instead, there are a number of different tasks he must master. How he meets these tasks will basically determine his self-concept and personality structure which will assume their stable form approximately by the time he is six years old.

THE THREE-YEAR-OLD

If you have sweated through the terrible two's with your youngster, you might have a hard time recognizing your three-year-old except for his physical appearance. The three-year-old is in a new stage of equilibrium. He's a much more pleasant person to have around; he has been through the difficult transition period from babyhood to true childhood, and he feels much surer of himself. No longer is he swept by the vacillating back-and-forth emotional storms of first adolescence. Since much of the anxiety of the transition period has passed, he is more comfortable with himself and doesn't need the protection of his inflexible rituals as much. He no longer insists on doing everything just one way—his way.

During the previous stage he could have won a medal for the world's greatest nonconformist; now he actually begins to take pleasure in conforming to what other people desire and in trying to please. He may surprise you by asking permission to do something that in the previous stage he simply went ahead and did. His new spirit of cooperation makes things easier on everybody and will win the approval, not only of parents, but of his older brothers and sisters.

Whereas in the previous stage it may have seemed to you that you couldn't reason with him about anything, you are able to now, in the preschool stage. (But this doesn't mean that you should give him long moral lectures, in the guise of reasoning with him.)

No longer is he the grand exalted ruler of the house, the little tyrant who wants everything his way—or else! He is not so domineering or dictatorial now, and his temper tantrums begin to fall by the wayside. He is beginning to share, to take his turn. His capacity to wait is increasing. He has a longer attention span and is better able to persevere at a task. In part, this is due to his emerging self-confidence and, in part, to the reduction of the anxieties of the previous transition stage. New confidence is shown in the increasing sureness of his motor control and muscular development. He is developing more patience in dressing himself and in playing with his toys. He is less likely to fly off the handle when something goes wrong.

In part, your three-year-old's increasing sureness in himself is due to his improved language ability. This enables him to understand other people better and to put his feelings into words. Able to communicate his feelings, he develops better control over his impulses, particularly negative ones. If he can say "I'm mad at you, Jimmy," he can more easily control his impulse to hit out at his playmate. With improved language ability, a whole new intellectual world opens up for the three-year-old . . . including a delightful new world of imagination and fantasy. He is beginning to love words and likes to hear new ones. At times you will see him carrying out his own little dramatic monologues, combining actions with words. By doing this he is increasing his command of language.

The three-year-old is beginning to enjoy play and companionship with his peers. In the first-adolescence stage he was not able to play with other children in the true meaning of the term. He was in the stage of "parallel play," in which he and another youngster were close together only geographically, but in play each was in his own separate little world. At three he has advanced to a new plateau of truly cooperative play with other children. He is developing the ability genuinely to interact with other children, to wait, to take his turn, to share, and to accept substitute toys.

Three is one of the most delightful ages of the preschool period, a time when your youngster is at peace with himself and with his world. He loves life, he loves his parents, he feels good about himself, and he likes to please. Fathers should take advantage of this enjoyable time, because the next stage of development is a zinger!

THE FOUR-YEAR-OLD

I have pointed out that in the first five years stages of equilibrium tend to be followed by stages of disequilibrium, and this includes the three-year-old stage of equilibrium. Once again, your child's behavior patterns need to be loosened up in order for him to attain a new and more mature integration. Around the fourth birthday the old equilibrium starts to break up. (Please remember that these chronological times are only very rough approximations. Your child could just as easily begin the four-year-old stage at three and a half or as late as four and a half.) At any rate, unless you have some idea of what the four-year-old stage means, you might very well say to yourself in dismay, "Where did my pleasant and cooperative three-year-old vanish?" Perhaps the best way I can describe the four-year-old in a sentence is to say that his behavior is very remininscent of the terrible two's, except that he is more mature and sophisticated, and, in general, easier to get along with.

Four-year-olds delight in playing together. Friendships are more important to them than they were at three, but, paradoxically, they may find it more difficult to get along with their friends than they did at three. An anthropologist, accustomed to studying the tribal life of primitive people, would find the tribal life of a group of four-year-olds equally fascinating. Their social life is apt to be stormy and violent. Once a clique has been formed, they will tend to exclude outsiders. There will be a great deal of demanding, threatening, commanding, shoving, and jostling. Bragging may be the one of their most important forms of verbal communication. Name calling will also be quite popular. A four-year-old is crude, blunt, and direct, with little consideration for other people's feelings.

There is much in the behavior of your four-year-old to make you suspect that you are dealing with a two-year-old who is older and heavier. His wrangles with other children will remind you of how he was at two. He may become bossy, belligerent, and rambunctious. He is prey to the same kind of emotional extremes he exhibited when he was two: shy one minute, brassily boisterous the next. He may become as fixated on rituals as he was at two and will insist on having everything just so. It may be very difficult for him to tolerate any change in his routines of eating, dressing, or sleeping. His emotional insecurity will be expressed by whining, crying, or frequent complaints.

Dr. Gesell suggests that the key phrase to sum up the behavior of a four-year-old is "out of bounds." He is out of bounds in his motor behavior: he will hit, kick, or sometimes throw fits of rage. Verbally, he tends to be out of bounds also. He loves to exaggerate, and his conversation is sprinkled liberally with exclamation marks.

Four-year-olds take a heightened interest in language. They are fascinated by words and the sounds of words and like to make up silly words. I remember one car ride with my oldest boy when he was four. We spent about half an hour playing a "word game" in which we would make up silly "words" to rhyme with one another.

One aspect of your four-year-old's out of bounds behavior with words is apt to throw you unless you are prepared for it. This is his use of four-letter words and "bathroom" language. He will now discover the shock value they have, especially if company is around. Sometimes these bathroom words are hilariously funny for him. A four-year-old will say to you, "Daddy, you know what I had for lunch today? I had a BM sandwich and a drink of pee-pee!" At this point he will dissolve into howls of laughter, overcome by his own wondrous sense of humor. The best way to handle your child's use of these four-letter words is simply to ignore them. If you make a big fuss over them you will be teaching him how he can get a rise out of you and will merely prolong his use of them. If you ignore them, knowing they are characteristics of this age, they will fade away, in time, and be heard no more when he is five.

Your four-year-old will also be out of bounds in his relationships with people: he will delight in defying requests and commands, chafe at limits, swagger, boast, and swear, and he will be apt to threaten other children: "I'll sock you!" He will have no sense of property rights, except for his rather quaint idea that everything he sees is his own property. Many fathers are quite horrified when they discover their four-year-old's attitude toward property. They react by feeling: "I'd better start out right now and teach this kid to respect private property and the rights of others, or I'll have a juvenile delinquent on my hands when he's a teen-ager!"

A father need not be alarmed if he understands the limitations of four-year-old logic about property. To a four-year-old, possession means ownership. He thinks a toy he took at a neighbor's house "belongs" to him, because he was playing with it, put it in his pocket, and brought it home! The father who understands the limitations of four-year-old logic will gently explain the situation to his child, realizing that it will take years to teach him to understand and respect the property of others.

The drive level of a four-year-old is fantastic. He will race up and down the stairs, run exuberantly through the house, and shut doors with a crash and a bang. His drive to converse is also very strong. He is a great talker and loves to hold forth on almost any subject. He is the young-man-on-a-soapbox, his own self-appointed commentator on the world, and, sometimes, his own audience. He has a tendency to talk on and on and run subjects into the ground. His use of questions may rise to new heights, and a father sometimes has the feeling that if his four-year-old asks him "Why?" just one more time he will explode.

However, the wise father can use his four-year-old's new fascination with words and language by channeling it into constructive activity. You can play all sorts of word games with your four-year-old. He loves to make up silly words and to rhyme words. He is fond of humor, exaggeration, and nonsense rhymes. Your four-year-old

"MY FATHER DOESN'T EVEN
BLINK WHEN I SAY BAD WORDS."

"WELL, LET'S GO TRY
SOME OUT ON MY FATHER. HE
GOES CRAZY AND MAYBE
HE'LL CALL YOUR FATHER AND
HELP HIM GET WELL."

takes great delight in such nonsense questions as, "Shall we get a hamburger today, or would you rather have an elephant sandwich?"

Your four-year-old child loves to dramatize and can make good use of hand or finger puppets. One of the best things you can do for him is to build him a simple puppet stage in your backyard that he can use for putting on his own impromptu puppet shows. (See Appendix B, "Toys and Inexpensive Playthings a Father Can Make for His Child," for details on how to make this stage.) Your youngster will also engage in lengthy dramatic play indoors and out, with his blocks, cars, trucks, ships, dolls, and toy people. Another very helpful plaything you can build for your four-year-old is a sandbox. Make it good and large so that he will have a great deal of room for play, and give him lots of plastic animals, dinosaurs, small toy men, women, and children to use in his dramatic play. If possible, locate the sandbox near a garden hose connection so that he can combine waterplay with sandplay if he wishes.

Stephen Leacock's description of the man who jumped on his horse and rode off rapidly in all directions fits the four-year-old perfectly. Four never seems to know precisely where he is going until he gets there. His strong drive level and fluidity of thought will lead him hither and yon with bewildering rapidity. He may start to draw a lion, but before he is through his drawing may have changed suddenly into a dinosaur or a house. When his parent asked him what he was painting, one four-year-old answered, "How should I know? I haven't finished it yet!"[1] Such an explanation seems entirely logical to a four-year-old. A parent can expect the same unexpected shifts of direction when his youngster is reporting on some happening of the day.

Because of the exuberant personality characteristics of this stage, four-year-olds need firmness. Here a father may truly come into his own, for many times father is able to be firmer than mother with a child at this age. A weak or vacillating parent can be overwhelmed by the four-year-old. "I can't do a thing with him!" wails many a frantic mother. When you are being firm with your youngster, remember that although he needs a firm hand he does not need a dictator. Do not expect instant obedience from your four-year-old. Allow for grumbling and defiance when he is called upon to perform some task. But be firm. Insist that he do what you tell him if it is a reasonable request. Also, remember that the four-year-old thrives on variety and a change of pace. If you see a potentially troublesome situation arising, "head him off at the pass" by having a new activity in mind which will intrigue him. The behavior of a four-year-old can easily deteriorate into out-of-bounds silliness if not controlled. Try to anticipate this and divert him with some intriguing activity.

So that's the four-year-old. Gesell sums him up in this way: "He can be quiet, noisy, calm, assertive, cosy, imperious, suggestible, independent, social, athletic, artistic, literal, fanciful, cooperative, indifferent, inquisitive, forthright, prolix, humorous, dogmatic, silly, and competitive."[2]

Translated into Basic English, Dr. Gesell's remarks mean that the typical four-year-old is quite a handful for a parent to manage! However, just about the time you are gritting your teeth and saying to your wife for the umpteenth time, "Jane, when did you say he was going to grow out of this stage?"—your little rascal turns five. And amazingly enough, his behavior does change. For, almost overnight, he seems to have left behind the disequilibrium of the four-year-old and entered the new equilibrium that goes with being five.

THE FIVE-YEAR-OLD

Most fathers find that five is a delightful age. The out-of-bounds behavior of the four-year-old has disappeared. Five is in harmony with himself and other people. He tends to be reliable, stable, and well adjusted. He is more secure within himself and so he can afford to be more calm, friendly, and not too demanding in his relationship with others. Whereas four will try impossible tasks and become unruly and frustrated when he fails, five will try only what he can accomplish; therefore, he usually succeeds. For example, in contrast to a four-year-old who may not know what he's going to draw until he is finished, the five-year-old will have a definite idea in his mind of what he is going to draw and complete the drawing as planned. Five likes to finish what he starts; four rambles on and on, but five knows when to stop. In contrast to his out-of-bounds behavior at four, your five-year-old will keep his behavior within reasonable limits.

A five-year-old child is happy and content with the "here and now" world he lives in. He is not in conflict with himself or with his environment. Other people are usually satisfied with him. He has now returned to the spirit of cooperation and wanting to please other people which he showed when he was three, only now he is on

"THIS IS HOW YOU ACTED
SOMETIMES WHEN YOU WERE FOUR."

"OH, I WAS JUST A *KID* THEN.
I'M GROWN UP NOW — I'M FIVE."

a more mature level of personality integration. Living in the present and oblivious of the past or future, he is a pragmatic being who tends to define things in terms of their use: "A pony is to ride; a cushion is to sit on." His thinking is concrete, and his ability to think abstractly is very meager. When a five-year-old was asked, "Do dogs run?" he answered, with delightful five-year-old logic, "I don't have a dog!"[3]

In spite of his love for his home and family, home is not quite enough for the five-year-old. He is ripe for enlarged community experiences. He loves the friendships and socialization of his peers in the neighborhood. He is capable of a great deal intellectually, more so than most adults realize. For this reason he is eager and ready to go to "school," which, to him, means kindergarten.

If your public-school system does not have a kindergarten, special thought should be given to his play day. In fact, if your public-school system does not have a kindergarten, perhaps you will join with other parents to try to see that this unfortunate situation is remedied. The child who does not go to kindergarten has missed a very important educational experience. If it is financially possible, I urge you to find a good private kindergarten and enroll your child. A five-year-old is capable of great intellectual development under the guidance of a skilled teacher. It is too valuable a year of potential learning to let it go to waste.

Your five-year-old is a remarkable balance of good qualities put together in one all-inclusive package. Dr. Gesell sums up the five-year-old as follows: "He presents a remarkable equilibrium of qualities and patterns: of self-sufficiency and sociality; of self-reliance and cultural conformity; of serenity and seriousness; of carefulness and conclusiveness; of politeness and insouciance; of friendliness and self-confidence."[4] Physically, your five-year-old has advanced considerably in poise and muscular skill. Emotionally, he is on a much more even keel. Intellectually, he has made dramatic strides since he was four and he is full of curiosity and enthusiasm for learning. All things considered, he is a joy to have around. Five is a truly delightful age when a child seems to take life as it comes and be content with it.

From these three brief sketches you can see that there are enormous psychological differences between a three-, a four-, and a five-year-old. If a father is not aware of these vast differences in psychological development he will not be able to deal with his children very successfully. For example, in disciplining his four-year-old, he may be expecting his child to obey like a five-year-old, and then scold him when he cannot. Or a father may conclude that his child is going to the dogs when his three-year-old conformity and desire to please gives way to the out-of-bounds rambunctiousness and nonconformity of the four-year-old.

However, in spite of the great differences in behavior between the three-, four-, and five-year-olds, all three groups have many things in common. This is why all three ages are grouped together under one stage of development: the preschool stage.

It is much more complex than the three stages that preceded it. Instead of having only one developmental task, as each of the preceding stages had, the preschool stage has *nine.* These nine developmental tasks cut across all three age groups, and run like a leitmotif in a piece of music throughout all three preschool years. The leitmotif may be different in the four-year-old and five-year-old from the three-year-old, but the theme is still recognizable.

So let's turn our attention to these leitmotifs, these nine developmental tasks your child must master during the three years that he spends in the preschool stage.

FULFILLING BIOLOGICAL NEEDS

First, and more basic than anything else, *your preschool child must fulfill his biological needs for both large-muscle and small-muscle development.*

Biology is more basic than psychology in the human animal. Your preschool child has an innate biological drive to release energy. He literally has to be on the go from dawn to dark. He needs to wiggle, move, climb, run and jump, and move around. Because adults are much more placid creatures biologically, it is easy for us to overlook or underestimate the importance of this dynamic aspect of our preschooler.

I remember a father's impatient criticism of his four-year-old, who was wiggling around in his seat in a restaurant: "Can't you sit still, for Pete's sake?" his father asked irritably. I felt like saying to the father (but didn't, of course): "No he can't sit still. And you couldn't sit still either, when you were only four!" That father, like many parents, was expecting a biological maturity of his four-year-old boy which was impossible.

Think of your preschooler as a biological factory. He takes in raw materials in the form of food and then uses them to manufacture vast supplies of energy, which need to be expended. This means that your youngster needs plenty of play space and play equipment both inside and outside. For the most part our adult-oriented houses are not equipped to hold a preschooler with boundless energy. To an adult, a door is something you shut quietly; to a preschooler it is something you slam; to an adult, stairs are something to walk sedately up or down; to a preschooler stairs are something to run up or down or to crawl on in outlandish positions. Our houses come equipped with nice white walls on which we can hang pictures; a preschooler may think of them as "blackboards" for scribbling or drawing.

Incidentally, wouldn't it make a lot of sense for a father to see that the walls in his preschooler's room were truly adapted to this stage of his development instead of to that of a nonexistent adult? You could do this very easily by covering the walls of your child's room with Cellotex and then with vinyl. The four walls of your child's room would then literally be one enormous blackboard. He could scribble and draw and, later, print to his heart's content. The walls could be used, still later, to pin up his pictures or printings or school work. Marks from watercolor felt markers or paints could easily be rubbed off the vinyl surface and leave the wall fresh for new artistic decorations. Used this way, the walls of your child's room could aid enormously in his intellectual development.

Remember that preschool children are not sedate and quiet little people. Biologically they need to run and jump and yell and cavort. Their biological needs often run counter to our adult needs for peace and quiet and order. This may make it difficult for us to be fully cooperative in letting our preschoolers work out their biological needs. However, if your preschooler does not have constructive outlets for his immense energy, he will surely find destructive ones. If you force your child to be too "good" and quiet during his preschool years, he will be at a disadvantage with his classmates when he is older. He will lack the basic foundation of muscular coordination which is necessary for him to develop reasonable skill in the games and sports (and hence in the social relationships) of school.

In addition, to a much greater degree than most parents realize, motor and muscular skills are the foundation stones for later intellectual skills. For example, in order to develop the fine muscle coordination needed to learn to print and write, a child first must go through a stage of scribbling. Scribbling is practicing the fine muscle coordination of fingers and thumb which he will use in printing and writing. So a child whose walls are adapted to promote free scribbling is going to be at an advantage compared to one who has little outlet in his home for such activities.

Muscular coordination in children is composed of two basic factors: *laterality* and *directionality*. Our laterality is like a map of our own internal space in relation to the symmetry of our "leftness" and our "rightness." Unless a child develops this internal map of laterality he cannot operate smoothly with either hand or leg, or with both hands and legs. We can think of directionality as the projection into space of our own laterality, that is, our awareness of left and right, up and down, before and behind. Whereas laterality is like a map of internal space, directionality is like a map of external space.

The point is that laterality and directionality are not innate. They must be learned. And they can only be learned when your child has lots of opportunities to climb and crawl and run and tumble and build with blocks. These internal and external maps depend upon muscular patterns and motor movements which are learned by your child during his preschool years. They may be thought of as the "knowledge of the muscles."

"But what does all this have to do with intellectual tasks such as reading?" you may ask. Much more than most fathers realize. For example, if a child has not developed a good sense of laterality he will make letter and word reversals in reading. Notice that the only difference between the letter "b" and the letter "d" is one of laterality. Once you understand this, it is easy to see why children confuse these two letters. And if your child has not developed a good sense of laterality by age five or six he is going to have trouble in distinguishing between a "b" and a "d." If you want to know more about the importance of good motor development and its relationship to later intellectual skills, I recommend an excellent book which discusses the subject in laymen's terms, *Success Through Play* by D. H. Radler and Newell Kephart. But if you give your child lots of opportunity for vigorous muscular play, you need not worry about his missing out on learning good laterality and directionality.

One of the best (and most enjoyable) things you can do for your preschool child is to take him to a nearby park and watch him play.

Play with him if you like, but don't feel obligated. He will probably ask you to push him on the swings, but he can manage the other play equipment by himself. He will call to you from time to time: "Daddy, look what I can do! Watch me!" He will be proud to show you his new "gymnastic" accomplishments. But much of the time he will be happy to play by himself needing only to know you are nearby. And, of course, if there are other children to play with he will have less need for your attention. Take along a book or magazine and use the spare time for reading or thinking or just enjoying the scene.

One of the things I noticed when I took my three children to the park was how few fathers brought their children compared to mothers. I think that's a shame. Fathers who don't do this are missing a lot of enjoyment and some wonderful opportunities to deepen their relationship with their children. If you have two or more preschoolers you may want to take them all to the park sometimes, and other times you may find it best to take just one.

Of course there are many other opportunities for developing closeness between a father and his preschool child while the child is also fulfilling his biological needs: on camping trips, at the beach, in the swimming pool in the backyard, or roughhousing and tussling in the family room. But the main message for fathers in connection with this first developmental task of the preschool stage is that you need to give your child ample opportunity to be a healthy, vivacious, exuberant biological animal.

A CONTROL SYSTEM

Closely allied with the first developmental task is task number two: to develop a control system for his emotions and impulses.

Here, again, biology is basic. When your child is born he is essentially a young animal with no control over his desires. When he wants to yell, he yells. When he feels like kicking, he kicks. As your child advances to toddlerhood, his control over his impulsive drives is still very primitive. If he trips over a toy, he will probably, in his frustration, kick it. If another child takes something from him, he may hit to get it back. If he doesn't like something another child does while playing in the sandbox, he may throw sand.

But between his third and sixth birthday, your child will be actively working to establish a control system for his emotional drives and impulses. How can you help him in this developmental task?

The first and most important thing is to understand that it *will take a great deal of time* to develop controls. Fathers are, typically, much more impatient than mothers with the amount of time it takes for a child to develop impulse control. I think the basic reason is not that mothers are innately any more knowledgeable about preschool children, but that mothers are around their children much more than fathers and learn, by trial and error, what they can reasonably expect. Fathers spend much more time in the world of adults and much less in the world of preschool children. Therefore, it's understandable when fathers assume that preschool children are adults in diminutive form. When you are exasperated at your preschooler for not being able to control some impulse, you may be expecting him to learn this control faster than is reasonable.

Often parents say to a child, "Don't you know what 'no' means?" Of course, the child comprehends intellectually what "no" means; but he has not yet developed an adequate control system to enable him to deal with the "no" and inhibit himself from antisocial action. Some fathers think that once a child comprehends the meaning of "no" intellectually, he will be able to obey that command instantaneously. But things don't work that way. You will need literally thousands of repetitions to teach your child the necessary habits to inhibit antisocial impulses until they are well established.

Remember when your child was first learning to speak? He didn't start speaking right away in complex sentences such as, "Timmy and I are going down to his house to play in his sandpile." He started speaking in one-word sentences: "out," "sandpile," "beach," "drink." Then he moved on to two-word sentences. Finally he graduated to more complex sentences. Fathers are usually very understanding and patient as their child's ability to handle language grows. They can be very amused and tolerant of his grammatical mistakes, his mispronunciations as he says "aminals" for "animals" or "chimley" for "chimney." But those same fathers become very impatient with their child's mistakes, blunders, and balkiness as his ability to control his impulses develops slowly (oh so slowly!) through the preschool years.

Give your child time. If you aid him wisely and skillfully, by the time he is six years old your child should have a reasonably good control system established. This control system will effectively inhibit him from hitting, throwing sand, stealing, and any other antisocial behavior that might get him into trouble in grade school or in neighborhood play. If you have done a good job of teaching impulse control in the preschool years, there should be relatively few occasions when you will need to spank him throughout the rest of his childhood.

There are two major mistakes which fathers may make in teaching impulse control.

One type of father makes no demands at all for impulse control and the child at age six is no further advanced than he was at age two. This type of child will freely hit other children, take their things, indulge in temper tantrums, and in general raise hell with his environment. However, this is a mistake that is made by a very small minority of parents.

Most parents, and particularly fathers, are much more likely to make the opposite type of mistake, which is to pressure the child to try to control his impulses too fast. This is why it is so important for fathers to know in general, what is reasonable to expect of his child at each age.

Pressuring a child to control his impulses faster than he can reasonably manage may cause many needless problems. Eating problems, excessive dawdling, nail-biting, fear of animals or the dark, nightmares—all these may be disguises for the child's response to too much pressure to control impulses too quickly. Make only gradually increasing demands for control of antisocial impulses. Three is a good age to begin, for three is a period of equilibrium and cooperation; your child has by then acquired enough skill in handling language so that his command of words helps him internalize controls.

By allowing him to say to his brother, "I hate you, Jimmy!" you are making it easier for him to inhibit his impulse to hit his brother or take his toys. Offer your child alternative outlets for his antisocial actions. "No, I won't let you hit your brother, Tommy. But I know you are mad and feel like hitting him, so you can punch this Bobo the Clown instead."

One very good suggestion for alternate outlets for a child's antisocial impulses is to provide what Dr. Ruth Hartley calls "buffets." These are creatures designed to take beatings without harmful effects. A buffet is basically a sturdy rag doll without a body. Your wife (or you, if you know how to sew!) can make one by using canvas, stuffed, for the head, with features embroidered in colored thread. The buffet is completed by a man's shirt or a woman's blouse sewed to the neck. Buffets should correspond to each member of your family: mother, father, and each age and child. These buffets can safely be used to drain off antisocial impulses and disturbed feelings.

Another way to release antisocial impulses and disturbed feelings safely is to play the turnaround game. It works this way: Say to your child, "I have a new game for us to play today. It's called the turnaround game and this is how you play it. We'll pretend for fifteen minutes [shorter if your tolerance time is shorter!] that you are the Daddy and I am the child. Whatever you tell me to do, I have to obey and do it." You will be surprised what will be accomplished through the use of this game, and what negative feelings and impulses a child can release safely.

One four-year-old, when first introduced to the game, said: "Okay, you've got to do your homework!" He got his older brother's arithmetic book and made his father do arithmetic problems as "homework" for fifteen minutes, while he stood over him and exclaimed: "Work harder! You're not working hard enough!"

Often, we fathers do not realize how many rules and restrictions our children feel they must conform to, and how they long, deep inside, for a chance to boss us around the way they feel we boss them. Playing the turnaround game gives them the chance to boss us safely and release a number of negative feelings. One word of caution: your child may be too afraid at first to let himself go and may need several sessions and much encouragement in order to feel comfortable about "bossing" you.

One of the best ways to help your child develop a system of control is to send him to nursery school when he is three. Under the guidance of an experienced teacher he will have many more opportunities for learning self-control than in informal and unsupervised backyard play. I will discuss this and other advantages of sending your child to nursery school later in this chapter.

This developmental task of learning to establish a control system for his impulses has been concerned with your child's *actions*. The next developmental task concerns your child's *feelings*.

LEARNING TO EXPRESS FEELINGS

Between his third and his sixth birthdays, your preschooler needs to learn to express his feelings and put them into words.

In the last chapter I emphasized how important it is to allow your child to express his feelings rather than bury them underground where they will come out in a disguised and harmful form. The years from three to six are years in which your child will establish some very basic attitudes about his feelings and emotions. Either he will come to believe that his feelings are dangerous and he had better keep them repressed, or he will learn to feel comfortable with his feelings, negative as well as positive.

As a psychologist, I have spent many years helping adults learn to express their feelings. Often, when adults who are anxious learn to express the feelings which cause them anxiety (usually hostile or sexual feelings), they no longer feel anxious and fearful. In many cases, when an adult with a phobia learns to express the feelings for which the phobia is a disguise, it vanishes; and when adults who are depressed learn to express the angry feelings which cause the depression, the depression often clears up. None of these adults would have their psychological problems of anxiety, depression, or psychosomatic symptoms if they had learned to express their feelings verbally during their preschool years! If you want to keep your child out of the psychologist's office when he is a grown-up, there is probably nothing more important than giving him the right to express his feelings in words when he is a preschooler.

So teach your child that "right" and "wrong," "good" and "bad," do not apply to feelings. There are no "bad" or "wrong" feelings. There are only "bad" or "wrong" actions. Even the law of our country allows us the right to make a distinction between our feelings and our actions. The law allows us to feel like killing somebody ("I was so mad at my boss I could cheerfully have killed him"). Only if we translate such a feeling into action will the law step in and say, "That's wrong." Shouldn't parents give children the same right that the law of our land gives to its citizens?

Most of us were, unfortunately, not allowed to express our negative feelings when we were children. I was certainly not allowed to tell my father or mother that I was angry or hated them. That would have been considered "sassing" or "talking back" or "lack of respect." I allow my children to express their feelings freely to me. But sometimes when one of them is saying, "You're mean and I hate you!" I will feel a surge of anger and seem to hear a voice inside me saying, "Don't you dare talk that way to me, young man; I'm your father!"

Of course I know that voice from within is not my scientific training about what is best for children. It is merely the echo of my father's voice from my own childhood and the mistaken way in which he raised me. But I don't choose to pass on those same mistakes to my children. So I have allowed them to express their feelings freely to me, both negative and positive. (However, although I know it's better for a child to be allowed to express his feelings, that doesn't mean I am always up to doing what I know is best. If I have had an especially trying day at the office or am otherwise on edge, I may say: "Okay, knock it off! Daddy doesn't want to hear any more of your feelings right now.")

I want to tell a story out of my own family to illustrate what allowing your child to express his feelings will do for him. One Saturday afternoon I came home and went into the bathroom to wash my hands. I noticed the usual vase with flowers in it on the bathroom sink, but this time the vase had a strange yellowish liquid in it. I bent down to sniff it and my suspicions were confirmed; it was *not* water! I began to think who might have done it. I immediately eliminated my wife and teen-age daughter as suspects. I eliminated one-year-old Rusty as a suspect because his aim wasn't that good. That left only six-year-old Randy. I hunted him up and confronted him with the evidence. "Randy," I said, "what made you pee in the vase?"

"I dunno," he said, in typical six-year-old fashion.

"You must have been mad about something to do that. What were you mad about?"

He finally admitted that he had been mad because his mother wouldn't let him go to the movies that afternoon. That's why he did the dastardly deed. So I said, "Randy, you know you are allowed to tell Mother and Daddy when you are angry at us. So the next time you are mad at one of us, tell us you're mad, but don't pee in the vase!"

There is a lot to be learned from this simple incident. It illustrates very clearly the alternatives a child has: either he can express his negative feelings in words, or he is going to pee in the vase! (Or engage in some other sneaky way of getting rid of his angry feelings through antisocial actions.)

Some fathers reading this may misinterpret me at this point and think I am saying they should allow their children to express their negative feelings at all times and places and at all ages. No, I do not advocate allowing all children to express their negative feelings anytime and anyplace. Children need to learn to keep back their negative feelings at times. They need to learn that telling the teacher at school they hate her will probably get them in trouble. Children also need to learn that other people have feelings, too. They need to learn to respect the feelings of other people and be gentle with them.

But right now I'm talking about preschool children. And preschool children are too young to be able to make distinctions between controlling their negative and positive feelings. If we prevent our preschool children from expressing their negative feelings we will be teaching them to repress their positive feelings as well. The net result is that we teach them to be emotionally inhibited. Children in their preschool years cannot be taught to deal gently with people's feelings without paying the price of inhibiting their spontaneity and emotional freedom.

The time to begin teaching your child that other people also have feelings is around the age of six. There will be plenty of time for him to learn that sometimes he needs to keep his feelings to himself or they will get him in trouble. In the grade-school years, you can teach your child to discriminate as to where certain feelings may safely be expressed and where it is not wise to express them. But the preschool years are the time to encourage children to express *all* their feelings, whether negative or positive.

SEPARATION FROM MOTHER

In the stage of first adolescence, your child is not yet ready to separate from mother. Mother is the center of a two-year-old's universe. This is why it is ordinarily not a good idea to send a two-year-old to nursery school. Emotionally, he is not ready for it. He is simply not prepared to leave his mother for three hours a day to play with children under the supervision of what to him is a "strange" woman, his teacher. If a working mother has to leave a two-year-old at a day-care center because of economic necessity, then, of course, there is no alternative. But ideally, a child should be three before attending nursery school or a day-care center.

At three, a child is ready to leave the stage of parallel play. He now craves companionship. He wants to learn to adapt to his peer group. He wants to separate from his mother and become more independent.

The easiest way for your child to accomplish this task is for you to send him to a good nursery school.

I am continually surprised to find many otherwise intelligent fathers who are amazingly naive about nursery school and what it can accomplish. I have had bankers and lawyers and doctors and executives say to me: "Well, nursery school is more or less just a baby-sitting service, isn't it?" To call a good nursery school a baby-sitting service reveals an astounding ignorance of what it can do both for your child's emotional and intellectual development. We will talk more about what nursery school can do for your child's intellectual development in the next chapter. Right now I want to concentrate on your child's *emotional* development.

Even though a three-year-old wants to become more independent, separate from his mother, and get out into the new world of his peers, he still has mixed feelings about leaving the security and protection of mother. You should not be surprised that he feels this "separation anxiety," **for,** after all, mother has been his "home base" for three solid years.

You would get valuable insight into how a three-year-old feels about separating from his mother if you could see inside the mind of a three-year-old on his first day in nursery school. He is thinking something like this:

> Mother has brought me to this new place. She said I'd like it and have lots of fun here, but I'm not so sure about that. Mother said that woman over there is my teacher. What is she like? Will she be nice to me? Will she take care of me? Who are all those strange children? I've never seen so many other new kids in one room together in all my life! Will they like me? Will they be nice to play with, or will they hurt me? I'm feeling scared. In fact, I'm not sure I like this place at all! Mother, don't leave me, don't desert me! I feel so scared I'm going to cry![5]

And that's exactly what a number of three-year-olds do on their first day in nursery school: they cry. It would be very instructive if fathers could visit nursery schools on opening day. They would find a number of crying children being held on teachers' laps and comforted.

All three-year-olds experience these feelings of "separation anxiety" to some degree. If your youngster is a secure and psychologically healthy child he may feel them only briefly. Then he will let himself be led into the group of other children and started on an activity. But even if a child is able to let mother go and join in the activities of the group, he still has mixed feelings down deep about letting mother go. Sometimes a child may express his feelings about separating from mother, not in words, but in the body language of physical symptoms. When it's time to leave for nursery school he may suddenly develop a pain in his legs, an upset stomach, or a headache.

Separating from mother and making it on his own with his peer group is a *big step* for your child. To you, his father, it may seem like nothing at all, but to him it is like a scary voyage through outer space to an unknown planet. How much easier is the task of separation from mother if he can attend nursery school.

Fathers think nothing of borrowing money to send a child to college, because they know how important a college education is. But how many fathers realize how important nursery school is to their child's emotional and intellectual development and think about borrowing money for this purpose? In nursery school your child has a skilled teacher to help him accomplish the developmental task of emotional separation from mother. In neighborhood play with other children there is no skilled teacher to aid him. Nursery school is of particular help to shy children in enabling them to achieve this task.

If it is at all possible, I strongly suggest you take a half day off from work after your child has been in nursery school for a month or so. Visit the school and see him in action. Sit unobtrusively in a corner so as not to disturb the class. It will be well worth your while for it will give you an idea of what goes on at nursery school, and how it aids in your child's development.

You can also indirectly aid your child in his task of separating from mother by spending the kind of time with him that I have mentioned in previous chapters. The child who sees little of his father up to the age of three has only his mother to rely on as a source of emotional support. Consequently, such a child will have a more difficult time separating from her than the child who also has the security of a strong emotional relationship with his father.

THE NEW WORLD OF HIS PEERS

The next developmental task your child must master is to learn the give and take of relating to other children, his peer group.

Fathers who belittle the importance of these early lessons in the art of human relations should stop and ask themselves: Of all the people I know who got fired from their jobs, what was the main reason that they were fired? If you analyze the situation you will probably find that it was not lack of technical skill, but an inability to get along with other people.

The principle lessons a child receives in the art of getting along with other people are learned in the years between three and six. It is in the world of his peers that a child learns his socializing skills. He learns how to share, to wait his turn, to ask for something from another child, to put his feelings into words. He learns how to stand up for his rights, to prevent other children from bullying him, to express his feelings without resorting to his fists, to participate as well as observe. He must learn to develop self-confidence in his dealings with other children. No child is born with these basic social and emotional skills. However, these skills in human relations, learned in early childhood, are vital to your child's success in later life.

Each child learns that the world of peer relationships is dramatically different from the world of his family. In the family he is loved and accepted just for himself. His accepted place in the family is by virtue of being born into it. But he has no accepted place in relationships with his peers. It is a different psychological world with an entirely new set of unwritten rules and demands. In a child's first group experience he comes face to face with his strengths and weaknesses. He wins acceptance, but he also suffers rejection. He begins to get his first lessons in the important psychological skills of give and take with other human beings.

Your child needs to play with other children and learn these socializing skills. Nursery school is an ideal place to learn them, because there his learning of these emotional skills is supervised and guided by a trained teacher. In this respect, nursery school is particularly advantageous for both the shy child and the overly aggressive child, both of whom need special help in learning these skills. Neighborhood play, while valuable, is still learning by trial and error. In neighborhood play, for example, there is no trained teacher to help a shy child become a member of the group, build up his self-confidence, and outgrow his shyness.

Guard against a tendency that some fathers have with shy children. Many times the father of a shy preschool child who hangs back from playing with others, will gloss over his child's fearful *feelings*. He will try to push or cajole the child to join the group and overcome his shyness. This is the wrong approach and will only cause the child to withdraw more deeply into his shell.

Instead, the father should use the feedback technique discussed in a previous chapter. Feed his feelings back to the child: "I know you're kind of scared playing with Bert because he seems so loud and rough," or "I guess you're feeling a little afraid of going next door to ask the new boy to play." By feeding back his feelings of fear and insecurity, the father is showing the shy child that he truly understands how he feels and that he has an ally. This is the best possible way for a father to encourage a shy child to do things he is afraid of. *After* using the feedback technique, the father might work out some plan to help his shy child ask another child over to play.

Fathers often feel that the best way to cure an overaggressive child is by administering a few good spankings. You will hear one father say to another: "What that kid needs is a good licking!" This is like trying to put out a fire by pouring gasoline on it. What the overly aggressive child needs is not spankings (except as a last resort when the father's own temper flares up), but firm physical restraints. When a preschool child is bullying or hitting a playmate a father should grab him firmly by both arms and restrain him physically from hitting the other child. At the same time he should say to him firmly and emphatically: "You must not hit Danny! If you are mad at him, tell him you are mad, but you must not hit him."

GENDER IDENTITY: MALE OR FEMALE

Your child's next developmental task in the preschool stage is to stabilize his gender identity as a male or female.

Up to the age of three, the gender identity of boys and girls is not very sharply delineated. Both sexes like to play with the same kind of toys. Boy toddlers and girl toddlers are equally delighted with pull toys, sandplay and waterplay, cuddly animals, and blocks. Of course, there are differences between boys and girls even in these early years, but the differences are not extreme or clearcut. Boys, in general, are more feisty and aggressive and physically more active. Girls, in general, tend to mature faster than boys in many areas, such as language development, but, by and large, a decided gender separation does not make its appearance until boys and girls turn three and enter the preschool stage. From this time on, boys and girls will be viewing themselves and the world through different psychological eyeglasses, and hence behaving differently.

The emotional and psychological differences between boys and girls and later between men and women are, in all probability, due to both innate biological factors, on the one hand, and the cultural differences in the way boys and girls are raised, on the other. Experts differ widely in their views as to how much of the explanation to assign to biology and how much to assign to cultural learning.

However, what is important to you as a father is to see to it that your child achieves a firm and solid gender identity during his preschool years. For the achievement of an identity as a member of one's own sex is a very important part of your child's self-concept and his mental health.

It is important for fathers to remember that in their very early years both boys and girls identify with their mother, and that she is the most important person in a very young child's life. This is to be expected, since it is mother who spends the most time with a very young child. If father were the one who spent the most time with his young child, the child would identify and model himself largely after him.

Little boys as well as little girls want to copy their mother. It is quite normal for a boy of three to tell his mother, "When I grow up I'm going to be a mommy, just like you!" It is not unusual for a little boy to want to put on his mother's shoes as well as father's shoes, or to use his mother's lipstick or perfume. Don't panic and think you have a "sissy" or a future homosexual on your hands if you observe your young boy doing these things.

Such behavior is typical of the earlier years, but in the years from three to six, boys and girls normally begin to go separate ways in their psychological development. Now, little boys begin increasingly to imitate their fathers and little girls to imitate their mothers. But children cannot do a very good job of imitation if the model is not around much of the time. In this respect I think it is far easier in our present society for little girls to accept and consolidate their gender identity than it is for little boys.

Contrast today's society with our society 100 years ago. At that time ours was a rural and small-town society. Little boys saw a great deal of their fathers and could unconsciously copy him and achieve his gender identity. Farm boys tagged along after their fathers and helped them with the chores. Businessmen in small towns came home for lunch and so did their children. Nowadays, many fathers work long hours, and a little boy may not see much of his father except on weekends.

There were few female teachers 100 years ago. Nowadays, a boy may not encounter his first male teacher until the fifth or sixth grade. The unfortunate effect of all of these factors is that young boys do not have much time exposure to male models whom they can imitate.

Today's family situation is further compounded by the effects of divorce on male children. Usually it is the mother who is awarded custody of the children. This is, of course, much easier on little girls because their mothers are still around for them to model themselves after. But what about little boys, who may see their father infrequently under such circumstances?

Given the circumstances I have just discussed, you would think that today's father would make extra efforts to spend time with his preschool children. Unfortunately, this is not often the case. Many fathers today are so driven by ambition and a compulsive need to be successful that they immerse themselves in work and find little time for their young children. One clergyman father first realized he was doing this when his five-year-old son asked to have an appointment to see him!

Fathers usually rationalize their obsessive fixation on work by telling themselves that they are working these long hours so that the family may be better provided for. Sometime in the future, when his children are older, the father believes he will be able to spend more time with them. This usually turns out to be a fallacy. These preschool years are very basic ones. It is during these years that a child, particularly a boy, has the most need of his father for a model. And this process of modeling goes on in very subtle and unconscious ways. The little boy doesn't get up in the morning and say to himself: "Today I am going to observe how my father acts when he drives the family to the beach and then I'll model myself after him!"

I had a very good example of unconscious modeling from father to older son to younger son some years ago. It happens that I have a peculiar method of eating hamburgers. I discard the bun and eat the meat with a fork to keep down my consumption of calories. Of course I never said to either of my boys: "You should eat your hamburger the way I do." But one day when we were all eating hamburgers in a family-type restaurant, my eight-year-old boy Randy suddenly called for a fork and proceeded to eat his hamburger the same way I was. No sooner had Randy started to eat his hamburger meat with a fork than Rusty, his two-year-old brother, wanted to do the same.

So if you spend time with your young children, never fear, they will model themselves after you. The best kind of time to spend with your preschool boy is when the two of you are alone, doing something together. Even the busiest father can find time to spend at least half an hour in the evening doing something with his preschooler. What that "something" is will vary from father to father, depending on the kind of things he enjoys. But no father should be so busy he cannot take ten minutes to read a story to his preschooler. And no father should be so busy. that he cannot spend an hour on Saturday and Sunday with his child. Of course, if you happen to be the father of six children of assorted ages, you will need to make compromises and alterations in the plans I am suggesting here!

Fathers need to get in the habit of taking their preschool children with them on everyday errands, such as a trip to the hardware store, the grocery store, an automobile repair shop, or a library. The father has to make the trip anyway, so why not take his youngster along? The catch is that many fathers do not think of these trips as anything special, just as a chore that has to be done. To a father, a trip to the hardware store may be nothing exciting, but to a preschool boy is is high adventure!

There are also many interesting trips that a father can share with his preschooler on weekends, which will not only be educational for the youngster, but help to build a close emotional bond between them. Here are some of the trips I have taken my children on when they were preschoolers: a fire station, a police station, a newspaper, a welding shop, a library, a bank, a produce market, an airport, a shoe repair shop, a body and fender shop, a foundry, a pie factory, and a post office. People are usually happy to show a small child around even though they may not be very skilled in explaining things in language he can understand. I discovered it was great fun for me to take my kids on these kinds of field trips, all within a half hour of my house. Usually adults don't get a chance to do things of this nature. You may feel hesitant about going to the fire station and asking: "Do you mind very much, old chap, if I sort of look over your fire engine?" But your child is your ticket to all sorts of unexpected adventures within easy driving distance. And that's exactly what I called them when I spoke to my children about the trip: "adventures."

There are many ways to extend your child's experience after you have gone on your "adventure" trip together. There is an excellent series of books published by G. P. Putnam, with titles such as *Let's Go to a Post Office, Let's Go to a Zoo, Let's Go to a Bank,* and many others. You can read one of these books to your child after you come back from your trip. You can encourage him to draw pictures or make up stories about the trip. You and he can even "write a book" about each adventure trip you take. Here's how you do it.

After you come back from your trip, you can tell him: "Remember the fire station we went to visit yesterday? Well, did you know that we can write a book about it? We can, because a book is just talk, written down. You're going to talk and I'm going to write it down. And that's how we write a book.

"Now, what do you want to say about our trip to the fire station?"

"Daddy and I went to visit the fire station."

"Good. That will be the first page of our book."

Then print, in large lower-case letters, on page one: "Daddy and I went to visit the fire station." Leave room for him to draw pictures or decorate the page with a picture of a fire engine or firemen. Then ask: "What do you want to say next about the fire station?"

"We saw a fireman and he let me climb on the fire engine."

Print that on the next page. Each page will have only one sentence on it. Do not correct or change what your child says about his trip. You print whatever he says, because it is *his* book, not your book. As long as your child is interested in dictating to you, print it. When his interest begins to lag, then you know you have come to the end of the book. Figure out an appropriate way to end it and stop. Print in capitals and lower-case letters, just as it is in a real book, even though your youngster isn't able to read it yet. Don't use all capitals, because you wouldn't find it printed that way in a real book.

Let your child choose the title for his book, and print it on the cover. Under the title print the words, "by Betty Smith," since your child is the author. If you have access to a Polaroid camera use it to take pictures at the fire station which include your child. One of these could be glued on the cover, and several of them could be used as illustrations on the inside pages.

After completing the book, read it out loud to him. Chances are he will demand that you read it several times. This book will have great meaning for him, because you and he produced it together.

If you have access to a Xerox or a copying machine at a nearby business office or library, you can add something unique to the book-making process. Your child will be fascinated to discover he can make copies of the pages of his very own book. Now he can make extra copies to give to a friend, send to his grandparents, or take to nursery school to show and tell. The praise he will get from other people to whom he sends his book will motivate him to continue his preschool writing career.

So in helping your child to write books on the trips you take together you are simultaneously helping him with his language development, the general development of his intelligence, and the acquisition of his gender identity as a male.

There is one special trip that every father should enjoy with his preschooler. Take your child to see where you work and what kind of work you do. You may need to give some thought to this. It is important that you explain your work to your youngster on a level that he can understand.

If a father's occupation is that of fireman or policeman or doctor or welder, it is easy to explain, and is one that a child can act out in his playtime. A lawyer or a computer programmer is going to have a more difficult time explaining his job in words and concepts his preschooler can understand.

For example, I took my children, when they were preschoolers, down to see my psychologist's office. I told them that I was a different kind of doctor, a doctor of psychology, not a doctor who gave shots. I said I was a "talking doctor." People who were unhappy came to talk with me in my office and I talked with them and helped them to feel happy again. I also showed them the playroom adjacent to my adult office where I see child patients and use play therapy techniques. That, of course, had an immediate appeal and my children loved to visit daddy's office on a Saturday or Sunday so they could play in the sandbox or with the toys and blocks and puppets.

If your child is going to look up to you as a model, it is very important that he have some idea, on his own intellectual level, of what kind of work you do and why it is important. He knows what kinds of things mother does because he is with her around the house and observes her in action. Unless you show him what you do and why it is important, he will visualize you merely as a person who disappears every morning to something called "work" and reappears in the evening.

You and your child can make a book called "My Daddy's Job" along the same lines I just suggested. In addition, your wife can encourage your child at home to act out in dramatic play situations, "Daddy's Job."

I hope I have not given you the impression that fathers only need spend time with preschool *boys* so that the boys can imitate and model themselves after them. A father is equally important to a preschool girl, not as a model to imitate, but as the first man in the little girl's life. You are the model for your daughter's future husband. If she sees very little of you, she is going to have a very pale and indistinct image. I will go into this more thoroughly when describing the "family romance" in the next chapter. Your little girl needs to know that you love her, and how can she if you are hardly ever around?

What about the father who is terribly busy and finds it very difficult to do the kinds of things I have suggested? Well, even the busiest father can take five minutes at lunch or a coffee break to phone a child at home. That five-minute call will mean a great deal to the child, because it tells him that Daddy cares. You can also keep a supply of little notes or cards at work, and send them through the mail to your preschooler. Young children seldom get mail, and they are thrilled to get a letter from dad. A father often sends postcards or phones his child when he is out of town on a business trip. But he rarely realizes that to a preschool child, father is as "far away" when he is at work as he is when he is hundreds of miles away on a business trip. So bridge the communication gap between work and home with a phone call or a postcard and let your youngster know you are thinking of him.

To summarize, your preschool boy needs contact with you so that he can imitate you and stabilize his gender identity as a male. Your preschool girl also needs contact with you so that she can use you as a model for a future husband. She needs to know that you, as the first man in her life, truly love her and care for her and rejoice in her little girl femininity.

But it is wise for you to remember that no child (or adult for that matter) is ever 100 percent "masculine" or 100 percent "feminine." If they were, how in the world could a child ever expect to understand the other sex at all? We need to avoid such gender stereotypes as "boys don't cry," "you don't need to teach a girl to think, just teach her to catch a husband," and the like. We want our boys to grow up to become men who are capable of showing such "feminine" traits as warmth and tenderness and the ability to cry and show deep feelings. And we want to help our girls grow up to be women who can be independant, think logically, and dare to be original and nonconforming.

Do not be rigid about what you teach your children about what is masculine and what is feminine behavior. You need to allow your preschoolers the opportunity to play out roles and feelings appropriate to the opposite sex as well as their own. It's not going to hurt a three-year-old boy to play house, or for his mother to teach him how to cook simple dishes or bake cookies. And it's not going to hurt a three-year-old girl to play with trucks and fire engines if that's what she wants to do. Encourage your preschoolers in their gender identities, but don't be rigid and stereotyped about it.

7
The Preschool Stage II

The next developmental task of your child in the preschool stage is to form his basic attitudes toward sexuality.

In previous chapters you learned that children do not become particularly interested in sex until they are about three years old. Until then, all a father needs to do is refrain from giving his child a negative sex education. But now, during the preschool stage, it is time to begin giving your child a *positive* sex education.

In discussing the previous developmental tasks of your child in the preschool stage and how you can help him master them, I have assumed that you have no particular emotional blockages that would interfere with your aiding your child in mastering his developmental tasks. And that assumption is probably correct. But when it comes to helping your child learn positive and healthy sexual attitudes, things may be different. You may very well have emotional blockages within you which make it difficult to aid him in this particular developmental task.

As a psychologist for more than twenty years who has been

dealing with the intimate problems of people, including sexual problems, I am well aware that many fathers bear scars themselves of misinformation, fear, or guilt about sex, which date back to their own preschool years. Is it any wonder that they find it hard to handle their children's upbringing on this particular subject? For twenty years, one of the routine questions I have asked patients is: "What kind of sex education did you get in your family?" And the answer from about 99 percent of the people has been: "None . . . the subject was never mentioned." I sympathize with that answer because my own sexual upbringing was just as unfortunate as that of the people I questioned. Sex was a hush-hush affair in my childhood, something you simply didn't talk about (except with other children, on the sly, of course!).

So I am well aware that some fathers reading this will find it difficult to talk about sex or answer their children's questions with the same degree of ease that they can discuss other subjects. However, it is well worth the effort to overcome your own emotional blockages, so that you can give your children a better sex education than your parents gave you. You can take some comfort in the fact that you will find it far easier to deal with your child's questions about sex when he is young than when he is older.

There are two aspects to giving your child a positive sex education in the preschool stage: (1) answering his questions and (2) giving him an overall, systematic viewpoint on sexuality, love, and the family.

Answer your child's questions about sex directly and honestly. Your goal should be to answer as simply and matter-of-factly as you would questions about why it rains or what makes the TV break down. Your child is not going to be worried or obsessed with thoughts about sex unless grown-ups teach him to be. If he asks his little naive questions and you say: "There will be plenty of time to talk about that when you're older," or "Why don't you ask your mother about that?" he will begin to feel that sex is a topic which is taboo and dirty (yet fascinating, because it is forbidden).

Usually, our young children's questions about sex come out of the clear blue sky when we least expect them. My oldest boy, Randy, was about three and a half when, one night, in the midst of our dinner table conversation he said, "Daddy, where do babies come from?" This, of course, is usually the first question children will ask about sex. I answered him something like this: "Randy, babies come from inside the mother. They grow in a special place called the uterus." Randy said, "Oh," and then asked: "What are we having for dessert tonight?"

This little interchange illustrates very clearly that children think of their questions about sex as being no different from questions about anything else. They want a short and simple answer. If they need a more detailed explanation they will ask more questions.

Incidentally, be sure you do not fall into the error of many parents who tell the child that babies grow in the mother's stomach. Not only is this anatomically incorrect, but it causes a child to have fantastic misconceptions and fantasies about sex and childbirth. He will wonder how the little baby is getting along down there in mother's stomach among the meatballs and spaghetti and salad she just had for dinner! So tell your child about the uterus rather than the stomach.

One of the thorny questions you may be called upon to answer concerns the difference between boys and girls. Sometime between the ages of three and six a child discovers that a boy has a penis and a girl does not. The healthier the family atmosphere about sex the less psychological shock such a discovery will cause. The more repressed and guilt-laden the general attitude toward sex, the more difficulty a little boy or girl will have in absorbing and making sense of what to him is a startling discovery.

Most parents expect a child to take this discovery as calmly as the discovery that monkeys can climb trees but dogs cannot. Unfortunately for parents, that is not the case. A young child's understanding is too limited for him to comprehend that boys are born with penises and girls are born with uteruses and without penises. Young boys and girls tend to believe that all children were originally born with penises, but that something unfortunate happened to the little girls. A cartoon shows a little girl getting a good look at her little brother taking a bath, and exclaiming: "Mommy, I think part of me is missing!"

Some little girls feel they were gypped, and are second-class citizens; or they may think they originally had a penis and have been deprived of it as a punishment. If your daughter has either of these reactions, you can reassure her by telling her that although girls do not have penises, they have something that boys do not have: a uterus. Explain that her uterus is a special little bag inside her body

"I'LL SHOW YOU YOURS IF YOU SHOW ME MINE. DARN! I ALWAYS GET THAT WRONG."

where babies grow and that when girls grow up they can have babies but men cannot. One little preschool girl whose mother explained this to her went around proudly exclaiming for the next few days: "I've got a uterus, I've got a uterus!"[1]

Little boys may also react with psychological distress to the discovery that girls and women do not have penises. Since the thinking of a preschool child is still primitive and unsophisticated, many boys conclude that girls have had their penises cut off and that they themselves could be punished in this way as well. This fear is clearly illustrated by the story of the five-year-old boy who asked his mother where she kept her penis. When she reminded him that she had already told him boys and men have penises but girls and women do not, he replied: "Yes, I remember now, that's where someone axed you one!"[2]

If the sexual atmosphere in your family is relaxed and healthy, and interest in sexual organs is taken casually, the fears that arise in both boys and girls when they discover the anatomical differences between the sexes will soon subside. I am taking the trouble to go into this point because it is important to realize that little boys and girls are going to have some irrational fears about the loss of their sex organs in spite of your rational explanations. Don't expect your rational explanations to cause your child's irrational fears to vanish overnight. In a healthy and open atmosphere these fears will fade by the end of the preschool stage.

It would be nice if we could rely on answering questions about sex honestly to provide children with all of the information they need in the preschool years. Unfortunately, merely answering questions will not do the job. For one thing, children are often afraid to ask about sex. They sense, from the reactions of adults and older children, that this is a taboo subject and that it is dangerous to ask too many questions about it.

This brings us to the second thing a father needs to do to help his child develop positive attitudes towards sexuality. He needs to give his child an overall, systematic view of sexuality which will enable his child to see the connection between sexuality, love, and the family. One of the best ways to do this is to read a book to him which will give him an overall view of the sexual process and its place in family living. There are three excellent books which do this, and I strongly recommend that you buy at least one of them and read it to your youngster. Each book approaches the subject in a slightly different

"A BABY LIVES
IN MOM'S STOMACH."

way. Since they are relatively inexpensive, I think it would be well worth the investment for you to buy all three of them:

The Wonderful Story of How You Were Born by Sidonie M. Gruenberg, Doubleday (get the revised edition 1970).
   If you decided to buy only one of the three, this is the one to get.

A Baby Is Born by Milton I. Levine and Jean H. Seligmann (Western Publishing Co., revised edition, paperback).

Growing Up by Karl De Schweinitz (Macmillan, 1968).

Don't make a big deal out of reading these books to your child. Rather, read them in the same matter-of-fact way you would read any other book. Answer any questions that your child asks in the same way as you would answer his questions about any other book.
   However, do not assume that because you have read the book once that your child will understand the information and attitudes presented. The anxiety-ridden and guilt-laden atmosphere about sex in our society will prevent a child from absorbing information about sex in the same matter-of-fact way that he absorbs information about baseball or science. For this reason, you will probably need to repeat explanations about sexual matters that you thought your child understood when you explained it before. As an example, although my daughter was twelve when our youngest child was born, she believed the doctor would make an incision in her mother's crotch in order to get the baby out! And my wife and I thought that we were raising a sexually enlightened daughter!
   So don't be impatient if you find yourself answering questions about sex and covering the same ground that you covered before. For the same reason, it is a good idea to read these books to your child several times. To be more specific, I would read them to him once when he is three, once when he is four, and once when he is five. Then put the books in his home library, so that he can consult them later on after he has learned to read by himself.
   The information in these books should take care of most of what your child needs to know about sex until he reaches the stage of preadolescence—around the age of eleven. At that point, a whole new era of sex education begins that will be discussed in chapter ten.

Next we come to that part of a positive sex education for pre-schoolers which is hardest for most parents to handle: what to do when your child starts playing with his sex organs.

Younger children touch their sex organs purely out of curiosity, in the same way that they touch their toes or ear lobes. There is nothing special about them. But now, in the preschool stage, the child discovers that his sex organs are a special kind of place. He discovers a special kind of pleasure by fondling or caressing his sexual organs. In earlier times people thought that nothing like this occurred until adolescence. Now we know that this type of pleasure in playing with one's sexual organs is a part of a child's normal development. What is the best way to handle it?

The best thing to do is to ignore it. If you do, after a while the child will stop and move on to some other activity. If you can be relaxed enough in your own feelings about sex to let him do this, there will be no problem at all.

So far we have discussed how to handle it if your child plays with his sex organs by himself. But suppose your child and other young children are indulging in sex play in a group? This traditionally takes the form of the "doctor" game, in which children take turns examining other "sick" children. Or it may take the more open form of "I'll show you mine if you'll show me yours!" This type of sex play is a perfectly normal part of this stage of development and, once a child's initial curiosity is satisfied, the fascination disappears. There is no need for you to worry about it.

Usually your wife rather than you discovers this type of sex play going on, so you rarely have to worry about how to handle it in person. Your wife can tell the children she knows that they are curious about each other's sex organs. However, now that their curiosity has been satisfied, they can play some other games. Then she gets the children started in a new activity. Since your wife will probably handle this she needs emotional support from you that she handled it wisely, and matter-of-factly. The main thing to remember is that during the years from three to six parents are not only conveying information to their children about sex, they are conveying attitudes and feelings. And it is not healthy for your child if you convey the feeling that sexuality and playing with his sex organs is a nasty and dirty thing.

One final aspect of a positive sex education for young children concerns personal nudity in the home. In the olden days, bathroom

"YOU MEAN *WE* GET TO STAND UP, BUT GIRLS CAN ONLY SIT DOWN?"

doors were locked and children never saw their parents in the nude. Now the pendulum seems to have swung to the other extreme. Today a number of parents allow children to see them nude even when the children are in their preteens. What is the best way to handle this situation?

In general, I believe that the modern relaxed attitudes toward nudity in the home are a much healthier way of educating our children sexually. For children up to the age of six an open-door policy toward nudity is best. This is in line with the open policy of a good nursery school where children of different sexes use the same bathroom rather than have separate bathrooms for "boys" and "girls" as there are later on in elementary school. A more relaxed and a healthier attitude toward sex and bodily functions is created if children and parents are free to be nude or partially so around the house, as long as the children are preschoolers. But after seven or eight, things begin to change. Children develop a kind of instinctive modesty around these ages. They begin to prefer to have the bathroom door closed when they are going to the toilet or taking a shower. It is important for parents to respect a child's need for privacy at this time.

Of course, I am speaking primarily of nudity between parents and children of the opposite sex. For a youngster of nine or ten or older to see his parent of the opposite sex nude may be too stimulating sexually. Precocious sexual stimulation can lead to psychological problems because it may be more than the child can handle comfortably. However, I think it does no harm for parents and children of the same sex to continue to see each other nude in a matter-of-fact way.

In summary, both parents and children will naturally develop more modesty about nudity in the home during grade-school days. But meanwhile, the preschool stage is the time for a much more relaxed attitude on both sides.

THE FAMILY ROMANCE

The next developmental task your preschooler must master is what I call the "family romance." This is referred to as the Oedipus complex, from the name of the royal hero of the ancient Greek legend, who killed his father and married his mother. I do not like the term "Oedipus complex" because it gives many parents the impression that it is unhealthy or neurotic. I vastly prefer the title "family romance" to emphasize that this is an entirely *normal* stage of development which all children go through between the ages of three and six. Many fathers seem unaware of this developmental stage, much to their detriment and that of their children. The family romance occurs differently for boys than for girls, so I will describe each separately. Let's start with the boy.

Sometime around the age of three, your little boy discovers that you have a different relationship with his mother than he has. Until then his intelligence had not matured sufficiently for him to make this discovery. His mother, of course, had always been the most important person in his young life. But whereas his previous feelings toward his mother had been babyish and dependent ones, around the age of three they undergo a change.

Now he begins to "fall in love" and develop romantic feelings about her. This is normal. All little boys feel this way. Some boys keep these feelings to themselves and never say anything. Others express their feelings more openly. Your little boy now wants mother all to himself and begins to fantasize a romantic attachment to her. Little boys at this age are often heard to say: "When I grow up, I'm going to marry Mommy!"

Instead of listening to these "cute" sayings with an amused smile, you need to take them quite seriously. These feelings and fantasies run very deep in your little boy. At this stage, *he* takes them very seriously, even if you do not. These romantic feelings towards his mother are nature's way of getting him ready for his eventual role as a husband. This family romance is a vital part of his psychological development, and very important for his future happiness.

A boy's mother is the first woman in his life, his first romantic love figure. And, on a deep unconscious level, his feelings toward his mother will usually dictate his choice of a wife later on. He will want to marry a woman who in some ways reminds him of his mother. And this is quite normal. We even have an old popular song based on this "family romance" theme: "I Want a Girl Just Like the Girl Who Married Dear Old Dad!"

However, Mother Nature doesn't want to let your little boy stay fixated on his mother forever. She wants him to get over it by the time he's six or seven, and most little boys do.

The catch to all this is that the "family romance" is also a "family triangle." Your little boy not only feels deep romantic fantasies about his mother, he also feels rivalrous and jealous of you, his father. His maturing intelligence is now telling him that you have a special relationship to his mother that he doesn't have. You go out with her in the evenings and he is not allowed to go along. You sleep with her in your bedroom and he has to sleep in his own bedroom. Therefore he begins to resent you.

If a father does not realize what is going on in the mind of his little boy at this stage, the resentment can really throw him for a loop. Not knowing that this is a normal stage, the father may think he did something wrong to cause his son to resent him. Or he may just conclude that his kid is a "spoiled brat" and begin to reject him emotionally and pay less attention to him.

I remember vividly the first time I got hit with the family romance when my oldest boy was three. I came home from work one day, greeted him affectionately at the door as I always did, only to have him slam the door in my face and say: "Go away! I want Mommy!" If I had not known what was going on psychologically, this could have been devastating to me as a father. Even knowing intellectually what was going on, it was still hard not to take it personally and react with hurt feelings.

But if *you* are on the "hot seat" with your little boy during this stage of development, what about him? These new feelings of rivalry and hostility toward you put your boy on a most uncomfortable spot. He loves you and needs you and looks up to you and imitates you. But how can he feel loving toward you and at the same time want you to go away so that he can have mother all to himself? At this point, a civil war is roiling deep inside your little boy. These mixed feelings are very difficult for him to tolerate.

In his primitive type of thinking he imagines that you also feel rivalrous and hostile toward him. Since you are much bigger and more powerful than he is, your youngster may develop fears that you will retaliate and punish him severely for having such wishes and fantasies. These fears he has towards you are often projected onto animals or other people. The boy may begin to show irrational fears of animals or burglars. Or he may have nightmares in which he is pursued by lions or monsters. These animals represent his fears that you will hurt or punish him for his hostile feelings.

In a normal, healthy family the little boy realizes gradually that his fantasies of replacing father are not going to come true. This is partly accomplished by the development of the intellectual ability to sort out reality from fantasy. (Remember how the four-year-old has trouble separating reality from fantasy?) Usually it will take all the years from three to six for your little boy fully to give up his romantic fantasies and adjust to the reality that his mother is your woman and not his. For example, my youngest son Rusty simply refused to let me read him his bedtime story from the time he was three until he was about five and a half. He absolutely insisted, sometimes tearfully, that mother *must* read the story to him. Even when mother was out, and I was putting him to bed, he refused to let me read the story. Around the age of five and a half, things began to change and he allowed me to read him his bedtime story. Once this new development took place, it was a sure sign he was outgrowing the stage of the family romance.

Sooner or later during this three-year stretch your little boy will begin to get the idea that he must give up his romantic fantasies about mother. Then he adopts the attitude: if you can't lick 'em, join 'em. Since he realizes he can't *be* father, he decides he wants to be *like* father. And so begins the process of identification with father. He will, as I have mentioned before in the section on gender identity, use you as a model and imitate you in many ways. Both of these processes (the gradual giving up of the romantic fantasies about mother, and the gradual abandonment of the rivalry with father) will take all three years of this developmental stage.

How can you help him accomplish this task?

First of all, you need to understand the psychological process going on in the mind of your little boy, and not take personally any rivalry or hostility directed at you. Secondly, it is important to spend time with him, as I mentioned in the previous discussion on gender identity. If you are a distant and absent figure, he is going to have more difficulty identifying with you and modeling himself after you. It will be harder to resolve the "family triangle" by giving up his fantasies about mother and wanting to be like you.

If a divorce takes place when a boy is between the ages of three and six, it also makes it harder for him to resolve the family romance. At this stage he wants his mother all to himself and his father out of the picture. Then, when a divorce occurs, it seems to the child's primitive and magical thinking that his wishes have suddenly been granted. The little boy begins to think that, perhaps, in some way which he cannot quite understand he is responsible for the divorce. He begins to feel very guilty. He may try desperately to make up to both parents for what he feels he caused.

If you go through a divorce during the time your little boy is in the preschool stage, you will need to help him realize he is not responsible for the divorce. Use the feedback technique and help him put his feelings about the situation into words. Don't worry if his feelings are irrational; just put them into your own words and mirror them back to him. Only after you have mirrored his own feelings back to him and let him know you understand how he feels should you explain rationally that he is in no way responsible for the divorce. You will also find *The Boys and Girls Book of Divorce* (described in Appendix E) very helpful to you and your child.

But in most healthy families, by the time your little boy is six he has resolved the family romance, passed safely through this very important phase, and now has within himself deep unconscious images of the type of woman he will later want to marry. He also has deep unconscious images of the type of husband he will be to such a woman. And you, as his father, will have provided him with these images of himself. Without successfully resolving the family romance between the years three to six, your son may not be able to find a marriage partner successfully in later life. You must be familiar with at least one man in his thirties or forties who was not able to cut the subconscious apron strings to mother and get married. Of course he is not usually aware that this is the reason. He will probably say: "The right girl just hasn't turned up yet."

Fathers who spend time with their preschool boys make it easier for them to resolve the family romance, identify with father, and master this developmental task.

The family romance of the little girl, quite naturally, takes a different pattern. Your little boy's first love figure is his mother. He will keep that same love figure, in a new romantic form, throughout the stage of the family romance. Not so with your little girl. She starts with the same first love figure: her mother. But unlike a little boy, she now has to shift her love figure from her mother to you, her father, (since she imitates her mother). This makes the family romance a more complicated procedure for her.

Some girls keep their feelings and fantasies to themselves, but others are quite open about them. Little girls in this stage can be very feminine and coquettish with their fathers. I have a vivid memory of my five-year-old daughter coming out of the shower one day. She took her towel, and like a shimmy dancer, twirled it around her hips as she said, archly, to me: "Hey, Daddy, look at me!"[3]

Your little girl faces a different psychological situation than a boy in actual time spent with the romanticized parent. In our present society, mothers are in the home most of the time, whereas fathers are away at work. A little boy gets to spend a great deal of time with his romanticized love, his mother. But a little girl must spend much of her day longing for her absent father. Her romanticized feelings are lived out more in fantasy.

In the same way that your little boy felt rivalrous and competitive toward you, your little girl begins to feel rivalrous and competitive with her mother. If she is frank and outspoken she may even say things like, "Mother, why don't you take a nice trip sometime? I could take very good care of Daddy while you're gone!" But these competitive feelings trouble your little girl. After all, she is dependent upon her mother for love and affection. She feels she must be a terrible person to wish that her mother would go away and never come back! She thinks that her mother knows how much she wants to get rid of her, and is terribly angry and wants to punish her. She may have nightmares during this period in which she is chased by a wicked witch or monster, an unconscious disguise for the vengeful mother of her fantasies.

Once again, in a normal family, your little girl learns that she cannot take her mother's place with you. This learning extends over the whole period from three to six years of age. Gradually she gives up her romantic longings to be your wife, and replaces them with the general outlines of the man she will one day love and marry. Gradually she renounces her rivalry with her mother and begins to identify with and model after her. Unconsciously she fills in the general outline of what kind of wife she will become in later life. And so your little girl, like your little boy, resolves the family triangle.

What can you do to help your little girl progress normally through the family romance and resolve it by the time she is six or seven?

First of all, spend time with her. Sometimes a father thinks it is important to spend time with their young boys, but figures his wife should spend time with their young girls because "that's woman's stuff." Such an attitude overlooks the important psychological fact that the young girl needs her father's time and attention during this stage even though it may be for different reasons than the young boy. Your preschool son needs your time and attention so that he can learn to model himself after you. Your preschool daughter needs your time and attention so that she can fill in a healthy unconscious image of the man she will later marry. I mentioned an old-time popular song based upon the boy's side of the family romance; there is also a girl's song based upon her side of the family romance: "My Heart Belongs to Daddy." So spend time with your preschool daughter and enjoy the romance while it lasts!

Of course, it is important that you and your wife do not allow a preschool son or daughter to drive a wedge between you during this period. If the two of you have a basically stable and loving relationship, your children will gradually outgrow their romantic fantasies during these preschool years. But if basic difficulties exist in your marriage, then, for example, a boy may succeed in getting his mother to treat him more as a "miniature lover" than as a child. It is not a healthy thing for the boy if mother delights too much in this kind of attention from a son because she feels her husband is not paying enough attention to her.

You and your wife must be on the alert during this time not to let your child find chinks in your marriage and use these tender spots to play "divide and conquer." Resist the romanticized relationship offered by your child with what we may call "tender rejection." Both of you need to make it clear to a preschool boy that he cannot marry mother when he grows up because she and daddy are already married and happy about it. Someday, when he is grown-up he will find a wife of his own. Meantime, he is his mother's special little boy and his daddy's special little boy, too, because both of you love him.

Similarly, make it clear to a preschool girl that she cannot marry daddy when she grows up, for he is already happily married to mommy. But she is your little girl and no one can ever take the special place she has in your affections. And, someday, she will find her own husband.

It is important not to ridicule or tease your youngsters for having these romantic fantasies. Remember that they are a normal part of your child's development and a normal preparation for his future marriage. But neither should you actively encourage your youngster in these fantasies. To do so only promotes an overly close romantic attachment which is difficult to break away from later on. However, if you and your wife are reasonable, mature people, with a relatively stable and happy marriage, your youngster should pass safely through the ups and downs of the family romance by the time he is six or seven.

SENSITIVITY TO INTELLECTUAL STIMULATION

The final developmental task for your youngster at the preschool stage is a period during which he is particularly responsive to intellectual stimulation. He should develop basic skills and attitudes toward learning which he will have the rest of his life.

A child's intelligence could be defined very simply as "a child's repertoire of basic learning skills." This means that every time a child's basic learning skills increase, his intelligence increases. Intelligence tests, or IQ tests, are good predictors of whether or not a child will be successful in school because of one simple fact: the intelligence tests sample the repertoire of basic learning skills. The larger the repertoire of basic learning skills, the higher the IQ and the greater the probability of success in school. The child who enters first grade with a large repertoire of learning skills will learn more easily than one with a small repertoire of skills.

Preschool years are ideal for your child to acquire these basic learning skills. They are golden years for your child to "learn how to learn." The more intellectual stimulation you give your child in these preschool years, without pushing or pressuring him, the brighter and more intelligent he will become, and the higher the IQ he will have as an adult.

What can a father do to help his child in his intellectual development during the years from three to six?

First of all, if it is at all possible financially, send him to a good nursery school when he turns three, and continue until he reaches five. At that time send him to public-school kindergarten if your state has a public kindergarten. If not, and it is financially possible, send him to a private kindergarten.

A good nursery school not only has much to offer for the emotional development of your child when he is three and four years old, but can also do great things for his intellectual development. My wife and I have for many years operated La Primera Preschool in Torrance, California. From my experience with our parents I have concluded that many fathers have very vague ideas about what their child learns in nursery school. I think this is unfortunate. If more fathers realized the tremendous value of nursery school and what can be done for the emotional and the intellectual development of their child in the preschool years, they would be eager to enroll their youngster. (My previous book *How to Parent* gave several pages of suggestions on how to find a good nursery school and I suggest you consult pages 178 to 181 in hardcover, and pages 197 to 200 in paperback.)

Kindergarten offers such marvelous opportunities for learning, and the five-year-old is ripe for learning. Therefore, it is an educational shame that at this writing so many children in the United States do not have the opportunity to go to a public kindergarten. This deplorable situation is due to the fact that many states do not begin elementary school until the first grade.

If your state has no public-school kindergarten, I suggest that you send your child to a private kindergarten if this is financially possible. The previous suggestions for finding a good nursery school will also help you find a good kindergarten.

Next, you can do many things at home which will also provide your child with an optimal amount of intellectual stimulation. There are three books that summarize the many and varied things you can do. I have put together a number of specific suggestions in *How to Parent,* Chapters Eleven and Twelve, "School Begins At Home," Part One and Part Two, and Chapter Thirteen, "How To Select Toys, Books, and Records For Your Child." I also suggest you buy a copy of *How To Raise A Brighter Child* by Joan Beck (Trident Press) and *Give Your Child A Superior Mind* by Siegfried and Therese Engelmann (Simon and Schuster). These three books will form a good basic reference library, guiding you in things to do at home which will help develop your child's repertoire of basic learning skills.

Before concluding this chapter I want to mention four of the principle ideas found in those three books: 1. You need to provide a stimulating "learning environment" in your home so that your child will have the tools and materials for his intellectual development. Since the main way in which a preschool child learns is through play, it is important that you select toys, books, and records with care. Toys, books and records are the textbooks of the preschool years.

Unfortunately, most parents lack the information that would guide them in a wise selection. The five-part appendix of this book has been designed to provide you with this information. Appendix A is a father's guide to buying toys for children of different ages and at various stages of development from birth through adolescence. Appendix B is a father's guide to inexpensive toys and play materials you can make or build. Appendix C is a father's guide to books for children. Appendix D is a father's guide to buying children's records. Appendix E is an annotated booklist for fathers to aid them in raising and educating their children.

Providing an optimal learning environment at home through toys, books, and records need not be an expensive and costly undertaking. All the books listed in Appendixes C and E can be obtained at your local library. Even if you live near a very small library, the book can usually be obtained through an interlibrary loan. Many libraries nowadays have record collections and you can check out records just as you do books.

Store-bought toys are expensive, to be sure. But are you aware of the fact that many toys with the most play value can be made out of free or inexpensive materials? These toys often do much more to develop your child's imagination and creativity than expensive battery-powered toys from the store. In addition, your child will especially cherish such toys because you, his father, made them for him.

2. You can also learn to play educational games with your child. You need to be realistic about this. Obviously you do not have the same amount of time to play educational games with your child as your wife does. But I want to emphasize that there are many educational games which you can play in your everyday encounters with your child. For example, when you take him with you to the hardware store, why not play a game in the car on the way?

One of the things you want your child to do is to come up with novel and original ideas. The ability to do this will have a great deal to do with how successful he is in later life. A very simple game you can play anywhere and which aids in developing his ability for novel and original thinking is the Wouldn't It Be Funny If . . . game. Tell him: "I've got a new game we can play. It's called: Wouldn't It Be Funny If. Here's how we play it. I'll start. Wouldn't it be funny if cats could talk and people meow? Now it's your turn."

You will probably be surprised at your child's novel ideas. You might want to enlarge on the implications of some of these ideas or ask your child to. For example: Wouldn't it be funny if rivers and lakes had salt water in them and oceans had fresh water? What would happen then? What things would be different about our lives if this were true? For example: Where would we get our drinking water if oceans had fresh water and rivers and lakes had salt water? By playing this game you are helping your youngster learn to think in a novel way. You are aiding him to develop his imagination and you are building up his confidence in his own ability to create new ideas.

One of the most important intellectual skills your child can possess is the ability to think abstractly: to take two seemingly unrelated facts or things and see what they have in common. In fact, this ability to see similarities in seemingly disparate objects or items is used in several well-known tests of intelligence. Dr. David Wechsler, the author of two widely used tests of intelligence states: "A well-constructed similarities test is one of the most reliable measures of intellectual ability".[4] For example, you have different levels of intellectual ability according to the way a child answers a simple question: In what way are an apple and an orange the same or alike? At the lowest level, a child may not be able to see at all how they are the same or alike. At a higher level a child may say they both have skins. At a still higher level of abstraction, he may say they are both fruits.

Two excellent games which will help your child learn to think abstractly are the Same Game and the Different Game. Let's start with the Same Game.

Say: Here's a new game we can play. It's called the Same Game. Watch me."

Then take any two objects and put them side by side. Start with something easy, such as a sock and a shoe or a pencil and a felt pen. Ask your child: "Tell me how this sock and this shoe are the same or alike." "Tell me all the ways they're alike that you can think of." Praise him for whatever he says that is correct, and say, "Good," or "Good thinking, Jerry!" Each time you praise your child and tell him he is a good thinker you are building up his self-confidence and increasing his self-assurance in tackling new intellectual tasks.

Gradually work your way up to harder things as your child gets older and more sophisticated in his thinking. How are a quarter and a cookie the same or alike? Are they both round? Will they both roll on the ground? Will both of them fall down if you try to balance them on edge? After your child has built up his confidence in playing this game, you can elaborate on some likenesses he has not thought of. If he says a cat and a tiger both have tails and cannot think of anything else, praise him for what he said and then add "And also you could say they are both the same because they're both animals."

When first playing this game with your youngster at three years of age, it is best to work with two concrete objects which you place next to each other. Later on, as he gets more expert at the game, you can play it in the car where you merely use the *names* of the objects.

The Different Game works much the same way. Take any two handy objects and put them next to each other. Now ask him: How many ways can you think of that this quarter and this cookie are different? You can eat a cookie, but you can't eat a quarter (without causing yourself trouble!) A quarter can be used in an ice-cream machine, but a cookie can't. And so on.

Another educational game which you can play anywhere and anytime with your preschool youngster is the What Is the Best Thing to Do If? John Dewey has stated that "thinking begins with a felt difficulty." He is emphasizing the fact that we do not think unless there is some difficulty or problem confronting us and this game is built around the idea. You create a difficult situation and see what your child can suggest to get out of the situation or solve the difficulty. For example: "Here's another new game I have for you, Terry. It's called What Is the Best Thing to Do? Here's how it goes: "What is the best thing to do if you are driving in a car with your family and you see a fire that is just starting in a field?" Here are some other questions you could use. What is the best thing to do if you accidentally break a friend's toy when you are playing at his house? Or what is the best thing to do if our family were out in the woods on a camping trip and you went for a walk and got lost?

Since there could be many different "correct" answers to this kind of question, this is also a good game to help your child build self-confidence in solving problems. Praise him for any answer he gives which makes reasonable sense. Remember that he is young and inexperienced in this type of thinking.

These are three examples of educational games which cost absolutely nothing and do not need a special time out. All three games can, of course, be played for many many years, but the preschool years are especially important because in these years your child is acquiring basic "learning to learn" skills, including confidence in his own abilities as a thinker and learner. You will find many other educational games in the three books I have recommended. Browse through them and try out the educational games with your child that appeal to you.

Preschoolers love to play games. If you call anything you are going to do with your preschooler a "game" he is sure to have a positive attitude toward it. It is also important, in playing these educational games with your child, to accept his ideas. Do not be critical and say, "That's not right" or "No, it wouldn't work that way." This will discourage him from producing new ideas and take the fun out of the game. He will learn to be more precise and accurate in his ideas and concepts as he matures and grows older. What you want to do in his preschool years is encourage him to produce ideas, without worrying how scientifically accurate they are.

3. You can read to your child. In fact, if you did absolutely nothing else for your child but read to him as many of the books as you could which I have listed in Appendix C, you would be doing fantastic things to stimulate his intellectual development. Dr. George Gallup, in a very important research study, found that 79 percent of high-achieving first graders were read to regularly in their early years as compared to 49 percent of low achievers.

When can you read to your child? I have already suggested that an ideal time is to incorporate the regular reading of a story to your child as part of his bedtime ritual, but this should not prevent you from reading to your child at any other time that strikes your fancy. Of course, you have to use your common sense. Don't expect your child to leap with joy to have you read to him if he's in the midst of an exciting TV program or engrossed in playing with his toys or his friends.

I think the most important thing for a father to keep in mind in selecting books to read to his child is that they should appeal to you too. Don't read some hackneyed twenty-nine- cent children's book that you think is dull and tasteless. Personally, I learned a great deal myself by reading science books to my preschoolers such as the Let's Read and Find Out science series by Crowell or the True Book series by Children's Press. I also thoroughly enjoyed reading such books of imagination as *Charlie and the Chocolate Factory* by Roald Dahl and the *Twenty-One Balloons* by William Guy Pene DuBois. So take Appendix C with you to your local library. Browse through it and find books that you yourself will get a kick out of reading to your youngster.

4. You can teach your child mathematics by playing special games

with him. Now don't panic, father! You don't have to have any mathematical knowledge at all to teach math in the way I am going to suggest. Many fathers, unless they are engineers or scientists, feel uneasy when it comes to math. Parents are feeling particularly uneasy these days since the arrival of the "new math" in elementary school. Fathers hear about things like "set theory" and "base four" and the "number line" and "modular arithmetic" and other concepts that are entirely new to them. They discover their children are learning to do arithmetic in elementary school by methods which are quite different from the methods they used. The net effect of all this is for many fathers to feel distinctly uneasy about the whole area of mathematics.

Let me reassure you at once. Math was my most difficult subject in school. When my sixth grader asked me for help with his "new math" homework, I often had to read quite a bit in *his* textbook in order to help him with *his* homework! But I had no trouble at all in playing mathematical games with my preschool children. The reason I had no trouble, and the reason you won't have any trouble, is that this way of teaching math to a preschooler assumes that the father knows nothing about the subject. Don't you feel more relaxed already?

You can teach math to your preschooler painlessly by using a parent's kit designed especially for that purpose. It is called the Cuisenaire Rods Parents Kit and can be obtained from the Cuisenaire Company of America at 12 Church Street, New Rochelle, New York 10805.

Georges Cuisenaire, a Belgian educator, invented this way of teaching arithmetic and math to children. The materials consist of a set of wooden rods of different colors and various lengths. By playing games with these colored rods your child can learn to add, subtract, multiply, and divide. Using these rods he can actually go into algebra in a small way. The kit has a complete set of rods, plus step by step instructions on how to use them. The child begins by playing very simple games and moves gradually to more complex ones.

All these mathematics games use concrete objects (the rods) that your child can manipulate. A preschool child can learn a great deal of arithmetic and math when it is solidly based upon the physical manipulation of concrete objects and materials, but a preschooler's ability to learn math in the abstract form of numbers is quite limited.

One of the reasons so many children and adults have difficulty with arithmetic and math is that they were expected to learn it by first exposing them to the task of manipulating abstract numbers and symbols on a piece of paper. Instead, they should have had previous years of experience in manipulating concrete objects and materials. And this is precisely the kind of experience you will be giving your preschool child when you play mathematics games with him using the Cuisenaire Rods.

It is not surprising that we have covered so much territory in discussing the nine developmental tasks of the preschool stage because, in the years from three to six, an astounding amount of emotional and intellectual growth takes place. Let me summarize what your child will have learned during this all-important stage:

He has fulfilled his biological needs for both large and small muscle development.

He has developed a control system for his impulses.

He has learned how to express his feelings in words.

He has separated himself from his mother.

He has learned the give and take of relationships with his peers.

Gender identity as a male or female has become stabilized.

His basic attitudes toward sexuality have been formed.

He has worked his way through a resolution of the "family romance."

He has gone through a period of development in which he is particularly responsive to intellectual stimulation, and, it is hoped, he has received an optimal amount of such stimulation.

So here he is. Your child has only been on this planet for five years, but he has already graduated from the most important "school" he will ever attend: the environment he has been living in during those early years. If you have followed through on the suggestions I made in this book, your child should now have a strong self-concept and a psychologically healthy and stable personality structure. If things have gone well, your child has developed a basic sense of self-esteem and a strong sense of self-identity. Your most important work as a father has been completed in helping him to build a solid emotional and intellectual foundation in these first five years of life.

Now your child is ready to launch out on the next stage of development, the stage of middle childhood.

8
Middle-Childhood Years I (Ages Six to Ten)

The next stage of development covers the period approximately from six to eleven years. It covers a longer span of time than any of the previous stages. Different investigators have used different names to label this period of development. The psychoanalysts call it the "latency period" because it is a period of sexual quiescence between the intense family romance or Oedipal complex and the sexual upheavals of adolescence. I do not think that is a very good name. The label "latency" seems to imply that since sexuality is latent rather than "up front," nothing much of importance is going on. This, of course, is not true. Many things which are new and important to the psychological and intellectual development of your child will be taking place during this period. In addition, sex is not at all as "latent" now as some psychoanalysts think! I remember one of my patients telling me how she and some girl friends had masturbated each other with soft hairbrushes when they were eight years old. That doesn't sound very latent!

Some investigators call this period the school years, which emphasizes the importance of school learning and school life to a child of this age. But this is also a somewhat misleading label, for it overlooks the importance of the home and family in psychological development. Other researchers call it the gang age or the group age, referring to the importance of a child's peers at this time; but this label also seems to underestimate the importance of the family.

The least misleading title I can give this stage of development is to call it the stage of middle childhood. This label does not overstress one aspect at the expense of others. It also emphasizes the relative tranquility of this stage of development as opposed to the dramatic ups and downs of the preschool years which lie behind the child and the stormy turmoil of adolescence which lies ahead. During this stage your child's personality persists in a relatively stabilized form until the arrival of the stage of preadolescence when your youngster turns eleven.

Oddly enough, the stage of middle childhood is the one adults know the least about. This is due to the fact that there has been less meaningful research at this stage than on preschool children and adolescents.

During this period your child loses much of his early interest in parents and adults and unites in a new society of children. Whereas in previous stages your child's life was family centered and home based, he now actively joins a new and separate society of his peers formed from among his same-age and same-sex friends.

The child of middle childhood learns to keep his thoughts and feelings to himself. Moreover, he begins to practice outright guile and deception with adults. A father knows a great deal about what is going on inside the head of his preschool child (if he is at all sensitive) and he knows a great deal about what goes on inside the head of his adolescent (because an adolescent often informs you exactly what he thinks). But a father may be at a great loss to figure out what is going on inside the head of his middle-years child. (Or he may assume he does know and be far, far off the mark. The formation of the typical "secret societies" of this age are a tipoff that at this age, the child does *not* want to communicate to adults what is going on in his thoughts and fantasies.

In spite of the fact that less is known scientifically about this stage than about any other, there is still much solid information about middle childhood which it is important to recognize.

As with the preschool stage, it may be helpful for the author to give a brief sketch of the characteristics of a "typical" child during each of the years of middle childhood.

THE SIX-YEAR-OLD

You will remember from the preschool stage that the five-year-old is at an age of equilibrim, a delightful time of life when he is at peace with himself and his world. Five is a delight to have around. Many a father will wish he could have his pleasant docile five-year-old back when the six-year-old stage arrives. Five was an age of consolidation and equilibrium. But around six, this equilibrium breaks up. Your child is thrusting out in new directions, trying new things, finding it difficult to adjust to other people because of new psychological urges within himself.

Six is an age of extremes. A confusing mixture of baby and child, parents may often find him quite difficult to handle. He is prey to violent emotions. One minute he may tell his mother how fond he is of her. The next minute, after she has mildly reproved him for something, he bursts out with: "I hate you! You're always picking on me!"

His mother is no longer the center of his universe, as she was when he was five. An astronomical revolution has taken place and now *he* wants to be the center of the universe. His unconscious motto seems to be: "Do things my way and we will get along just fine!" He may become very demanding and his behavior will remind you of the stage of first adolescence.

Conflict with his mother at this age is Nature's way of getting him out of the secure nest of home and family and into the widening world of school and neighborhood. It is as if the only way he can be weaned from home to the society of school and his peers is to make him so obnoxious to his mother that she can't stand him. Often his mother will tell you when you come home from work: "He was impossible! I couldn't do a thing with him today." He is usually worse with her than with anybody else. This is due to his five-year dependency on her. Often a six-year-old cannot break that dependency easily and smoothly, but only by a psychological uprising, complete with violent emotions and lots of negativism.

This is an age when his father can often guide and manage him best. He will respond positively to your firm commands whereas he

"DO THINGS MY WAY
AND WE WILL GET ALONG JUST FINE."

may respond negatively to even the most gentle suggestions from his mother. (At times though, he acts on the premise that it is only fair for him to be equally as obnoxious with you as he is with his mother!)

Six is full of boundless energy, and all his muscles cry out for action. He is on the go every moment he is awake: running, crawling, climbing, pulling, pushing, jumping, and hollering. Parents naively think that the furniture in their house is for sitting and the floors are for walking on. Six knows better. To him the sofa in the living room is just the thing to use to build a fort, with the addition of some old boards from the garage and part of an old carpet he found in the cellar. The floors of the living room seem ideally designed to crawl on or roll around on. Mother and daddy's bed makes an ideal trampoline. Noise and violence seem to characterize his activity play: "Bang, you're dead! I hate you, you stinker! Gimme that or I'll sock you!"

Six is Mr. Wiggle-and-Squirm. He expends an enormous amount of energy just sitting still. But of course he is *not* sitting still! He wriggles, writhes, and contorts his body into various grotesque shapes while he carries on whatever activity engages him at the moment. Mealtime is no exception. At this age, a child's reaction to being told to sit up straight at the dinner table is to suffer an attack of, what the humorist B. M. Atkinson calls, "Roman Spine," which he defines as "A sudden collapse of the backbone, occurring always at mealtime and rendering a child incapable of sitting up straight at the table; believed to be a psychic regression to the Roman days of dining horizontally on couches, a position celebrated in the history of eating as being the only one that ever came naturally to a child. A corollary condition, occurring mostly in small boys is Scooter Foot, a temporary binding of the crotch bones which prevents the child from keeping both feet under the table at the same time, the stray foot always being poised upright alongside the chair, thus making it appear that he is riding a scooter instead of sitting at a table."[1] Six-year-old boys are enormously hard on clothes. The badges by which they are quickly recognized include holes in the pants at the knee, shoes with scuffed toes, and shredded elbows of sweaters.

Six loves to be in the limelight and monopolize the conversation. He delights in making up his own jokes or making himself the center of attention with impromptu show-off stunts. He loves to brag and exaggerate wildly as to what he can do. He can be infuriatingly dogmatic about something he knows absolutely nothing about. Six is a good beginner but a poor finisher. This holds true for eating getting dressed, taking his bath or anything else. He is easely distracted and at times can be the world's champion dawdler. Robert Paul Smith has amusingly sketched this characteristic quality of the six-year-old in the following "translations from the children":

> "I'm all dressed."
>   He has his undershirt on.
> "I'm all dressed except my shoes."
>   He does not have his undershirt on.
> "I'm just tying my shoelaces."
>   He's looking for his shoes.[2]

First grade opens a completely new world of experience for a six-year-old. It is his first encounter with formal schooling (as compared to the much more informal and flexible schooling in nursery school and kindergarten). In first grade he has to do many things that are somewhat foreign to his six-year-old temperament. He has to learn to sit still in his seat, to persevere at a task, to raise his hand and wait until he is called on to speak, to wait his turn at an activity, to resist the temptation to chatter with classmates. These things to not come easily and naturally to a six-year-old, in particular to a rambunctious, feisty, six-year-old *boy*. Adults are not aware of the psychological pressure that a six-year-old feels in conforming to the demands and regulations of first grade.

I remember vividly when my daughter Robin was a first grader. During the first few weeks, when she got home at the end of the school day, she let out a bloodcurdling screech that lasted for a minute or two. This was her method of letting off steam that had been building up in her all day. And Robin was very much a quiet and well-behaved child in school! The new pressures and demands of first grade are usually managed more easily by the child who has had nursery school and kindergarten experience. First grade is usually hardest on the child who has had no prior experience of adjusting to the demands of school, a new teacher, and new and strange children.

It is very probable that much of the changed behavior and obnoxious attitudes of the six-year-old are due to the effects of his first encounters with formal schooling. A child's first experience with daily competition at school and on the playground often cause much

"I'M ALL DRESSED."

more emotional pressure on him than parents realize. For the first time in his young life he is required to be away from the emotional shelter of home and mother and follow the directions of adults other than his parents for five of six hours a day. This is emotionally draining for a six-year-old. Deep down inside, many children are lonesome for their mothers and their homes, especially if a younger brother or sister is still at home enjoying mother's attention and the simple, easygoing play of early childhood. Saturdays, when the pressure of school life is over, the six-year-old may be a changed child, bounding out of bed early in the morning to watch TV or just "mess around" with the nondemanding type of play he cannot indulge in during the school day.

The new school day is *long* for a six-year-old. He is tired, both physically and emotionally, at the end of it. When he comes home he wants to be able to relax and just "fool around." A mother may be astonished when her six-year-old responds with tears or an angry outburst to a simple request that he change clothes. She wonders what got into him, not realizing that physically he is tired and emotionally he feels he cannot tolerate one single more command after what to him are long hours of obeying adult regulations. Therefore it is important to be sure that your six-year-old has adequate time for rest and sleep at night. It is also important to allow some time just to "blow off steam" when he comes home from school. The period immediately following the school day is no time for a parent to make psychological demands on a six-year-old.

A typical six-year-old will enjoy the fun part of school, but find to his dismay that it also involves what one first grader called "a lot of mean old work!"[3] But he does enjoy coming home and proudly showing off what he did in school: his drawings and printing and the stories he is learning to read.

It is typical of the extreme mood swings of six that he will love school one day and hate it the next. This usually means that on a day when he gets recognition and praise he loves school and his teacher. But if things don't go well the next day, he will hate it. Robert Paul Smith has caught this aspect of the six-year-old's attitude toward school life very well:

> "Miss McPhetridge is mean."
> He's being taught to read.
> "Miss McPhetridge hates me."

He's not learning how to read.
"Miss McPhetridge is peachy."
He's learned how to read.[4]

In addition to school, his peer group assumes enormous importance to the six-year-old. At this time your child enters what Dr.
Ruth Hartley calls "the year of the swarm." Six loves company and
feels ill at ease unless he is with a group of his contemporaries.
Paradoxically, the members of the swarm often go their own way
without paying much attention to the others. Still, they seem happy
somehow as long as they are all together in a clump.

Teasing and name-calling now make their frequent appearance in
the group life of six-year-olds. Your child needs to learn how to
handle teasing and to be able to trade insults with others without
losing his composure. In any kind of competition, whether at school
or in play, six is not a graceful loser, so don't expect it. Every defeat
in a game is a crushing blow to his ego. It is best not to expect six to
play well at games that have rigid rules and to be upset when he
breaks the rules in order to win. If all goes well he will be warm,
enthusiastic, and eager; but if things go badly, you may get emotional outbursts, tears, and temper tantrums.

New fears may make an appearance in your child's life at six.
Among the most common fears are: fear of some kind of bodily
injury; fear of rain, thunder, wind, or fire; fear of various kinds of
wild animals or insects; fear of the dark; fear of dark closets, attics,
and cellars. Six may also be troubled by nightmares involving wild
animals, witches, ghosts, or monsters. Don't poke fun or ridicule
him, hoping to shame him out of these fears. No matter how
irrational the fear may be, use the feedback technique and let him
know that you understand how frightened he feels. Then you become his ally and help him feel stronger inside.

One reason for the sudden appearance of fears in six-year-olds is
that so much seems to be expected of them and they do not feel
they can perform adequately. They feel frustrated and angry inside.
The fear that this hidden anger will be discovered by their parents
who will punish them for these feelings, is unconsciously projected
onto wild animals or monsters in phobias and nightmares.

An additional reason for the appearance of fears is that children of
this age notice much more about the world than they did before. But
much of what they register they only partially understand. Partial

understanding gives rise to fears and insecurities. For example, when Rusty was six and first heard I was going to be on television, his reaction was a sudden look of fright: "You mean you're not going to be here at home with me any more, Daddy?" To him "being on television" meant I was going to some vague place called "television" and would no longer live at home with him and the family. When I explained that I was just going to drive over to Hollywood where the television studio was located, be on a show, and be home again that night, then he was relaxed and happy.

Even though six spends most of his time at school or with his neighborhood gang, and comparatively little time with his parents, it would be a great error to conclude that he no longer needs you and his mother. He very definitely needs to know you are *there* in the background while he explores the new worlds of school and gang. And after a period of apparent indifference to you, he may astonish you by asking you out of the blue, to spend some special time with him.

I hope I have not given you the impression that six is just a hellion on wheels and nothing more. This is an expansive age and your six-year-old is branching out psychologically in many new directions. He is a young explorer, setting out across unknown seas and, as befits a young explorer, he is full of courage and derring-do. He is on the lookout for new experiences. He savors life to the fullest, and meets it head-on. He is delightful in his vigor and energy and enthusiasm. Enjoy him when he is on the positive, enthusiastic side and try to roll with the punches when he is in a negative, unhappy mood. And take comfort in the thought that a new year of equilibrium is just around the corner when he reaches seven!

THE SEVEN-YEAR-OLD

If six is an age of extremes and exploring into new psychological worlds of school and gang, seven is an age of assimilation. Ruminating over the various life experiences he has had until now, he mentally incorporates them into his concept of self and world.

The brash and noisy behavior of the six-year-old begins to ebb. Seven is a calmer age that is easier to live with, much more rational, and more reasonable to deal with. The blind thrusting out into new experience so characteristic of the six-year-old disappears. Seven likes to talk things over and will accept parental explanations of limits with much better grace than he did before.

Your child is more eager to be liked, more cooperative, more anxious to please. He is a better listener than he was last year. He is more tactful and does not meet life head-on as he did at six. Whereas six would thrust out into a new undertaking without anybody's approval, seven likes adult approval before starting on a new project. He finishes things better than he did at six; he has a greater capacity for persevering. In general, he is a pleasant and responsive member of the family most of the time.

But seven can also be quite withdrawn at times. In fact, he can be downright morose and dejected. When he feels he did not do well at school or in competition with his peers, he may sink into a black mood of self-pity when he feels "nobody wants me around" and "I guess I'm just no good." At times like these, seven believes that people are against him, they don't like him, and they are picking on him. He may be convinced that other kids cheat at the games they play, his brothers or sisters get away with murder but he gets punished, and that his parents are grossly unfair to him. This type of attitude is summed up beautifully in the middle-childhood chant: "Nobody loves me, everybody hates me, I'm going out and eat worms!"

Parents should learn to respect the hidden inner life of their seven-year-olds. As Dr. Gesell puts it, "We cannot do justice to the psychology of the seven-year-old unless we recognize the importance of his private mental activities."[5] His self-absorption accounts for his occasional brooding and times of sadness, sulkiness, and complaining.

Seven is a time for mulling things over and sorting things out in the privacy of his own mind. He is much more introverted than he was at six. His inner mental musing is a psychological device by which he absorbs and reorganizes his life's experiences. Parents need to understand that when a seven-year-old is off in his own little world daydreaming or wool-gathering he is really *working*. He is trying to understand the meaning of all the life experiences he is having at school, with his gang, and at home. These meanings he is sorting out in his inner world are basically *feelings*. And these feelings need to be worked over and put into some kind of meaningful arrangement.

Just as he needed to practice endlessly going up and down stairs when he was a toddler, at seven he needs to practice endlessly thinking things over about life and its meaning on a seven-year-old level. The six-year-old was a man of action; the seven-year-old is a man of reflection. He mulls things over endlessly in terms of their repercussions upon his personal and private self.

It is particularly important for fathers to understand the value of this introspection to a seven-year-old. Otherwise, when he sees his son sprawled in front of a TV set, lost in the electronic world before him, or sitting staring out the window, he may become impatient with him and snap: "Hey, come on, haven't you got anything more important to do than just mope around the house like this all the time?" A father needs to understand that his child is often actively working mentally when he just sits and does nothing.

Don't get the impression that your seven-year-old is a melancholy Prince Hamlet, however, who broods excessively on the paradoxes of life and death. He feels life in every pore. He not only sits and thinks, but he continues to run and jump, to climb trees, to scuff and tussle with his friends, to play cops and robbers and commandos. He has active and silly spells as well as pensive moods. Although very self-absorbed, your seven-year-old is not only increasingly aware of the finer nuances of his own feelings, but he is now becoming sensitive to the feelings of others.

This should be a good year at school for your seven-year-old. Generally speaking, a second-grade teacher has an easier time of it than a first-grade teacher. Your youngster has a year of school experience behind him and he is more accustomed to its demands. He is now over the hump with reading compared to first grade, where learning to read at times seems like a very difficult task. His increased socialization skills make school life go more smoothly.

He likes a personal relationship with his teacher. He is very pleased when she praises him. He likes to be near her, to talk to her and touch her. He enjoys asking her permission before starting a new task. The wise second-grade teacher knows that this need for a personal relationship with her is a part of the developmental stage of the seven-year-old. With this in mind, she will quietly circulate around the room so that she can give each child that needed personal touch.

Although at seven he does not demand the companionship of his group as much as he did at six, and he spends a considerable amount

"I HATE BEING ANGRY"

of time by himself, his gang is still important to him. Seven is a for-and-against age. Several children are likely to gang up against another child; cliques are formed; some kids are "out" and others are "in." It is not unusual to see a lone youngster sobbing his way home from school on one side of the street while a group of four or five kids on the other side taunt him with: "Cry baby, cry baby, run along home!" Many seven-year-old boys have trouble with older boys who bully them.

Physical combat often goes along with the age of seven, especially with boys. The typical "fight," however, is more likely to be a mixture of wrestling and boxing, with more shoving than punching. Two boys often spend more time trying to scare each other with threats of what they will do than actually punching one another.

Seven also needs romping, shouting play as he did at six, and for the same reasons. He still has a fantastic store of energy and this kind of boisterous play is both an outlet for energy and a way of letting off emotional steam.

A seven-year-old is very definite in his insistence on "fairness." "It isn't fair!" is one of his most vociferous complaints. The wise father will note with amusement, however, that his seven-year-old often has a double standard of fairness. He is far more concerned when someone has been unfair to him than when he is unfair to someone else.

Swapping begins to make its appearance in the group life of the seven-year-old. This will continue unabated through the age of ten as a prized socializing activity. What do sevens swap? Anything and everything, from trading stamps and baseball cards to games they own. The psychological value of swapping is that it enables seven to relate to his peers in a relaxed, nondemanding way.

Seven is sometimes the age at which a child is first enrolled at summer camp. Often this is a mistake. It is better to begin by sending a child to day camp when he is seven or eight, working up to camp for a whole week when he is eight or nine. Many times fathers send their sons to camp at an early age so they will learn to be independent and assertive and aggressive. This is particularly true if the son is on the passive and introverted side. The father feels: "Camp will be good for him; it'll toughen him up!" But if the camp experience is rushed into at too early an age, the whole procedure may backfire. The results of the camp experience may be exactly the opposite of what the father was hoping to accomplish. The timid boy will become even more timid. And the boy who is poor at physical activities and sports will find them more distasteful and scary than ever.

Seven not only gets along much better with his mother than he did at six, but he also reaches out for a closer and deeper relationship with his father. This is especially true for boys. Your typical seven-year-old boy will enjoy participating in activities "where there are no women around": going camping or fishing, going for a walk where you can talk over "male-type" things such as baseball averages or how to fix cars, going to baseball games or other sports events, shopping together for hobby equipment, going for a trip to the hardware store for new tools for the home workshop, working on a car together. Mother and sisters may be treated with kindly but amused condescension by a seven-year-old boy.

However, it is well to emphasize that you need to be true to your own nature. Don't feel you have to pretend an interest in cars or sports if you have none. Be yourself. Do with your boy the things that you genuinely like. Don't pretend an interest in activities that are regarded as typically masculine if you do not really enjoy them. For example, I happen to enjoy camping, hiking and backpacking, and attending various sports events, and I did all of these things with my boys in their years of middle childhood. But I have never been particularly interested in fishing or in the inner working of cars, and so I did not engage in either of these activities with my two boys.

Seven years is an important time for father-daughter relationships as well. The seven-year-old girl is also reaching out for relationships beyond her mother at this developmental stage. This is an excellent time for a father to help a girl appreciate her femininity. Do this by a special invitation out to lunch, or taking her for a walk, or going to a special movie she might like but her brother wouldn't, and being sure to compliment her when she is dressed up for some special occasion and continuing to read her a story at bedtime.

Seven years is a good time for a father, if, due to the pressure of work, he has not spent much time alone with a son or daughter. Your youngster is reaching out psychologically for a closer relationship. Your children will welcome the opportunity to spend time with you even though your relationship may not have been as close in the earlier ages as they would have liked. Now is the time to forge a deep emotional relationship that will be so all-important later when adolescence rears its disturbing head. For if you have not established a solid, close relationship during the years of middle childhood, it is going to be very difficult, if not impossible, to establish such a relationship during adolescence.

To sum up the seven-year-old: This is generally a good year for both child and parents. Your seven-year-old is more stable, relaxed, and cooperative than he was at six. Praise is the key to handling him. He thrives on praise but is sensitive to criticism and disapproval and may burst into tears when reprimanded. Seven is an introspective time, and your child at this age has a psychological need to mull over and assimilate his life experiences in order to fill out his concept of himself and his world.

THE EIGHT-YEAR-OLD

Six was an expansive age; seven was a more inward age. Eight is another expansive age. Seven tended to withdraw from the world; eight goes out to meet the world with gusto and verve. Less sensitive than he was at seven, less within himself, he is less apt to withdraw. He is ready to tackle anything. He is busy and active, constantly on the go, enjoying new experiences, forever trying out new things and making new friends. The typical eight-year-old is exuberant, expansive, and ready for anything.

Eight is leaving behind the more serious, thoughtful, inward self of seven. It is as if the eight-year-old were "trying out against the world the self which he was so busy consolidating at seven," as Dr. Gesell phrases it.[6] Whereas seven liked to be alone much of the time, eight abhors playing alone. He demands not only the presence of another person, but his complete attention and participation. If that other person happens to be his mother, he often becomes extremely demanding of her time and attention.

According to Dr. Gesell there are three traits which particularly characterize the behavior of the eight-year-old: "speediness, expansiveness," and a new word coined by Dr. Gesell, "evaluativeness." An eight-year-old is nothing if not speedy. His psychomotor tempo is heightened and he does everything in high gear. He is full of impatience. "I can't wait!" is a characteristic phrase of the eight-year-old, whether it refers to the time dinner will be ready or to a friend's birthday party next week.

Dr. Gesell sums up the expansiveness characteristic of eight in a striking metaphor: "As a hungry amoeba thrusts out one pseudopod after another, the hungry eight year old mind actively spreads into new territory."[7] Evidence of the inroads of an eight-year-old into the larger culture is indicated by his passion for collecting. He collects anything and everything: pebbles and rocks, stamps, postcards, souvenirs. You name it and he collects it. Weekend trips and vacations are occasions for him to find new treasures: shells, rocks, seaweed, driftwood, old boards and sticks, etc.

Parents often see little value in many of the things their eight-year-old collects, but to him they are wondrous treasures. The collections are stored in his treasure box, his bureau and desk drawers, his closet, as well as in a boy's pockets or a girl's handbag. His interest in acquiring possessions is, however, usually not matched by an equal interest in taking care of them, although he sometimes likes to classify, arrange, and organize things. He can become particularly incensed if a younger brother or sister gets into his prized possessions.

By "evaluativeness" Dr. Gesell means the eight-year-old's tendency to appraise what happens to him and what he causes to happen. He constantly evaluates his activities and those of others. This interest in appraising and evaluating is part of his drive to become more grown-up. He definitely demands that adults treat him more like a grown-up. :"Whaddaya think I am, a baby?" he will say.

Eight loves to dramatize and exaggerate, and his characteristic dramatic exaggerations of childhood events may bring forth amused smiles from adults. He likes to dramatize air raids, accidents, fighting, and bombing with his toys. He loves to impersonate characters in the TV shows or movies he has seen and the books he has read. Girls are quieter, more verbal, and more sedentary in their dramatizing than boys. Dolls are often used by girls for their dramatizing. Girls may also put on special little "shows" for neighborhood audiences of other children at this age.

Closely allied to his new propensity to dramatize himself is the characteristic bravado of the eight-year-old. Although he may feel inwardly unsure of himself in tackling some new activity, he would "just die" before he admitted this to anyone. The need to seem completely self-sufficient and assured may cause him to present an indifferent stoic front to the world at times.

He may appear to be completely unmoved by adult scoldings or lectures. He will listen in stony silence to punishments meted out for misbehavior, and proclaim "I didn't want to go outside and play today, anyway!" when grounded for some wrongdoing.

In spite of his occasional stoic front, he will burst into tears at the hint of a frustration, especially when he is overtired. The tears are a reaction to being deprived of something he wanted very much, doing something he knows he shouldn't, or being disappointed over his performance at school or play.

Some fathers are taken aback when they encounter tears at this age. They feel that by now a boy should have given up crying—a thing they regard as having been appropriate when he was smaller but not at this age. This is a mistake. Tears can be expected readily from children up to the age of twelve, and boys are no exception. There is nothing unmanly about crying and a father should accept a son's tears without telling him, "Stop that crying; you're too old for that." (As a matter of fact we are never too old for that. Mother Nature does not turn off our tear ducts even when we have reached the ripe old age of twenty-one!!)

In school the eight-year-old is not emotionally as dependent on his teacher as he was in second grade. He has less need for a close personal relationship. He relates to her now in a more formal way and regards her as an impersonal figure of authority who regulates and rules the classroom. Emotionally, his school group is now more important to him than his teacher.

In school and out he is hungry for facts. His eager, curious mind soaks up facts about anything and everything, especially unusual information such as can be found in the *Guinness Book of World Records*. Armed with his new-found facts he delights in asking questions of younger children which they cannot answer.

Mothers report that their eight-year-old is much more communicative about school life and what goes on than he was at six or seven. Sometimes he may come home from school bursting with news: "You wouldn't believe what happened at school today—it was fantastic!"

In keeping with his new-found knowledge he often assumes a know-it-all tone in his comments about the world.

The "gang" continues to be important to him. To remain a member in good standing, he will have to prove his worth by conforming to the "Code of the West." This gang code includes many values which probably were never stressed at home: daring, physical strength, agility, comradeship, ingenuity, and even slyness.

Eight marks the beginning of a very definite change in the pre-ferred sex of playmates (if this has not already occurred). Boys and girls now definitely segregate themselves in their play. Girls will usually do this by quietly drawing away from boys and seeking the company of other girls. Boys, however, do this much more crudely and ostentatiously, making it clear to all concerned that girls are "dumb," "stupid," "silly," and totally unworthy of their attention.

Eight usually marks a difference in a child's choice of friends. When he was younger the child believed that he must be accepted by every one of his peers, indiscriminately. Occasionally he cried if even a disagreeable classmate deserted him to play with someone else. But now, at eight, his self-confidence is greater and he no longer feels he has to please everyone. He begins to pick and choose among the children he knows. He selects a few to be his best friends and does not bother too much with those he has discarded.

Eight is also the age when the chum or special friend usually makes his appearance. These friends are almost always of the same sex. Nothing remotely like the relationship to the chum has ever appeared before. This is a very significant step for him to take in his maturing interpersonal relationships. For the first time in his life, your child develops a real sensitivity to what matters to another person, and how what he says and does affects the feelings of others. An intense and important experience, it is very valuable for your child's emotional growth. This relationship with a chum usually is your child's first major realistic attachment to another person out-side his own family. The intimate exchange of feelings helps diminish your child's feelings of isolation at this age. It helps him to under-stand how another person feels and manages the same problems he is struggling to master. This is the early foundation for his capacity to form deep, meaningful, and lasting friendships in later life.

This is your child's first experience with intimacy that develops from common personality traits and interests rather than through family ties. Experiences of this positive relationship with a chum become a foundation, not only for friendships in later life, but for marriage (even though the chum is of the same sex). Relationships with a chum may continue through the age of ten, although usually not with the same friend.

Your child will have a constant need to be with his chum. An altruistic attitude develops in which his friend's welfare becomes almost as important as his own. However, as with any intimate personal relationship, not all is sweetness and light. There is also much arguing and disagreeing, getting mad, and then making up.

Parents seem unaware of the positive emotional growth which the relationship with a chum enables their child to experience. Parents often react in negative ways to the importance of a chum in their child's life. "Why do you always have to play with Jimmy?" they will say. "Why don't you have somebody else over to the house?" Parents complain: "All I hear is Jimmy likes this and Jimmy likes that—you'd think my boy didn't know anybody else in the world existed besides Jimmy!" In such cases you should guard against showing such jealousy of the emotional importance of the chum. Do not ridicule or poke fun at the relationship.

The importance of the chum in a one-to-one relationship does not negate the equal importance of the total gang to which your child belongs. The secrecy of the gang is a large part of the fun of belonging and is an indication of a child's need to create his own miniature society which is independent of adults. Secrecy is the child's way of maintaining privacy and individuality.

You will win real points if you can furnish the gang with an indoor meeting place in the cellar or attic or garage, or if you provide them with the scrap materials to build a tree house or fort, such as old lumber, old shingles, tarpaper, or bricks—or old furniture to use inside the gang's hideaway.

You will also win points by inviting the gang to come in for snacks every now and then. Your home will become known to the group as a "neat" place where the "eats" are good. In spite of the fact that the gang ignores your adult presence, and regards you rather as a machine that dispenses treats and "goodies," never fear, you are still much appreciated by your eight-year-old for being hospitable to his friends rather than antagonistic.

Eight is also the time for organized groups such as the Cub Scouts (Brownies for girls started earlier at seven) Little League and Pop Warner Football for boys of nine and seven respectively, and AYSO Soccer for both boys and girls from the ages of seven on. The experience with an organized group can help a youngster learn to act in cooperation with his team and adjust to definite regulations and requirements. Organized group life can help to focus many of the energies that were so hard to direct a year or so ago.

Money, property, ownership and possessions are of great importance in the cultural organization of the eight-year-old mind. Money is all important. Parents may be disturbed by his money-mad nature, but it is nothing to worry about. The one sure way to motivate an eight-year-old is by the promise of earning money. The eight-year-old loves to gaze in store windows, browse in shops, and even indulge in a good deal of imaginative spending. Eight is a good time to begin an allowance if you have not already done so.

Eight-year-olds also continue to love to barter. They love TV and comic books. In fact, the interest in comic books usually reaches a peak around the ages of eight and nine. Eight loves to buy, collect, and swap his favorite comic books. The average eight-year-old devotes many passionate hours a week to watching TV and reading comic books. These are simple, undemanding media: they offer easy, relaxing fun for your child. After the time he spends meeting the demands and pressures of school, watching TV or reading comic books is the equivalent of what a relaxing weekend is for you after a regular workweek. So please don't scold your youngster for watching TV and reading comic books and pester him to read more "good literature." He is not only enjoying himself with these relaxing media, but he is soaking up more information than you are aware.

Of course, comic books are not the only things an eight-year-old likes to read, but there is no doubt that they are his favorites. Eight years is also the time when spontaneous reading makes its appearance since he feels much more at home with reading than he did in the first and second grade. You can capitalize on this new interest in reading, or sometimes stimulate it, by taking him to the library or bookstore. If you take him to the bookstore, let him choose whatever paperback book he wishes. Don't attempt to dictate his choice or get him to read one of the classics. As long as he chooses the book himself he will be motivated to read it, and any type of reading helps him develop reading skills.

If he does not have a bookcase, now is the time to buy or make one. He is ready for a more personal relationship with his books and he will welcome personalized bookplates as a birthday or special gift. He also likes to look at pictorial magazines and pore for hours over mail-order catalogs. He delights in sending for things through the mail. And nothing pleases him as much as receiving mail of his own. A wise father will capitalize on this and clip out items from a newspaper or magazine that he knows will interest his child and send them through the mail. From time to time, a paperback book called *1001 Things You Can Get Free,* or some similar title, will appear which tells how to get free pamphlets or articles by writing various companies. Such a book makes a much appreciated gift for an eight-year-old.

An interest in horror shows and movies which have titles like "Gallons of Blood" or "Buckets of Gore" is now making its appearance and will continue through at least age ten. Sometimes parents, particularly mothers, feel that these shows are too "brutal" and are bad for their children. Fathers can be reassuring about this, for this kind of interest is perfectly normal. Seeing horror shows and scary movies is one way your child masters his fears. This explains why youngsters avidly seek out movies and TV shows of this nature.

An interest in table games is now at its height. Take advantage of this as another avenue of strengthening and deepening your relationship. Your child will enjoy playing checkers, dominoes, Parchesi, and even a rudimentary and primitive form of chess. Two-handed card games, such as slap jack, crazy eights, and war, especially appeal to children. A very good book for a father to buy at this point is *Packs of Fun* by Bill Severn (David McKay Co). Monopoly is a very good family game which the eight-year-old enjoys. You can also teach him to play blackjack and a simple form of poker known as 727. Both of these games will also indirectly help him in his counting.

To summarize the eight-year-old, he has consolidated the self he was mulling over at seven, and he is now energetically trying it out on the world. He is vigorous and active and experimenting with all sorts of new activities and interpersonal relationships. He is trying to be more grown up and he demands that adults treat him like an adult. For this reason spankings should disappear from the parent's discipline reportoire. Being deprived of a favorite TV program will usually be much more effective as a discipline measure.

THE NINE-YEAR-OLD

In many ways the nine-year-old is a continuation and extension of what he was at eight, only at a more mature level of psychological integration. It is harder to tell an eight-year-old from a nine-year-old by his behavior, for example, than it is to tell a three-year-old from a four-year-old. These ages of middle childhood merge much more than the ages of early childhood, where there are very dramatic differences between a two-, three-, four-, and five-year-old.

Remember that three traits particularly characterized the behavior of the eight-year-old: speediness, expansiveness, and evaluativeness. These traits continue to operate at the nine-year-old level but at a higher plane of maturity and integration.

Nine is still speedy, but his speed is under better control and does not come in such sharp, erratic bursts as it did before.

The expansiveness of eight was influenced much more by what was going on in his immediate environment. The expansiveness of nine comes more from within. The exploration of his world is much more self-motivated.

The evaluations of nine are deeper and more discriminating. He has new powers of self-appraisal and social judgment which he did not possess at eight. He is able to experience and express more sophisticated and finer shades of feeling.

Perhaps the key words describing the characteristics that set off nine the most sharply from eight are *individuality* and *self-motivation*.

The nine-year-old is much more of an individual than at any previous age. His gestures, his enthusiasms, his ways of laughing and talking, his humor, even his table manners are all stamped with his own individuality. Fathers should respect their nine-year-old as an individual with a very real personality of his own. His abilities are clearly apparent and his own real and unique interests are beginning to flower.

Your nine-year-old responds best if treated with the same courtesy you would treat a grown-up; that is, learn to take into account his own unique preferences and eccentricities. Approach him in an adult way and he responds well. He will enter eagerly into making plans for an activity, whether for a project in the garage workshop or a family outing. He is more cooperative and responsive when included in making the plans than when he is told, "This is what we are going to do." A father accustomed to making decisions without consulting his child may have to shift psychic gears to accommodate his nine-year-old's new grown-upness.

Your nine-year-old will respond well to increased independence and the opportunity to make his own choices and decisions. He likes to be more on his own. He can enjoy an overnight visit to a friend's house or a trip downtown by himself on the bus. Even an airplane trip by himself to visit relatives is not above the capabilities of some nine-year-olds.

However, precisely because he seems so mature and capable in many ways, you may overestimate his maturity at times and expect too much from him. Remember that, at times, he will need to revert to the behavior of a young child. Don't be disappointed when he does. Be willing to help without ridiculing or teasing him for being "childish."

Self-motivation is one of the basic characteristics of nine. He is much more self-sufficient and on his own than he was at eight. He has a growing capacity to use his own initiative, with only slight cues from his environment. Typically this gives him a preoccupied businesslike air both at home and at school.

The attention span of the nine-year-old has greatly increased. In persevering at tasks, the eight-year-old is much more dependent on environmental support—the pressure of the group or the stimulation of an adult. But the nine year old can persevere much longer. He may spend all afternoon working with his erector set, building something in the garage workshop, or creating an elaborate city in his backyard sandbox. He has a new capacity to set his mind to a task and see it through.

However, the fact that his attention can be sustained for a longer time does not mean that you should plan activities of too long a duration for him. His own interest and self-motivation in a project are important factors as to how long his attention span will be. He can sustain a project over a long period of time, planning and carrying out the whole thing with an almost adult carefulness, as long as it is *his* project. But as soon as it no longer interests him he drops it. Forced or required attention for too long a period of time can be very wearing to him. You can quickly detect this by his sighs of tension and restlessness.

Nine is interested in perfecting his skills. He enjoys doing the same thing over and over again until he masters it, such as learning to use a skateboard or to pitch horseshoes. He is particularly anxious to learn various play skills. He wants to be a good ballplayer, to pitch and catch well. He wants to learn how to swim and roller-skate and ice-skate and ski. Nine wants to develop skills which will give him status in the eyes of other children.

It is good for father to take the time with his nine-year-old to encourage him to learn how to do things and to help him to do them well. Show him how to open a knife and use it safely, how to use different kinds of woodworking tools. Show him how to throw a baseball and how to catch it, how to bat and how to bunt, how to throw a football pass, how to make a lay-up shot in basketball.

However, don't overdo the teaching of techniques and skills. Although your child wants to learn how to do things, his ability and capacity for sustained interest may not equal his initial enthusiasm. It is very important that you teach him skills in the spirit of fun and enjoyment. Praise him for each step of progress he makes. Do not demand perfection of performance and do not let yourself become a nag. Let your child lead the way. You supply the knowledge he needs when he expresses a readiness for it.

Nine has great interest in sports of all kinds: baseball, football, swimming, and for some boys, basketball. He likes hand and body wrestling, bicycling, roller-skating, ice-skating, skateboarding, kite flying. Climbing rocks is a particularly irresistible sport to most nine-year-old boys. So is throwing stones in a stream.

This is a good year, if you enjoy it yourself, to help your child get acquainted with nature and the great outdoors. Take simple, easy hikes and try outdoor camping. Picnics in the woods or at the beach or river or lake are enjoyed immensely by nine-year-olds. Camping is a particularly good activity for the whole family, and promotes a real "family feeling" as children of all ages pitch in with the chores and the fun.

The urge to play an instrument may be strong at nine. This may be the time to begin piano or guitar or recorder lessons. First lessons should be considered a trial exposure to the instrument, with no blame attached if the project doesn't pan out.

Learning to play an instrument should be-a pleasure, not a chore. You need the right kind of teacher—someone who not only has the required technical skill in playing the instrument, but who knows how to keep lessons alive and stimulating. It is sometimes wise to rent rather than buy an instrument to see if it is going to "take" with your child. Sometimes when parents have bought an instrument for their child, they get on his back about regular practicing. Resist the temptation. Remind him, but do not nag him; using the word "rehearse" or "play" is psychologically much better than the word "practice" in motivating your child.

Above all, resist the temptation to push your child into music lessons or any other activity if he gives you clear indications that he is not psychologically ready.

Many parents start their youngsters in some activity too soon and expect results too quickly. They send them to camp too early, before the children are emotionally ready. They start music lessons too soon, and they push their youngsters into instruction in tennis or riding before their physical coordination has matured sufficiently for them to handle these activities successfully. As a result, the child acquires a bad attitude toward particular activities before he has a chance to develop a real interest in them.

It is important also to remember that your nine-year-old needs free time when he can just take it easy, idle around the yard or neighborhood, lie down on the grass and watch the clouds, and in general "let his motor idle." I feel strongly that our middle-children's lives are becoming increasingly overorganized, with mother spending many of her afternoons chauffeuring youngsters from one activity to another.

Children need free time to create their own self-motivated activities, their own special forms of play. They cannot do this if their time is continually blueprinted and preprogrammed by their parents.

Your nine-year-old is very independent. He does not want to be babied or treated as though he is still a very young child in need of constant supervision and protection. In fact, it may hurt our feelings when he shows more interest in getting together with his gang instead of joining a special family excursion which his parents had so benevolently planned for him.

His friends are the main focus of nine's attention. He wants to be like the others in his gang, to talk like them and look like them. If the current fashion for his friends is to wear shirttails out, he also must wear his shirttails out.

Friends and membership in the group mean a great deal to nine-year-olds. They are great conformists, afraid of that which is different. They often exclude a child from the group who is different, whether by virtue of being unusually bright or unusually slow, or speaking with an accent, or dressing differently from them or being handicapped in some way.

Clubs and gangs are stronger now than when your child was eight. The influence of the group is greater. He enjoys his secret clubs in their hideaways with their passwords, codes, dress, bulletins, and taboos. Girls also have clubs in which much time is devoted to giggling and whispering. The purpose of a secret club is to achieve a sense of solidarity among members, a sense of "we-ness" which is achieved by excluding outsiders. The flavor of a middle-childhood club is well illustrated by the following quotation from the *New Yorker*:

The rules of a secret society of nine- and ten-year-old girls in a certain community on Long Island that shall here be nameless are as follows:

1. Do not tell a white lie unless necessary.
2. Do not hurt anyone in any way.
3. Do not hit anyone except Ronny.
4. Do not tell a black lie.
5. Do not use words worse than "brat."
6. Do not curse at all.
7. Do not make faces except at Ronny.
8. Do not be selfish.
9. Do not make a hog or a pig of yourself.
10. Do not tattle except on Ronny.
11. Do not steal except from Ronny.
12. Do not destroy other people's property, except Ronny's.
13. Do not be a sneak.
14. Do not be grumpy except to Ronny.
15. Do not answer back except to Ronny.[8]

Sometimes parents worry about youngsters "wasting so much time in these foolish gangs and clubs." A father wonders, "Why do they spend so much time just sitting around talking and doing nothing?" It is important to realize that in bickering with one another or in "idle chatter," nines are testing their ideas on others their own age. They are sharing their feelings—their doubts and worries. They are also learning the technique of carrying on a conversation and acquiring important socialization skills. The play of the nine-year-old does not have to be active to be productive.

Boys and girls have separate clubs and each sex expresses a certain lofty disdain for the other. Bragging to each other, spying on each other, and teasing each other serves definite psychological functions for the two sexes. The secret, underground interest in the opposite sex can only be adequately disguised by expressing contempt for them. This is charmingly illustrated by a nine-year-old girl's comment about boys: "Boys are loathsome creatures. I enjoy watching them!"[9]

The school life of the nine-year-old, with its changes from third to fourth grade, is often a huge psychological step. The world of the fourth, fifth, and sixth grader is quite a different world from that of the first, second, or third grader. A typical nine enjoys school, although teachers report that fourth is a difficult grade to teach.

Nine has a much greater capacity for independent work than he did at eight. He is anxious to get good marks and works for them, but can be easily discouraged by failure. He has a better critical evaluation of his own abilities, and more self-discipline. He especially likes to read for facts and information, and the more unusual the facts are the better he likes them. He will like to tell his father: "Dad, did you know that . . . ?"

Wide variations in scholastic ability begin to be apparent at this age, much more so than in the earlier grades. Many nine-year-olds are avid readers; others are hardly interested in books at all.

This is the year in which marked reading disabilities become evident and begin to affect the total personality of the child. Parents should be on the alert for signs of reading disability. The help of a special reading tutor or guidance teacher may be necessary. His schoolteacher or principal will refer you to a person who can give such special help. Or your child may need to be evaluated by a psychologist, particularly one who specializes in educational problems.

With regard to his personal life, nine has his appetite under better control than he did at eight. He is very positive in his food likes and dislikes, and states them quite frankly. He does not appreciate "gourmet cooking" preferring hamburgers, hot dogs, and spaghetti.

It would be a mistake to assume that nine's newly found self-motivation extends to bathing, washing, or doing chores. In this respect he suffers from a peculiar psychological affliction which the humorist B.M. Atkinson calls "Glenn's Exit." He characterizes this as "a psychic phenomenon in which a small boy will be around the house for hours but within ten seconds of being called for a meal or a job, will, for all practical purposes, disappear from the face of the earth. Occurs always in conjunction with LAGGARD'S EAR. The boy, though normally possessed of a sense of hearing that enables him to detect the tinkle of an ice-cream wagon's bell five miles away, will, on this occasion, lose the use of both ears, and, though no farther away than the next yard, will be unable to hear his own name called, no matter how many times or how eloquently his mother bellows it."[9]

Nine often has to be reminded to take his daily bath. He also needs to be reminded to wash his hands before meals and to brush his teeth. Usually, he takes such reminders good-naturedly, as though he had been planning to do these things all along, but they had somehow slipped his mind. A nine-year-old (boy, particularly) has little aversion to wearing old or dirty clothes. Some boys could cheerfully wear their pants until they were almost able to stand upright by themselves.

Nine is beginning to develop an ethical sense. He understands more about truth and honesty, property rights, and personal rights of individuals. Fairness plays a large part in the thinking of a nine-year-old. He takes criticism or punishment if he believes it is fair, but becomes quite indignant or bitter if he thinks his parents or teacher are unfair. There are many arguments between nine-year-olds over the issue of "fairness" in games or sports, with the youngsters taking different sides at different times. This is a good sign. It shows that at this age, the child is trying to develop ethical standards.

Some nines are great worriers. They may worry about failing in school or doing the wrong thing in a social situation. Once again a father can be of great help to his nine-year-old, not by rushing in with premature reassurance that does not really reassure, but by using the feedback technique. This gives the child a chance to air his concerns to a sympathetic listener and get the worries off his chest.

In general, nine is so busy with the many and varied activities of his own life that he makes far fewer demands on his parents than he did at earlier ages. Nine demands much less of his mother's time than in previous years. He is extremely busy with self-appointed tasks. He likes to do endlessly what he enjoys doing. He may like to see the same movie again and again. A nine-year-old enjoys himself roller-skating or skateboarding for hours at a time. Girls often play endlessly with dolls.

In summary, the nine-year-old has developed as a very real personality in his own right. He is beginning to think for himself and to develop his own ideas and points of view. He understands explanations. He is realistic and, generally, reasonable. He is interested in doing things well and is beginning to have a strong sense of right and wrong. He is self-motivated and can occupy himself happily throughout the week in innumerable activities of his own choosing. He is busy and absorbed in his own affairs, and vigorous in carrying them out.

THE TEN-YEAR-OLD

In the same way that early childhood comes to a kind of consummation at age five, middle childhood comes to the same sort of consummation at ten. In fact, one of the best ways to describe the ten-year-old is to say that his behavior reminds you of a five-year-old, except that it is on a much higher level of emotional and mental integration.

The five-year-old, you will remember, was reliable, stable, well-adjusted, self-contained, and in focus. He was content to live in the world of the here and now and was generally not in conflict with himself or his environment. He was satisfied with himself and others were satisfied with him. Five was a delightful age when your child took life as it came and was content with it.

All of the above observations could describe the ten-year-old equally well. The five-year-old was a delight to have around, and so, in general, is the ten-year-old.

Parents should really enjoy this year for it is the last of its kind! Eleven will usher in a new and upsetting stage of preadolescence, and you will often wonder: Where did my wonderful and easy-to-get-along-with ten-year-old vanish?

Ten is, to sum it up in one phrase, a golden year of developmental equipoise. It is a year of consummation in which the ten-year-old assimilates, consolidates, and balances the psychological resources and qualities he has attained up to now. It is a plateau year, before the upthrust of new and unsettling developmental forces at age eleven.

Parents enjoy having a ten-year-old around because he is happy, outgoing, and hearty. He is a good student and a good sport. He is tolerant, easygoing, and carefree. These are some of the words parents or adult friends use to describe a ten-year-old: sincere, happy, casual, relaxed, companionable, poised, friendly, frank and open. He loves sports and likes to be outdoors. He feels closer to his family and home than he did at nine. He is proud of his family and loyal to them. He gets along well with both mother and father. He recognizes the authority of his parents and will obey fairly cheerfully. He participates in activities with the whole family, such as picnics or weekend trips. He handles his interpersonal relations in an engaging, likable manner.

His prevailing emotional attitude is positive, calm, and poised. One ten-year-old unwittingly summed up the basic emotional climate of this age by saying: "I don't like to be cross." [10] The general emotional mood of ten is contentment with himself and his world.

However, all is not completely sweetness and light in the world of the ten-year-old. At times, he is given to sharp outbursts of anger during which he may cry or strike out with primitive, childish violence. Angry outbursts are almost always exhibited toward someone his own age or younger. Very seldom are they directed toward adults.

His anger is often focused toward younger brothers or sisters, particularly between the ages of six and nine. In part, this is due to sibling jealousy; but it is also because those obnoxious qualities in younger siblings remind him of qualities which he has so recently overcome in himself. He hates to be reminded of how unreasonable he was, and the behavior of younger brothers and sisters does exactly this. He illustrates a tendency, quite prevalent among adults, to make scapegoats of other people for precisely those qualities we hate in ourselves. The ten-year-old is much better in his relationships with very young siblings up to the age of five. They look up to him as an admired older brother and he often derives pleasure in showing them how to do things.

The angry outbursts of ten are usually brief, explosive, and shallow. Ten has a good emotional exhaust system at his disposal. The anger is quickly expended, and the basic goodness and equanimity of his personality asserts itself again. His temperament is on the whole easygoing and tolerant. If you ask him to make a choice between two alternative ways, he often shrugs his shoulders and says: "Sometimes yes, sometimes no." His shoulder shrugs are characteristic of his tolerance of spirit at this age.

In comparison with the intense emotions of nine he is more relaxed. He has an unconcerned poise and self-assurance. If he can acquire the new skills, fine; if not, then that's the way the old fruitcake crumbles. At nine he indulged frequently in self-evaluations and more or less conscientous self-criticism. At ten his emotional climate has changed. He is less self-conscious and more easygoing. The taut bow-string quality of a year ago is being replaced by a looser, softer personality make-up.

However, in spite of ten's generally pliant and cooperative nature, washing and taking good care of his clothes and room are not high on his priority list. This holds particularly true for boys who, if left to

"I DON'T CARE IF CAPTAIN ZOWIE *IS* ON. YOU'VE ALREADY WATCHED TV 7.3 HOURS TODAY."

their own devices could go cheerfully for weeks at a time without taking a bath. Ten typically "hangs up his clothes on the floor." Or as one girl put it: "We sling our things down somewhere," but added with characteristic ten-year-old cooperativeness, "we have to hang them up afterward."[11]

Ten-year-olds, particularly boys, continue to be hard on clothes. This stems from the basically different attitudes of adults and children towards clothes and the way they should be treated. This has been described wryly by B. M. Atkinson in writing of the psychological aberration known as "Germ Shoe, a delusional antiseptic in which a child . . . comes to believe that all shoes are contaminated and, when being put on the foot, should never be touched by the human hand. Instead of sitting down and slipping the shoe onto the foot, the child will remain standing and screw the foot into the shoe. As this maneuver is executed with all the grace and delicacy of a man stamping out a cigarette, a new pair of shoes will, within a week, cease to look like a pair of shoes and start looking like a pair of catcher's mitts."[12]

Knowing ten's love of old, well-worn, and casual clothes, you would not expect him to be overmeticulous about the care of his room. And you would be right! As one ten-year-old boy put it: "My room's a mess. If it was neat I couldn't tell where anything was. Books piled all on top of things. More *friendly*, more natural that way."[13]

When it comes to the matter of chores around the house, ten feels little drive to work. Some days he's good about doing a job; other days he's not. He works best when he is working alongside his mother or father in getting a particular job done. He is at his worst when left completely to his own devices. In view of this, it would be wise for fathers to be quite flexible in their work demands on ten.

But ten's erratic work habits can easily be overlooked in view of his devotion to his family. He thinks his mother and father are "the greatest," though he may not always verbalize this to them as to his friends or his teacher. He is very happy and contented with his homelife.

Both boys and girls get along well with their mothers at this age. They depend on her and look up to her. Girls, especially, like to confide in her. They want to feel that she is their friend and they can trust her. Boys may like to surprise mother by bringing her breakfast in bed on a weekend morning. Both boys and girls tend to be demonstrative in their affection for mother at this age, with sudden physical expressions of warmth shown through hugs and kisses.

Father is also important to both sons and daughters at this age. Girls especially look up to father and adore and idolize him. Ten respects his parents and likes to quote them as authorities: "My mother says" and "My dad says" appears frequently in conversations with friends and teacher.

This is the age for a father really to enjoy companionship and shared times of fun with a son or daughter. Take your child on a trip or a hike, play ball with him or take him to ball games and sports events, go swimming, skating, or just "mess around" with him. He will love it and so will you. Take him out to lunch or a movie, take him to visit you at your office or place of work; he will be thrilled.

The following conversation between a ten- and an eleven-year-old girl shows the basically positive relationship to parents of the ten-year-old even at times of stress and conflict:

Eleven-year-old Mary: Don't you hate your mother? Mine's just rotten today. I'd like to see her dead.

Ten-year-old Barbara: Don't you realize you'd never see her again? You can be angry at your mother, but you don't need to hate her.[13]

Ten's relationships with younger siblings are the only fly in the family ointment. Fathers should be alert to the fact that rarely does the ten-year-old start the conflict. Often it is the younger brother or sister who pesters and pesters ten until he finally retaliates with fisticuffs. Then the younger sibling, a paragon of innocence, runs crying to father or mother: "Larry hit me!" If a father immediately blames ten in such a situation, he will feel his parent is mean and unfair, and there is something to be said for his feelings in this case.

Ten loves his friends, all of them. Clubs of all kinds are relished. Of all ages we have considered, ten is the readiest to respond to the group. He is more a man of action than of thought, and he is happy with the variety of activities that occupy his day. Ten-year-olds love to play more than anything else, and school may sometimes be considered an interruption to the more important task of play!

He especially likes outdoor play, mostly for the sheer joy of exercising his body and working off energy, whether it be roller-skating, climbing, skateboarding, swimming, or above all—running.

Boys and girls tend to differ in their choice of outdoor activities. Girls' activities are quieter, such as hopscotch, roller-skating, double-dutch, jumprope, and horseback riding.

Although outdoor play is usually preferred, ten can spend hours indoors happily occupied with his friends. He likes table games, such as Monopoly, Parcheesi, and various card games. He also continues to enjoy his collections. Girls like to "write plays," dress up in costume, and perform. Animals and pets are particularly enjoyed by the ten-year-old, but he is still not mature enough to be held fully responsible for its care.

Ten loves to construct things, model planes or cars or boats from hobby kits, or build with an Erector set, or put together various things in a home workshop. He continues to enjoy comic books, movies, and TV. Cartoons, Westerns, blood-and-thunder films, war movies, mysteries, movies about animals, and slapstick comedies are his favorites. Walt Disney movies will usually make a hit with ten-year-olds of both sexes.

Ten's ethical sense continues to grow and mature. He is no longer thinking entirely like a child: He develops a strong sense of justice and a strict moral code. In keeping with the psychological develop-ment fact that negative ethics precedes positive ethics, ten is usually more concerned with what is wrong than what is right. He is definitely concerned about fairness. However, although he is capable of lofty ethical sentiments, when it comes to actual practice he does not always measure up to the mark! (But, then, adults do not always practice what they preach either, as ten is beginning to discover to his dismay.)

Parents generally complain about the table manners of ten (as they have about the table manners of six, seven, eight, and nine!) As one boy reported, in characteristically ten-year-old fashion: "I wouldn't say they were bad, and I wouldn't say they were good!" Ten likes more kinds of food this year than in previous years, but his favorites still continue to be hamburger, roast beef, hot dogs, and steak, along with potatoes in any form: baked, French fried, and mashed.

Boys and girls are beginning to go their separate ways this year when it comes to physical development and awareness of sex.

Girls of ten, in contrast to boys, will show the first slight but unmistakable signs of approaching adolescence. The childish body of the ten-year-old girl now begins to undergo a slight softening and rounding, especially in the hip region. Few girls will begin to menstruate before their eleventh year, but ten is definitely the time to prepare a girl for it. Schools often have health education films on menstruation for fifth-grade girls, but the mother should also prepare her daughter for this event.

Because of their more advanced sexual and social development at this age, girls are more sex-aware than boys. However, they are usually less outspoken about it. Girls do not tell the same kinds of so-called "dirty jokes" with sex or elimination connotations as boys do. (However, ten-year-old boys who tell these jokes in their gang are often quite naive as to the full meanings of the jokes they relate with such glibness and gusto.) Girls are more apt to be embarrassed than boys in receiving sex information. To parents it appears sometimes as if the girl has forgotten the information they gave her at an earlier age! Nevertheless, in spite of their embarrassment, girls are keenly interested in seeing books about sex and babies. A good book to provide is *Girls and Sex* by Dr. Wardell Pomeroy (Delacorte Press.) Parents should not let a ten-year-old girl's embarrassment about sex deter them from giving her a good book such as this. For as Dr. Gesell comments, girls "tend to hide these books and later to confess that they have read them many times!"[14]

Your ten-year-old boy's sex awareness is not up to that of a ten-year-old girl. He questions very little, and when he does it is apt to be in an offhand manner. However, it is also a good idea to give him a book to read on sex. *Facts About Sex* by Dr. Sol Gordon is ideal. It is a very short book—only forty-three pages in all, and admirably suited to ten-year-old comprehension and attention span.

Although a ten-year-old boy is not very interested, it is good for him to know the true facts about various aspects of sex which up till now he may not have encountered. Otherwise, he has no other way to acquire sound sexual knowledge except through members of his gang, an educational process which could appropriately be labeled "the blind leading the blind."

Dr. Gordon's book is particularly helpful to a boy, for it includes the correct definitions of the so called "dirty words" of sex. Ten will see these four-letter words written in bathroom walls at school and hear them spoken by older boys, but he is usually too embarrassed to admit he does not know what they mean. This book will set him straight and take the foolish snicker out of slang words. This is a book which your boy can keep and refer to a year or so later when he feels the need for further clarification of points which he did not fully understand emotionally in his first reading.

When it comes to school, ten generally enjoys it. He likes his teacher and enjoys learning. Teachers report that, in general, the fifth grade is not as emotionally wearing as teaching the fourth grade. Ten-year-olds like a lot of oral discussion in class. He will accept his teacher as an authority and quote her word as law to his parents (even as, at other times, ten will quote his father or mother as an authority to his teacher or his friends.)

Ten loves to memorize. He perceives and listens well. Fathers should take advantage of the fact that this is a great age for educational TV. Father can be on the lookout for good documentary shows on politics or current events, and he and his ten-year-old can watch them together. Ten will especially enjoy it if he is allowed to stay up later than usual to watch a special TV show.

Since ten is interested in facts and is at a cooperative and receptive age, a wise father will use this year to introduce various grown-up topics which are mentioned in current magazines, newspapers, and on TV. Included among these can be stories which give factual accounts of drugs and drug abuse. These seeds, dropped at the receptive age of ten, may help him to withstand the temptation of drugs in adolescence, since he will be armed with facts on the subject.

Parents should be careful not to lecture or preach or drive the subject into the ground, for then it will backfire. Just be sure to include news items on drugs and drug abuse along with other interesting bits of information about current events. And this is the year to do it. The facts that he is willing to listen to at ten will be emotionally rejected when he is eleven and in the rebellious stage of preadolescence.

In summary, ten is a golden age of poise and equanimity—the summation and fulfillment of all the years which go to make up middle childhood. It is a plateau year, soon to be interrupted by the upward thrust of the growth forces of the preadolescent stage. Ten is a period of live and let live. Consideration for others, getting permission to do things, and generally fitting smoothly into the family group seem to come naturally to ten.

And so my special message to fathers about this age is: enjoy your ten-year-old to the utmost, for preadolsecence is on its way when his eleventh birthday rolls around! And when the hurricane warnings of preadolescence are up, the wise father battens down the family hatches and prepares for the emotional storm he knows is coming!

This concludes our year-by-year survey of middle childhood. In spite of the diversity of these years, your child's personality exists in a relatively consistent and stabilized form from the ages of six through ten, which is why we group all of these years together in the stage of middle childhood.

Since I'm afraid you may have gotten lost in the specific descriptions of each year, I want to give you a psychological overview of the total stage of middle childhood, and what is unique about it as a developmental stage.

AN OVERVIEW OF MIDDLE CHILDHOOD

You remember that the closing of the preschool stage brought about a stable integration of your child's personality. This stable equilibrium lasts throughout middle childhood, from approximately his sixth to his eleventh birthday.

After his sixth birthday, your child's primary socialization has been completed. Up to that time, the family has been his society almost exclusively. This is true even if he has been fortunate enough to attend nursery school and kindergarten, which are still basically regarded as psychological side-trips by your child. His self-concept has been formed by viewing himself in the mirrors of the members of his family: his mother, father, and brothers and sisters. His parental standards have been partly but not completely internalized, and it is these standards that will guide him when he is away from his parents.

During the preschool years your child was loved and accepted simply for *being*, for being a member of the family, not for what he could do or accomplish. Now, for the first time in his young life, all that changes. Now, his self-concept will be formed mainly not by looking into the mirrors of his family members, but by viewing himself in the mirrors of the outside world, the larger society. And in the mirrors of the larger society, his self-concept will depend to a great degree not on who he is, but on *what he can do.*

In the years of middle childhood, your child enters two new worlds: the world of school and the world of his "gang" or peer group. In school, his teacher and other adults and children evaluate him in terms of what he can do, what skills he can learn. In the gang, he is also evaluated in terms of what he can do, not in terms of what he is. The following description of Tony, a middle-years child who is rejected by his peer group, brings this out very clearly:

> Tony had no friends because he didn't know how to do anything. He couldn't catch a ball or shoot a basket, or stand up on roller skates. He wasn't a sissy; he was just dull, a fact which had been brought home to him rather pointedly by his contemporaries.[15]

The functions of these two new worlds is to prepare your child to live in the larger society rather than just within the bosom of his family. In the preschool years he learned his self-identity almost exclusively in relation to one world; the world of his family. Now he faces the psychological task of learning his self-identity in relation to three different worlds at the same time. Moreover, the three worlds have conflicting standards. What defines good behavior at home is not necessarily what defines good behavior at school, and certainly not what defines good behavior in the gang. A child may get away with certain breaches of behavior at home because he is cute and able to manipulate mother and father. He learns that this will not work at school with his teacher and other children. Mother and father and teacher may want him to reveal "who broke the window!" But to "snitch" on a fellow gang member is by no means good or acceptable behavior to his peers.

Trying to forge a self-concept in relation to three different worlds or societies, is it any wonder that a child has difficulty with his behavior during these years of middle childhood? It is as if he is simultaneously being taught Spanish and French and Italian and expected never to make any mistakes or confuse the words of the three languages.

What then is the development task of this stage? Your child is learning *mastery* versus *inadequacy*. His self-identity is now based on how well he masters the specific skills and accomplishments that are demanded in school, in his peer group, and at home. A good self-identity depends on your child feeling secure in the knowledge that he can do things that are demanded of him. A child wants to be recognized for his competence, for what he can do. If he is not able to master tasks and skills demanded of him by school and his contemporaries, he feels a sense of inadequacy and inferiority.

In other words, in the middle years of childhood your child is leaving the security of home and family and venturing out into a much larger universe, the world of his society and even of the world as a whole. In the preschool years he might have been aware *intellectually* of the larger society outside his home and family, but *emotionally* he was only dimly aware that a larger world existed. Now he has come to a point of an awareness of his individual aloneness as a self in the vast and emotionally overpowering world. In the preschool years, your child must deal with a sense of inferiority due to his small size in a world of grown-up giants. But in middle childhood a new dimension is added. Now, for the first time, your child understands intellectually how vast and complex the world is and how small he is and how little he knows about how to deal with it.

Your child handles the problem of how to deal with the larger society in two main ways. First, on a realistic level, he attempts to learn the skills he needs at school and with his peers. At school he learns to read, to handle math and arithmetic, to think logically, to deal with abstractions: he finds out about new and strange things and places. He attempts to learn the skills required to give him acceptance by his gang, to throw and catch a ball, to compete in group games, etc. By learning the required skills of school and gang, your child establishes a feeling of competence, of mastery: without these skills he feels inadequate and inferior.

However, your child also needs *emotional* strength to deal with the larger society. Since he is setting sail from his emotional moorings of home and family, he needs to find new emotional support. This he finds in his peer group. He now replaces his psychological dependence on parental authority with a new dependence on peer-group authority. By conforming to the minutest detail of what his gang expects of him, the child shows them that he belongs and that he is entitled to the emotional security of their loyalty and support.

Your child not only finds emotional support in belonging to the society of his peers, but he also finds reassurance through various magical psychological devices which make up the ritual of middle childhood. Perhaps a good way to illustrate these magical devices of middle childhood would be to compare them with the behavior of an adult suffering from a compulsion neurosis.

Adult compulsions take many forms. I remember dealing with a patient who felt compelled to arrange and rearrange the toilet articles on his bureau in a very exact and precise order before he could leave to go to work in the morning. Such a compulsion neurosis takes the form of a psychological ritual which needs to be carried out in precisely a certain way or the person becomes very anxious and fearful. The purpose of these psychological rituals is to ward off anxiety and to make the adult feel emotionally more comfortable and relaxed. In other words, the psychological ritual serves as a kind of tranquilizer against anxiety.

The rituals of middle childhood are similar in many ways to adult neurotic symptoms. At this stage, children love ritual for its own sake. Unconsciously they use it to give themselves a sense of magical power over what, at times, seems like a vast and frightening world with which they feel they cannot cope.

Children have used ritual chants and games for centuries. Children's games and chants in use today have been traced back to the Middle Ages and even beyond to Roman times. For example, the painting "Children's Games," by the sixteenth-century Flemish painter Brueghel, shows children engaged in playing a myriad of games that not only go back much earlier than the sixteenth century, but many of which can be found today in any contemporary American playground or neighborhood street or vacant lot. They are games children teach other children, rather than games that adults teach children, such as hopscotch, hide-and-seek, red rover, keep-away, etc.

Along with games go chants that children have used for years and will probably continue to use; "It's raining, it's pouring; The old man is snoring"; "Margie's mad/And I'm glad/And I know what will please her;/A bottle of wine to make her shine/And Timmy Jones to squeeze her"; "I scream,/You scream,/We all scream/For ice cream." And who could forget the traditional children's chant signaling the end of the school year: "No more school, no more books,/No more teacher's dirty looks." These chants may be empty of literal meaning for the child, (he may like school a great deal, for example!) but the need to say them is there, for they give the child a sense of emotional security.

Along with these magical chants there are the magical, superstitious observances of middle childhood: avoiding stepping on the cracks in the sidewalk ("Step on a crack, break your mother's back") touching every lamp post or fence rail. There are also what to adults are the child's meaningless stunts with his body: He learns how to look cross-eyed, to rub his stomach while he pats his head, to contort his face into various horrendous shapes, and even, perhaps, to wiggle his ears. Another ritualized way of dealing with the world is through the enthusiastic gathering of collections during middle childhood. To mother or father, the collections of rocks, castoff broken pieces of wood, and rusted metal implements may make no sense at all. But the child will protest vigorously if mother wants to throw away some part of his valuable collection.

Typical middle-childhood behavior may appear ridiculous or foolish to grown-ups in exactly the same way that the compulsions of an adult neurotic seem ridiculous to someone who does not suffer from that compulsion. Once a parent understands that these magical ways ward off anxiety and help a child deal with a new and threatening world, then the parent can understand the meaning of these strange bits of behavior and accept them with amused grown-up tolerance.

Rituals and collections provide a magical domination over reality. They make a child feel comfortable in the grown-up world where he has not yet learned all of its *realistic* skills and competencies. Ritual behavior is, in part, a substitute for practical accomplishments. A child reduces the complex world of the grown-ups to a scale that he can manage. The wise parent learns the meaning of these ritualized bits of behavior and allows the child to practice them. When he feels more comfortable and adequate in the adult world he will give up his childhood rituals.

Parents need to understand the ambivalent attitude that a child at this stage takes toward his family. Dr. Barbara Biber has summed up his mixed feelings toward his family in an incisive sentence: "A child of this age," says Dr. Biber, "is looking for ways to belong to his family and feel free of them at the same time".[16]

Let's look at both sides of the child's ambivalent feelings. First, a child needs to feel free of his parents. In the years of middle childhood he dethrones his parents. Not only does he dethrone his parents, but he becomes disillusioned about them. To his parents these may seem like bad things for a child to do. And yet, for a child to be dis-illusioned about parents, he must first cherish illusions about them. For a child to de-throne his parents, he must first place his parents unrealistically on a throne. And the preschool child does both of these. He places his parents on a throne and cherishes illusions that they are all-knowing and all-powerful.

This was brought home most clearly to me when my youngest son Rusty was about three years old and asked a question about something. I have forgotten the exact question, but I recall that it was something I didn't know the answer to. So I told him "Rusty, I don't know the answer to that question." Just as if he hadn't heard my reply, he asked me the question again. Again, I said "Rusty, I told you already; Daddy doesn't know the answer to that question." "Yes you do, Daddy," he said emphatically, "you know everything! Now tell me the answer!"

Flattering as it may be to have such godlike qualities ascribed to us, our children must give up these ideas and replace them with a more realistic assessment. And yet, how difficult it is for us to take when our middle-childhood children see us as human beings after all, with the faults, foibles, psychological warts, and inconsistencies of human beings!

Now your child begins to see you and your wife in a realistic perspective. He criticizes and complains of the parental inconsistency of which he is aware for the first time. Mother taught him not to lie, but she may tell a lie in order to get out of a social engagement. The child overhears grown-ups talking about sharp business reactions or cheating on income-taxes. He becomes aware that adults tell children always to be honest but, at times, are dishonest themselves. And so, in this stage your child will, especially if he is psychologically secure and happy, from time to time point out your inconsistencies and inadequacies as a person and a parent.

It is important for you to remember that your child's attack on your vulnerable points is *an important aspect of his growth.* Each flaw he sees in your "godlike perfection" is another building brick in the structure of his own selfhood and independence. You will especially endear yourself to him if you are able to admit your mistakes and imperfections rather than try to cover them up in injured dignity.

Your child wants freedom to express his own independent preferences in many areas: his clothes, his books and records, the way his room is furnished and decorated. He wants a voice in everything that involves him, and the wise parent gives him a voice (though not necessarily always the deciding voice!) in planning weekends, choice of movies and recreational events, and vacations.

A curious thing happens to the ears of children in the stage of middle childhood. First of all, they completely tune out when it comes to parental requests for picking up, straightening out their room, taking out the trash, or doing other household chores. On the other hand, parents are often amazed how finely tuned in the same children's ears are to pick up choice bits of neighborhood or office gossip. New types of psychological radar are developing which enables a child to pick up information about the adult world.

A nine-year-old patient of mine once relayed some choice bit of gossip about his parents' home. "Where did you hear that?" I inquired. "Oh, grown-ups don't notice me," he said, "I'm a good spy!"

Your child is now learning that other children have different ideas about things than he does. He is learning that other adults such as teachers, family friends, Boy Scout leaders, and church school teachers have different ideas and values from those of his parents. He begins to compare and test the ideas and values of his parents and family against these new and strange ideas and values of the outside world. In so doing, he goes beyond the egocentric world of his family and is able to view life in a larger perspective.

In other words, your child is going through a very important psychological process in which he is withdrawing his emotional energy from his parents and family and reinvesting this emotional energy in others: his schoolteacher, other adults, and his peers in school and in the neighborhood.

Yet to stop there, would be to give you a very incomplete and misleading view of your middle-childhood child. For at the same time that he is seeking to wean himself from his family, he is, paradoxically, still looking for new and more mature ways to belong to his family. At times the need to be independent will be predominant, and it will seem to you as if your child uses his home only as a dormitory for sleeping. As soon as he gets home from school he is trying to see how fast he can get back outside to be with his beloved neighborhood gang. But at other times his need for dependence predominates, and he wants to be taken care of, especially when he is sick or troubled.

Even when he is not sick or hurt or in trouble, your child still needs mother and father as ego-ideals and important emotional allies in his struggle to learn how to cope with the grown-up world. This is an especially important time for one-to-one relationships with your middle-childhood son and daughter. Your son needs time with you spent in various ways so that he can fully incorporate you as an ideal figure to imitate. Your daughter equally needs time with you so that she can learn how to relate to men. You are the first and most important man in her life and how she relates to other men will basically be determined by the kind of father you are.

The stage, therefore, is a particularly good time to correct any mistakes you feel you made in previous stages of your child's development. (And what parent can honestly say: "No, I made no mistakes at all with my children in their preschool years!") In spite of the importance of his peer group, this stage is one in which your son or daughter is also reaching out to you for a deeper and more mature relationship than he experienced in the preschool years. If you made mistakes in earlier years, now is your opportunity to make a fresh start in your father-child relationship. For once your child becomes an adolescent it is very difficult for a parent to start over and establish a new and more positive relationship. If you made mistakes, don't be afraid to admit them to your child. You might say: "Larry, I guess I was too busy with my work when you were younger and I didn't spend enough time with you, but things will be different now"; or, "Betty, I think I have been expecting too much of you as a child. I guess I've been expecting you to act more like a grown-up, but I'm beginning to see things a little differently now. So maybe we can sort of start over again, huh?" If you are able to admit human mistakes and frailties, you will build a deeper and more positive relationship with your child.

In some respects, today's youngster going through the stage of middle childhood will be very similar to what you experienced in your own childhood. But in other repects, a child today will be light-years away from the middle childhood children experienced in the past. This has been summed up by someone who quipped, "If Booth Tarkington wrote his novel *Seventeen* today, he'd have to call it *Twelve!*"

Urbanization, the information explosion, and the mass media have wrought vast changes in today's child. Today's middle-childhood boy and girl are infinitely more sophisticated than they were ten or twenty or fifty years ago. Today's child is much more aware of aspects of the adult world. Children are brighter than they used to be. They are more sensitive to what is going on in the world. They are capable of asking more thoughtful and penetrating questions. Children learn faster than they used to, not only because of increased educational technology in the schools, but because of all the information they are bombarded with through the mass media.

It is most important for you to be aware of the increased sophistication and precocity of your child; otherwise you will unconsciously expect him to behave as you did when you were a child. Of course, in some respects he *will:* He will still be building forts and tree houses in the backyard, forming secret clubs, and chanting traditional childhood chants. But in other respects he will be infinitely more sophisticated than you were. He will understand and study subjects in school which you did not get to until you were older. He will be studying about some branches of knowledge that simply did not exist when you were his age. He will have a much more sophisticated awareness of sex than you did at his age.

So you can only partly expect to understand what his middle childhood is like by remembering what you were like in those days. In many ways his middle childhood will be something entirely new on this planet. You cannot expect to understand it merely by summoning up remembrances and feelings from your own childhood.

9
Middle-Childhood Years II

In the first five years of his life, your child's self-concept was formed by gazing into mirrors in only one world: the world of his family. In the stage of middle childhood his self-concept will be formed by looking into mirrors in three different worlds: the school, the "gang," and the family. Let's take a more detailed look at each.

THE WORLD OF THE SCHOOL

The purpose of a school is to teach children the knowledge and skills they will need later to function as self-sufficient adults. School is a major socializing agency. It is your child's first experience with being evaluated or judged on the basis of his achievement, on merit alone. Since your child is evaluated according to his achievement, it is especially important *not* to let him feel your love is dependent on what kind of a report card he brings home or his class standing. More than ever before, your child needs to know you love him just because he *is*. He needs to feel that your love is not contingent on how well he achieves in school or elsewhere.

Many parents are not aware of the stress a young child experiences when he begins elementary school. To a first grader, school is a strange and, in part, a frightening experience. If he has not been to nursery school or kindergarten, it becomes doubly strange and frightening. Any person who has seen the emotional upset of first graders who have never been separated for long stretches of time from their mothers will understand how big an emotional step this is.

Even if your child attended nursery school and kindergarten, first grade represents a new and strange experience. Nursery school and kindergarten are not formal learning situations. Learning takes place through the medium of informal play and concrete learning materials such as blocks and cars and trucks. First grade confronts the child with learning through abstract symbols rather than concrete experiences. For most children first grade means learning to read.

A first grader soon learns that his teacher is very different from his mother. She does not cater to him. She may ignore his individual needs, especially in a class with twenty-five or thirty other children (nursery-school classes are much smaller.) He cannot evade school rules by being appealing and using the wiles that worked so well at home. Whereas at home he might count on rubber rules that stretch when he tests them, in school the rules are rigid enough to withstand the assaults of the whole class.

It is important to recognize that starting first grade is a big emotional step for your child. Part of him wants to be that more mature, more independent going-to-school child, but a part of him fearfully still wishes to remain the dependent, take-care-of-me-at-home child. Deal sympathetically with the unconscious ways in which your child seeks to avoid school. He may complain of pain in his legs, an upset stomach, a headache or some other physical symptom which would mean he has to stay home from school. Reflect back his feelings with the feedback technique. "I understand how much your leg hurts this morning," or, "Yes, that headache makes you feel miserable this morning; here, I'll get you an aspirin." But after reflecting his feelings and letting him know you understand how he feels, then you need to be firm that he must go to school because that is what is expected of him. This will usually solve the problem.

After a few weeks, when he feels more comfortable at school, the physical symptoms usually disappear. Of course if your child should develop an actual phobia of school and cry hysterically at the idea of going to school in the morning, you may need professional help from a psychologist or a psychiatrist. In most cases of school phobia the problem is not a fear of school, but a fear of separating from mother and the feeling that he cannot manage without her around.

Assuming that your child has overcome his initial emotional hurdles in beginning first grade, what can you do to help him relate to the world of school?

First of all, you need to know what he will be taught in grades one through six, the years of elementary school. Luckily, a fine overview of what he will learn in the different subject areas of elementary school is available as a paperback. It is called *A Parent's Guide To Children's Education* by Nancy Larrick. In my opinion, this is an indispensable reference book for the elementary-school years for any parent to own. The only weakness of the book is its inadequate coverage of new math and the fact that new English is not dealt with at all. The book is full of practical suggestions to help you enrich your child's education at home.

It is important to realize that something is happening in elementary school and will continue to happen in junior high school, high school, and college which did not occur when you were in school. In your elementary school, the curriculum of the school changed very, very slowly—what you were taught in elementary school was not vastly different from what your father and mother were taught. This is no longer true. The school curriculum is changing and continuing to change at an accelerated rate. We have "new math" and "new English" and we are also running into "new biology" and "new chemistry" and "new physics" and "new history."

Curriculum today is being modified and changed by the information explosion in ways which did not occur in past times. The main responsibility for the information explosion rests with the computer. It is difficult for the layman to appreciate the fantastic impact of the computer on every field of organized knowledge. Alvin Toffler has documented its importance very well in his book *Future Shock*, which should be required reading for every parent.

To be very specific, what does this mean to you? It means that you cannot rely upon the memory of your own school experiences to help your child. To keep up, you will probably have to take an adult education course or two yourself. Only then can you communicate meaningfully with your child about what he is learning.

The information explosion means that all learning for both children and their parents is now lifelong learning. Some fathers feel threatened by this. When his child comes home spouting new and strange terms such as, "base five" or "modular arithmetic" or "phonemes" or "transformation grammar" the father says: "That's a stupid way to do something. When I was in school. . . ." I hope you will not react this way, but will regard the new approaches to learning as a challenge and an interesting opportunity for *both* of you to learn some new things about the universe.

Dr. Larrick's book will tell you what children-in-general will be studying and learning in the elementary grades. But your child is not children-in-general. He is this particular child in this particular school with this particular teacher. Therefore, it is important for you to learn all that you can about the particular school your child is attending and what his teacher is like. Attend Parent's Night and Parent Education Week and Open School Week activities whenever these are held.

Above all, get to know your child's teacher. One of the best ways to help your child throughout his school career is to become friends with his teachers. I am not implying that you should apple-polish or browbeat them, but treat them courteously and with warmth and respect, as you would treat a valued business associate.

If you take the time to become friends with your child's teacher, it is simply human nature that in a large class of thirty or more she is going to pay attention to your child. The teacher will feel she has a friendly ally in educating your child, and that you and she are engaged in a common task. You would be surprised how few parents do this. It is probably easier to do in a smaller community, and yet Dr. Benjamin Fine quotes a teacher as saying, "I've taught in this town for more than thirty years, and in all that time only three of my pupil's families ever invited me to dinner. No matter what we do or how long we stay, we're essentially strangers in the community."[1] So get to know your child's teacher and treat her as a human being. She will respond!

But suppose you have reason to believe that your child is being taught by an incompetent or neurotic teacher? We need to be honest and admit that this does happen at times. One way to make sure this does not happen to your child is to take half a day off from work after school has been in session for about a month in the fall, and visit your child's class in action. You will need permission for this from the principal. But don't let the school know ahead of time

"I KNOW IT'S 2 A.M. BUT I'M JUST GETTING THE HANG OF THIS *MODERN MATH.*"

when you plan to visit so that you will see the class as it actually is. It will help you get the feeling of what school is like for your youngster and what kind of teacher he has.

In most instances, the teacher will be quite adequate for the job, but there are situations where your child is in the hands of an incompetent or neurotic person. Your child will usually complain in such circumstances. Do not leave him to the mercies of such a teacher. Be sure of your facts, and then go to the principal, or if necessary, the superintendent. See that your child is transferred to another class. If parents are tactful, but firm and insistent, this can be done. Remember that you have rights as a taxpayer if your child is attending a public school. You also have rights as the person who is footing the bill if your child attends a private school.

Second, the most important skill your child will learn in elementary school is reading. Reading is the key to all other subjects. If you followed through on the things I suggested in the earlier chapters of this book, your child is prepared to learn to read in first grade—or he may already have learned to read in kindergarten. What can you do in elementary school to help him learn to become a good reader?

First, continue to read to him as you have been doing in his preschool years. Just because he has learned to read himself, does not mean he wants you to quit reading to him, particularly at bedtime. Reading to him creates emotional closeness between the two of you and is also a way of telling him that books and love of books are important.

Second, you can surround him with books. If you have not already put bookshelves in his room, do it now that he is in elementary school. Make regular trips to the library and encourage him to find books he will enjoy reading. Help him to make a personal friend of the children's librarian, who can aid him in finding interesting books he may not be aware of. Take him to your local bookstore. Let him select a book to buy, and add it to his growing home library. Help him to make a friend of the owner or manager of the bookstore.

Above all, remember that the paperback book is the friend of the child. Particularly in junior high and high school he seems to take to paperback books more naturally than he does to the more forbidding hardbacks. More and more good children's books are coming out in paperback, and this, of course, makes things easier on your family budget.

See if you can acquire a revolving bookrack for paperback books similar to the kind in drugstores and markets. Put it in your child's room, and let him select paperback books for it. You can also surprise him by bringing home paperback books you think he will like. The elementary-school child will particularly enjoy his revolving bookcase. He will probably be more motivated to pick out a book to read since it is displayed jacket outward, instead of spine outward as in the customary bookcase.

Third, adopt the principle that as long as your child is reading something, things are going well, regardless of what he is reading. Some parents worry about their child reading comic books or Charley Brown books instead of "good literature." This is a mistake. Give your child free rein to read whatever he wants. His taste will mature as he grows older.

Fourth, once your child has learned to read reasonably fluently, in the third or fourth grade, you can institute a new "going to bed" rule. Tuck him in with the usual ritual at his accustomed bedtime, but tell him that since he is a little older now you will let him read in bed for a while until he feels sleepy. He will usually be delighted at this privilege, and may begin the habit of reading for a half hour or so before going to sleep. He is getting rest by lying in bed, and at the same time he is learning to love reading and books by that half hour or so of free reading time. If you find he is abusing the privilege and staying up hours past his bedtime, of course, you will need to tell him that it is late and he must turn out his light and go to bed.

Fifth, arrange for a subscription to one or two children's magazines that he will enjoy. *Jack and Jill* is good for children from four to ten, *Child Life* for children from four to twelve, *Children's Digest* for children eight to twelve, *Boy's Life* for boys eight to sixteen, *The American Girl* for girls nine to sixteen.

Once your child has developed some special leisure-time interests in the later grades of elementary school (grades 4, 5, and 6), give him a subscription to some magazine that fits his particular interests and hobbies. Consult your librarian about this. Tell her your child's hobbies and interests and she will be able to help you find a magazine that fits your child's particular interests. For example, *Sports Illustrated,* for a sports-minded boy; *National Geographic* for a child with those interests; *Popular Mechanics* for the mechanically minded boy, etc.

I suggest all these different ways to help your child learn to love reading and the printed word because, in general, TV is more attractive to the school-age child than reading. I can remember that as a child I loved to read, but I also loved to go to the movies. If the choice lay between reading and the movies I would always choose the movies. But, at that time, the movies were usually only available on weekends. Now "movies" are available to your child every afternoon, evening, and weekend in the form of TV. Make special efforts to help your child acquire a love of books and reading. Without your help, it probably will not happen.

Next to reading, math is probably the most important subject in the entire elementary-school curriculum. If you followed the suggestions made for teaching math in the preschool years given in the earlier chapters of this book and in *How To Parent,* then your child should have a rich background of mathematical experience in manipulating concrete objects. One of the things that makes math difficult for many children is that they are expected to master math through the manipulation of abstract math symbols (such as numerals on paper which they add, subtract, multiply, and divide) without any prior extensive background with concrete objects which the abstract symbols stand for.

So if you have already been using the Cuisenaire Rods to play math games with your child, you can continue these through the early grades of elementary school to help him master arithmetic and math.

But you yourself need to learn something about the new math, unless you happen to be a scientist or an engineer. There are a number of books on new math for parents, but I recommend these three entitled: *Mathematics Enrichment: Program A, Program B, and Program C* by George Spooner (Harcourt Brace, 1962). These three are all programmed books (teaching machines in book form). Very few fathers have ever heard of these books, and the reason is not hard to discover. They are actually written for sixth graders! However, I have personally read, enjoyed, and learned from them. I think it is the most painless way possible for a father to learn the basics of the new math as it applies to what is taught in elementary school.

An excellent way to help your child in elementary school is to equip your home with some basic educational tools. If you have been following my recommendations in earlier chapters, you already have some. You have a large blackboard in your child's room. You have bulletin boards in his room and in the family room where he can pin up his drawings or stories.

When he enters elementary school you need to add more educational aids. You need a good dictionary and an atlas. In addition, I suggest you give your child a paperback dictionary, which he will probably end up using more than the hardbound one.

As for encyclopedias, you can get either *World Book Encyclopedia* or *Compton's* for your fifth or sixth grader to use.

A paperback book such as the yearly *Almanac* or the *Guinness Book of Records* may fascinate your youngster in the later grades of elementary school.

A tape or cassette recorder has hundreds of educational uses. Youngsters can use them for recording portions of radio or TV broadcasts, presenting homemade dramas, and practicing speeches at home for delivery at school, among other things.

Fifth, you can continue to play educational games with your child as you did in his preschool years. Educational games should be fun. If they are not fun for either one of you they become a burden and lose their gamelike quality. The word "game" is generally a magic word for a child of any age. When you say "Let's play a game" you can usually count on your school-age child to respond. But if he is not interested in playing the game at that time, forget about it until later.

There are various educational games such as Scrabble, Scribbage, Educational Bingo or Lotto, Risk, Monopoly, Facts in Five, etc., which you can find at your local toystore, or bookstore or the toy section of a department store. If you are fortunate enough to live close to an educational-supply store that sells to both teachers and parents, you will find a gold mine of educational games not found in the average toystore or department store. I will not list such games in detail because children are individuals by the time they are in middle childhood, and an educational game which would appeal to one child will leave another cold. You need to find the kind of game that your particular child enjoys playing.

Even more valuable than store-bought games are the "games" you store in your head and that can be played on a drive with the family or at the dinner table. By middle childhood your youngster is capable of more sophisticated educational games than he was as a preschooler. For example, twenty questions is an excellent game that aids children in their logical thinking. And let's not forget the old favorite—charades. The family chooses sides, picks book titles, movie titles, or song titles and tries by using non-verbal gestures, to act out the different words of the title for their team.

Educational games are great because they introduce a child to a field of learning or to learning skills in a pleasant, easy way. They can aid your child in developing his ability to think logically, to develop scientific hypotheses and check them out, to develop his vocabulary, to think abstractly and see relationships, to develop his memory, and to build his self-confidence in being able to think through situations and succeed in mental undertakings.

Sixth, you can help your youngster learn how to study. It is incredible, and yet true, that although studying is involved in every grade, schools generally do not teach children *how* to study. By "how to study" I mean such things as how to take notes in class, the difference between reading a book and *studying* a book, how to take different kinds of tests (such as objective tests versus essay tests), and the like. Children will be doing these things from their later elementary years throughout college, and yet you cannot rely upon the schools to teach these basic skills.

What can you as a father do to teach your child how to study? Start when he is in the fourth or fifth grade and begins to have homework. Don't begin sooner because he usually is not ready to learn methods of study and should not be having homework until that time.

First of all, it is important for your child to have a regular place to study. The ideal place would be at a desk in his room since he will be freer from distracting influences there. His quiet place for study should be away from the sounds of TV or phonograph, and he should not have to contend with brothers or sisters bothering him. He should also not be allowed to study with a radio or phonograph going as "background," in spite of his protestations that "a little good ol' music doesn't hurt my studying a bit!"

Second, your child should have a regular time for study. There is no one "ideal" time which will suit all children, but there is one time which should generally be avoided: the time immediately after he comes home from school. Some parents insist on this as study time with the idea that "You get your study done first and then you can play." In general, this is a poor psychological time, since your child has been cooped up in school studying in one form or another all day. He needs the time immediately after school for uninhibited play: to run and yell and be boisterous and work off all of his exuberant energy.

Some children may study best immediately before dinner, some after dinner. Usually parents find that the time immediately after dinner is good, but if your child prefers a different time, and he will stick to it, that's fine. One thing to be avoided is to let your child watch TV immediately after dinner and then expect him to do his studying later. This means he will start his studying when he is tired at the tag end of his day. In addition, he will probably set up a clamor to "Let me watch just one more TV program, Dad, and then I'll do my studying." Far better to set the study hour immediately after dinner, and when he finishes his studies then he can watch TV. This motivates him not to dawdle since he wants to finish up quickly in order to watch television.

It is important to get your child in the habit of a regular place and a regular time for study when he is in the fourth or fifth grade. Then he will consider study as a fixed routine in the same way that he takes bedtime as a fixed routine. If you wait until he is in junior high to teach him regular habits of study it is generally too late.

You can teach your child the difference between *reading* a book or a chapter and *studying* a book or a chapter. Chances are that nobody at school will teach him this. Explain to him that now that he is in the fourth or fifth grade he is old enough to know the difference between reading and studying. Explain that you read a book only once, but when you *study* a book you will need to read it *several* times, because the purpose of study is to transfer the facts from the book to your brain so that you can remember them. When you read a book for pleasure you don't particularly care whether you remember the material.

It is a safe bet that 99 out of 100 children (to state it conservatively) are under the impression that they have "studied" a chapter of a book when they have merely read it once. Explain that there is a special method of studying a chapter or a book.

The first step is to preread the chapter. Prereading gives an overall view of what the chapter or lesson is all about. In your own words, tell and show him how to preread. First he reads the title of the chapter. That gives him the main idea of what the chapter is all about. Then he reads all subtitles. This will give him an idea of the main divisions of the material in the chapter. Then he needs to read the bold-faced print at the beginning of each section or paragraph. If there are any charts or graphs he should look them over carefully. (Most youngsters ignore these completely). If he understands the charts and graphs these will usually help him a great deal in understanding the chapter as a whole.

If there are questions for study or review at the end of the chapter (and there usually are in school textbooks) he should read these carefully. These questions usually summarize what the author feels are the key points. Many textbooks also have a formal summary in the last paragraph or last section and your child should read this carefully. When he has completed his prereading, he should summarize the main points and what the chapter is all about out loud. If he can't do this, he has not done an effective job of prereading.

Take a chapter from one of your child's books and go through this procedure, following each of the steps I have outlined and show your child how to do it. Tell him what you are doing, in the same manner that a sportscaster might describe a football game. If he feels he knows how to do it, have him go through the next chapter and preread it, telling you out loud what he is doing at each step of the process.

Try to be patient as your child learns this procedure, because chances are that it is completely new to him and no schoolteacher has ever explained it. The purpose of skimming and prereading is to get an idea of what the material is all about so that a child can do a more effective job when he actually reads the chapter.

Second, teach him to read the chapter for study instead of reading it only for pleasure. In elementary school your son probably does not own his textbooks and, therefore, is not allowed to mark or write in them. This is most unfortunate from the point of view of learning how to study. Most children are under the impression that it is a major crime to mark a book, even if you own it.

It will be very helpful if each spring you can find out what textbooks your child will be using in the fall and arrange to buy individual copies. The relatively small amount of money that you spend, will be well repaid if it helps your child lean how to *study*, instead of merely how to read. If you have an educational bookstore or supply store near you, you can probably purchase them there. If not, your nearest bookstore can order them for you (or you can order them direct from the publisher, allowing about a month to get the book.) If your child owns the book then he can underline it and otherwise mark the most important passages.

Don't try to accomplish too much at one sitting. Teach him to preread the chapter one night and to study the chapter the following night.

When you teach him how to study the chapter, show him that reading purely for pleasure is a *passive* way to read but when reading for study, the approach is an *active* one. The best way to demonstrate this with a chapter is by using a question-and-answer method.

Teach him to change the title of the first section or paragraph of the book from a statement into a question. If the title of the first section is "Civilization Comes to the Tigris-Euphrates Valley," show him that he needs to change that statement into a question: "Why did civilization come to the Tigris-Euphrates Valley?" Then he reads the section in order to answer the question—"Civilization came to the Tigris-Euphrates Valley because: . . ." listing the various reasons given in that section of the chapter. And so he continues through the chapter, section by section, changing statements into questions and reading in order to get the answers. Go through part of the chapter aloud this way yourself, and then let him do the next part to see if he grasps the process.

As he goes through the chapter, teach him how to underline or check the most important parts. Explain to him that by marking the important points he will only need to review these portions when it is time to study for a test, rather than the entire chapter. After your youngster learns to read a chapter this way have him answer the questions at the end out loud to see if he has grasped the main points of the material. Then have him summarize the main points of the entire chapter. If he cannot do this, he has not studied the chapter effectively. He then needs to go back and clarify the parts of the chapter about which he is still confused.

The naive parent may assume that the foregoing method of studying will be taught in school. Ha! A whole course in Study Skills could profitably be used in the fifth grade and repeated again in junior high and high school. But you will look in vain in the curricula of public and private schools for such a course. Not a single youngster I have worked with in my years of clinical practice was taught such study skills in school. My oldest daughter was not taught such study skills; my oldest son was fortunate enough to have an excellent sixth-grade teacher who did teach him these study skills, but his fourth- and fifth-grade teachers did not.

I think your best bet is to assume that your child will not be taught these study skills at all unless you do it. And I personally think that teaching these skills can best be done by the father. Our elementary-school children are so surrounded by women teachers that they cannot help associating education with female influences. I think it is good to have father teach them because not only does it show his interest in them and their schooling, but it associates a male influence with learning and education. When it comes to the education of their children, the role of many fathers in our society is limited to passing judgment on report cards. Fathers are often more patient and businesslike in teaching study skills than mothers. However, if you are very impatient with your children about how fast they learn, and tend to lecture or scold, let your wife teach the study skills.

Your child needs to know other study skills, such as how to take notes, how to study for examinations (your child should study differently for an objective-type examination, such as multiple choice or true-false, than for an essay-type examination), how to write a research report, how to study a foreign language, how to study math and science, etc. Time and space do not permit me to go into detail. But I urgently suggest you buy two very important paperback books for your child's present and future library. They are: *How to Study* by Clifford Morgan and James Deese (McGraw Hill, 1969), and *How to Study* by Lester and Alice Crow (Collier Books, 1963). Both of these are written for high-school or college students, but you can adapt the material and use it to teach your child how to take notes, study for examinations, etc. In addition, your child can read them himself as an aid to learning to cope with the different and more intensive study required in high school.

I have written about the positive things you can do at this stage of development to help your child in school. Now I want to warn you what *not* to do. Do *not* do the things which will turn your child into an underachiever.

What is an underachiever? This term is bandied about rather loosely at times. I feel it should be restricted to mean a child who is typically doing very poorly in school (getting D's and F's, for example) when his intelligence level shows he is capable of doing very well. Every psychologist who deals with children or adolescents runs into these cases. Let me paint you a picture of the "typical" underachiever, made up of a composite of underachievers I have dealt with over the years in clinical practice.

Tommy is in the fifth or sixth or seventh grade. He is brought to me by his parents because of his problems in school. He is getting D's and F's and, in general, doing very poorly. He may or may not be a behavior problem in school in addition to his educational difficulties. Some underachievers are polite and quiet in class; others are disrupters. But the main thing that bothers his parents and that causes them to bring him to see a psychologist is his poor performance in school. I interview the parents, then give the child a complete battery of intelligence and personality tests; the tests are followed by a clinical interview.

This is the picture that emerges in about 99 cases out of 100. On the individual test of intelligence that I use, the Wechsler Intelligence Scale for Children, the child typically tests out at a high intelligence level, usually at the ninetieth percentile or over. This means that he is quite capable of A and B work, but he is actually pulling down D's and F's. What has caused him to be achieving considerably lower than his intelligence level shows him to be capable of doing?

In all probability, there are two psychological factors at work. First, the parents have exerted strong emotional pressure on the child to achieve, and in the elementary and junior-high years this means "achieve in school." Parents are usually either unaware they have put this kind of pressure on the child or are reluctant to admit it. Typically, they say that they have "only been trying to give him some help with his schoolwork," or they have been "reminding" him to do his homework or something like that. Pressuring him? Heavens no! But whether they are aware of it or not, their child has clearly received the unconscious message from them: "We will love you if you achieve, and it is terribly important to achieve in school."

The second psychological factor that produces an underachiever is a "passive-aggressive" personality structure. This means that the child was not allowed to express angry feelings freely in words. Instead, his parents clamped on a very tight lid. The child had to repress these feelings and drive them underground. And so he develops an overwhelming fear of his own angry feelings.

Since he is not allowed to express his angry feelings openly and get them out of his system, he must express them in some hidden and covert form. He is aggressive, but in a "passive" way. Typically, he is a pleasant and somewhat submissive child. He does not rebel against his parents and defy them openly. But since they made school achievement such an emotionally important issue, he unconsciously strikes back where it hurts. Their self-esteem is wounded by his poor school performance. He expresses his anger, in a "passive" way by school failure. As one child put it, "They can take away the TV and my allowance but they can't take away my failing grades."[2] These, then, are the twin causes of underachievement: emotional pressure by the parents for achievement, particularly in school, plus refusal to allow their child to express his angry feelings directly through words. If you have followed my advice in previous chapters you are allowing your child to express all his feelings (including his angry feelings), and get them out of his system. Then angry feelings come out directly and will not need to come out in an indirect attack on you through school failure.

The second point that I want to stress is to avoid making your child's school achievement an emotion-laden issue. How can you do this? First, in the attitude you take toward homework. I have already said that there is no valid educational reason for a child to have homework in grades one to three. Children are already spending what for them is a long educational day in those grades. There is no sound reason to put additional pressure on them after the school day is over. Homework should not begin until at least grade four or grade five.

When homework does begin, you can provide the place and time for him to study as discussed previously. You can show him how to study and develop study skills. (And the only reason you are showing him the study skills is because the school doesn't do it. If you are lucky enough to have a teacher or school that instructs your child in study skills then, of course, you don't need to.) But beyond that, you should leave your child and his homework strictly alone, *unless* he specifically requests your help.

In other words, make it clear to your child that his homework is his "work," just as your job is the work that you do. Too many parents make homework their responsibility rather than the child's. Do not supervise his homework. Do not check his homework to see if it is correct. Above all, you should not nag him about getting it finished.

Make it clear that what he does about his homework is up to him, but that if he has difficulty and needs your help, of course you will

"...NOW I MIX A LITTLE BIT OF *BAD GRADES* WITH SOME *TERRIBLE SCHOOL BEHAVIOUR* AND I SHOULD GET DAD TO BOIL."

be happy to do so. If you do this and really stick by it, then homework need never become an emotional battleground between you, and your child can never use homework as "emotional blackmail" against you.

In addition to homework, the attitude you take toward report cards and your child's grades is also important. Whenever I think of grades I am reminded of a panel discussion in which I participated, along with several other educators and psychologists, moderated by the principal of a local school. The five panel members disagreed vehemently about many of the goals and methods of education. But in one thing we were in unanimous agreement.

We agreed it would be a good thing educationally for children in the elementary and junior-high years if report cards and grades were abolished, or if, at most, a pass-fail system were used. We agreed that it is difficult, if not impossible, to sum up a child's work in a particular subject in any fair or meaningful way, with *one*, all-inclusive mark of A, B, C, D, or F. We all agreed that parent-teacher conferences *without grades* would be a much better way of handling things. We also agreed that the reason grades would probably *not* be abolished in elementary and junior-high years would be that parents would continue to demand them.

Various studies have shown that there is a very low correlation between grades in elementary and junior-high school and success in later life. Stories of famous businessmen and scientists are full of instances where the successful man had a poor report card sometime in the early school years. Some teachers grade very leniently, others very strictly. And yet parents continue to place a magical value on grades as if a report card set an absolute value on their child.

By now some father reading this may be thinking: "Well what are you saying, Dr. Dodson? Are you telling me just to ignore my child's report card and act as if it isn't important at all?" No, I'm not saying that. In accordance with the principles of positive reinforcement which I discussed in the chapter on discipline, I'm suggesting that when your child brings home his report card you praise him for his good grades and *ignore his poor grades.* In that way you are positively reinforcing good work in school, but you are not discouraging him by "verbal spankings" over his not-so-good grades. Above all, you are not investing his bad grades with such a heavy emotional meaning that he can use them as "emotional blackmail" against you by becoming an underachiever.

If you want further enlightenment on the subject of the under-achieving child and how to prevent your child from becoming an underachiever or how to help him if he is already an underachiever, I recommend the book *Bright Child—Poor Grades* by Barry Bricklin, Ph.D. and Patricia Bricklin, Ph.D. (which is in paperback by Dell Publishing Company). If your child needs professional help for poor school achievement, you can consult a college or university educational or psychological clinic or a psychologist in private practice.

So far I have discussed what you can do to help your child in the world of school. I have said nothing at all about the quality of the school your child attends. In spite of the great value most parents place on the importance of education for their children, the experience of many children in both public and private schools in this country is still the same as that of Penrod Schofield, described so graphically many years ago by Booth Tarkington:

> To Penrod school was merely a state of confinement, envenomed by mathematics. For interminable periods he was forced to listen to information concerning matters about which he had no curiosity whatever; and he had to read over and over the dullest passages in books that bored him into stupors, while always there overhung the preposterous task of improvising plausible evasions to conceal the fact that he did not know what he had no wish to know. . . . he had been told that school was for his own good; in fact, he had been told and told and told, but the words conveying this information, meaningless at first, assumed, with each repetition, more and more the character of dull and unsolicited insult. He was wholly unable to imagine circumstances, present or future, under which any of the instruction and training he was now receiving could be of the slightest possible use or benefit to himself.[3]

Schools have generally improved a great deal since Booth Tarkington wrote, and yet, in many respects, today's school still fail to provide our children with a truly meaningful educational experience.

All concerned parents should read two books which describe in grisly detail the miseducation that still goes on in our contemporary schools.

Crisis in the Classroom by Charles Silberman is an account of a two-year, in-depth study of a representative sample of public and private schools in the United States, based on a study undertaken by the Carnegie Corporation. *How Children Fail* by John Holt (now published in paperback by Dell Books, 1970) is one man's account of the failure of America's schools to give a meaningful education to children, and what can be done about it.

Holt starts with the shocking proposition that "most children in school fail."[4] He then proceeds to document this proposition by pointing out that for children who drop out of high school and college the failure is absolute. Close to 40 percent of those who begin high school drop out before they finish. When it comes to college, the figure is one in three. But Holt points out that there is an important sense in which *almost all children* in our American schools fail:

> Except for a handful . . . they fail to develop more than a tiny part of the tremendous capacity for learning, understanding, and creating with which they were born and of which they made full use during the first two or three years of their lives."[5]

Holt states that these children fail because they are "afraid, bored, and confused."

> They are afraid, above all else, of failing, of disappointing or displeasing the many anxious adults around them, whose limitless hopes and expectations for them hang over their heads like a cloud. They are bored because the things they are given and told to do in school are so trivial, so dull, and make such limited and narrow demands on the wide spectrum of their intelligence, capabilities, and talents. They are confused because most of the torrent of words that pours over them in school makes little or no sense. It often flatly contradicts other things they have been told, and hardly ever has any relation to what they really know—to the rough model of reality that they carry around in their minds."[6]

As merely one example of many which could be cited of the failure of American schools to educate America's children, consider the matter of learning how to write. The one subject every child takes each year, from first grade through twelfth, is English. Presumably one of the major goals of English would be to teach a student to write:. to write clear, correct English sentences that communicate effectively. If this is, in truth, one of the major goals of the teaching of English it is certainly not being accomplished.

Ask the high-school teacher of *any* subject that involves written work, and he will tell you sadly that students are very poor in their written work. Ask any instructor of freshman English in any college in the country whether his students can write clearly and well, and he will answer in the negative.

Clearly something is drastically wrong. What is it? Incredible as it may seem, the main reason that students do not learn to write is that by and large *nobody teaches them to write!* You may say, "But what about all of the years they took English?" The sad fact is that English courses do not usually include instruction in writing. They instruct in grammar and literature.

How does a person learn to write? How do professional writers, the writers of newspaper and magazine articles and books, learn to write? Simple. *They learn to write by writing* and by having someone with more experience go over their work and show them how to improve. This could be done in English classes, but by and large it is not. English teachers do not instruct children to write things that are meaningful and they do not go over the writing individually to show the children how to improve it. A full documentation of how and why English teachers in our public and private schools do not teach children to write can be found in *How They Murdered the Second R* by George Reimer (W. W. Norton, 1969).

This is not a book on why American schools need to be changed or how to change them. But I include this critical evaluation of American schools for several reasons. Like most parents, you may be naive about how poor the quality of education is in many of our schools. If so, a reading of Holt and Silberman's books may enlighten you and, possibly, motivate you to try to do something about it. At least, by introducing you to a critical evaluation of the miseducation that goes on in American schools you may view your local schools without rose-colored glasses. You will then be more tolerant as your child struggles to cope with what he is offered as "education."

Some of you may think, "But what about private schools? Surely they must be much better." Unfortunately that does not seem to be the case, as a reading of Silberman's study which deals with *both* public and private schools, shows all too clearly. The only thing you can say for sure about most private schools is that they generally have smaller classes. And all other things being equal, a teacher can do a better job teaching fifteen or twenty children than she can teaching thirty or forty.

If you are thinking of sending your child to a private school, do not view it as a panacea or a magic road to a fine education. Above all, do not go by the school's "fine reputation" in the community, whatever that may mean. Visit the school yourself, talk with the principal and teachers, and, above all, sit in on a full day's classes (but don't tell the school in advance that you're coming.) This is the only real way you can judge the education that goes on in a school. You might find, for example, that you could see no difference in the quality of education received in the local public school versus a private school. If so, why invest your money in a private school? On the other hand, you may see quite a difference, and feel that it would be well worth your while to spend the extra money.

The only way you can really tell what goes on in a school is to visit and see it in action on a more or less "typical" day—not on a day when everybody is putting their best foot forward, such as during National Education Week.

I have spent a good deal of time on what you can do to help your child in the world of the school because the attitudes toward school and learning and study which your child forms in the elementary years will, to a large extent, determine his attitudes to these things in high school and college. The world of school is a very important world to your child in these years of middle childhood, but the world we discuss next is also most important: the world of the "gang."

THE WORLD OF THE GANG

Psychologists and educators speak of the "peer group" and its importance to the child at this stage, but I prefer to use the homier term "gang." By the way, when I use the word "gang" please do not confuse it with some antisocial or juvenile delinquent group. Parents need to be aware of the psychological reasons for the existence of the gang and its importance to your child.

During the years of middle childhood, your child is leaving the small intimate world of his family and seeking a separate identity in the larger world, the world of society. This is a scary task for him, and so he seeks emotional support by belonging to a gang. He cannot manage complete freedom of self yet, only freedom from his parents and his preschool dependence on them. As he casts off this dependence, he takes on an equally strong dependence on the gang. He feels he must be just like its other members in every way. The psychological importance of conformity to the gang is expressed whimsically in one eight-year-old's lament that, "Everybody in my class has poison ivy except me!"[7]

The gang is a new world for your child, with new social rules to which he feels he must conform. He gains a new pair of self-concept eyeglasses in relation to his peer group. The gang has its own standards of what makes a good member. Its standards of approval include such things as loyalty to the group, willingness to compromise in matters of conflict, not being a crybaby, not snitching to teachers and other adults, not being a sorehead when you lose, and being good in certain skills, particularly sports.

The gang works out its own social organization, which is completely independent of adults. This is different from the social organization of the peer group in nursery school and kindergarten, which was not so secretive or independent of adults. This gang subculture becomes like a special little society within our larger society, with traditions, values, games, and rules of its own. In many respects, this gang subculture has many of the aspects of primitive cultures, aspects an anthropologist would immediately recognize. The gang subculture is handed down by word of mouth, and it is very conservative and resistant to alien influences (in this case, the world of adults.)

Nevertheless, this subculture is very important to the psychological development of your child. Buoyed by the support of his gang, he will learn many valuable socialization skills. And, furthermore, he will learn these skills *independent of adult evaluations*. This is the reason for the secrecy which is so characteristic of children and their gangs. Secret clubs flourish in this stage of childhood as they do at no other. Booth Tarkington's description of the founding of the

'Independent Order of Infadelaty" by Penrod and Sam is evidence that the psychological need for secret societies in middle childhood has not changed much since the early years of this century:

> ... no one could remember who first suggested the founding of a secret order, or society, as a measure of exclusiveness and to keep the shack sacred to members only; but it was an idea that presently began to be more absorbing and satisfactory than even the shack itself. The outward manifestations of it might have been observed ... in a few ceremonial observances exposed to the public eye. As an instance of these latter, Mrs. Williams, happening to glance from a window, about four o'clock one afternoon, found her attention arrested by what seemed to be a flag-raising before the door of the shack. Sam and Herman and Verman stood in attitudes of rigid attention, shoulder to shoulder, while Penrod Schofield, facing them, was apparently delivering some sort of exhortation, which he read from a scribbled sheet of foolscap. Concluding this, he lifted from the ground a long and somewhat warped clothes-prop, from one end of which hung a whitish flag or pennon, bearing an inscription. Sam and Herman and Verman lifted their right hands, while Penrod placed the other end of the clothes-prop in a hole in the ground, with the pennon fluttering high above the shack. He then raised his own right hand, while the four boys repeated something in concert. It was inaudible to Mrs. Williams; but she was able to make out the inscription upon the pennon. It consisted of the peculiar phrase "In-Or-In" done in black paint upon a muslin ground, and consequently seeming to be in need of a blotter.[8]

Parents are often baffled by the uncommunicativeness of their child, and complain that he has become a stranger to his family. It is normal for a child to be this way, and it is important for you not to take it personally as a reflection on your relationship.

The psychological fact is that during middle childhood children see life in vastly different terms from adults. Children are learning to cope with life without adults pulling the strings. This has been seen very clearly by Robert Paul Smith in his delightful book, *Where Did You Go? Out. What Did You Do? Nothing.* He comments as follows on the vast gulf between the adult mind and the child mind at this stage:

> I think we were right about grownups being the natural enemies of kids, because we knew that what they wanted us to do was to be like them. And that was for the birds.
> "Hey, mother, you know what? Ted Fenster's kid brother eats dirt." "Well, don't let me catch you doing it," said your mother. "Go-wan," a kid would say. "Eats dirt? You mean really eats dirt? Yer full of it." "He'll do it for a penny," you said, and you went off to find Ted Fenster's kid brother, and by God he ate dirt, lots of it, spoonfuls of it, for a penny.[9]

It is important for parents to keep in mind that the "good boy," the boy who still clings to parental standards and is so overly "adultized" as to be unable to mingle freely with the gang on their terms, is missing out on some important social learning. All gangs carry out some activities that adults consider undesirable, whether the gangs are from rural areas, small towns, or large cities. Parents often worry about their children being under "bad influence" with undesirable friends. Here is where a sensible father can often recognize that there is a big difference between boyish pranks and mischief, on the one hand, and juvenile delinquency, on the other. In today's world, there is less amused tolerance of childhood mischief, and the "boys will be boys" attitude of yesteryear is not as widespread. Girls' gangs at this age are much more sedate and docile than boys' gangs.

One characteristic of the gang stage is the strict separation of the sexes. Each sex excludes the other during middle childhood for a very simple psychological reason: Each sex is trying to become more secure in its own gender identity. It seems easiest to do this by excluding the opposite sex from the activities of the gang. In our society boys are generally less secure than girls in their gender identities, and this may account for the fact that boys overdramatize the exclusion of girls from their group in much more sensational and emotion-laden terms than girls do when excluding boys.

The gang is important to middle-childhood boys and girls. It is the child's first experience with a subculture not directed or dominated by adults. For this reason the boys' and girls' gangs are very important for their future development as men and women. We may look upon their juvenile business operations, clubs, and secret societies with an amused adult eye. But these experiences help to train boys and girls for their future roles in life. Typical of these childish business ventures is the G and T Cap Gun Sales Company, described by Bentz Plagemann:

> The G and T Cap Gun Sales Company, a merger of those two brilliant tycoons, Goggle and Tory, had been formed after the Great Beebee Gun Crisis for the express purpose of unloading all those toy guns, now of interest only to "little kids." Partnership papers were drawn up and suitably sealed and filed away in the executive office of the company, located in Goggle's bedroom. . . . The executive office was connected to the showroom sales office in the tree house by a two-way telephone system, although this never really functioned properly, in spite of all the effort which went into it. "One, two, three, testing" Tory would say, in the tree house. "Can you hear me?" "Yes," Goggle would say, in his bedroom, "But not on the telephone."[10]

Many of the most important activities engaged in by gangs are not organized, in any sense of the word, but can best be described as "hanging around" or "doing nothing." Robert Paul Smith describes these activities from his own childhood as follows:

> . . .we spent an awful lot of time doing nothing. There was an occupation called "just running around." It was no game. It had no rules. It didn't start and it didn't stop . . . a good deal of the time we just plain ran around. . . . making piles. Tearing things down. Throwing rocks at things. . . . Breaking sticks in half. . . . Catching tadpoles. Looking for arrowheads. Getting our feet wet. Playing with mud. And sand. And water. You understand, not doing anything. . . . We swung on swings. We went for walks. . . . We watched things: we watched each other patch bicycle tires with rubber bands. We watched men dig ditches, climb telephone poles . . . our mothers making jam, our sisters skipping rope . . . we strung spools on strings; we tied each other up with string, and belts and clothesline. We sat in boxes; we sat under porches; we sat on roofs; we sat on limbs of trees. . . . We looked at things like knives and immies and grasshoppers and clouds and

dogs and people. We skipped and hopped and jumped. Not going anywhere—just skipping and hopping and jumping and galloping. We sang and whistled and jumped and screamed. What I mean, Jack, we did a lot of nothing."[11]

When boys do play more organized things they play games such as cowboys and Indians, cops and robbers, hide and seek, red rover, prisoner's base, marbles, kiteflying, bike riding, roller-skating, skateboarding, ice-skating. When boys engage in sports by themselves, without organized adult leagues such as the Little League, they play baseball and football with innumerable arguments about the rules and what constitutes cheating. Indoors, they play cards, build models, or collect most anything. Or the gang may play petty pranks upon girls, other boys, and adults, that are on the edge of vandalism. Direct defiance of adults is much more common in boy gangs than in girl gangs. In all these things there is an emphasis on being able to do what the toughest boy can do, competition in terms of physical skill and bravery, and an emancipation from adult restraints and standards.

Girls' gangs are more sedate and less rebellious. Girls spend more free time at home, and they are usually much closer to their parents during this stage. This probably reflects the fact that the gender identity of girls is more secure. Therefore, they do not need to flee the home as much as boys do. Girls, unlike boys, do not value themselves or fill in their self-concept eyeglasses according to their athletic abilities, bravery, or leadership abilities.

Girls spend time playing with dolls, dressing up in mother's cast-off clothes, playing house, cooking, and sewing. They play jacks, hopscotch, and skipping rope. Girls indulge more in quiet activities than boys do. They love to chatter and enjoy sharing secrets. Secret clubs are enjoyed as much by girls as by boys. But girls are less competitive in their peer-group activities. They are more interested in other people and the intricacies of interpersonal relationships. Like boys, they form cliques and exclude outsiders. The girl who is a loner, and isn't accepted by her peer-group gang, may have a difficult time.

What can you do to aid your boy or girl in relation to this gang stage of his development?

1. Try to understand the psychological importance to your child of a gang that is free of adult influences. Accept this need and don't

take it as a personal rejection when your child prefers the company of the gang to your company. This is particularly difficult for a father who has planned to take his son to a baseball game or on a fishing trip only to find that the gang has other, more important plans for that day. Try to remember it is a sign you have done a good job as a father when your son has the courage to tell you he would prefer to be with the gang that day rather than be with you! There will be other days when he will prefer to go fishing or to the ballgame with you.

2. If you have a place at your house for the gang to play or to meet, it will be a considerable help to your child at this age. A basement recreation room (preferably armor-plated!) or a garage or backyard may furnish just such a gang meeting place. You do not need elaborate equipment for the gang's home base. The important thing is to have a place where children can make their fill of noise without getting into trouble.

One of the best things you could provide is a "junkyard park" in your backyard. Some of the Scandianavian countries have these, and the idea can be adapted very simply to any reasonably ample backyard. Fence off a portion of your yard for your children's play area. A sandbox should probably be first on your construction list. While you are at it, make it a *large* sandbox, so that a group of children can play in it at the same time. A hose connection going to the sandbox makes it doubly fascinating because of the addition of water play to sand play. Buy an ample supply of plastic animals, soldiers, and astronauts at your local toy store. The addition of odd sizes of scrap wood from a cabinet shop or salvaged from a nearby construction site, will furnish hours upon hours of building activity.

In addition to the sandbox, collect a large supply of odds and ends of scrap lumber and wooden boxes. Simply leave these in a pile in the "junkyard park" for the gang to construct whatever they wish. As my ten-year-old boy said when I asked him what he was going to do with a large, long board he brought home one day: "Dad, a board is always useful for something!" You also need several hammers and a large supply of stout nails, kept in the garage or in a special place. Now your child and his gang can build and rebuild houses and forts and shacks to their heart's content. The concept of a "junkyard park" fits the nature of middle-childhood boys so beautifully that once you try it you will wonder why all families with boys of this age do not provide them with something like this to channel their immense energies constructively.

Robert Paul Smith gives his pleasurable recollections of the hut he built at this age:

> The hut . . . was a place where we could live. I have been trying hard to remember just how we started to build it. Certainly there was no foundation. I seem to remember building the first wall in one piece, boards and tarpaper hammered onto a couple of two-by-fours, and the two-by-fours extending below, the whole structure raised and the extensions going into holes, and rocks being jammed around. I imagine we put the second wall up the same way, and ran roof beams across the top so that it stood up. The roof, if memory serves, and I am getting pretty dubious about that, was something that was lying around the lot. An abandoned cellar door, perhaps. . . . I remember repairing it, and expanding it, and putting a better door in it, a hasp and lock. I remember packing rocks from the rockpile around the perimeter, to strengthen the hut—it was then a fortress—against any attack. I remember tamping down the dirt floor, and finding a piece of lineoleum and a gunnysack to brighten the corner which was mine. . . . It was ours. It belonged to us. And if you were not one of us, you could not come in. We had rules, oh Lord, how we had rules. We had passwords. We had oaths. We had conclaves.[12]

3. You can help your child with physical skills that will not only give him status with his peers, but will be the source of healthy exercise and fun. I am speaking particularly now of boys, although girls may also need your help in learning sports such as swimming, skiing, tennis, or golf. You can help a boy to become reasonably good at sports such as baseball, football, soccer, and basketball. You can coach him in the basic skills, such as how to catch a baseball or football, dribble a soccer ball, hit and throw a baseball, or throw a forward pass with a football. And you can give him the opportunity to practice these things with you.

Chances are the physical-education teacher in elementary school will not teach your child these basic skills, nor will your boy have the opportunity to *practice* them when playing with the gang. For when

he is with the gang they are playing, not practicing fundamentals.
But keep practice sessions fun and handle them in a relaxed way,
rather than after the manner of a marine drill sergeant trying to whip
a raw recruit into line.

In addition to the basic skills of baseball, football, soccer, and
basketball, you can teach your child to ride a bike, roller-skate,
ice-skate, and swim. But don't expect too much too fast when you
are teaching basic skills. Fathers often expect children to learn
physical skills faster than they are able to. The father gets impatient
and irritated, and what started out as a relaxed get-together turns
into a tense and unpleasant session.

4. You can help your child with the kinds of socialization skills he
needs to relate to the members of his gang. Sometimes a child is not
able to handle insults or teasing. You can help him with this by
repeating the incident and suggesting a few choice insults to bandy
back at the other guys.

Or your boy may be timid and shy of body contact. Here some
not-too-pushy rough-housing or Indian wrestling with you may be of
help. If he has trouble taking care of himself with bullies, a class in
self-defense or karate for children may prove helpful. If your child is
an only child, he may find it harder to adjust to the rough-and-
tumble ways of the gang than if he has brothers and sisters. (When
your kids bicker and fight, console yourself with the thought that
"at least family in-fighting is helping him with his peer-group
relationships!")

5. You can teach your child the basic skills of using tools such as a
hammer, saw, plane, pliers, wrench, etc. This is the best age for
learning to use *real tools*. Once he has learned well, he will not be
dependent on you for him to work on all kinds of projects in his
home workshop.

6. You can encourage overnight visits with a friend. Arrange for
him to invite different friends over to spend the night, and they will
in turn invite your child. Remember that this is an exciting adventure
for a child, so bedtime rules can be relaxed a bit for these occasions.
As Bentz Plagemann describes it:

> ... When boys spend the night together it means exactly
> that. It has nothing to do with sleeping. They giggle and
> talk and climb out on the roof. They build railroad bridges

with the Erector set at two o'clock in the morning . . . and
they go downstairs to eat cold peas from the icebox, or
scoop the frosting off the chocolate cake.[13]

However, a relaxation of the rules does not mean that they can
make noise that disturbs you late at night. No matter when a child of
this age goes to bed he still seems to wake up at approximately the
same time in the morning. Overnight visits and slumber parties are
equally popular with girls. Also, you can encourage your child to
bring along a friend on weekend trips or vacations.

What about friends of whom you disapprove? My rule of thumb is
that even if you do not consider certain youngsters the best influence, you should not forbid your child to play with them unless
the others are getting into real trouble with juvenile delinquent actions
such as stealing or using drugs. Otherwise grin and bear it and let the
friendship run its course. Meanwhile, make sure there is ample
opportunity to invite other friends over as well.

7. You can send your child to camp in the summer. It is best not
to begin this too abruptly, for being away from home for the first
time for two weeks, or even for one week, may be unsettling for
your youngster. The best way is to begin with day camp at ages seven
and eight, and make the first going-away camp for no more than a
week at age nine. By ten and eleven, your child will be ready for
camp for two weeks at a time. He may even plead for three weeks if
he really enjoys it and the camp is geared to his psychological needs.

The YMCA and YWCA generally run very good and inexpensive
summer camps for children. In addition, there are numerous private
camps. You will need to look into these carefully to find out the
qualifications of the camp directors and the counselors. By all means
visit the camp with your child before you decide.

8. Encourage your child to join organized groups such as the Cub
Scouts, Girl Scouts, Indian Guides, or Indian Princesses. Cub-
scouting is part of the overall Boy Scout program and covers boys
from eight to ten, preparing them to become boy scouts at eleven
years of age. Cub-scouting offers an opportunity for a father-son
involvement in various activities which are of great interest to
middle-childhood boys. I recommend it, but even more I recommend
the Indian Guide program offered by the YMCA. The father is
involved with Cub Scout activities, but the bulk of the program is

run by the den mother. This, in my opinion, is a psychological mistake. A boy at this age needs another female-dominated activity like he needs a hole in the head. I hope the day will come when the Boy Scout organization recognizes this and arranges for Cub Scouts to be run by a den father rather than a den mother.

In contrast to Cub Scouts, the entire Indian Guide program is run by fathers, which fits the psychological needs of a boy of this age better. There is also an excellent Indian Princess group sponsored by the YMCA for fathers and daughters which I recommend enthusiastically. The Girl Scouts and Brownies offer the same values for girls as do the Cub Scouts for boys at this age, and I recommend them.

Finally we come to the question of adult-organized sports programs such as Little League, Pop Warner football, and others. I must confess to mixed feelings about these adult-organized sports. Some boys benefit from them, but they are physically and psychologically bad for others. Pediatricians are familiar with injuries known as "Little League elbow" and "Little League shoulder." It is difficult to prevent boys of this age from straining muscles. A boy may not notice or he may be reluctant to tell his coach that his arm hurts, hating above all else to be called "chicken" or to think of himself as weak; and so he may not admit that he is tired or that his arm hurts. The musculature is not yet strong enough to take some of this adult-oriented activity.

In addition to the physical strain that may be involved in Little League or Pop Warner football, there is the emotional strain and pressure of performing before a crowd.

Psychologically, I feel that this is too young an age for a child to be exposed to this kind of psychological pressure. When children play baseball, football, soccer or basketball among themselves, they are not exposed to the same kind of competitive pressure as in Little League or Pop Warner, where they must contend with a referee or umpire, a competitive atmosphere, and emotionally involved adults.

My feeling is that if my son definitely wanted to play in Little League or Pop Warner I would probably let him, but I would not encourage it. I also warn the reader that I am biased. I agree strongly with the American Academy of Pediatrics, which suggests that the beginning age for competitive sports should not be earlier than twelve. This makes much more psychological and physical sense to me. Perhaps the only exception I make to my feeling that middle-childhood children should not participate in organized competitive sports would be soccer. Soccer is much less demanding on a child of this age, both physically and psychologically, than baseball or football. In soccer there is less psychological pressure on individuals, and more team spirit.

THE WORLD OF THE FAMILY

I have emphasized how important the new worlds of the school and his gang are for your child. But it would be a huge mistake to underrate the importance of the world of the family during these middle-childhood years. Remember the words of Dr. Barbara Biber which I quoted earlier as a key to understanding the child at this stage: She emphasizes that the child is "looking for ways to belong to his family and feel free of them at the same time."[14]

Do not be fooled by your child's Declaration of Independence from the family at this stage. Underneath the growing-up self is the babyhood self, and this stage is lived out in constant oscillation between the two. At times, your child will appear very mature, independent, and self-sufficient and want little to do with his parents. At other times, particularly when things are difficult in school or with his gang or he is sick or feeling physically or psychologically under par, he will revert to the dependent child with whom you were familiar in the preschool stage.

In previous sections I have emphasized how important it is that your child learn to separate himself from you and the family and find his place in the new world of school and the gang. I want to emphasize that this is very much a back and forth process: your child takes two steps toward psychological separation from the family followed by one step back.

It is the ambivalent, back-and-forth nature of this psychological process that helps to make the middle childhood years difficult for parents. At times a father will see how uncommunicative his eight-year-old is and adjust reluctantly to the idea that his son just doesn't seem to be interested in being close to him anymore. However, the very next day the boy may have a special need for a close talk with his father. But due to his previous observations the father's psychological radar will not pick up the hints his son is throwing out.

A father needs to realize that his middle-childhood boy or girl is in the paradoxical process of both (1) identifying with his parents, and

(2) resisting his parents and growing away from them. Since children of this age so often disobey their parents' commands in their *actions*, it is particularly important for parents to recognize that parental *feelings* and *attitudes* are being absorbed. Middle-childhood years are very important because the values and attitudes of the parents are being passed on to the child. If more parents realized this, they would breathe an enormous sigh of relief.

These are the years during which your child is learning to develop his conscience. Developing a conscience means learning to be a parent to himself. He will be the same kind of parent to himself that you and his mother have been to him. If you have been overstrict and authoritarian, he will develop an overstrict conscience. He will worry excessively over minor things and whether he is "doing what is right." If you have been overpermissive, he will feel he can get away with murder and not develop adequate controls on his exploitative impulses. If you have made reasonable demands on him, consistent with what can be expected at his age and stage of development, then he will make reasonable demands on himself in relation to what he expects and the standards he sets for himself.

In other words, during these years your child is forming an image of the adult he wishes to be. He will use other adults as models and he will quote to you what his teacher or Scoutmaster or Sunday-school teacher or gym coach say to him. But you and his mother are still his most important models for the adult he will become. This basic fact is often easy for parents to overlook. When their child "tunes them out," answers in monosyllables, and regards home as a place to grab a quick bite to eat and a bed for the night, many parents wrongly conclude that they have lost all influence over their child. Not so. Not so at all.

So it is important for a father to take the initiative in seeking companionship with his son or daughter during these middle-childhood years even though they will rebuff your interest and initiative from time to time.

One of the best things fathers can do with this age child is to join the Indian Guides with their boys in grades one, two, and three, and the Indian Princesses with their girls. I have recommended this earlier in the chapter and in greater detail, but it is such an excellent activity, I want to mention it again. Both of these groups are sponsored by the YMCA. Typically, they will involve hour-long meetings twice a month and an outing or camping trip once a month.

The Indian Princesses program did not exist when my girl was in middle childhood, but I have participated for the full three-year program of Indian Guides with both of my boys. We visited such places as an Indian Museum, a railroad museum, an airport-control tower, the zoo, tidepools, and took various hiking and camping trips. This type of program exposes a child to the give and take of group life with his peers, while at the same time deepening his identification with his father.

The same psychological values of Indian Guides and Indian Princesses can be found in Cub Scouts, Brownies, and Girl Scouts. Some of the same values can also be found in Little League and other adult-organized sports.

In addition to participating with your boy or girl in group activities, fathers should not neglect the many opportunities for one-to-one relationships. Exactly what a particular father wants to do with his child will depend on the father's own interests. If he has no interest in fishing, it is certainly foolish to take his nine-year-old boy fishing. Oftentimes a grandfather may be able to supply the interest and companionship with the boy in some area in which the father is not interested. For example, my boys' grandfather, who is an expert, enthusiastic fisherman, taught them how to fish, since this is not my cup of tea.

Let me mention some of the general things that a father may spend time doing on a one-to-one basis with a middle-childhood boy. First, he can take him along when he needs to buy something at a hardware store or nursery or sporting-goods store. He can invite him for a walk to the library or to an ice-cream or grocery store. He can teach him some of the basic skills such as catching or throwing a football or baseball, batting, or shooting a basketball. He can take him to spectator sports such as baseball, football, soccer, basketball, or hockey games. He can take him hiking, camping, or fishing. Incidentally, it often helps for your middle-childhood youngster to take a friend along on a hike or picnic or weekend camping trip. The addition of a friend makes things psychologically much easier for you. You can take your boy to a movie, either walk-in or drive-in.

With a middle-childhood girl, you can take her out to lunch, which will be a special treat and a valued experience. Fathers often are interested in spending time with their middle-childhood sons, but many are at a loss as to what to do with a middle-childhood girl. Fathers forget that they are the model for the kind of husband their middle-childhood girl will be looking for in later life. That's why a warm relationship with father is valuable for a girl, however it is expressed.

There is no reason that you cannot take your little girl shopping, or on trips to stores, or walks to an ice-cream store or library or hiking or camping the same as your little boy. And she, also, will be thrilled to have you take her to a special movie all by herself.

With both boys and girls, you can play two-person table games such as checkers, Chinese checkers, dominoes, chess, and various two-person card games such as slapjack and crazy eights.

But above all, be responsive to the many spontaneous occasions for closeness and camaraderie with your children. Don't be deceived by their facades of independence and aloofness. Remember the baby self underneath the growing-up self, and be aware that they still need a strong emotional relationship with you and their mother.

I have stressed the importance of one-to-one relationships and one-to-one times with your middle-childhood youngster, but do not overlook the importance of family activities. A family game-time after dinner for a half hour or so is a custom that could well be adopted by many families. Games such as twenty questions, Scrabble, charades, Parcheesi, lotto, and various card games could be played. Everybody in the family takes turns choosing the game, with one person choosing one night and another, the next.

Our family has always enjoyed drive-in movies, and these work out much better for us than walk-in movies. For one thing, you can take babies to drive-in movies easily. And the younger members of the family can go to sleep comfortably when they get tired or bored.

Our family has also enjoyed camping trips, first using a station wagon and later a camper. Children are much more cooperative about helping with things like building a fire, cooking, and cleaning up on a camping trip than when they are at home.

Activities for the whole family bring us to the difficult topic of sibling rivalry. It has been my experience as a psychologist that no topic is of keener interest following a lecture on child psychology, than the question of how to handle sibling rivalry and the bickering and in-fighting among children.

The first thing to understand is the cause of sibling rivalry: Each child, deep down, wishes he could somehow get rid of his brothers and sisters and have 100 percent of his parents' love and attention. This is the reason for the almost constant bickering and fighting that goes on between brothers and sisters. In fact, the greatest ill feeling a child has towards a brother or sister is usually directed toward that sib born directly after him. Once this basic cause of their rivalry is understood, you can see that sibling fighting can never be *eliminated* from a family; it can only be *moderated.*

The best way to handle sibling bickering and fighting is through the "time-out" technique I referred to in chapter 5 on discipline. When two children are quarreling send each to a neutral place for a five-minute quiet time. That way, their fighting is not rewarded or reinforced by parental attention. Each sibling merely gets to spend five minutes in a boring place. The use of the time-out also eliminates the need for the parent to act in the role of judge and referee, having to decide who started the fight, etc.

The question of sibling bickering leads naturally to the topic of how fathers can successfully discipline the middle-childhood youngster.

The first thing is for a father to accept the *childishness* of children. Of course this will vary a good deal with your general understanding of children and how loose or "uptight" you are around them. But my general observation of many, many fathers around children, particularly middle-childhood *boys,* is that fathers really expect the child to be calm, decorous, prompt, courteous, unselfish, quick to do any chores assigned, clean, careful not to tear his clothing or get it dirty, always willing to listen to adult instructions, and always careful to keep his room clean and his clothes hung up. Middle-childhood boys (and girls, too) are obviously *not* that way. The sooner a father accepts all their immature, childish qualities the easier it will be, and the better the relationship he will have with his child. In this respect a father would do well to heed the words of Aunt Sarah Crim, ninety years old, speaking to Penrod's mother about him and summing up the stage of middle childhood very well:

> You don't expect boys to be civilized, do you? You might as well expect eggs to crow. No; you've got to take boys as they are and learn to know them as they are.[15]

Second, many parents fear that if children acquire a bad habit, and it is not corrected immediately, the child will keep the bad habit forever. If an eight-year-old boy has a great aversion to washing or taking a bath the parents fear he will be this way as an adult. If a nine-year-old girl lies when it is easier to lie than to face some uncomfortable truth, her parents are afraid she will end up as an adult who cannot be trusted to tell the truth.

I want to reassure fathers that unpleasant habits which characterize a child's behavior as part of middle childhood will be outgrown with proper parental understanding and discipline. The middle-childhood youngster is by no means a miniature model of what he will be like as an adult! I wish that somehow the fathers who are staid, respectable teachers, bankers, repairmen, insurance agents, actors, engineers, bricklayers, or physicians could see sound movies of their own behavior at the age of seven or eight or nine! I have a hunch that such a movie would enable them to relax and not worry so much about the "bad" habits of their offspring.

Third, I have noticed that the method of discipline most used by fathers is the lecture, whether it is short or long. I have observed the lecture method being used on informal family outings, at parks, on airplane trips, at Indian Guide meetings, in restaurants, and just about everywhere you see a father and his youngster in interaction. After hearing the enormous torrent of words loosed at children by their fathers, I can only conclude that fathers sincerely believe that the way to change a child's behavior is to deliver a good stiff lecture explaining why that behavior is wrong. His theory seems to be that the child will feel so bad that he will never do *that* again! Or that the child will see that he *should* work harder at his math since he brought home a low grade, and he will respond to a careful, logically reasoned-out lecture on what he should do.

Of course the actual result of being on the receiving end of a lecture (particularly one delivered in front of other people) is that the child is made to feel ashamed, inadequate, and resentful. These feelings ensure that he will be even less likely to take his father's suggestions.

Fourth, instead of lectures, learn to praise your child. Again, in my observations of fathers in interaction with their children I hear very little praise on the part of the father. But praise is the greatest reward or reinforcement at your disposal in order to encourage your child to behave in desirable ways and avoid undesirable ways. Even the child who seems most independent and aloof from the family is still affected by praise from his parents although he may not respond to it overtly. Get into the habit of being on the lookout for behavior that you can praise. If your eight-year-old hangs up his pants but drapes his shirt and socks over the chair in his room, praise him for hanging up the pants and ignore the rest of his behavior!

Fifth, if you have followed positive methods of discipline in general, you will probably have no emotional need to spank your child after the age of eight of nine. If you are still exploding emotionally and spanking him quite frequently throughout middle childhood, it would probably be best for you to seek some professional help yourself. If punishment is used as a method of discipline, depriving the child of something such as a favorite TV show is probably the best technique.

Sixth, the middle-childhood youngster now wants and needs to have a voice in decisions that affect him. Fathers must learn to shift gears from the way in which they simply used to tell the preschool child what to do and what not to do. Increasingly, the middle-childhood youngster should have a voice in family decisions which affect him: whether to acquire a pet and what kind, what movie to see, what kind of a camping trip to take, where to spend a vacation. This doesn't mean that he should have the *controlling* voice in the final family decision, but he should be consulted.

Finally we come to an area which is a very tender one, and yet one in which a father can have a great deal to contribute. This is the area of sex education.

For over twenty years in clinical practice one of the routine questions I have asked my patients is, "What sex education did you get in your home?" And the answer from about 99 percent of them is: "None—the subject was never discussed." So the myth of the father-son talk about the so-called "facts of life" is just that: a myth.

Almost every study of where children acquire sexual information has shown that they get it from their peers. Learning about such things as coitus, contraceptives, prostitution, homosexuality, etc., almost always comes from peers. Children interact and exchange sexual information on a sporadic, hit-or-miss and usually guilt-laden basis. With respect to sexual information, the children's world resembles a secret society anxiously keeping information from parents.

This is an unfortunate state of affairs. Let any father reading this ask himself a simple question: Did your father give you *any* sexual information in *any* form during the years of middle childhood? Wouldn't you have been very grateful if he had, and if you had been reassured about the whole anxiety-ridden and guilt-laden subject of sex?

You remember, I suggested in the preschool years that you read three books on sexuality, love, and marriage to your child. This information is fine for that period, but the years of middle childhood are another story. The preschool child is more apt to ask his parents direct, innocent questions about sex than the school-age child. The middle-childhood youngster is much warier about expressing his feelings and violating adult taboos. He may have questions he would like answered about sex, but he will hesitate to ask.

There is one other factor that complicates the picture of sex learning in middle childhood. Today's children are generally much more sophisticated than any previous generation. The mass media, movies, TV, magazines, are all much more frank and explicit about sex than they were even a decade ago. And yet, in spite of all of their seeming sophistication, today's middle-childhood boy and girl are still woefully ignorant about sex and in great need of knowledge and reassurance. How can a father help?

Let me begin by giving an unorthodox suggestion. Most families will take children only to Walt Disney and other "family"-type movies. Our family has not done this. We never believed in censoring what movies or TV shows our children saw or what books they read. We took our children along to any adult movies that we wanted to see. Consequently, going to drive-in movies has served as a surprising source of sex education for our children. I remember, for example, one movie in which the word "prostitute" was used, and my nine-year-old daughter turned and asked me, "Daddy, what's a prostitute?" "Robin," I said, "A prostitute is a woman who has sexual intercourse with a man for money." "Oh," she said, and we went on seeing the movie.

I have already mentioned giving Dr. Sol Gordon's book *Facts About Sex* to your child at the age of ten. Another book you might consider at ten is *The Sex Book,* available in paperback. This is an excellent book covering all aspects of sexuality and illustrated with nude photographs. Some parents may find this much too strong for their taste, and if it would embarrass you to give such a book to your child, don't do it. But if after examining the book you would feel comfortable giving it to your child then I think the child would find it very helpful and guilt-reducing.

The point is that middle-childhood youngsters want to know a lot more about sex than just where babies come from. There are many aspects of sexuality that puzzle and confuse them. Fathers can play a vital role in helping to impart this knowledge. Many times, both parents and children feel more comfortable when the knowledge is imparted by way of books. Even though parents themselves may be quite free and at ease about sexual matters, the child may not feel at ease about discussing sexual matters with them. One ten-year-old told her teacher: "My parents are very understanding and all that, but there are some things it's easier to talk about with other people."

However, the least every father can do is discuss sexual matters as freely and objectively as other matters, give his middle-childhood youngster some helpful books on the subject, and tell him that he is always available to answer any questions the child has.

From this discussion of the role of the family in the life of the middle-childhood boy and girl you can clearly see that the school and the gang are by no means the only important influences on the child. The family is still a very crucial influence. And, within the family, the father has a most critical role to play.

In our next chapter we will turn from the relative stability of middle childhood to the tumultuous next stage of development: preadolescence.

10
The Preadolescent Stage (Ages Eleven and Twelve)

It might be well to contrast the ten-year-old, as the height of the stage of middle childhood, with the eleven-year-old, as the beginning of the stage of preadolescence.

A typical ten-year-old likes to get along with adults as well as with his peer group. This is a period of contentment. Although he is devoted to his gangs and groups, he is also able to show consideration for others and to adjust reasonably well to adult requirements

However, the psychological growth forces of adolescence are at work underneath the surface of the ten-year-old's placid and out-going behavior. These adolescent growth forces erupt sometime during the eleventh year, and usher in the stage of preadolescence.

The eleven-year-old suddenly develops an indifference to parental standards and either overtly or covertly resists parental and school authority. Parents may complain that their eleven-year-old has lost all semblance of table manners and is abrasive with brothers or sisters as well as his parents. This phenomenon is not limited to the United

States. As a Canadian parent expressed it, "All of a sudden my eleven-year-old girl has gotten 'cheeky'." To put it succinctly, the eleven-year-old becomes obnoxious to live with. He challenges his parents constantly. He suddenly becomes a juvenile shyster lawyer: he loves to argue over fine points and prove his parents wrong. Getting him to cooperate on household chores now becomes a monumental task. Parents may call him "selfish and completely self-centered."

In school, the eleven-year-old is typically restless and talkative. He likes to pass notes in class, play tricks on his classmates, and gossip. He is quite critical of adults and their shortcomings. For these reasons, sixth graders are not easy to teach. The job demands a teacher who is interesting and challenging, but who can be firm and not let the class get out of hand.

I want to emphasize again that while this general description is true of all preadolescents, there will be enormous individual variations in the way different children, even in the same family, go through this stage. Some children will pass through relatively easily, without causing their parent's blood pressure to go up to dangerous levels. Others will be so obnoxious and difficult that parents will often feel like tossing the youngster out of the house or sending him to live with distant relatives until the stage is past. For example, my oldest daughter Robin went through this stage fairly easily, with only a few slammed doors, crying jags, and temper outbursts. My oldest boy, Randy, on the other hand, was so difficult as an eleven-year-old that we would fantasize that some new science-fiction machine had just been invented that would keep a child in a deep freeze for about two years. Fortunately, for our sanity as parents, by the time he turned twelve he had mellowed considerably and was much easier to live with.

The preadolescent stage roughly covers the years from eleven to thirteen. During this stage, boys and girls are even more widely separated psychologically than before. For example, if boys see scenes of kissing in a movie, they will display great disgust and aversion. This is a basic defense mechanism against the emergence of puberty and a compelling interest in the opposite sex. Boys of this age are usually not ready to cope with their heterosexual feelings, and so they run away from them by restricting themselves to all-male companionship.

"LET'S SEE—IT'S EITHER HIS IMPRESSION OF THE EATING SCENE FROM *TOM JONES* OR HE'S REGRESSED BACK TO EARLY CAVEMAN"

"SEE, I *TOLD* YOU IT WOULD STILL BE DISGUSTING AFTER WATCHIN' IT 6 TIMES!"

Unless parents have a psychological understanding of this stage of development, they are liable to be very upset by it. "I just can't understand what has gotten into my boy!" a parent will complain.

Parents need to understand that the stability of middle childhood cannot go on permanently, or a child would never grow up psychologically and become an adult. In order to pave the way for the new constellation of psychological patterns which constitutes adulthood, the old childhood patterns must be broken up. The first step in the breakup takes place in preadolescence. Once a parent realizes that the defiance and moody belligerence which is so characteristic of preadolescence is part of normal growth and development, he is better able to take this period in his stride.

Previous developmental stages have each had *positive* developmental tasks for your child to master. This is the first developmental period in which the purpose of the stage, paradoxically, is *disorganization*. This is not a permanent disorganization of your child's personality, of course, but a disorganization which is a prerequisite for future psychological growth, so that a *higher* organization of his personality can occur. In order for your child to work his way toward adulthood, he has to destroy part of what he has been like as a child and become "something else" in various ways.

The real psychological growth of your child towards adulthood takes place during adolescence, the years from thirteen to twenty-one. Preadolescence is a stage of preliminary loosening-up of your child's personality structure in order that the changes of adolescence may take place. Preadolescence is, in Fritz Redl's vivid phrase, "comparable to soaking the beans before you cook them."[1] "Yes, yes," the parent will say, "but why does my kid have to soak his beans in such an obnoxious manner? Couldn't he soak them in some nicer way?" Yes, he could, and while that might make him much more pleasant around the house it would not achieve the psychological goal of this stage, which is to disorganize and break up his psychological equilibrium of middle childhood.

Biologically your child is in a sort of twilight zone at this stage. He is not exactly a child any longer, but he is not an adolescent either. His body is changing as it prepares for puberty. But he is usually quite unaware of these hormonal and glandular changes.

An anthropologist studying a group of preadolescents would probably notice first of all their extreme physical restlessness. Mother

Nature has endowed the child at this age with such enormous amounts of physical energy that the ordinary and polite measures of civilization are not sufficient to use it all up. Running seems to be more natural to preadolescents than walking. And as Fritz Redl comments, "The word 'sitting' is a euphemism if applied to what they do with a table and a chair."[2] Their hands are constantly manipulating something: folding up the pages of books they are reading, twisting, tapping pencils, or playing with various miscellaneous objects collected in their pockets or purses. Funny gestures and bodily antics spring up for no apparent reason. Children who painfully and laboriously learned reasonable table manners now suddenly seem to revert back to caveman days.

One mother tried patiently to explain to her preadolescent son about his eating habits that

> he really didn't have to use both hands . . . and it was customary to . . . swallow one mouthful before taking another, and it wasn't considered polite to mix all the food on the plate together like wet cement, and you buttered only one bite of bread at a time instead of lathering it, and most foods were chewed rather than swallowed whole, and . . . you sat straight in your chair with your feet under the table, since the chair was not a saddled horse you were riding in a handicap, and you paused now and then between bites to take a breath of air, or even to address a polite word to your neighbor . . . and you did not exhale loudly after drinking, and you did not scratch yourself at the table, and it was not considered polite to remove food from your mouth to examine it doubtfully before putting it back in.[3]

The ravenous appetites of preadolescents are notorious and are another manifestation of the imperious biological demands of this period. One mother reports that her preadolescent girl "has two hobbies in her life, eating and talking."[4] Bentz Plagemann describes a typical after-school snack of preadolescent boys:

> After school the scholars approached our house like the rabble storming the Bastille. They swept up the driveway in a scatter of gravel like grapeshot, and attacked the kitchen, which fell without struggle, after Kate had learned to leave the sandwich things out on the table and retreat.

The carnage afterward, the crushed milk cartons and evis-
cerated bread wrappers and violated peanut-butter jars,
was terrible to behold. Nature had failed to equip the
boys with hinged jaws, like boa constrictors, but in spite of
this they managed to stuff into their mouths the towering
concoctions they made of cold beef and cheese and any
other tasty condiments they found lying around loose,
such as lime Jello or mashed potatoes or ketchup or
marshmallow fluff or pickles, and afterward, refreshed and
belching, they would depart like a plague of locusts, leaving a silence broken only by the drip of spilled milk falling
between the cracks of the table.[5]

The biological activity and physical restlessness is usually much
easier for parents to take than is the negativism and general "cussed-
ness" their preadolescent youngster displays in the area of parent-
child relationships. Even children who obviously love their parents
and have a basically good relationship with them will develop moods
and attitudes of distrust, suspicion, and irritability. At times you will
begin to think that your preadolescent's unconscious motto is,
"Down with my parents, but up with everybody else!" As Fritz Redl
puts it:

The worst meal at the neighbors, at which they weren't
even welcome, may be described more glowingly in its
glory than the best-planned feast that you arranged for
their birthday. The silliest antics, the most irrelevent possessions or skills of neighbors will be admired way beyond
any well-rooted qualities and superior achievements of
father and mother.[6]

Your preadolescent is against any and all the restraints and requirements of family living. The most reasonable requests of
parents—for coming home at a prearranged time, going to bed at a
reasonable hour, wearing a sweater or coat if it is cold—all are
responded to as if he were living under the cruel and capricious rule
of power-hungry dictators masquerading temporarily as his parents.
Harassed parents find that daily life with a preadolescent in the home
is a constant round of mind-rasping irritations about minor things
and seemingly irrational flareups of resentfulness.

If there are younger brothers or sisters in the family, the behavior
of the preadolescent toward them seems to reach a new high of

"THE LOCUSTS HAVE MOVED ON TO PILLAGE ANOTHER UNSUSPECTING KITCHEN."

intolerabilitv. The repressed jealousy of his younger brother or sister, which had been kept in a state of equilibrium, now breaks out again with new intensity often to the amazement of the parents who thought the two children were "finally learning to get along well together."

The standards and values of the parents which had been assimilated into the child's personality in middle childhood now temporarily lose their power and become ineffectual. The child's individual conscience seems diluted and his control of antisocial impulses is weakened. The youngster has a great deal of trouble living up to standards of behavior which he had no difficulty with a few years ago.

But in addition to the conflict with his parents that is so characteristic of this stage, the preadolescent emotional turmoil goes beyond the relationship between the child and his parents. Jimmy's father and mother become more than father and mother: they are suddenly the representatives of the value system of the adult society he must fight in order to prepare himself for his own adulthood. In other words, many of the rebellious actions of preadolescents toward parents are not really aimed at parents at all. They are aimed at adults—which parents represent. Although it is sometimes hard to realize, parents are emotional bystanders to the rebellion of their preadolescents against adult society in general. Such rebellion is not only perfectly normal; it is absolutely *necessary* to get ready emotionally for adolescence.

Up till now your youngster has lived within the psychological confines of the adult value system. "Good" and "bad," "right" and "wrong" were defined by the value system of adults. Although he may have disobeyed the adult value system at times, deep down he felt he was wrong when he did so.

Now, for the first time in his psychological history, in a dim and fumbling way he begins to question the value of the system itself. He enters into allegiance with the value system of his peers. And the peer code of values differs considerably from adult values. In the adult value code, for example, a "good" child is one who studies hard in school, is well liked by the teacher, and obeys the rules and constraints of the adults, such as parents, teachers, Boy Scout leaders and church-school teachers who govern his behavior. All these values are turned upside down by the values of the peer group.

Generally speaking, the more acceptable to adults a preadolescent is, the more unacceptable he will be to the society of his peers. This was true even in Booth Tarkington's day early in this century: Georgie Basset was the idol of the adults in the neighborhood but was thoroughly detested by the gang of boys led by Penrod and Sam. Gang activities which are most enjoyed by preadolescents are those that are considered somewhat subversive according to adults' values and standards.

Some adult values are clearly rejected by peer standards; others may be compatible at some times but conflicting at other times. The actual group life of preadolescent gangs ranges from indulging in smoking or other forbidden activities to out-and-out vandalism, stealing, or other delinquent actions. But whether the gang is mildly rebellious or an out-and-out delinquent group, the psychological attitude remains the same. It is essential that the gang indulge in some activities that defy the adult code and about which the adults know nothing. It is remarkable that so many parents adopt a completely "see no evil" attitude to this very important phase of child development.

However, the change from the adult code to the code of his gang is not an easy process for a preadolescent. The transition from adult values to peer values is full of conflict and psychological pain. He wants to be admired by his gang on the basis of the peer code. But at the same time he still loves his parents and hates to see them unhappy or disappointed.

I can recall vividly my own transition from adult values to peer values during this period. I had always been a good student in school and gotten along well with my teachers. But in the seventh grade I became aware that being well thought of by your teacher did not sit so well with the gang of boys I palled around with. So I began to make fun of my teachers behind their backs and imitate their mannerisms to my classmates. This made me quite the sport with my peers. One of my seventh-grade teachers, a very friendly and understanding woman, happened to catch me mocking her to the rest of the class. She kept me in after school for it. She was rather shocked and puzzled by my behavior, since she had done nothing to deserve my derision. She was absolutely right; it had nothing to do with her personally. I was mocking her as a representative of adult society in order to make my points with my peers.

I can also remember that in the seventh grade I went through a sudden burst of petty thievery. I stole magazines from the corner drugstore, records from the neighborhood music store, and candy bars from the school cafeteria. This made me quite a "big wheel" with my gang. Luckily for me my parents never found out about these activities. This came to a halt when the local druggist discovered me attempting to make off with a magazine stuffed inside my jacket and made me put it back. He told me that if it ever happened again he would have to tell my parents. That brought my life of crime to an abrupt end.

Along with the substitution of peer values for adult values, the preadolescent begins to step on the parental toes exactly where it will hurt the most. For a number of years the preadolescent child has had ample leisure time to engage in a psychological study of his parents. He now puts this counterintelligence activity to work. When he needs to prove how emancipated he is, he will choose precisely those actions and attitudes which will irritate his parents the most. In other words, the preadolescent "symptoms" he will develop are in accordance with his thoroughgoing study of the psychology of his parents. If his parents are moralistic and anti-sex, that will be the area he concentrates on to shock and horrify them. If he knows that school grades are very important to his parents, he will suddenly begin to get D's and F's. Wherever his parents are emotionally vulnerable, there he will stage his psychological commando raids. And he will know by the anguished complaints that he has struck exactly where it hurts the most.

A classic instance of how a preadolescent finds one of the tender places of his parent's psyche and presses on it is given by Dr. Flanders Dunbar:

> An eleven year old boy and his father went to a shoe shop to get white sneakers but there were none in his size in white. Father and the salesman tried to persuade him that blue or red ones were just as good.
>
> The boy got up with dignity and said: "There are other shops in town that will have white sneakers in my size. Let's go, Dad." On the way to the door he said "Daddy, you cared more about disappointing the salesman than you did about disappointing me. I've noticed that before. Daddy, you are afraid to say what you think and what you want, and if you don't reform, you'll never get along in the world.[7]

A very penetrating analysis of his father, wouldn't you say? And that is very typical of the clarity with which a preadolescent can see the weaknesses and foibles of his parents.

"DON'T BOTHER TO WAIT UP FOR ME."

Unpleasant as it may be, our preadolescents are going to step on our psychological toes. And they are going to rebel not only against us as parents, but against the whole adult society for which we stand. It is important for us to realize that no matter how uncomfortable it is for us, every preadolescent needs the chance to have some type of wild behavior come out in one way or another. The preadolescent who never steps on adult corns, defies adult rules, or gets into trouble is going to have a great deal of difficulty making it satisfactorily through adolescence and into adulthood. It is important for parents not to take personally these typically preadolescent shenanigans.

Having given a general overview of this stage, let's now zoom down and take a closer look at the eleven-year-old and the twelve-year-old.

THE ELEVEN-YEAR-OLD

In the same way that the five-year-old is a consummation of the preschool years, the ten-year-old is a consummation of middle childhood, the years from six through ten. The eleven-year-old, however, represents an entirely new period of growth. We have called this new stage preadolescence, but, in one sense, the eleven-year-old is entering adolescence itself.

For eleven is outgrowing middle childhood with a crash and a bang. He is suddenly very self-assertive, often in ways that are irritating to adults and particularly to his parents. He is restive, talkative, and inquisitive. He likes to be in motion and on the go. He wriggles a great deal. He develops a new and voracious appetite. He loves to argue and will do so at every opportunity. He interrupts other people but delights in going on talking jags himself. He rushes through the house like a whirlwind, slamming doors and making noise. He keeps his radio or record player or TV operating at a sound level 50 decibels higher than adults can stand.

Most of all, he is subject to moods and emotional changes he has never experienced before in his entire ten years on this planet. Dr. Gesell expresses quite well the feelings of many parents about this entirely new phenomenon they have to deal with in the person of their eleven-year-old:

> There may well be an odd, vague, uncomfortable feeling
> in the minds of the parents of eleven year olds. It is as

though some force of nature were grabbing hold of their offspring—as though he were acting under some influence quite apart from those of the tangible environment in which he lives.[8]

Suddenly their self-contained, reasonable, and agreeable ten-year-old seems to have been replaced by an awkward, loutish stranger. This stranger is often disagreeable, argumentative, resentful, fidgety, rude, and sulky. Eleven knows he feels grumpy at times, but often he does not know why. He may wake up in the morning feeling cross, peevish, and mopey. Anger is a very common emotion for the eleven-year-old. He is frequently subject to outbursts of hostility which are most often directed against his younger brothers or sisters. Disappointments and hurt feelings are also frequent. Some disappointments and frustrations may bring on hot tears, and eleven-year-old boys are just as apt to cry as eleven-year-old girls.

His emotional life has sudden peaks of intensity. It is difficult to cope with an eleven-year-old who suddenly lets out a blast of emotion all out of proportion to the situation at hand. He can fly into a rage at the drop of a cross word. He can change abruptly and give way to a burst of laughter and joy. His voice can rise several decibels in as many seconds. But what is most amazing of all to parents is that he is completely oblivious to the fact that adults consider these moods and emotions difficult to live with. ("Who—me—hard to get along with? G'wan—you gotta be kidding, Dad!")

Fathers need to remember that these emotional changes are phenomena of growth. The whole biological and psychological organism of the child is undergoing profound changes. The changes in his emotions are only part of an all-pervasive process of *developmental reorganization*. We cannot see the subtle changes in body chemistry and the structural growth of the nervous system which heralds the beginning of adolescence; these changes are taking place silently but powerfully. That is why I said that in one sense we can speak of the eleventh year as heralding the beginning of adolescence.

It is good for us to remember that *biological changes in children are more basic than psychological changes.* Throughout the stage of middle childhood, your youngster's biological system was more or less in equilibrium. With preadolescence, vast biological upheavals play havoc with this previously well-established balance. There is a marked increase in activity level. Your child becomes a perpetual-motion machine with an enormous appetite. Not only does his appetite for food increase, but also his psychological appetite for new experiences, particularly in interpersonal relations.

Even physiological functions such as temperature control become unsteady at this age, and tend to fluctuate between extremes. He usually complains of feeling either too hot or too cold. I remember how my oldest boy, Randy, would manifest this in a typical eleven-year-old way. When we were camping with the Boy Scouts in the hot desert, he would want to hike with a jacket on. But when camping in the cool mountains, he would strongly resist wearing a jacket, claiming he was too hot!

Typically, an eleven-year-old behaves better away from home. At school, for example, he does not have to contend with siblings and his own jealousy, nor does he have to work up to the same emotional pitch to break his childhood dependence on his parents. At school he is with his peer group, and he likes to mingle and compete with them. For example, when Randy was eleven, my wife and I sometimes joked that maybe there are two, absolutely look-alike editions of Randy Dodson: the obnoxious, cantankerous Randy we knew at home, and the outgoing, enthusiastic, cooperative Randy known to his schoolteacher and Boy Scout leader. During a parent conference, when his schoolteacher praised him for his behavior, we looked at each other as if to say: "Are you sure she's talking about the same boy who lives at our house?"

As preadolescence begins, it is as if the eleven-year-old, who has never had a golf club in his hand before, were about to be initiated into the mysteries of driving and putting. We would not be surprised if his performance at his first golf lessons were somewhat awkward and erratic. Instead of golf, however, what the preadolescent is actually beginning to take lessons in, at this age, is the social behavior and the interpersonal relationships of adolescence.

Once a father grasps this concept, then the erratic and awkward social behavior of his eleven-year-old begins to make sense. To many fathers there is not much rhyme or reason to the after-school activities of an eleven-year-old. He spends a great deal of time just "messing around," with lots of horseplay, outbursts of laughter, teasing, sometimes temper flareups—a whole rich gamut of emotional interactions with his playmates. These can be thought of as his awkward attempts at interpersonal "driving" and "putting" by a rank beginner at the sociological "golf game."

The social life of boys at this age is more crude and rough than that of girls, which is more subtle, complex, and emotionally rich. Girls show more of a tendency to form cliques, with much sociological including and excluding: plotting, grouping, quarreling, and making up.

Both boys and girls have self-organized, loosely formed clubs, which constitute the stage setting for their training exercises in social relationships. The preadolescent is shifting emotional gears. He can no longer be classified simply as a child; he is becoming a youth. His emotions are going through a new and dynamic training process. One of the characteristics of this training process is the recurring pattern of antagonism followed by reconciliation.

Parents are often bewildered by the ups and downs in the friendships of their eleven-year-olds. But this should be viewed as the first awkward learnings of the social relationships of adolescence. As one girl commented: "I like everybody, but we have to quarrel to break up the smoothness."[9] In other words, the preadolescent is learning to define his new self by responding both positively and negatively to his peers.

Boys and girls do not get along too well at this age. If you were to look only on the surface, you would miss the underlying attraction which is usually expressed in teasing. One boy expressed a typical attitude toward girls when he said, "We don't mind girls but we don't usually play with them. I guess we would if we had to."[10]

However, underneath the apparent disdain toward the opposite sex the sexual attractions of adolescence are beginning to stir. On the boys' side this is expressed as teasing. As one boy said about girls, "There's not a better target around."[11] And the girls, in spite of their outward protestations, really enjoy the joking, teasing attitude of the boys. It is as if each sex is saying to the other: "Officially I can't allow myself and my peers to know that the opposite sex is of any great interest to me. But if I can disguise my feelings through teasing and being teased then I can express my positive attraction through a kind of behavioral code."

A boy may have a "girl friend" in the sense of a girl he likes in his own private thoughts. But no one else, not even his best friend and certainly not the girl herself, will have the faintest idea that he has any interest in her.

Unfortunately for parents, the eleven-year-old's behavior is at its worst within the family circle. It is important for a father to remember

"OFICIALLY, I CAN'T LET HER
KNOW THAT I LIKE HER, BUT I CAN
RUN OVER AND PULL HER HAIR
TO LET HER KNOW I'M AROUND."

that the rebelliousness, cantankerousness, argumentativeness, resistance to household chores, and abrasiveness with his younger siblings,
are all samples of an eleven-year-old's early adolescent self-
assertiveness. Although your youngster is experienced in living out the
role of a child, he is very inexperienced in living the role of an
adolescent. The abrasive ineptness of his social behavior at eleven is due
to the fact that he is just *beginning* to learn how to make the
interpersonal adjustment of adolescence. In this respect, he reminds us
of the child of two and a half who wants to inform another child he
would like to play with him in the sandbox, and does so by throwing
sand at him!

Eleven often challenges other people, particularly his parents, to get
responses which give him a psychological leverage to work against.
He is throwing his own new-found preadolescent self up against the
selves of other people in order to help him define who he is and who
they are. This self-definition is found through confrontation with
others, particularly parents. He challenges his parents with criticism
and accusations in order to get a response. To the eleven-year-old, as
to any child, any kind of response is better than none. He will often
lash out at his parents without really understanding why he is acting
in this way.

Fathers need to realize that the unpleasant qualities of eleven—his
belligerence, his argumentativeness, his defensiveness—are expressions
of his search for selfhood: a selfhood which is radically different
from the self he has had for so many years as a child. He is finding his
own self by reacting against other selves. In this he is giving expression
to a psychological theme which we have mentioned as crucial to
understanding the negativism of the stage of first adolescence (between two and three years). We will see later that this same theme is
critical for an understanding of the stage of second adolescence
(between the years of thirteen and twenty-one): *negative self-
identity must precede positive self-identity.* The child first must react
negatively to what the parents want him to be and do before he can
find out, in a positive fashion, what he himself wants.

So it is important to understand what the underlying growth
forces of the eleven-year-old are trying to accomplish. Otherwise a
father may simply throw up his hands, declare that his eleven-year-
old is a spoiled, selfish brat, and feel tempted to give up on the whole
enterprise.

But even if a father does understand the positive growth forces underneath the negativism and rebelliousness of his eleven-year-old, it is still no easy stage to live through. For example, even though I had the psychological understanding of what was happening to my oldest boy at this stage, I found him most difficult and exasperating. I was probably at my worst as a parent during the year that he was eleven. Fortunately for my peace of mind, he settled down considerably by the time he was twelve and was much easier to live with.

Amazingly enough, eleven often seems to be completely deaf, dumb, and blind to his abrasiveness and its effect on others. "What do you mean, my rude outbursts?" he may reply to his father in a challenging and belligerent tone. That he is unaware of his loud, boorish, and rude ways is reflected in the defensive attitude he often presents when he says things like "Everybody is always picking on me!" or, "You guys seem to think everything I do is wrong."

As I have mentioned previously, never forget that not only psychologically but *biologically* your eleven-year-old is different than during his previous ten years on the earth. It is as if he has been injected by an enormous hypodermic syringe full of biological energy. As Dr. Gesell comments, "His activity, especially when he is in any way confined . . . is so constant that one almost becomes seasick watching him."[12]

Eating is one of his favorite activities. He may often follow fads and eat large quantities of one food. The intense emotionality of eleven is shown also by his response to different foods. He may now "hate and despise" some food he was very fond of a few years ago. Fluctuations in appetite often seem to follow fluctuations in mood: "Some days can't get a thing down—other days I'm hungry as a bear."[13]

Getting eleven to bed is often a painful and exasperating process. In keeping with his new drive to be more independent and "grown-up." Eleven demands later hours, and wages pitched battles against going to bed. He will use any excuse to delay bedtime. Almost any bedtime a parent chooses is denounced as "too early" or "that's for babies."

Fathers are often more effective in getting eleven to bed at a reasonable hour than mothers. In part, this is due to the fact that mother has been trying to cope with his unreasonableness ever since he came home from school. Trying to deal with his resistance to bedtime may be, to her, the proverbial last straw. Above all, parents should be flexible with regard to eleven's bedtime, realizing that to him it is a symbol of his new attempts at independence and assertiveness.

Two suggestions may be of help to you at this point. First, tell your eleven-year-old he needs to go to bed at a certain time, but that he can read in bed for a half hour or so until he gets sleepy. If he can curl up with a favorite book, magazine, or comic book for a while, it will often lessen his resistance to going to bed. Second, give him increased latitude in his bedtime over the weekend, and also during vacation periods.

With regard to chores or work around the house, eleven is very difficult to contend with. Whatever his previous attitude toward work, he is now almost sure to hate all household chores. Furthermore, he will expend enormous energy in getting out of doing a task, or in doing it in ways that clearly negate the intention of the parent who requested it. If he is required to make his bed, for example, he may throw a coverlet over a collection of toys, books, and junk on top of the bed and consider that the bed is "made." In contrast to his remarkable reluctance to lift a finger to do any work at home, he expends a fantastic amount of energy doing work he voluntarily chooses, such as building a tree house or fort. Or a girl who has stubbornly balked at cleaning up the kitchen may suddenly erupt with a spurt of energy and bake a cake, a pie, and a batch of cookies for the family, simply because that is work she has *chosen* to do.

Parents report that trying to get eleven to take care of his room is a frustrating, never-ending task. My suggestion is this: ask yourself, "Is it really so important that his room be clean and tidy?" Parents tend to forget that this eleven-year-old stage is not going to last forever. Personally, I feel that the emotional wear and tear would be much less on parents if they woud close the door so as not to see the shambles inside. Then a clean-up campaign could be staged at appropriate intervals.

Clothes, of course, are often slung all over the room rather than being hung up. When eleven can't find his shoes or socks, or whatever, he will not admit to any responsibility for this. But he will complain bitterly to the world in general: "Why can't a guy ever find his shoes around this house?" (Only to discover five minutes later that he had stuck them underneath the TV in the family room!)

In general, eleven-year-old boys do not care much for clothes and would cheerfully wear the same shirt and pants for weeks at a time. Eleven-year-old girls are much more aware of clothes and may love to dress up. They often have definite ideas of what they want to buy and what they will wear.

When it comes to school, many eleven-year-olds continue to like it. Others may have great difficulty adjusting to school. The high energy level and newly-found critical attitudes of eleven make him difficult for a teacher to handle. If school is enjoyed, it is often because the eleven-year-old's friends are there. His need for continued contact with his peer group is insatiable, even when he gets along poorly with them. He teases, torments, pokes, chases, or hits his classmates. Eleven-year-olds are restless, talkative, and critical. They can't stand sitting in one place, but like to browse around the classroom, pass notes, play tricks, and gossip. As Dr. Gesell puts it, describing a group at school. "If eleven is allowed to go his own way without sufficient adult guidance, his ways and actions are a little reminiscent of those of the jungle."[14]

For all these reasons, a group of sixth graders is by no means an easy class to teach. It demands a teacher who is not an educational dictator, but who has a firm control of the class and does not let eleven-year-old expansiveness get out of hand. A weak, vacillating, or wishy-washy teacher has had it with sixth graders. If, in addition, the teacher has a good sense of humor and can crack jokes or tell funny stories, so much the better. A good sixth-grade teacher is not easy to find, and if your youngster is fortunate enough to have one, be sure to show your appreciation.

But even with the best of teaching, your eleven-year-old may fatigue rapidly, either physiologically or emotionally, or both. This fatigue may show up in an inconsistent learning pattern. One day he will do very well, but the next day his school performance may be disastrous.

A wise parent makes allowances for this type of erratic performance from his sixth grader. In fact, one of the best things you can do for your eleven-year-old is to give him two or three surprise days off during the year. This gives him a great psychological lift, and, perhaps, a fresh attitude toward school, particularly if he has been complaining.

In general, as we have seen, eleven gets on better in school, church school. Boy Scouts or Girl Scouts, or other activities outside the home than he does with his family. You and his mother have definitely lost your parental halos. Having studied the two of you for a number of years he is now very much aware of your weaknesses and foibles. He usually has no hesitation in pointing out to you where he thinks you are wrong on something. One youngster puts it this way: "My father keeps insisting he's right when I have proven him wrong."[15] Above all else, eleven loves to argue and make finicky legalistic points, particularly when he has done something he knows he shouldn't. As one parent reports it, "She is exuberantly defensive."[16]

However, life isn't *completely* negative in your relationship with your eleven-year-old. Don't conclude from his feisty and obnoxious ways that your eleven-year-old wants to have nothing to do with you, his father. In spite of the fact that he will make loud anti-parental noises at home and frequently challenge you, don't make the mistake of thinking that you are not important to him. You are. Even though he may reject some of the overtures you make, it is important that you make them; he would feel bad if you did not. Also remember that although *all* eleven-year-olds have some degree of obnoxiousness in them, some are much easier to get along with than others. If your preadolescent happens to be one of the easier-to-get along-with type, enjoy him and take the time to do things with him. If your preadolescent is more difficult, there will still be times when he will like to be with you and do things together.

During the eleventh year, probably more than any year we have looked at so far, it is especially important to plan things to do as a twosome, without your requiring anything whatsoever of him during that time. These times of togetherness should simply consist of being together and doing something that you mutually enjoy. A child's need for such times in which nothing is demanded of him is illustrated beautifully by a youngster in Rochester, New York who wrote in an essay on "What My Dog Means to Me":

> My dog means somebody nice and quiet to be with. He does not say "Do" like my mother, of "Don't" like my father, or "Stop" like my big brother. My Dog Spot and I just sit together quietly and I like him and he likes me. [17]

There is probably no other age child who gets along as badly with younger brothers and sisters as eleven. He is often fantastically jealous and will accuse parents bitterly, saying, "You like Timmy better than me because you do all kinds of things for him you never do for me!" (This kind of accusation often leaves a father thunderstruck, because he may have just done something particularly nice for the eleven-year-old which he didn't do for the younger sibling!)

In such situations, it is important not to take a purely rational approach to the matter but to understand the feelings involved and use the feedback technique. For example, I recall one family camping trip when Randy was eleven and Rusty was five. Randy was acting so obnoxiously to Rusty that I finally suggested we walk down the canyon for a little and talk. I asked him what was bugging him and he finally burst out: "You and Mom love Rusty more than you love me, and I just hate it!"

"Tell me why you feel we love Rusty more than you."

"Isn't that obvious? You're always doing things for him and you never do anything nice for me!"

(I resisted the temptation to point out that we had allowed Randy to bring a friend along on the camping trip, but we hadn't let Rusty do this.)

Instead of responding rationally to his feelings and telling him we did love him and we did not do more things for Rusty, I simply encouraged him to tell me his feelings. I used the feedback technique to let him know I understood how he felt. We took about fifteen minutes, with him pouring out his feelings of anger and jealousy and me reflecting them back by means of the feedback technique. When he had fully expressed how he felt I gave him a hug and suggested we head back for camp. Randy did not become an angel overnight after that father-and-son dialogue, but he was easier to live with and he got along much better with Rusty on the rest of the trip.

In spite of all of his difficulties and conflicts with other members of the family, eleven rarely chooses to be alone. Generally he seeks out the midst of the family circle. He is a great watcher of the other family members, and above all, an avid talker.

So there he is—the eleven-year-old. The child of this age is aptly called a *pre*adolescent. For at age eleven we see clearly for the first time many of the psychological changes that will be so typical of adolescence.

His physiological and psychological pace of growth is beginning to accelerate and there is an enormous increase in activity level and expenditure of energy. He is caught in the phase of negative self-identity which precedes the finding of a positive self-identity. He is aggressively (and often obnoxiously) trying out new patterns of interpersonal relations in order to define who he is. Relationships with parents and above all with younger siblings are full of conflict. He is often consumed by self-doubt and insecurity and may be very defensive at times. He may find school unrewarding and be difficult to handle. (However, in general he gets along better at school than at home.) Only his relationships with his peers remain reasonably smooth. When engaged in building a tree house or a fort or occupied with one of the many clubs he organizes he is capable of exuberant happiness.

The father who is feeling dismayed about the difficult behavior of his eleven-year-old can take heart. Although many of the same psychological themes are present at age twelve, they are considerably mellowed. These preadolescent personality characteristics are so difficult to live with in the eleven-year-old because it is the first time in his whole life he has had to contend with them. By the time he is twelve his anxieties and insecurities have quieted down a great deal. Feeling more comfortable within himself, he is a much easier child to have around.

THE TWELVE-YEAR-OLD

Somehow Mother Nature knows that parents could not endure a solid two years of the behavior characteristic of the eleven-year-old. So she has wisely arranged that the preadolescent behavior so typical of the eleven-year-old will mellow during the twelfth year. The eleven-year-old was often thrusting out blindly and crudely to win new status. In many respects the twelve-year-old feels he has won this new status. So he can now afford to relax his pushy efforts and be more gracious and agreeable. To sum up the difference in a sentence: it is as if eleven was searching for his self, but twelve is beginning to find it.

One twelve-year-old's comment sums up the typical attitude toward self: "I'm not bad, though I'm not too good. If you're too good, kids don't like you."[18] This comment also underlines the vast importance of his peer group. Both boys and girls are anxious to know how their peers think and feel about things. They do not like to be out of step. The way their peers dress, wear their hair, the kinds of music and social attitudes that are "in" at the moment are of great importance.

An overall view of the twelve is that the eleven-year-old searching-for-self personality structure is being integrated and pulled together. He is more reasonable and tolerant, with a new-found dash of humor which parents and teachers recognize as a very positive asset.

Enthusiasm is another important trait of the twelve-year-old. If he is interested in anything at all (a movie, a baseball team, pizza, or science) he is *ardently* interested. Typical twelve-year-old comments about things they like are: "I *love* pepperoni pizza"; and "It was just divine"; and "*All right!* that's really super!" He is equally "enthusiastic" on the negative side. "I just *hate* liver." His enthusiasm propels him into tasks he has chosen himself (*not* those that adults have chosen for him!) with great vigor and elan. In school, for example, he likes the challenge of debates and discussions. With boys, much of their enthusiasm is given over to sports. They not only like to play baseball, football, soccer, or basketball, but they are avid fans and follow their favorite teams and players with all-consuming interest.

Since twelve is so enthusiastic and outgoing and often expends such enormous energy, he also periodically needs time to calm down and recuperate, both physiologically and psychologically. Some twelves have periods of extreme fatigue when they hate everybody and everything that makes any demands on them. Others may develop a cold and need to rest up for a day or two. Still others may get their batteries recharged by just fooling around aimlessly, doing nothing in particular. The wise father will allow his twelve-year-old to do this, knowing it is psychologically important for the child to let his emotional motor idle. He will not make demands on the youngster during this time of "just messing around."

The physiological changes that make preadolescence different from middle childhood are reflected in twelve's appetite. His appetite, like that of eleven, is still enormous. Parents will often describe his stomach as a "bottomless pit." Twelve typically loves a big snack when he comes home from school in the afternoon. Again, at bedtime he often suffers from hunger pangs which require a snack. Parents, not suffering from preadolescent hunger pangs themselves, sometimes deny such snacks to their youngsters because they feel the child is being "pampered." This is a mistake. It is important to understand that the enormous appetite of preadolescents is an entirely normal growth phenomenon, and reflects basic physiological changes taking place in the total body organism of the child.

Twelve has usually given up the abrasive arguments and fights about bedtime he had when he was eleven. Once again, allowing him to read in bed is a big boon, and lessens his resistance. He often likes to keep his radio on after he is in bed as a "sociable companion."

There are fewer arguments about clothes and what kind to wear. Twelves definitely want to be in on the choice of clothes. Girls, especially, want to try on clothes to see how they look rather than have mother bring home things she has picked out.

There is no reason why mother should always be the one who goes shopping with a twelve-year-old boy or girl. It is a good thing for father also to take a son or daughter on a shopping trip. Girls enjoy shopping for clothes with their fathers, particularly when lunch or a snack is included in the trip.

Twelve is usually much better at choosing clothes than at taking care of them and hanging them up. The room of your twelve-year-old is *slightly* better than that of eleven, but not enormously so. Not only is his room usually strewn with clothes, but his various collections are all over the place. A helpful thing to provide for a twelve-year-old is a bulletin board for his room. Then he will have a special place to pin up all the bits and pieces of memorabilia that are so important to him: pictures of sports stars, cartoons torn from magazines, pages from *Mad* magazine, photos of movie stars or rock musicians, etc.

When it comes to work around the house, twelve is not as belligerently resistant as he was at eleven. He is not going to *volunteer* to do chores around the home, but he is more cooperative when reminded. Boys may now be washing the car, cleaning up the garage or home workshop, or doing some rough-and-ready carpentry such as fixing a broken fence. Girls may be interested in cooking and will take pride in learning to prepare new and special dishes, with mother's help; and more reluctantly, they may even care to clean or dust the house.

The emotions of twelve are more calm and settled than those of eleven. The disagreeable, belligerent, argumentative ways of eleven have not entirely disappeared, but they have settled down to a more tolerable level. As Dr. Gesell puts it, the twelve-year-old shows a "miraculous smoothing out" compared to his eleven-year-old self.[19] Much of the time parents find him good-natured, able to listen to reason, and a pleasure to have around. However, he will still have angry flare-ups from time to time and, as at age eleven, these will typically be directed at younger siblings.

One of twelve's particularly redeeming features is his new-found sense of humor. For example, an eleven-year-old might say to his overweight father, "You look gross with that big pot on you. You really ought to work out at a gym, you know." A twelve-year-old might say to his overweight dad, "Pop, you have what I would call a unique physique!"

School is a very different environment for the twelve-year-old than it was at eleven. In most school systems, he now graduates from elementary school and enters junior high. This is a drastic change for him. In elementary school the sixth grader is "top of the heap," looked up to by all of the younger grades. Now, as a seventh grader, he is suddenly low man on the totem pole in a new and strange environment.

Instead of the security of a regular room and one teacher, he now goes to a different room for each class, taught by a different teacher. This is upsetting to his dependent feelings. He unconsciously feels that he has no *one* person to "take care of him" as his teacher did in elementary school.

It is a big psychological step moving from elementary to junior high. Be prepared to sympathize and use the feedback technique for any tales of woe your twelve-year-old brings home from school. Recognize that a particular beef or gripe of the youngster may be a screen for his deeper feeling (of which he is usually unaware) that "junior high is a new and strange world and I don't have any one teacher to take care of me."

As was true for the teacher of sixth graders, the teacher of seventh graders also needs a firm hand and a sure touch with discipline. If a seventh-grade teacher is weak or unsure with a class, the children sense this very quickly and proceed to "give him the business." They may throw spitballs, cough in unison at prearranged times, or do other things to get the class in an uproar.

Although they share some things, in common, many school interests of seventh-grade boys and girls begin to diverge sharply. Although both boys and girls like mystery and adventure stories, their reading tastes differ considerably in other respects. Boys love to read about sports, hot rods, motorcycles, and, perhaps, hunting and fishing. Girls like to read stories about late-adolescent girls which involve romance and a career. Many boys like an elective subject such as shop, and many girls like home economics. However, expecially today, many boys and girls are crossing these stereotype lines and experimenting with subjects traditionally allocated to the other sex. Girls are usually enthusiastic about cooking and sewing. When they cook, their primary interest is to eat the results. Boys enjoy baseball, basketball, football, and soccer, and girls continue to like softball, dodge ball, and volleyball.

Twelve's whole personality structure has mellowed, as compared to what it was at eleven. This is certainly true of his interpersonal relationships, both within the family and outside it. Within the family he gets along better with both parents and siblings. Not that he has suddenly become an angel, but, as one mother reports it, "He's over the hump."[20] Twelve himself may recognize that he gets along better with his parents. One twelve-year-old girl commented: "Father is less strict. He changed gradually." Then on second thought she added, "I think it was me."[21]

Typically, twelve's relationship with parents are improved more than his relationship with younger siblings, who still bug him because they get into his things and tease him. If twelve is fortunate enough to have an older sibling (fifteen or older) he may admire or even idolize this older brother or sister. He may tend to confide in a sympathetic older sibling instead of in his parents.

For many twelve-year-olds, this is an age of considerable boy-girl activity and interest, but interest in the opposite sex may be shown in strange and wondrous ways. A girl may have a boy whom she likes and feels is her boyfriend but the boy in question may be completely ignorant of her interest! The same may be true of a boy and his alleged girl friend. Both boys and girls often shift interest from one friend to another. Girls on the whole are more interested in boys than vice versa. Boys show their interest in girls by teasing them, chasing them, snatching a girl's purse, or some other devious and indirect way of letting the girl know they are interested.

With respect to physical development and sexual awareness, this is a period when many girls grow rapidly both in height and weight. By the end of the twelfth year, for example, the average girl has achieved over 95 percent of her mature height. During this year there is usually a definite filling out of the breasts and some growth of underarm hair.

For most girls, menstruation starts sometime during the twelfth year. It is to be hoped that your daughter has been prepared for her first menstruation both at home and in school before the event takes place.

When menstruation actually occurs, it is typical of our culture that a mother and daughter discuss this together, but father never mentions it. I think this is unfortunate. By a father's silence he seems to be saying "This is something that is not quite acceptable to men, because you notice I never mention the subject."

Instead of keeping silent when your daughter first begins to menstruate I suggest you quietly express your approval to her when just the two of you are together. You might say something of this nature: "Jeannette, I understand you've started to menstruate. I'm glad to hear that, and I'm proud that you're developing into a very attractive young woman." Don't, of course, repeat such phrases mechanically. Put them in the words you would use naturally, and don't worry if your daughter seems somewhat embarrassed that you mentioned the subject. It is still better for you to comment naturally and openly on it than to be silent. It is important for your daughter to know that not only her mother has a positive attitude toward menstruation, but that you do also.

At some opportune moment, remind your twelve-year-old daughter that you are willing to answer any questions she has about sex or boy-girl relationships. Sometimes fathers feel that the sex education of a daughter is entirely mother's job. Generally, a girl will ask questions and discuss sex more openly with her mother than her father. But that doesn't mean father should stay out of the picture. Preadolescent girls also need a man's point of view and a father's perspective on sex questions.

Twelve-year-old boys are more apt to be interested in the physical aspects of sexuality than girls are. This is the stage when boys will be interested in pictures of nude girls, *Playboy* magazine, and "dirty" jokes in which sexual and excretory functions are both the source of the humor.

Many boys begin to masturbate during this year. If you have not previously spoken to your son and reassured him that masturbation is normal (and that you yourself did it when you were a teen-ager) now is the time to do it. If you have not previously given him Sol Gordon's *Facts About Sex* or Dr. Wardell Pomeroy's *Boys and Sex*, by all means do so now.

When my boy Randy had his twelfth birthday I gave him a present of Dr. Pomeroy's *Boys and Sex* (not at the family birthday party, but afterwards in his room, when just the two of us were present). I used the occasion as an opportunity for a very short discussion of sex. In spite of the fact that sex questions had been answered and sex discussed quite openly in our home, he was somewhat ill at ease.

I told him that his mother and I had always tried to answer any questions he had about sex openly and honestly. And he had read several books on sex and babies and human reproduction at an elementary-school level.

But I added that now that he was twelve and almost a teen-ager, he was at a new level of sexual development. His sex glands were now maturing and secreting hormones into his bloodstream. These hormones would cause him to think about sex and girls and cause his sex organs to become more sensitive and develop new capacities for sensory pleasure. At this point he interrupted, and said, "I know all about that puberty stuff, Dad. Dr. Schaefer told us all about it (referring to a very good fifth-grade sex education class he had)."

I decided to pursue the subject a little further.

"Did Dr. Schaefer tell you about wet dreams?"

"Yeah."

"And did he tell you about masturbation?"

"Yeah—he told us all about it."

"And did he tell you it's a normal thing and that almost all teen-age boys do it?"

"Yeah, he told us all about that, too."

At this point I decided that Dr. Schaefer had covered the ground adequately, and simply said: "Well, this book deals with all kinds of information about sex you may wonder about this year or in several years to come. And if you don't understand anything or have any question about sex you can always ask your mother or me."

In spite of the fact that the school physician had obviously covered the subject adequately, and in spite of Randy's being somewhat ill at ease in our discussion, I still felt it was helpful for Randy to hear this general message from me personally: "Sex is a natural and normal thing. Masturbation is normal. In our family we can talk over sex naturally and openly, and if you have any questions you can ask your mother or me."

Twelve-year-old boys and girls are by no means alike in how free they feel to ask questions and discuss sexual subjects with father or mother. A shy son or daughter might much prefer to get sexual information from a more detached source than a parent, such as a counselor at school or a Boy Scout or Girl Scout leader, whereas a more open and uninhibited child will bombard a father or mother with a series of frank and intimate questions about sex.

Sometimes a father can get thrown by some of these intimate but honest queries from his twelve-year-old. For example, I remember one father, a therapy patient of mine, who told me two questions his twelve-and-one-half-year-old daughter asked him that almost caused him to have apoplexy. She asked, "How often do you and Mom have intercourse?" and followed up that bombshell by inquiring, "Can I watch sometime?" Dumbfounded, he mumbled, "I'll have to think about those questions for a bit" and beat a hasty retreat!

In his next therapy hour, this father asked me how I thought he should answer questions like that. He didn't want to handle his daughter as his parents had where sex was hush-hush and all questions about it were taboo, but questions like that really threw him. I pointed out that he certainly did *not* have to answer questions about his own and his wife's sex life. I suggested he tell his daughter that she certainly had the right to ask him any questions about sex she wanted to, and that he was glad she felt free enough to ask him any question at all. He would try to answer all questions that pertained to her and her sex life now and in the future. However, sex is a deeply personal relationship between a man and a woman. So he would not answer questions about his and his wife's own sex life because that was personal and private. For the same reason, he would not let his daughter watch when he and his wife had intercourse. I suggested he tell his daughter that he respected her rights to privacy and, in the same way, she needed to respect his and her mother's rights of privacy.

All of which goes to show that when you discuss sex with a twelve-year-old, you can't tell what might come up!

It is also important and helpful for a father and his daughter to have the same kind of general talk as with his son. Fortunately, Dr. Pomeroy has written a book for preadolescent girls as well as boys: *Girls and Sex.* If you have not already made this available to your daughter at an earlier age, the twelfth birthday is a good time to do so. Even though your twelve-year-old daughter may be somewhat embarrassed to have a dialogue with you about sex, on a deeper level of personality it is very reassuring to her.

Give her a book on the subject, reassure her that masturbation is normal, and offer to answer any questions she may have, both now and in the future. In too many families even if mother and daughter are able to communicate about sex, a daughter may grow up and get married without ever exchanging a word about this important area with her father. To the unconscious mind of the daughter it is as if the father, by his silence is saying: "Sex is taboo and must not be talked about." Since you are the main model for the man she will untimately marry, do not unwittingly set up road blocks which will prevent her from communicating with her husband about sex.

So, there he is—the twelve year old—still an in-betweener, living in the psychological no-man's land between childhood and adolescence. He is definitely no longer a child. He is a mellowed version of the obnoxious, argumentative eleven-year-old. But he is not yet "over the hump" into full-blown early adolescence, which is the next stage of his psychological development.

HANDLING THE PREADOLESCENT

I have described as clearly as possible, what children are like in the preadolescent stage. Now we come to the most crucial part of this chapter: How can a father handle his child in an intelligent way during this difficult stage? I want to make several suggestions to help a father survive life with his preadolescent.

First and foremost, realize that the obnoxious behavior of this stage is temporary. Even within the bounds of the stage itself the cantankerous personality of the eleven-year-old will mellow and be easier to live with when he is twelve.

I am always surprised that in this halfway psychologically enlightened age, so few fathers realize that preadolescence is a *normal* stage and that it is *temporary*. So many fathers react as if the obnoxious behavior of their eleven-year-old were going to continue year after year unless they do something immediately to prevent it. You'll hear them say something like "The way kids behave nowadays is due to all of this damned permissiveness in our society. I'm going to let him know once and for all who's boss in this house!" Then the father cracks down on the preadolescent like a ton of bricks—with the result that any psychologist could have predicted: the youngster's behavior gets worse. He becomes either more forthrightly defiant and even more difficult to control, or else he becomes compliant outwardly but carries on forbidden activities behind his father's back. So parental crackdowns and parental rigidities in discipline only make difficult behavior worse. One way to avoid this unfortunate parental reaction is to realize that the behavior of your preadolescent, although difficult, is temporary. In time he will outgrow it.

Second, try to avoid parental counterhysterics. "You know what that crazy kid of mine did the other day? Boy, I'm gonna tan his fanny so he'll never try that again!" This kind of parental reaction takes a mild problem in parent-child relationships and puffs it up until it becomes a major problem. Dr. Fritz Redl, an outstanding authority on parent-child relationships, comments:

> It seems to me that 90 percent of the more serious problems between children and parents or teachers on which I have ever been consulted could have been easily avoided. They were not inherent in the actual problems of growth. They were produced by the hysterical ways in which the adults reacted to them.[22]

By advising you to avoid parental counterhysterics, I do not mean you should let your preadolescent do whatever he pleases or that you should never say "no" to him. But the way you discipline him should be as free as possible from your own hysteric overemotionalism. The following example is the kind of thing we need to avoid.

A mother who was one of my patients phoned me one morning, very much upset. "Dr. Dodson, my daughter (who was 12) has been using marijuana!"

"How do you know?" I asked.

"I found a bag full of it, hidden under her clothes in her bureau drawer! This is tragic—I've got to see you right away about this!"

I looked at my schedule book. "Mrs. Jones," I said, "I can't see you today or tomorrow. The earliest I can see you is Thursday. Now don't say anything to your daughter, try not to panic, and we will have lots of time to talk it over on Thursday."

Mrs. Jones reluctantly accepted the idea that she couldn't see me until Thursday, talked a few more minutes on the phone, and then we ended the conversation.

That afternoon she called me back, and from the tone of her voice you could almost see the shamefaced look on her face:

"Dr. Dodson, we won't need to bother about that Thursday

appointment after all. It seems that what I found was a bag of catnip!"

So when dealing with your preadolescent try to keep cool and don't hypo his minor problems into major ones by parental counterhysterics.

Third, with respect to discipline, preadolescence is above all the time when a father needs to distinguish between what is important and needs his firm intervention, and what is unimportant and can be left alone. Preadolescents are difficult enough to cope with without a father fighting on all fronts at once! Save your heavy parental artillery for really important things and don't try to shoot down bees with a cannon.

Fourth, try not to respond to the provocative behavior of your preadolescent. The behavior which you find so obnoxious and annoying has been unconsciously programmed to get your goat, and it will usually succeed! Instead of getting excited and condemning your preadolescent's strange and novel behavior, try a "delayed reaction" instead of an immediate, worried, excited, and condemning response. Try to see what is behind his choice of friends you think are dreadful, his goofing off and failing in school, his smoking, and defying your reasonable restrictions, or whatever. Don't be taken in by surface behavior. Don't fight the behavior itself, but look underneath it to the feelings and attitudes your youngster is expressing. Say to yourself: "This surface behavior of my child—his failing grades in school where he used to get good grades, his smoking—is a message to me in code. Let's see if I can learn to read the code and find out what kind of a message he is sending me."

Fifth, try to provide growth opportunities where the "wild" behavior of preadolescence can emerge safely. No matter how unhappy it may make you, it is still a fact that every preadolescent youngster needs a chance for "wild" behavior to come out in some form or another. If it cannot come out in a socially approved setting, it will erupt in socially disapproved action.

For example, let's suppose your eleven-year-old boy needs the experience of some kind of life situation where he can prove to himself and others that he is independent, aggressive kid and no longer mother's little boy. If you provide him with the opportunity, for example, to attend the kind of summer camp where he can go on a backpacking or canoe trip in the wilderness, he can prove his self-reliance and independence without getting himself or anyone else in trouble. But if he has no life situations to try his independence then he may start stealing from the supermarket to prove his point to himself and his peers.

I can vividly recall that my own overprotective parents refused to allow me to join the Boy Scouts for fear I might "get hurt." This was probably one of the reasons I started stealing at this age, to prove to myself and my friends that I was a tough guy and not a mama's boy.

Sixth, respect your youngster's newfound independence at this stage. This is hard for a father to do with a preadolescent. For ten years you have been accustomed to treating him like a child. You have been talking to him like to a child. You have been praising him and punishing him as you punish and praise a child.

Just as he has reached this new developmental stage in which he is no longer a child, you, as a father, must, move up to a new developmental stage in handling him. You have to "promote" him to a new level where he is more on an equal footing with you. This will continue throughout adolescence and when he becomes a young adult, the two of you will relate to each other on the more or less equal footing of two adults, one of whom is older than the other. And this process needs to begin when he is eleven! I'm sure you won't find it easy to change ten years of habits overnight. But you need to *learn* how to respect his new and awkward ventures at independence and accord him a more adult status.

Seventh, don't take the rebellion of this stage personally. So many fathers do. They feel quite hurt or angry or both at the perplexing and difficult behavior of their preadolescent. They react as if the behavior is aimed at *them.* It is not. Father is merely a representative of the whole adult society against which the preadolescent is rebelling. Try to think of yourself as an innocent bystander to your preadolescent's rebellious assertiveness. That should enable you to "keep your cool" and deal with it in a more productive way.

Eighth, let me give you three basic rules that will sum up what a father needs to do in order to survive the preadolescent stage:

Rule 1. Roll with the punches!

Rule 2. Roll with the punches!

Rule 3. Roll with the punches!

11
Early Adolescence I: (Ages Thirteen to Fifteen)

Of all the psychological stages of development your son and daughter must negotiate from birth to adulthood, adolescence is the most complex and difficult. It is difficult for them; it is difficult for you. Adolescence is confusing to the adolescent himself, and it is equally confusing to his parents and teachers. Little wonder that Anna Freud, famous for her work with children and adolescents, writes: "There are few situations in life that are more difficult to cope with than an adolescent son or daughter during the attempt to liberate himself."[1]

In speaking of adolescence, I refer to the transition from childhood to adulthood in the United States (and to a lesser extent in other comparable complex, industrialized countries.) In primitive societies, there is no equivalent for our concept of adolescence. In some primitive tribes, in fact, the transition from childhood to adulthood is so smooth that nobody takes particular notice of the process. What is more usual in primitive societies compared to our own, is that the young person who is on the threshold of adulthood goes through a vastly time-shortened ceremonial adolescence.

Adulthood is conferred upon youths in primitive societies by ceremonies which are called by various names: rites of passage, puberty rites, or initiation rites. Many of these initiation ceremonies are ordeals which serve at least partly as tests of character. These ceremonies seldom last more than a few weeks. Once the initiation rite is over, the young person has attained full adult status and is treated accordingly. Such a passage from childhood to adulthood is clear-cut and dramatic. Before the initiation rite the youth is a child and is clearly and unmistakably treated as such. After the successful performance of the rite, he is an adult and is definitely treated as an adult.

Young people in our society have no such clear-cut rites of passage. In complex technological societies such as ours, a child needs many years of experience before he is ready to assume the adult role. Even within our own society, the length of the stage of adolescence will vary enormously depending on the young person himself, the socioeconomic class in which he grows up, the type of job he aspires to, and other factors. As Theodore Lidz points out: "The youth whose father is a laborer and who leaves school at sixteen to take a semiskilled job and marries at eighteen has a very brief adolescence. In contrast, the graduate student who is still undecided about his career at twenty-three and has another three or four years of study ahead of him may be considered an adolescent in some respects, for he is still unprepared to assume adult responsibilities at the high level for which he is preparing."[2]

It should be clear, then, that the phenomenon of adolescence does not have firm and fixed boundaries. However, let us arbitrarily define adolescence as that stage of development which takes place between puberty and the attainment of adulthood. Neither of these terms can be defined precisely as to the time of their occurrence. "Puberty" will occur at varying times among any group of preadolescent boys and girls, although, in general, the boys will lag about two years behind the girls. However, for the sake of clarity I will define puberty as beginning around the twelfth or thirteenth year, and thus designate age thirteen as the rough-and-ready time for the beginning of the adolescent stage.

And what seer could possibly define the precise time when any individual attains "adulthood?" Therefore, I arbitrarily set that time on the occasion of the twenty-first birthday. So, for practical purposes, I am defining the stage of adolescence as that period of life between the age of thirteen and twenty-one. On one side of that period, your youngster is a child. When he emerges from the adolescent stage he is an adult, functioning independently of his family, having chosen his vocation, and capable of full adult sexuality.

Within the eight years which make up this crucial period there are enormous psychological gaps among different age groups. A fourteen-year-old is vastly different psychologically from a nineteen-year-old, and the two would not occupy the same "psychological life space." It will clarify things further if I subdivide adolescence into two periods: early adolescence and late adolescence. Remember, there is considerable psychological overlap in making such subdivisions. Nevertheless, I will arbitrarily define "early adolescence" as encompassing the years thirteen, fourteen, and fifteen, with late adolescence beginning at age sixteen, and continuing through twenty.

What is the central developmental task common to both early and late adolescence? It is to form a separate ego identity for oneself. In this sense, the adolescent is silently and unconsciously asking for the first time in his life the question: Who am I? He never raised this question with himself as a child. By the time he passes successfully through the stage of adolescence he will answer that question.

In early adolescence the teen-ager is still trying to answer the question "Who am I?" pretty much within the framework of his family, although with considerable rebellion. In late adolescence, he is grappling with that question within the larger framework of his society in which he is attempting to cope with the very real questions of occupational choice and marital choice.

To put a slightly different twist on it, before adolescence a youngster has no ego identity because he is still dependent on his family. After moving successfully through adolescence the youth does have an ego identity because he has now become independent of his parents and family. Put this way, adolescence is seen as a voyage from dependence to independence.

However, the trip from dependence to independence is not clear-cut and straightforward. It is more like three steps toward independence, followed by two steps backward to dependence. Remember the story I mentioned in chapter four on the first adolescence of the teenage girl who vacillated back and forth on the question of whether or not she wanted her mother to help her select her clothes? Here is a similar true account, cited by Dr. O. Spurgeon English:

> One boy of seventeen wrote his father from boarding school, protesting all the advice he had been getting from him about working harder and making better grades.
>
> "You seem to forget that I am grown up now," he said in his letter. "I'm no longer a child and resent being treated like one. Please respect my independence and let me live my own life. Just remember, Dad, that from now on I am on my own and need no further help from anyone."
>
> The following evening this same "emancipated" son telephoned home and reversed charges to ask for an extra twenty-five dollars to meet some unexpected expenses that had arisen![3]

If there is one key that will help parents to understand the baffling world of the adolescent, it is found in this story and in the previous one I mentioned. Each adolescent is a civil war within himself. Part of him wants to become emotionally independent of his parents and stand on his own two feet. But part wants to remain a dependent child with all the comfort and security associated with still being emotionally dependent on one's parents. A father needs to understand that his teen-ager will fluctuate from day to day and week to week (and sometimes from hour to hour!) between the wish to be independent and the need to be dependent. Once a father grasps this, many of the seemingly baffling inconsistencies of adolescence will fall into place.

So much for the total phase of adolescence. Now let's talk more specifically about early adolescence, from the thirteenth to the sixteenth birthday.

Early adolescence begins with puberty, the time in life when your child's sex glands begin to function. The word "puberty" comes from a Latin word *pubertas* meaning "adult." Although there are enormous variations among teen-agers, girls generally begin puberty sometime during their twelfth year. Boys, lagging behind by approximately two years, begin sometime during their fourteenth year. Puberty is marked in girls by the first menstruation; in boys the most reliable indication of the coming of puberty is the presence of spermatozoa in the urine, which is detectable under a microscope. However, puberty does not happen all at once, and it is not a clear-cut phenomenon either for boys or girls. The first menstruation for girls may be skimpy and irregular, sometimes with months intervening between flows. Boys may have frequent erections but not be able to ejaculate.

Whether early or late, when puberty arrives it means that your child must now cope with an entirely new phenomenon within himself: sexual urges. One important aspect of finding his ego identity is learning to handle his new sexual urges. Coping with sex urges in early adolescence is crude and blind compared to the more sophisticated journey toward sexual maturity in late adolescence.

With the onset of puberty, a teen-ager must adjust to a changing body. Secondary sex characteristics appear now. The girl's breasts begin to develop, her hips widen, and underarm hair and pubic hair begins to grow. Boys also develop underarm hair and pubic hair as well as a fine fuzz on the face which is the signal that in several years they will need to begin shaving. Both boys and girls go through the typical "adolescent growth spurt" during which parents find that no sooner have they bought their adolescent a new dress or outfit than the teen-ager has outgrown it.

The important point is this. Not only does the early adolescent need to adjust to a new and powerful set of sexual impulses, he also must adjust to a new body: a body vastly different from the one he was accustomed to as a child. He is suddenly taller, heavier, of a different build, with a different facial appearance, including, perhaps, the typical adolescent acne. Remember that adolescents have intense feelings. If they think of themselves as too tall or too short, too fat or too thin, too full-breasted or too flat-chested, too pimply, too thin-faced or too fat-faced—all of these things will affect their self-concept. Is it any wonder that many early adolescents feel physically and socially awkward? Adults have had so many years to become familiar with their bodies, that they take them for granted. The early adolescent cannot take his body for granted; it is too new to him and he is too uncomfortable with it. You would be surprised at how the effects of an early adolescent self-image will linger on in later life. A former patient of mine, a strikingly beautiful woman in her thirties, still thought of herself as unattractive. She had been overweight in adolescence and she still unconsciously had a concept of herself as physically unattractive.

The youngster whose puberty and body growth come either particularly early or particularly late often has difficulties adjusting to this. The girl whose puberty comes early, who outstrips her classmates in size, whose suddenly womanish contours set her off from her friends, or who has to cope with the onset of sexual feelings much earlier than her friends, may have great difficulty handling the new and strange feelings associated with this precocious physical and sexual development.

On the other side of the coin, the girl whose puberty comes particularly late and who emotionally does not understand her friends' sudden interest in boys may feel alone and estranged from formerly close friends. She may feel very much behind in her development and worry when, if ever, she will finally become a woman.

Early maturation is much less upsetting to a boy than is late development. Early maturation does not change a boy's body image as drastically as it does a girl's. He may even welcome it because, in his eyes, it makes him more of a "stud" and gives him increased status with his gang. Late maturation is more upsetting because the other boys may tease him that he isn't "with it" yet.

In addition to adjusting to sexual changes and changes in his body and body image, the early adolescent now begins in earnest what he had been working towards tentatively in preadolescence: overcoming his emotional attachment to his parents and family and achieving emotional independence.

Since an adolescent spends many years being emotionally attached to parents, it is not easy to break away. The most typical way is to revolt against them and find flaws in them. It is not easy for a parent to withstand these attacks on his authority and character. Unfortunately many parents take these attacks personally. It would be extremely reassuring to many parents to realize that rather than being an expression of genuine and basic hostility to his parents, the violence and intensity of the adolescent revolt is usually really an indication of how much he loves them! By becoming hostile and critical he can cut the emotional cords of childhood attachment and launch out as a person in his own right.

But the adolescent is still too shaky in his self-confidence to stand on his own emotionally. He needs to belong to a group which can give him the emotional security he craves in order to be able to cut the ties to his parents. This security he finds in his peer group. So the banner of early adolescence contains two words: "Revolt" and "Conform"! He succeeds in revolting against his parents, only by conforming rigidly to his peer group and becoming a slavish imitator of their ways and mores. Since he is still in the process of achieving his own inner identity, he must take comfort in identifying with his group: dressing as they do, wearing his hair as they do, listening to the same music, having the same folk heroes, talking the same special language. This is the paradox of adolescence: the rebels and non-conformists in relation to the adult culture are at the same time the most conservative of conformists with regard to the youth culture! Parents always find it amusing that the same adolescent who criticizes them so fiercely for being conformists in their dress or habits is almost totally unaware that he is doing the very same thing in relation to his peer culture.

Within the youth culture, the early adolescent takes his first insecure and shaky steps in developing toward mature sexuality. In early adolescence these steps are very primitive. Relations between the sexes are complicated by the fact that, as mentioned previously, boys tend to lag about two years behind girls in both their physical and psychological development. For this reason, at a dance of eighth of ninth graders the girls are on one side of the dance floor, willing and eager to dance, and the boys on the other, busily engaged in rapping, horsing around with one another, and pretending they are not afraid to ask the girls to dance.

Early-adolescent boys, particularly, may have "split personalities" in their sexual development. On the one hand, they may be avid readers of *Playboy* magazine, earnest collectors of sexy pictures of women, and may masturbate quite often. They may have an active and vivid fantasy life when it comes to sex, either about movie stars, Playboy bunnies, or women beyond adolescence. However, when it comes to asking a real live girl, a female contemporary, for a date or kissing her or making sexual advances they may be immobilized with fear. Although sexual freedom seems to be moving down to earlier age levels in our society, at the present time there is still not much active sexual involvement in the mature sense of the word between boys and girls until late adolescence. (Although boys and girls in lower socioeconomic classes tend toward sexual involvement at much earlier ages.)

Another very important development which takes place in early adolescence is often overlooked or not given its proper attention by parents, perhaps because it takes place so quietly. I am referring to the giant step forward which the early adolescent takes in his intellectual development. Although it is not as dramatic or outwardly

as noticeable as the sexual and bodily changes of adolescence, there is a spurt in intellectual functioning which corresponds to the physical growth spurt.

This intellectual growth, which has far-reaching implications for adolescent functioning, consists of four basic aspects:

To begin with, the adolescent is now able, for the first time in his life, to think logically about verbal propositions. Contrast this with the way he thought as a child. Although previously he has been able to reason out problems and solve them, his problem-solving and thinking abilities have been limited in a very important way.

Although a child can reason about physical objects, he cannot reason about verbal propositions. For example, if you show a child three toy cars of different sizes he can reason, without having to compare them directly, that if car A is bigger than car B, and car B is bigger than car C, that means that car A is bigger than car C. However, if you ask the child "if Bill is taller than Jim and Jim is taller than Tommy, which one of the three is the tallest?" he ordinarily cannot answer this correctly, although this problem merely states in verbal propositions the problem of the three cars. But an adolescent can answer this question.

Second, the adolescent is now developing the ability to introspect and probe into his own thinking. In fact, during the times that he may seem to be just loafing around, "doing nothing," he is far from "doing nothing." Instead, he is busy introspecting. Typically, children do not do this. Early adolescents talk for the first time about their own ideas, beliefs, and hunches, and know that these are *theirs*. Children state that certain things are true or not true, but do not realize that these statements are really ideas in their own mind rather than necessarily true out in the world of reality.

Third, adolescents begin for the first time to understand metaphor and to be able to grasp nonliteral interpretation of language. Parents may feel this is a rather minor feat, but they should not underestimate its importance. Children are very literal in their interpretation of language. A child has great difficulty in understanding that a word like "skunk" can be applied to a person, because he can't grasp that a human being can be like a skunk in certain respects but not in others. The early adolescent's ability to understand metaphor enormously expands his comprehension, not only of language, but of life. He no longer needs to take everything literally, and he begins to grasp the multiple meanings in a word or term or gesture.

Fourth, for the first time the early adolescent is able to think in terms of ideals and contrary-to-fact conditions. This contrasts with the way he was as a child when he lived exclusively in the here and now. If you say to a child, "Let's suppose you live in China instead of California," he may reply, "But I live in California!" The early adolescent, however, could accept that contrary-to-fact proposition and reason from it.

This newfound ability to think in terms of ideals and contrary-to-fact situations has far-reaching consequences. It enables him to plan realistically for the future, including his future occupation, in ways he was incapable of as a child. This ability to think in terms of ideals also gives him the basis for a new and different perspective on his parents, his teachers, his school, his community, nation, and world. The adolescent can now compare all these people and social structures with ideal versions of them in his mind. These comparisons are also the basis for adolescent disillusionment and are part of the adolescent's attack on his parents as a way of emancipating himself emotionally.

The capacity to think in terms of ideals is also responsible for the idealism which is so characteristic of many adolescents. Adults often overlook or depreciate this, but adolescent idealism is genuine and a very important force in molding the emerging ego identity. The idealism may take the form of a passion for remaking society. It is also no accident that adolescence is the time when so many young people undergo deep and profound religious conversions. When your adolescent says to you, "The trouble with adults today is that they're so materialistic," don't get on your high horse and reply, "Who do you think is paying your bills, particularly your clothing and telephone bills, young lady?" Instead, realize that your daughter's comment is her way of expressing her concern that many people in society are missing the importance of philosophical or spiritual values in life.

The early adolescent's new capacities for intellectual functioning, for reasoning about what the future will bring, and for attempting to govern his life by means of ideals—all these new types of mental abilities enable him to cope with his drives and feelings more effectively. This is particularly helpful at this time in life when he is attempting to handle his newfound sexual impulses and their insistent demands.

After this overview of early adolescence, let's turn to a more detailed inspection of the thirteen-, fourteen-, and fifteen-year-old. Once again, remember that these age profiles are very generalized descriptions of adolescents, based mainly on American middle-class teen-agers, and are not characteristic of adolescents everywhere. They should certainly never be used by a parent to say, "Well, thirteen-year-olds are supposed to have developed such and such. But my Betsy hasn't developed that yet. She must be sadly behind her peer group, and I'd better do something about that." These age profiles should not be used to rank your child as "successful" or "unsuccessful" compared to his peer group. Their only aim is to provide a generalized description so that you can have a more sympathetic understanding of what children of a certain age group are like. One of the main mistakes of parents is to expect children and adolescents to be more mature in their behavior than they are capable of being. These age profiles are given in the hope that you, as a parent, will lower unrealistic adult expectations for your adolescent, and give him the freedom to behave like the thirteen-, fourteen-, or fifteen-year-old that he really is.

THE THIRTEEN-YEAR-OLD

Perhaps the key to understanding the thirteen-year-old is to think of this age as a period in which the adolescent is "inner-directed." The typical outgoingness of the twelve-year-old is now replaced by a turning inwards, a preoccupation with self, and a somewhat moody giving over to internal reveries.

Thirteen is not particularly communicative with parents or adults. He may suddenly become distant and unapproachable. Attempts of adults, particularly parents, to talk to him are often rejected as "prying." Thirteen is beginning his real rebellion, but it is often a silent rebellion. Perhaps it is just as well, sometimes, that we do *not* know what thoughts are going on in their heads!

Thirteen is often "touchy." This is the age of the slammed door and the sulky retreat to his room. Thirteen is very sensitive to real or imagined slights from others. In many respects thirteen may be the least happy of the adolescent years. For many young people it is a nowhere year. Phyllis McGinley has captured this feeling very well in her poem, "Portrait of Girl with Comic Book," and I want to quote part of it here:

> Thirteen's no age at all. Thirteen is nothing.
> It is not wit, or powder on the face,
> Or Wednesday matinees, or misses' clothing,
> Or intellect, or grace . . .
>
> Thirteen keeps diaries and tropical fish
> (A month, at most); scorns jump-ropes in the spring;
> Could not, would fortune grant it, name its wish;
> Wants nothing, everything;
> Has secrets from itself, friends it despises;
> Admits none to the terrors that it feels;
> Owns half a hundred masks but no disguises;
> And walks upon its heels.[4]

Thirteen's turning inward also leads to a search for self-understanding, and a preoccupation with himself. He compares his real self with an idealized self. Due to his adolescent growth spurt, he may agonize over being too tall or too short, too fat or too thin or too weak. Thirteen is a great worrier. What does he worry about? Anything and everything. He worries about his appearance. He worries about school. He worries about what kind of a job he can get in later life. He worries whether he will be successful. He even worries that he is going to worry! As one thirteen put it very perceptively, "I'm going through a stage when everything bothers me."[5]

Many parents take the emotional and social withdrawal of thirteen from them and the family very personally. It often hurts their feelings. Or they may become alarmed and feel they must have made some grave parental errors and that is the reason for their youngster's actions.

I hope you will not jump to conclusions of this kind. Instead, try to understand that this emotional and social withdrawal is a very necessary part of your adolescent's growth at this time.

His emotional "inwardizing" is what enables him to have a deepening and expanding sense of self. A wealth of new experiences are now rushing in upon your thirteen-year-old—his adolescent growth spurt and his new body image, his new sexual awareness, his intellectual growth spurt, and his new awareness of the outside world. All of these new experiences, which hit him with a tremendous psycholog-ical impact, must be mulled over and made a part of his personality structure and the new ego identity he is slowly and painfully con-structing. The inwardizing of thirteen is thus a positive and con-structive growth force. You, as a father, need to understand the reasons for this inwardizing and respect it. Dr. Gesell gives a helpful example:

> A 13-year-old boy joins the family group to enjoy an evening TV program. He is interested, but in the middle of the program his face suddenly assumes a detached and serious expression. He rises unceremoniously and without a word he goes to his room—to cogitate, to ruminate.[6]

Such behavior is *not* an escape from reality for a thirteen year old. On the contrary, he is probing more deeply into *his own psychologi-cal reality* by such inwardizing behavior.

Adults are inclined to speak of the "idle musings" of adolescents. But these musings are *not* idle! They involve wishes, fantasies, ideas, ambitions. They may lead to significant decisions for his future life. He is clarifying and organizing his experiences by inward rehearsal and self-scrutiny.

Sometimes, when an early adolescent is wrapped up in his own thoughts, he may look sullen and glum to his parents. But in actuality he may not be feeling that way at all. If we tease or josh him in a misguided effort to "get him out of his blue funk" we may do him an injustice.

Both boys and girls withdraw from close, confidential relation-ships with their parents at this age. A mother may particularly take this personally if a son, or more usually, a daughter, has had a close relationship with her up to now. You may need to be emotionally supportive of your wife if she feels as if the adolescent is rejecting her rather than going through a typical developmental stage.

Thirteen is also more discriminating than he was at twelve in his choice of friends and companions. Typically, he has fewer friends and is more likely to play by himself or with a chosen friend.

Thirteen is famous as the age in which the mirror is discovered. In fact, he uses the mirror, in Dr. Gesell's vivid phrase, as a "develop-mental device," an auxilliary laboratory tool in constructing his sense of self-identity. Long hours are spent in front of a mirror by *both* boys and girls, in order to try to see how they *really* look.

They carefully study the mirror image to see what changes in dress, hairstyle, makeup, and even facial expression look like. (Any father who has unexpectedly come upon his adolescent practicing smiling or scowling in front of the mirror will attest to that last one!) But the mirror also may lead to agonizing concern if the reflected image does not look as he thinks it should. (If acne blights the facial picture, or the new hairdo does not somehow come off!) But disappointments and all, the mirror plays a constructive role in aiding the early adolescent to define a realistic sense of selfhood.

Movies and the TV screen are another sort of mirror used by the early adolescent. Here he sees an extraordinary variety of youths and grown-ups who represent potential parts of the self he would like to be. In his reading of books, magazines, and comic books he is also consciously or unconsciously identifying himself with characters and personalities.

But it is with his peer group at school and in the neighborhood that he encounters the most powerful images of all—the flesh-and-blood images of his age mates. He feels he must be one of them, in dress, hairstyle, social conventions, slang, etc. One of the important ways of being by himself and yet being connected with his peer group is by using the telephone. One mother defines her daughter's best friend as "a girl permanently connected to my daughter by a telephone line."

Parents report that thirteen is beginning to pay much more attention to his personal appearance. This is partly in keeping with his newfound developmental device, the mirror. Youngsters who have previously been sloppy may now look much better.

Unfortunately for most parents, thirteen's new interest in his personal appearance does not result in a corresponding new interest in taking better care of his clothes or his room. However, his room is one of thirteen's favorite haunts. He spends quite a bit of time there, listening to his radio or records or tapes, doing his homework, reading or just "messing around."

With regard to his emotions, the exuberance and enthusiasm of twelve have been calmed down. Emotionally, thirteen is a time of quieting down in a minor emotional key, with periods of marked moodiness described variously by parents as pessimism, sullenness, secretiveness, or "blue funk."

His emotions are affected by the central theme of withdrawal and hibernation. Many thirteens want to hide or cover up their feelings.

Often they only let their most intimate friends know how they really feel about something.

Expressions of affection and love do not come easily to thirteen. He is more standoffish. Parents should not push him in this respect.

Thirteen's feelings are easily hurt and it is especially important for a father to recognize this. A father's joshing or teasing remark may cut a sensitive thirteen to the quick.

A father may have tended to criticize his youngster about the care of his clothes, or his table manners, or not keeping his room cleaned up, or not helping more around the house, or not working harder at his school subjects. Criticizing a child for such things rarely motivates him to change. A father could wisely give it up entirely. Thirteen is very touchy and will interpret such criticism as nagging or bugging, and will only result in a further withdrawal from the family than would ordinarily occur.

Fathers need to realize that time is on their side. All the things they feel like urging and prodding their adolescents to do will ultimately be accomplished. Thirteen is not going to stay permanently fixated in the way he presently picks up his clothes and takes care of his room!

Thirteen is constantly annoyed by his younger siblings, especially those between six and eleven. Often when he withdraws to his room it is to get away from them.

There is considerable difference between boys and girls in their relationship to their own sex. Friendship is very important to thirteen-year-old girls because they need someone to confide in, someone to whom they can tell their cherished secrets and observations. Girls often go around in threesomes. The threesome may suddenly become a twosome, as two of the girls gang up against the third. Thirteen-year-old girls are very vulnerable to hurt feelings occasioned by being on the outs of the ever-shifting cliques.

Thirteen-year-old boys tend not to have the same closely knit groups. Boys are more likely to clump together in groups of four or five, with each member considering all the others to be his best friends. Boys do not need the intimate atmosphere of shared confidences that girls do. Boys group together, not so much to talk and confide, but to *do* things with their friends—to play basketball or baseball or some other sport, to go to the movies, or to go fishing.

Although a boy may have started masturbating and may have an active sex life in fantasy, he tends to be shy and inhibited in his actual approach to a thirteen-year-old girl. Although they may go to parties or dances from time to time, thirteen-year-old boys do very little dating. Thirteen-year-old girls may be scornful of their male contemporaries and calling them "drips" or "idiots," they may want to date older boys, who are more on their own level of maturity.

The interests and activities of thirteen-year-olds are becoming more individualized. The pursuit of special hobbies and the expression of interest in one specific line are growing more common. Boys typically may be interested in radio, photography, designing cars and planes, and the ever popular model construction. Boys continue to be sports minded as they were at eleven and twelve. Girls may be interested in sewing, knitting, macramé, and cooking. Girls often enjoy creative expression through drawing, painting, or writing. Parents are usually pleasantly surprised to find how little time thirteen spends glued to the television screen, as opposed to earlier years.

Reading increases during this age, and both books and magazines are devoured. Science and sports magazines are big with boys and *Mad* magazine goes over well with both sexes. Music is becoming very important to the thirteen-year-old and he loves to listen to his favorite musical groups.

To summarize, thirteen is an "inwardizing" year of inner consolidation of psychological resources. He has been hit very powerfully by the stimuli of the adolescent growth spurt, his new and changed bodily appearance, and his newfound sexual urges. He withdraws within his inner psychological castle to be able the better to cope with these powerful stimuli.

He is taking the first big but shaky steps along the road to constructing his own ego identity. He is beginning to see himself more clearly. First and foremost, he is concerned about his *outer self*, his external appearance. He is drawn to a mirror as to a magnet for the information it can give him about his hair, his clothes, his facial grimaces and gestures, and his total bodily appearance.

But his *inner self* is also scrutinized with his newly discovered mental powers of observation. He can now stand off and observe himself in a more or less adult manner. He may lack the power to change certain behavior traits at the moment but he can at least acknowledge to himself that at times he can flare up in anger or be lazy or selfish or inconsiderate of others. The ability to see himself as others do represents a major psychological step forward.

Though parents may tend to be upset with thirteen's withdrawal, his touchiness, and moodiness, this time of psychological hibernation is a very valuable developmental period as your early adolescent seeks to form his own ego identity.

THE FOURTEEN-YEAR-OLD

By age fourteen the early adolescent has had a year to adjust to the impact of the new stimuli of his growth spurt, his changing body image and his new sexual feelings and impulses. Consequently, he does not need to retreat into himself as much as he did at thirteen, and he moves out of his "introspective-hermit" stance. At fourteen he is typically more outgoing, with a new self-assurance. He is much less guarded, "touchy," and sensitive. He gets along better with both parents and siblings. He is more open about expressing his feelings and does not keep them to himself as he did last year.

A parent might have needed to walk on eggshells with his thirteen-year-old. This is no longer true for fourteen. He is more capable of an easy give and take with other people, and generates a friendly and more relaxed atmosphere around him. He is no longer fearful that every question asked by another person is a prying into his personal affairs, so he talks more freely, in an outgoing, straightforward manner. His whole personality structure undergoes a new expansiveness. His basic relationships within the family are more genial and less tense.

Fourteen is an age when friendship and socialization with his gang again become very important. Boys band in groups and girls do the same. Fourteen spends a huge amount of his free time in social gatherings of one sort or another. In addition to such group gatherings, a great deal of socialization goes on over the telephone which gets considerably increased usage past age thirteen. Girls are particularly avid users of "Mother Bell" and her communication device. The importance of the telephone to fourteen-year-old communication is illustrated by this rhyme which appeared in a high school anthology of poetry:

> The telephone was invented
> For the use of communication;

> But now-a-days its basic use
> Is for teen-age conversation.
> In future years, I predict
> Our parents will combine
> And banish all our telephones
> To keep us off the line![7]

The incessant chatter of fourteens, either in person or by phone should not be thought of as "idle talk." Talk is a means by which fourteen learns about human personality and social relationships. Girls use conversation in this way more than boys. What do they talk about? Parents, teachers, boys, movie stars, musical groups and folk heroes, and, above all—themselves. They talk about anything and everything. Talk is thus used by the fourteen-year-old as a sort of do-it-yourself course in applied human psychology.

Fourteen is beginning to use his intelligence in new ways. He develops a new competency in his use of language, particularly in comprehension of words and fluency in using them. He takes a new and genuine pleasure in mastering new words and putting them to conversational use. His use of logical and rational thinking also takes a decided upswing at this age. The famous philosopher and humanitarian Albert Schweitzer, for example, relates that in his fourteenth year he felt a "passionate need to think."[8] Because of his new powers of reasoning, fourteen is now capable of self-criticism which he has not made use of before. Along with this new capacity for self-evaluation is a new degree of self-acceptance.

The physical and sexual development of boys and of girls at this age are, in general, quite different. Very few girls have not menstruated by their fourteenth year, and the majority are well established in their menstrual patterns. The typical fourteen-year-old girl's body resembles that of a young woman more than that of the child she used to be. Her adult height growth is nearly completed during this year; her breasts approach full adult size; and her pubic hair is full and dense.

In contrast, fourteen is a transition year for most boys. At thirteen, most youngsters still look like boys; by fifteen most will look like men. Fourteen is a no-man's land. This is the period of most rapid height growth for the majority of boys.

By the end of the fourteenth year, a large majority of boys will experience ejaculation in one form or another. For some this will take the form of their first nocturnal emissions or "wet dreams," as they are more commonly known. For others the source of their first ejaculation will be masturbation. Many boys have been masturbating since they were twelve; others may not begin until fourteen; others will begin still later.

Fourteen is an age when both boys and girls need and seek information about sex. There is a new level of sex information which fourteen has reached and he now has questions about intercourse, birth control, venereal disease, homosexuality, prostitution, and other topics. The greater explicitness of sexual matters in movies and the mass media are also causing fourteen year olds to be more searching and sophisticated in the questions they ask. A fourteen-year-old boy, for example, may purchase *Playboy* magazine at the drugstore and read quite adult and sophisticated articles about sex (and look at the photographs of the nudes as well).

At this point it may be very helpful to give your fourteen-year-old son or daughter a copy of Dr. David Reuben's book, *Everything You Always Wanted to Know about Sex (But Were Afraid to Ask)*, which can be obtained in paperback. (Even though there are some factual mistakes, on the whole it offers a great deal of useful information to an adolescent boy and girl.)

An example from my clinical practice may highlight the intense need for sexual information by means of such a book. Several years ago I had a fourteen-year-old boy in therapy who was an under-achiever in school, and quite resistant to reading his assignments and doing his lessons. His father was particularly concerned because, according to him, "The boy just has no interest in reading whatso-ever." In one therapy session the teen-ager brought up the topic of sex, I inquired if he would be interested in reading a good book on sex if I could get his parents to buy it. The boy was amazed. "Sure I would!" he said. "Could you really get them to buy me one?" That night I phoned his father, who agreed to buy the book.

The following week the father told me what had happened. He gave him the book after dinner. The boy thanked him effusively, and immediately went upstairs to his room with the book under his arm. He closed his door and apparently read steadily until eleven o'clock, when his mother noticed the light under his door and said, "Hey, it's past your bedtime!" "Just a few minutes more, Mom, until I finish this part!" he said. After the father related, the incident to me, I commented, "And this is the boy you said had no interest in reading!"

Fourteen not only wants information on sex, he wants the

opportunity to discuss various sexual topics and work out his own value judgments about them. If your son or daughter wants to discuss these things and you feel comfortable about it, this may be a not-to-be-missed opportunity, for in the later adolescent years he will not want to discuss such subjects with a parent. On the other hand, your fourteen-year-old may prefer to talk over such subjects in a more neutral atmosphere than that of the family, such as a sex-education class in school or a church-school class or young people's group.

With regard to his emotional life, fourteen has taken a decided turn for the better. In general, he rushes out to meet life enthusiastically and eagerly. He does not have the "closed" type of personality he did at thirteen, and more openly expresses both affectionate and angry feelings. He does not keep things bottled up. Happy moods are far more common than sad ones. Parents may particularly appreciate the nice touch of humor he may develop at this age. However, from time to time he may have outbursts of violent anger or unhappy crying. Sometimes fathers expect that at this age, an adolescent, especially a boy, is "too old to cry." Then the boy gets a little lecture, exhorting him to be more manly, take things bravely, and stop crying. Fathers must understand that crying is an appropriate response to deep feelings of unhappiness *at any age*, including adulthood and old age. Our tear ducts have been provided by Mother Nature for a reason, and they do not dry up when we reach the age of twenty-one.

In general, fourteen is made of tougher emotional stuff than thirteen; he is not as vulnerable; on the whole, fourteen accepts himself as he is. This self-acceptance usually results in a happy and salutary change in the family atmosphere. His parents are now able to communicate with him much more easily, and the whole family relationship takes a turn for the better. Throughout the thirteenth year, parents often anticipated some kind of unpleasant, negative, or critical response from thirteen to their communications. The more positive and outgoing responses of fourteen are a huge relief.

This does not mean that all is complete sweetness and light. There are still disputes about hours of coming in at night, homework, clothes, care of room, household chores, and other matters. It is still important for parents to make a distinction between feelings and actions, allowing your youngster to express his feelings, but being firm about what actions you permit and what you do not. As one fourteen-year-old girl put it, "It's most important for a father to have a firm hand and keep things in order."9

This is the year in which the expanding social interests of *both* boys and girls include a real and genuine pull toward the opposite sex. Boys don't stand on the sidelines as much at dances and parties. They mix better with girls and are able to carry on a conversation better. Fourteen-year-old girls, however, still prefer to go to parties and on dates with older boys, since they are more mature. The parties most enjoyed are those that erupt spontaneously with little advance planning. This kind of party usually occurs in the summer-time and with older boys.

Boys go in more for double-dating at this age than individual dating; individual dating is more common with girls. Dating activities may include a movie, a sports event, swimming or skating, parties, picnics, or parties at home.

There is considerable contrast between boys' and girls' interest in sports. Girls do not have the drive and push for sports that boys do. Boys are not only keenly interested in participating in sports, but they follow their favorite college and professional teams avidly. Fourteen spends a great deal of time in social gatherings, where the sexes are separate or in mixed company. The social gatherings are fluid and shifting. Membership in after-school clubs is of great interest. Each school will have its own variety of club and there should be at least one club that will interest your youngster. There are athletic clubs, science clubs, musical clubs, drama clubs, bowling clubs, chess clubs, and 57 other varieties.

Interest in records, jazz, and rock music, which was strong at thirteen, increases at fourteen. Boys are often intensely interested in cars and motorcycles at this age. They delight in reading "hot rod" or motorcycle magazines.

So there he is—your fourteen-year-old—typically exuberant, out-going and enthusiastic. Gone is the touchy, hermitlike isolation of thirteen; on the whole he is a happier and more integrated person, in the family, at school, and in his extracurricular activities.

THE FIFTEEN-YEAR-OLD

Unfortunately for parents, the outgoing, friendly, and enthusiastic demeanor of their fourteen-year-old gives way to a period of disequilibrium at fifteen. The contrast with the mood of the previous year has caused some observers to label this period the "fifteen-year-old slump."

Since he entered the stage of early adolescence your child has been pushing toward adulthood in great strides. Let me sketch it out this way from a year-by-year perspective. Age thirteen is when your youngster is bombarded by the new adolescent stimuli of a physical growth spurt, a new body image, and new and intense sexual drives. He finds these new stimuli hard to cope with and responds by withdrawing into his shell. By fourteen he has learned to cope with these new stimuli and he can, therefore, be more enthusiastic, self-affirming, and outgoing. But age fifteen is a transitional period to the next stage: late adolescence. In late adolescence, your son or daughter must cope in a truly serious manner with assuming his own self-identity. This means thinking seriously about what vocation he will pursue and what education he will need to prepare for this vocation, and learning to relate to the opposite sex in a fully mature and adult manner. The stage of late adolescence begins at approximately sixteen, but your fifteen-year-old catches glimpses of it, and finds even this difficult to cope with.

The important thing to understand is that at fifteen your adolescent is beginning in earnest to separate himself from parents and other adults. This is the time when an adolescent often would rather "die" than be seen with his parents. If he absolutely has to go with his parents to some school or social function he will often hang back two or three steps behind as if to say to possible onlookers, "I'm really not with these people walking ahead of me!" Fifteen-year-olds typically refuse all invitations to participate in family outings or activities, preferring to be by themselves or with their peers. If forced to attend, they make it abundantly clear to everybody that they are not pleased to be there.

Your greatest psychological problem as a father will be the danger of taking your adolescent's detachment from the family as if it were a personal rejection of you. It is not. It is a necessary psychological growth process: a drive for independence, freedom, and selfhood.

Related to this drive for independence, is a tendency of the fifteen-year-old to be guarded and uncommunicative that will remind you of the way he was at thirteen. Fifteen is waving the banner of freedom and independence, and he resents anything that limits or infringes. What to you may be perfectly reasonable questions about where he is going and what he will be doing, will be often taken by him as if you are using Gestapo interrogation techniques.

The rising spirit of independence is often expressed in very crude and naive forms. These may include such things as keeping to himself, not responding to greetings when he comes home, fiercely resisting all restrictions on his behavior no matter how reasonable they are, dashing out of the house in the midst of a conversation and slamming the door. Some fifteens engage their parents in a cold war, so that the parents feel they are harboring a hostile, sullen, and silent stranger in their midst. However, other parents find their fifteen-year-old reasonably easy to get along with, but very seclusive.

The important thing to remember, as a father, is that whether the manifestations of a new spirit of independence are severe or mild, they are to be respected and taken seriously. In his own mind, your fifteen-year-old is no longer a child. He does not want to be treated in any way similar to the way children are handled. In his mind, he is on the verge of adulthood even though you can see that this is far from being the case. This typical bright flame of independence is seen very clearly in the comment of one fifteen-year-old girl. She quite seriously stated that she would like to be a rich woman and give scholarships so that all fifteen-year-old girls could go to school away from home![10] (Incidentally, perhaps I should point out that I am opposed to sending high-school teen-agers away to boarding school. In spite of their fierce demand for independence, they still need the security of home and family, no matter how much they rebel against it. College is the time for an adolescent to go away from home, not high school.)

In addition to his fierce addiction to independence, the fifteen-year-old is entering a new phase of increasing self-awareness and perceptiveness. In this sense, he is, as Dr. Gesell puts it, "not an enlarged, super-version of Fourteen, but rather a Sixteen in the making."[11]

He is learning to be more observant of the personality characteristics of both his peers and adults. He is able to be more analytic and objective about he personality traits of his parents (often to their dismay!) Fifteen also zeroes in on the personality characteristics of his teachers and may often be quite critical. For this reason, teaching this age group is not an easy job.

Fourteen, you remember, was more likely to take life as he found it and accept himself and life for what they are. Fifteen is more serious and complex. Fifteen could well be termed Mr. Amateur Psychologist. For he is consumed with an intense desire to understand himself and other people. He wants to know why he feels as he does about other people and situations, and why he acts as he does.

The feelings of fourteen are crude and simple, compared to the new complexities of feeling at fifteen. He is learning to be aware of subtler and more complex feelings. This new awareness expresses itself in new sensitivities, new irritabilities, new delights, and new suspicions. The new awareness of feelings extends into intellectual and aesthetic areas. This makes him capable of understanding literary and artistic expressions which would have passed over his head at fourteen.

What adults often think of as lazy or apathetic behavior is merely fifteen's need to be alone. He is apparently doing "nothing." But, in actuality, he is mulling things over so that he can more clearly and precisely understand his own feelings or those of another person. After all these years, I can still remember that when I was fifteen I spent a whole Saturday evening in my room listening to what I thought of as "romantic" music on my record player, and mulling over what to do with my life and what vocation to choose.

At times the drive to increased self-awareness of fifteen may take a negative and critical turn against himself. He may have times of feeling depressed, discouraged, or just plain confused. One of the reasons for the depressed feelings at this age is that adolescents are just now becoming *emotionally* aware that the happy dependence of childhood is gone. Suddenly they are *emotionally* beginning to grasp the fact that they are on the threshold of adulthood, which involves making basic decisions about career and marriage. In comparison to fourteen, the fifteen-year-old is able to project himself much more realistically into the adult future. In this sense, whereas fourteen has both feet planted happily in the stage of early adolescence, fifteen has one foot in early adolescence, and one foot tentatively and hesitantly in the next stage of late adolescence. All in all, fifteen is a quiet, somber, and thoughtful period. Incidentally, parents should not be fooled when some fifteens try to cover up the gloomy and discouraged side of themselves by giving the impression of being "tough" or "hard-boiled."

Parents are likely to see more of the somber, glum, and apathetic side of fifteen than are his peers. He likes to be with groups, at school and in the community. He is gregarious, and enjoys gatherings of his peers, even though he plays the isolationist role at home. He likes spontaneous, informal groupings that include both boys and girls.

It is the group life with his peers that enables many fifteens to enjoy school, for otherwise they are often very critical of school and their teachers. School life becomes a way of loosening their emotional ties to home and family and achieving more independence. However, even though fifteen moves in groups, the close circle of friends may not be as important to him as they were at fourteen.

Fifteen prefers spontaneous and changing interpersonal relationships. He likes the casual atmosphere of some "hangout," where both sexes can be together, such as a soft-drink bar, a hamburger shop, or an ice-cream parlor. He wants to be where he can sit and talk, have a coke, listen to a juke box or dance. He likes a place where he can drift in and out as the mood strikes him.

Fifteens generally are not easy to teach. Teachers of high-school sophomores speak of this year as the "Fifteen-year-old slump." (Incidentally, the word "sophomore" is derived from two Greek words, one meaning "wise," and the other meaning "foolish"!) Parents may feel that this describes their fifteen-year-old perfectly. For at time he seems so worldly wise and, at other times, he seems unbelievably foolish.

Although fifteen is in rebellion against authority at school and at home, his adjustment to the requirements of school and home depends to a considerable extent on how the authority handles his rebellion. One key to the handling of fifteen-year-olds, for both teachers and parents, is a wise nonresponse to his opinionated and provocative remarks. Some fifteens delight in hurling such remarks as, "You and mother are so shallow and materialistic in your outlook on life," or "I've decided I'm a Communist," or "This family is hopelessly old-fashioned; it belongs in the nineteenth century!" Many parents rise to such bait with a highly defensive attitude, and the verbal battle is on. Similar conflicts arise between students and teachers who unwisely respond defensively to such provocative remarks.

Fifteen is a disastrous year in school for some students, especially boys, as shown by the rise in dropouts following this year. For rebellious boys who are not doing well and who hate school, parents would do well to consider an alternative solution: a half-day work experience. This may be of enormous help to some boys if the right type of apprentice job can be found in relation to the high-school courses he is taking (a helper in a garage or motorcycle shop, a worker in a business office or on a farm, etc.). A successful work experience can sometimes bring about a dramatic change in a boy's attitude to himself, to life, and to the reduced schedule of school subjects.

Boy-girl relationships have become more sophisticated at fifteen, although, as usual, the girls are outwardly more interested in boys than vice versa. One boy expresses a typical male attitude at this age as follows: "Never been to a dance yet that required the taking of a girl!"[12]

Fifteens almost always have a good time at parties or in group activities. Sex is very much on the minds of many fifteens although there is enormous variation in "how far" an individual will go with members of the opposite sex. At one extreme, there is no apparent interest at all in the opposite sex, and no dating at all. Parents should not be deceived by this apparent lack of interest, for although the adolescent may not actually have dates, in the safe secrecy of his own mind he has *thought* a great deal about it. Other fifteens have no interest in sex, such as the boy who is absorbed in sports or the girl who is entirely devoted to her studies and girl-type activities. However, other fifteens may be having intercourse with relative frequency, usually with only one partner rather than promiscuously with a number of partners.

Boys are still quite avidly interested in sports, both as participants and spectators. Boys are also especially interested in care of motor-cycles, particularly because of the possible imminence of getting a driver's license. This is the year when driver-education courses are given in high school, and most adolescents are quite eager to take them. Some boys are merely interested in learning to drive; others show a great mechanical interest in cars, and like to hang around garages and pick up information. If you happen to know a great deal about cars or motorcycles and enjoy tinkering, your interests may become an excellent meeting ground and communication bridge between you and your fifteen-year-old.

Girls are usually quite different in their activities from boys except for their common interest in meeting in social groups. Girls, in general, are less active and less sports minded. If a girl is interested in sports, she is more likely to be interested in participating in in-dividual sports such as skiing, ice-skating, swimming, tennis, sailing, or horseback-riding. Girls like to sit around and talk; boys prefer to be engaged in some activity. Much of the girls' conversation centers on that old familiar, favorite topic: boys!

This ends our brief description of fifteen—not an easy age to understand. Indeed, at times fifteen is an age in which it is hard for the adolescent to understand himself! His battle cry, whether expressed silently and passively, or loudly and agressively, is: "I want more independence; I don't want to be treated like a kid anymore!" To parents he seems rebellious, critical, and at times ungrateful, confused, dissatisfied, and glum. However, all of these negative emotions should be viewed as the outer husk of positive growth forces. These positive growth forces will usher in the healthy self-confidence and nondefensive independence which usually begins to flower at sixteen.

Now that I have given you an overview of the stage of early adolescence and sketched in the psychological age profiles of a typical thirteen-, fourteen-, and fifteen-year-old, I want to turn to what you as a father can do to help your adolescent achieve his maximum emotional and intellectual growth. In addition, I want to suggest how you can avoid many of the needless problems and hassles that many parents get into with their adolescent sons and daughters during this stage.

12
Early Adolescence II: What Parents Can Do

Perhaps a more realistic title for this chapter would be: "What Parents Can Do to Guide Themselves More Wisely During Their Son Or Daughter's Early Adolescence." In the last chapter I pointed out some of the typical biological and psychological changes that will be taking place in your teen-ager between his thirteenth and sixteenth birthdays. That, unfortunately, is where many magazine articles and books stop. They talk about the psychological changes erupting in the adolescent, but ignore the psychological forces breaking forth in the parent in response.

In these articles and books the parent is provided with a set of "cookbook" rules and recipes as to how he should manage his adolescent through this or that phase of his growth. Unfortunately, they overlook the existence of psychological forces in the parent *of which he is not aware*, since they are on an unconscious level. And it is precisely these unconscious forces that will probably prevent him from handling his adolescent in a reasonable and sensible manner.

If it were not for the existence of unconscious psychological forces both in the adolescent and the parent, we could say that adolescence is basically a learning experience of approximately eight years' duration. During this time the adolescent is practicing the adult role under the experienced coaching of a friendly adult, his parent. I want to use a dramatic and exaggerated analogy to clarify how unconscious psychological forces in both learner and coach make the period of adolescence such a difficult one for both of them.

Suppose, for example, that the father of an adolescent girl of fifteen is an excellent tennis player. Imagine that all she needs to do during her fifteenth year is to learn to play a good game of tennis. And all he needs to do in relation to her is to teach her how to play tennis. He establishes a routine of regular practice sessions and gives her instruction in forehand, backhand, how to serve, volley, rush the net, etc.

At first, things go well. She is mastering the different strokes and techniques of the game under her father's expert coaching. Then, all of a sudden, strange and upsetting things begin to happen. One morning she blows up and screams at her father: "I hate you; you're always prying into my personal business!" She doesn't show up for her regularly scheduled session that afternoon. When her father asks what happened and why she didn't come to the tennis court, she does not even reply. The next day, as she is practicing volleying, she deliberately hits the ball at her father as hard as she can. When he remonstrates with her, she mutters something sullenly under her breath.

The effect of all of this is to make her father absolutely furious. "Here I am spending so much of my valuable time trying to teach her tennis and she treats me with such ingratitude!" he thinks. With angry feelings seething inside, it becomes very difficult for him to teach her tennis in a friendly or encouraging manner. Things are particularly difficult for him to handle because he is completely bewildered by his daughter's behavior. He has no idea why she is acting this way. But he resolves to grit his teeth and put up with it because, after all, his job is to teach her to play tennis.

Just as he is beginning to adjust to her vicious and angry outbursts, she suddenly shows up on the court in a bikini instead of tennis clothes. She very obviously wiggles her body and flaunts her breasts as she practices tennis shots. He is upset to discover that he is having intense sexual feelings. He thinks to himself: "This is terrible; I shouldn't be having horny thoughts toward my own daughter!" To make matters worse, she suggests quite brazenly that they could repair to a nearby bar for a couple of drinks after the morning's practice, and then check into a motel and "live it up." At that point, her father explodes: "What kind of ugly talk is that, young lady? Is this the child I raised to be a decent and respectable girl, talking like a tramp?"

Some fathers, reading this analogy, may think it completely foolish and farfetched. Yet I mean to show you in this chapter that the psychological interchanges that took place between father and daughter and disrupted the coaching of tennis are exactly the same kinds of psychological interchanges, *on an unconscious level,* that disrupt the attempts of a father who seeks to guide a son or daughter through those difficult years.

Let's take a bird's-eye view of child development up to the adolescent years, so that we can see more clearly the immense psychological changes that a father has to cope with when his child reaches adolescence.

For many years a father has been accustomed to seeing his son or daughter behave like a child. He takes for granted this child who comes home from school or school activities anxious to tell his parents about them. He takes for granted a child who, though disobedient at times, nevertheless is generally eager for help with projects and to go to the movies or fishing or camping or on weekend trips with the family.

Now, suddenly, this child is no longer a child. Almost overnight, there is a stranger in the family, who looks like the child of the past, but who acts quite differently. This stranger is at times uncommunicative, seclusive, unreasonable, sarcastic, and is subject, without rhyme or reason, to sudden and frequent outbursts of emotion. Any attempts to reach this stranger in a friendly fashion are usually met with even further withdrawal.

As if this weren't enough for a poor father to cope with, Mother Nature adds still another upsetting stimulus to this "former child." Do you remember the "family romance" I described in chapter five when discussing the preschool stage? It is the time when the pre-school boy begins to feel romantic toward his mother and rivalrous with his father, and it is a normal stage of development. By the time he is six, the normal boy gets over this rivalry and wants to be like his father. He now knows he cannot marry mommy, so he wants to marry a woman like mommy when he grows up. The same thing happens to little girls in reverse. If a father understands this normal "family triangle" at this age, he can handle it adequately and it need cause no concern.

From about age six until puberty, the family romance lies dormant. In some respects (but not all, by any means!) the child from six to puberty can be thought of as "neuter." But suddenly, with the onslaught of puberty, all that changes with dramatic intensity. The former "child" is now a full-blown, but by no means mature or sophisticated, *sexual being.*

The new sexuality of his child may be a difficult thing for a father to adjust to. For one thing, the "family romance" reappears during the adolescent years. But this time it is very different from the simple attraction of the preschool years. Then the child's sex glands had not developed and his urges were nowhere nearly as intense as they are in early adolescence. How difficult a problem this is for many mothers and fathers can be seen by the "conspiracy of silence" which exists on the subject of the "family romance" during the adolescent years.

Thousands of articles are published, in popular magazines on the subject of raising children. But I have yet to see a single article discuss in any depth this subject of the "family romance" during adolescence. In fact, some fathers reading this will be shocked that I assert that such a thing takes place. But shocking or not, it happens. The "family romance" of the preschool years occurs all over again, but on a higher, more complex and sexualized level. Teen-age boys develop a romantic and sexualized interest in their mothers and regard their fathers as rivals; teen-age girls develop a romantic and sexualized interest in their fathers and regard their mothers as rivals. This normally takes place on an unconscious rather than a conscious level.

I want to emphasize that this is a *normal* part of the development of adolescence. Its purpose, as in the preschool years is to prepare the boy and girl for a romantic and sexualized attachment to a spouse. In early adolescence the attachment is still to the parent of the opposite sex. By late adolescence, if the psychological development of the teen-ager has proceeded normally, he will have broken away from the attachment to his mother, and moved on to mature heterosexual relationships with girls. The girl will have broken away from her attachment to her father, and moved on to the same type of relationships with boys.

Some fathers are blissfully unaware of such things because romantic and sexual feelings do not emerge directly and obviously. The disguised form may be so remote from the original romantic and sexual feeling it is no wonder the bewildered parent does not pick up any connection between the two.

For example, the mother of a fourteen-year-old boy came to me for counseling to help her handle her son. She said, "I don't know what's gotten into him. I'm at the end of my rope trying to cope with him." I asked what it was about his behavior that was so disturbing, and she told me: "I'm a good cook and he used to love my cooking, but now he hates it and doesn't hesitate to tell me. The other day, when I put dinner on the table he said, 'Do I have to eat this garbage?' He criticizes everything I do. He tells me I'm getting fat and ought to diet. He seems to be trying deliberately to be as obnoxious as possible. And he's not this way with his father. What's wrong? Have I done something terribly bad as a parent?" I told her I would give the boy a thorough psychological evaluation and report my results. Then we would see what needed to be done to handle the situation.

Once I completed the testing, the situation became quite clear. I called the mother in to explain what was going on. I told her: "Your son is beginning to feel romantic and sexual feelings toward you, and these are scaring the living daylights out of him.

"He doesn't know how to handle these feelings because they are taking place mostly at an unconscious level. The only way he is able to cope with them at the present time if to be as obnoxious as he possibly can—to put emotional distance between the two of you. That's the only way he feels safe in the face of new and disturbing romantic and sexual feelings, feelings which he believes are wrong to have toward you, since you are his mother. Far from being an indication that he hates you, his obnoxious behavior is actually his way of coping with intense affectionate feelings for you."

The test results indicated that the boy was a normal adolescent and did not need psychotherapy. Once his mother understood what was going on, she could cope with it, even though his obnoxious behavior did get on her nerves at times. The behavior persisted for about six or seven months, and then he found himself a girl friend.

Lo and behold! he didn't need to be obnoxious toward his mother anymore!

Here is another example, by Dr. Anita Bell, of a situation between a father and his fourteen-year-old girl. She had well-developed breasts, wore bras, and no longer looked like a child. She would frequently turn to her father and complain about the way her mother treated her. She would hug her father and sit on his lap, causing him to feel a momentary sexual arousal. She frequently sat astride, facing him, while on his lap as she chatted about the happenings of the day. To his amazement and embarrassment he found himself having erections at such times. The father accepted these flirtatious overtures from his daughter, but denied the implications they had for him by thinking of his daughter as only a child. She cooperated in this fantasy by behaving as a very young child at such moments and not like a fourteen-year-old.

About a year later, however, his daughter began to go out with boys, and the father reacted with self-righteous protests that his daughter was too young. But his righteous attitude was his psychological defense mechanism against his own sexual feelings toward his daughter. In actuality, his daughter had withdrawn emotionally from him and was trying to find a new love object in the boys she was dating. But the father, unaware of his own feelings, could not tolerate this and so could not help his daughter resolve the "family romance" in a normal manner.[1]

This last example brings up another problem. Parents have to face the fact that their child is no longer a "neuter" but a highly charged sexual being with romantic and sexual feelings toward his parents. In addition, the parents now must cope with new sexual feelings toward their adolescents. What makes this particularly difficult is that in our culture nobody tells parents that they are going to have such feelings toward their own teen-agers. There is a vast conspiracy of silence in this area. Over it hangs the dreadful, unutterable, unspoken word: "incest."

Of course, to use the word "incest" to describe what I am talking about is to misunderstand the situation completely. Remember what I have emphasized again and again throughout this book: *there is a wide difference between feelings and actions.* Incest consists of actions. Although it does occur in our society, it happens in an infinitesimally small number of families where actual sexual relations take place between father and daughter or, in rarer cases, between mother and son.

I am not talking about *actions* at all, but about *feelings.* In every family where there are teen-agers; the teen-ager has sexual feelings about the parent of the opposite sex and the parent has sexual feelings about the teen-ager. Many parents have repressed these feelings completely and have no conscious awareness of them. They believe it would be terrible wrong to have such feelings toward their own children. Of course, it would be wrong and psychologically destructive to engage in sexual *acts* with one's own children. But psychological *feelings* are normal and cannot be helped. There is no mechanism provided by which a father's sex glands can function normally at all times *except* when his good-looking daughter walks by!

So I'm trying to break the conspiracy of silence and tell you that it is quite normal for a father to have romantic and sexual feelings and fantasies about his teen-age daughter and for her to have them about him. The same goes for his wife and a teen-age son. What is important is that you accept the *normality* of such feelings and not repress them into your unconscious mind and think that you are "dirty" or "bad." When fathers repress such feelings, it prevents them from being truly helpful to their daughters in guiding them through the family romance until they find a man of their own.

For example, a sixteen-year-old girl I had in therapy a few years ago was quite bewildered by her father's behavior towards her. She told me: "He used to be such a good father and we were so close. Then a few years ago he started treating me like he wouldn't touch me with a ten-foot pole. He finds fault with the boys I date, and he accuses me of things I've never done. I've never had sexual relations with a boy, but my father calls me names like 'slut' or 'tramp.' And I haven't done anything bad at all!" she told me with tears in her eyes. The problem was that with the onset of puberty, the father couldn't handle his own sexual feelings toward his daughter, or even admit to himself that he had such feelings. That was the reason he was treating her so severely.

Acknowledge to yourself that it is normal and natural to have romantic and sexual feelings toward a teen-age daughter. Accept the feelings and keep them to yourself. Do not tell your daughter because to do so would probably frighten her. Just accept both her romantic and sexual feelings for you and your romantic and sexual feelings for her as a normal and natural part of the family romance during adolescence.

You might as well learn to enjoy the situation in early adolescence because, by late adolescence, your daughter probably will be dating regularly and you will no longer be the object of her romantic fantiasies. I remember one day when my own daughter was fourteen and we were talking together in the living room. She looked up at me as a teen-age girl might look up at the star halfback on the football team, and said: "Oh, Daddy, I'm so lucky to have a father like you, because you're so intelligent and educated and just seem to know everything about everything!"

When moments like that come, father, you might as well enjoy them because your daughter is *not* going to say things like that when she's seventeen or nineteen!

I have spent some time describing the reactions of *both* parent and adolescent to the revival of the family romance. However, I don't want to overemphasize it or make you think it is the most important thing about parent-child relationships in adolescence. It is not; for even more important is the adolescent's quest for independence.

Let us put together the two most difficult things a father has to cope with when a child enters puberty and early adolescence. For many years he has regarded his son or daughter as a *neuter child.* Now, suddenly, with the beginning of puberty and adolescence a father must cope with a son or daughter who is no longer neuter, but sexual, no longer a child, but a *half-adult.* It is not an easy job!

FROM CHILD TO HALF-ADULT

Let me use an analogy to illustrate the difficulties of handling the transition your youngster goes through from being a child to being a half-adult.

During my career I have taught every grade, from nursery through college and graduate school. There is no question but that the hardest grades to teach, the children who are the most difficult to cope with, are grades seven and eight, the years of early adolescence.

Through the fifth grade, children look to their teacher as an authority. Oh, they may disobey or break the rules occasionally, but in their heart of hearts they feel they are wrong to do so. They will quote you to their friends or other people: "My teacher says . . ." In the sixth grade this attitude begins to change and by the seventh and eighth grades you have definitely been dethroned. They have ceased being obedient (or occasionally disobedient) children, and are now challenging and provoking half-adults.

The same thing that happens to teachers of early adolescents happens to parents of early adolescents. Deep inside of us, some sort of monologue like this is going on: "I feel emotionally discarded by my child. This really hurts me deeply although I don't like to admit it to myself. My youngster doesn't seem to want to be involved with me and the family anymore. Our home is just a place where he eats and sleeps and talks endlessly on the telephone. How could he treat me this way after all the things I've done for him?"

At this point, for many parents the down-deep hurt feelings shift gear into angry feelings, and the parent begins to say to himself: "Maybe I've just been too easy and permissive with this kid. I've let him get away with murder and that's why he's acting like this: defying me and smarting off and not being cooperative around the house. So I'll get tough and let him know once and for all who's boss around here. He'll toe the line or else!"

Of course, once a parent adopts such a hard-nosed attitude, then what had been essentially normal emotional withdrawal and normal rebellion becomes escalated into a bitter and fruitless conflict. The more the parent drops emotional bombs on the adolescent, the more guerilla warfare he engages in, and so the parent-adolescent warfare escalates, ending in a complete breakdown in communications.

To prevent such situations from occurring, I have stressed in this book the importance of learning to view adolescent rebellion as a *positive step forward* in the development of your teen-ager. However, even though *we are intellectually* able to view it as a positive step forward, it still hurts our feelings when our adolescent son or daughter rebels and withdraws emotionally. Parents need to acknowledge the existence of these hurt feelings, to tolerate them, and to work them through. It usually helps a great deal if we talk to parents of other adolescents and find that their youngsters are acting in the same way. It has been my observation that fathers, as compared to mothers, repress and block out their hurt feelings in this situation. All the father is aware of is that he is angry at his adolescent's behavior, but he is often unaware that underneath his angry feelings are hurt feelings. It is important for a father to get the hurt feelings to the surface and be able to talk about them to his wife or a friend. As long as the hurt feelings are repressed and unconscious he cannot deal with them.

Once again, the most comforting thing I can say to a father about his reactions to his adolescent's behavior, is this: You may feel that you are losing your son and daughter and that you are very unimportant in their lives. Don't be deceived by their surface behavior. You are still important to them, but you are no longer important in the same way as when they were children. You are now important in a new and somewhat uncomfortable way: the way a parent is important to someone who is no longer a child but a half-adult. But hang in there. Don't get discouraged and give up! For when your child emerges from adolescence, you will be important to him in a new way: the way an older adult parent is important to a young adult son or daughter.

Textbooks emphasize how much turmoil and stress there is in the life of the adolescent and how difficult it is for him to achieve the psychological growth required during those years. I am trying to point out that exactly the same thing holds true for parents. A great deal of difficult and unpleasant psychological growth is required of parents as they adjust to the drastic behavior changes their youngsters go through in the adolescent years. Sometimes I think that all parents of adolescents should have free group-therapy classes once a week! There we could pour out our psychological woes to each other and receive emotional support, thus helping ourselves guide our parental canoes down the treacherous rapids of our children's adolescence.

ADOLESCENTS AND DRUGS

If there is anything more scary to deal with than drugs I don't know what it would be. The plain fact is that drugs frighten parents. The drug world and the drug scene are mysterious. Parents feel inadequate to deal with it. The cure for mystery is information. So I want to give you information about drugs and the drug scene that will enable you either to prevent your youngster from using drugs or to know what to do if he is.

First we need to define some terms.

A *drug* is a chemical substance that has an effect on the body or mind. A *psychoactive* drug can be defined as a drug that alters the mind in some way. When we talk about adolescents and drugs we are not talking about aspirin, but about psychoactive drugs such as marijuana, LSD, speed, alcohol, or barbiturates. I see no point in making nit-picking distinctions and saying, "Well, technically, you can say that marijuana and alcohol are not drugs." I think it is simpler to classify *anything* used to alter consciousness as a psychoactive drug. The important thing is that, functionally, many different kinds of chemical substances are used by adolescents to make themselves feel better, turn themselves on, or alter their consciousness. Some years ago the word spread that if you took banana-peel scrapings and dried them and smoked them they would work almost as well as marijuana. In such a case, banana-peel scrapings would be functionally defined as a psychoactive drug.

A *drug experimenter* is any adolescent who has tried, for any reason at all, one or more psychoactive drugs. A drug experimenter tries one or more drugs and after a few experimentations, goes no further.

A *drug abuser* is any adolescent who has gone beyond brief experimentation, and uses drugs excessively in order to meet some psychological need. It does not matter what kind of drugs are used, whether they are physically addictive or nonaddictive. If the adolescent is using them excessively as a chemical crutch, he is a drug abuser.

A *drug addict* is any adolescent who uses a drug which produces both physical and emotional craving. A classical example of such a drug is heroin. A person who takes heroin develops a tolerance so that he requires larger and larger amounts of the drug to produce the same effect. The adolescent is then both physically and emotionally dependent upon the drug. If the use of an addicting drug, such as heroin, is stopped abruptly, the period of withdrawal is characterized by both extremely distressing physical symptoms and unpleasant emotional reactions.

It is important to have clear-cut definitions because, unfortunately, some parents lump all drugs together as if the effects of one drug were the same as the effects of another. Or a parent may find out his adolescent has experimented once or twice by smoking marijuana and angrily accuse him of being a "no-good drug addict" in spite of the fact that marijuana, according to all present scientific evidence, cannot be classed as an addictive drug like heroin.

HOW TO PREVENT DRUG ABUSE

Some parents want to prevent their teen-ager from ever touching a
drug. In other words, they want answers that will prevent their
adolescent from ever becoming a drug experimenter. Such parents
no doubt believe that the healthiest adolescents psychologically
are the ones who have never touched drugs. I'm afraid I must
disagree. It is true that many psychologically healthy adolescents
never experiment with drugs. But it is also true that many psychologically healthy adolescents *do* experiment. In fact, the behavior of
some adolescents who never experiment with drugs is based not upon
psychological strength but upon psychological weakness. They do
not experiment because they are too cowed and intimidated to
indulge in any form of typical adolescent rebellion, including experimentation with drugs. These are often the "mama's boys" or
"goody-goody" teen-agers who never get up their courage to rebel in
adolescence, and then may go through a delayed and pathological
adolescent rebellion in their 30s or 40s.

What I am saying is that it is not realistic for you to expect that
your teen-ager will go through adolescence without ever experimenting with drugs. From various research studies of high-school and
college students, the odds are against it. Furthermore, you may never
even know that your youngster has experimented. My advice is that
parents need to be concerned with preventing an adolescent from
becoming a *drug abuser* or a *drug addict* and not a *drug
experimenter*.

What leads any person, whether adolescent or adult, to become a
drug abuser or a drug addict? The person who turns to drug abuse is
doing it to solve an emotional problem or to meet an emotional
need. If he could meet the need or solve the problem without a
chemical crutch, he would not need to turn to drugs.

Sometimes I jokingly say to my adult patients, "You know, there is
hardly an emotional problem for which people come to psychotherapy
that couldn't be *temporarily* cured by three stiff martinis!" Anxiety
attacks, depression, marital unhappiness, obsessions and compulsions . . . all of these things can be blotted out temporarily by three
martinis. Of course, after the effect of the alcohol wears off, the
underlying problem is still there because the person has done nothing
to change it. The same is true of drug abuse. Drugs don't solve

emotional problems in any fundamental way; they just blot out the problem or the need temporarily.

The first thing you can do to prevent your child from becoming a drug abuser is to raise him so that he has a psychologically healthy personality. If you have been raising your child in accordance with the psychological principles set forth in this book so that his basic psychological needs have been met, he has a strong and healthy self-concept, and he is able to love himself and love others, then, it is hoped, the problem of drug abuse will never arise. However, there are some specific things you can concentrate on as an emotional in-surance policy against drug abuse.

First: The strength of your relationship with your child is one of your best safeguards against drug abuse. If you have a strong, deep, loving relationship, the chances are that he will go through a normal rather than abnormal rebellion in adolescence. Drug abuse is one symptom of an abnormal rebellion. Some fathers are preoccupied with work and spend little time with their adolescents. This leaves an emotional void in their lives and they may turn to drugs to fill it. You can prevent this by spending time with your child in the early years and learning to enjoy him as a person.

Second: You can help your child avoid becoming a drug abuser by maintaining open, genuine, two-way communication with him through all of the preadolescent years. As I have stressed repeatedly, it is important to allow your child to express his feelings verbally and let him know you understand how he feels by your use of the feedback technique. Some adolescents turn to drugs to vent their bottled-up, angry feelings. But if you have allowed your youngster to express his feelings openly, including his angry feelings, he will know he can express his feelings directly and verbally and does not need to express them indirectly through the use of drugs. Remember the incident I described in chapter six about Randy peeing in the vase as a way of indirectly expressing his angry feelings? Well, a lot of adolescents "pee in the vase," and strike back at their parents by becoming drug abusers.

Open and genuine communication of feelings is valuable for an-other reason. Suppose your teen-ager feels he can communicate freely with you about other subjects, but that when it comes to drugs you do not want to listen. If so, you are robbing him of the chance to absorb some psychological strength from you in order to resist the temptation to take drugs. If he says to you: "You know, Dad, I've been wondering—what would really be so bad about trying marijuana?" and your response is: "That doesn't sound like straight thinking son. Surely you know all of the dangers of a drug like marijuana," your answer effectively cuts off all further communication. He surely isn't going to seek you out to talk over his feelings and wishes and fantasies and ambivalent desires about marijuana. But suppose you responded something like this: "You've really been seriously wondering about marijuana and thinking it might be interesting to try it. Tell me more about your feelings." With such a response you are leaving the door open for further communication and perhaps a meaningful talk. Maybe all your teen-ager needs is the opportunity to discuss his thoughts and ambivalent feelings about marijuana freely in order to obtain from you the psychological strength he needs to resist the temptation to try it.

Drug addiction among teen-agers spreads like a communicable disease. Those who are already drug abusers act as "evangelists" to convert their friends to their way of life. In most instances the persons who "turn on" a teen-ager to drugs are not the stereotyped "dirty old men who are drug pushers" but some of his friends. Therefore your youngster will probably need to be strong enough to resist the group pressure of his friends in order not to become a drug abuser.

If your adolescent is having an internal struggle about whether or not to go along with his friends' entreaties to try drugs, with whom can he talk over his feelings? Not his friends, certainly! They are heavily involved in trying to persuade him to try drugs. But if you can maintain an open, nonjudgmental attitude, it is possible he may be able to talk over his mixed feelings with you. On the one hand he doesn't want to disappoint his friends; on the other hand he wants to stay away from drugs. Several really deep and meaningful talks with you may give him the psychological strength to avoid going along with the "crowd" and becoming a drug abuser.

Third: You can help your teen-ager avoid becoming a drug user by providing sound, accurate information about drugs in the years before adolescence, the years from five to thirteen. How can you do this? By doing what I call "sowing seeds." When you see an article in a newspaper or magazine that is relevant to a particular drug or the drug problem in general, you can introduce this into the conversation at mealtimes, while driving in the car, etc. You say something like: "I noticed in the paper today that a teen-ager died of an overdose of speed"; or "I see the National Institute of Mental Health is doing research to see if they can determine what the difference might be between teen-agers who smoke marijuana and those who don't." It is very important that you bring up these news items in the same way you would bring up news items about anything else. Avoid preaching or moralizing.

You can also read books on drugs to your school-age child just as you read books on many other subjects. For example, *The Ups and Downs of Drugs* by Kathleen Elgin and John Osterritter M.D., is a good one, and you could read this to a nine-or ten-year-old. Don't make the reading of a book on drugs any special thing that would cause it to be emotionally different to the child than a book you would read to him on any other subject.

If you do this kind of thing in a low-key way in the years leading up to adolescence, your child will have a good deal of reliable information on drugs. By the time he reaches adolescence he should have absorbed the idea that drugs are dangerous things to fool around with. If your school has a good program on drug education in the lower grades or early junior-high school, so much the better. But remember that your youngster's primary information (or nonin-formation) about drugs and attitudes toward drugs are going to come from his parents.

Once your youngster enters early adolescence he needs information on drugs at a higher and more sophisticated level in the same way that he needs information on sex at a higher and more sophisticated level. For one thing, he will be subjected to the pressures of the various specious arguments and rallying clichés of his con-temporaries. If you and he have a good and open communication, you may be sure that he will throw these up to you, such as, "Well, you older generation have your martinis and cocktails; why shouldn't we have our joints?" To answer such questions, you should, first of all, know the facts, the hard cold facts about the various drugs that are currently being used. Oftentimes, it is the adolescent who knows more factually about drugs than the parent. If the adolescent knows this it reduces the authority of the parents on the subject of drugs to zero.

How can a parent get the information he needs? I suggest you read at least one book that carefully and scientifically covers the current American drug scene. I have listed several in Appendix E. What you are seeking in such a book is accurate and impartial scientific information about the effects of the different drugs, and the potential and actual dangers of each.

But above all, take all this information into consideration and formulate a comprehensive viewpoint on drugs, a "philosophy of drugs," as it were. Only when you do this can an adolescent know where you stand on drugs in general and each drug in particular. Your adolescent may not agree with your views on drugs, but he will respect you because, first, you do have accurate information, and second, you know where you stand and are not wishy-washy on the subject.

It is particularly important for a father to admit that the older generation is *also* involved in the problem of drugs. One of the things that fuels the anger of adolescents is what they view (and I think correctly) as the hypocrisy of the adults, who think of drugs as strictly an adolescent problem. As Joel Fort, M.D., an authority on the subject makes clear, it is simply not true that the problem of drugs is confined to adolescents. It pervades our whole culture much more than we are aware:

> If you pick 20 adults at random, the odds are that 15 of them drink moderately, two are problem drinkers, and one is a desperate alcoholic. Two who use alcohol are also using marijuana, a couple are taking tranquilizers on doctors' orders and one or two have been popping barbiturates to relieve insomnia and are perilously close to addiction. Three or four have taken amphetamines to stay awake or to lose weight and nearly all of them drink caffeine, another stimulant. Ten or 12 of this group of 20 continue to smoke tobacco even after the medical hazards of that habit have been amply documented. One has probably taken acid or mescaline. . . . The drug culture, as the newspapers call it, doesn't just belong to the kids; everyone's in it together. . . . Today, 35,000,000 Americans use sedatives, stimulants, or tranquilizers, mostly obtained legally through their doctors. Despite this medical supervision, between 500,000 and 1,000,000 of these people have become abusers.[2]

Much more than most adults realize, our total American culture has become a drug culture. All of us are familiar with the television commercials which tell us that the cure for jangly nerves, upset

"MY PARENTS ARE AGAINST ME USING DRUGS, BUT THIS IS *THEIR* COLLECTION."

stomachs, and pounding headaches is to pop a pill. Do we think that our children, who see these commercials for 10 years before they become adolescents, are immune from their message? And what is that message? It is this: when anything troubles you, a pill will cure it!   •

I think it strengthens your rapport with your child if you can honestly admit that drugs are a problem of *both* parents and adolescents in our culture, and is not by any means confined to teenagers. For example, more than 125 million prescriptions for sedatives and tranquilizers and more than 25 million prescriptions for stimulants are written by physicians each year in the United States. In truth, we are a nation of pill takers. If you admit this honestly to your adolescent you will probably increase your chances for open and honest communication.

Fourth, the example you set for your teen-ager is one of the most powerful deterrents he can have against drug abuse. One of the best things you could do, for example, is to check your medicine cabinet and throw out any medication that is not a current prescription taken on a physician's orders and absolutely needed. A great deal of drug taking, particularly at the junior-high level, begins when a son or daughter experiments with drugs found in the family medicine cabinet. If your adolescent knows that you are firmly and unalterably opposed to the use of drugs and do not use them yourself (as tranquilizers against life's difficulties, as aids to sleep, or as aids to losing weight), it will be one of the strongest deterrents to drug use you can give him.

Fifth, parents need to do all they can to enable their teen-ager to get involved in constructive and meaningful activities. The adolescent needs to have goals and a cause he believes in which is greater than himself. Remember the adolescent idealism I discussed in the last chapter. Your youngster needs an outlet to express his new ideas. If he doesn't find it he may turn to drugs. As one of our leading authorities on drugs, Dr. Donald Louria, puts it, "Over and over again I see young users who appear to have no goals and are committed to nothing. They say, in one way or another, 'I'm not really interested in anything.' "[3]

Let me give you a specific example of the kind of meaningful activities for young people I'm talking about. In the area where I live there is a young minister, Mel Knight, who really knows how to get young people involved in projects to which they commit themselves.

For example, every Easter vacation he manages to have a project organized where the young people of his church and area can see that their efforts make a difference in the lives of other people. One Easter, ninety adolescents traveled by bus from Los Angeles to San Felipe, Mexico, where, in one week, they built a one-story, eight-room high school as part of an American-Mexican self-help project.

In order to participate in the Easter project, the teen-age volunteers raised a total of $6,000: by working on a Rose Parade Float, by writing, publishing, and selling "Theological Notebooks," and by dedicating the concrete blocks used for construction by contributions of 25 cents a block. Each volunteer was responsible for selling 20 blocks. Adult sponsors of the project managed to get a total of $48,000 in materials and building equipment contributed. An engineer who donated his time as construction boss said that the building would normally have taken three to four months to complete. But the teen-agers, with good planning ahead of time and hard work on the job, finished it in eight days. Furthermore, the job was not a sloppy, amateurish venture. The walls didn't vary three-quarters of an inch, corner to corner.

Here is what one of the girls who worked on the project said afterwards: "I think it's a privilege to be able to help people, who even though they are so very poor, are still happy. I'm not giving up anything at all. I'm gaining, really gaining something."[4] In other Easter projects, the teen-agers from Mr. Knight's church have built a playground and a crafts museum at an Indian school in Tucson, a basketball court at an orphanage in Ensenada, and a health clinic for the Yurok Indians near Trinidad, California.

These are the kinds of intriguing, dynamic, and constructive activities in which our young people need to be involved. There are certainly enough problems in our society which our young people can assist in solving. They can become involved in projects initiated by their church or synagogue. They can volunteer for help with any number of social agencies. For example, they can volunteer to help with Head Start or day-care centers; they can become Candy Stripers, they can help man the hot line that deals with teen-age problems, they can visit old people in nursing homes who feel that nobody cares for them, they can give voluntary service to the political party of their choice. Or, on another level, they may become immersed in the world of sports. I know a number of teen-agers who wouldn't consider using drugs because sports are too important to them.

What it boils down to is this: *many of our teen-agers feel very unimportant.* They feel that they are no longer children, but they are not yet adults. They dwell in a no-man's land where they are neither fish nor fowl, bird nor beast. Give them a chance to feel important; to know that they have something to believe in, a cause to fight for which is bigger and more important than they are. If we give them this opportunity we can prevent the psychological vacuum in their lives that so many adolescents fill with drugs.

However, once again the example we set is crucial. If you spend your time either at work or relaxing at home in front of the television set, and show little concern about the unsolved problems of our society, it is unlikely that your adolescent son or daughter is going to get involved in trying to solve those problems either.

I have tried not to be too narrow and detailed about "constructive, meaningful activities." Certainly the kinds of constructive meaningful activities available are going to be different on a farm in South Dakota, in a small town in Georgia, and in Chicago or the suburbs of San Francisco. But regardless of where you live, the principle is the same: an adolescent who believes in a cause bigger than himself, who is working at constructive extra-school activities which he thinks of as challenging and worthwhile, is far less likely to turn to drugs than the adolescent who has no idealistic beliefs to motivate him and who lives a life of apathy and boredom.

I have suggested five things you can do to prevent your adolescent from becoming a drug abuser. Unfortunately, many parents, in their zeal to prevent their child from becoming a drug abuser, unwittingly do some things which have the very opposite effect. Some things, instead of turning their child away from drug abuse, drive him toward it. So I want to mention five things for you to *avoid* in dealing with your adolescent in relation to drugs.

First, avoid prying and becoming a "parental private detective." Many parents resort to this when their child becomes an adolescent. Due to their enormous fear that their child will use drugs, they act as private detectives investigating their own child. They listen in on phone conversations for clues as to whether their youngster is using drugs. They go through their teen-ager's room with a fine-tooth comb looking for tell-tale evidence of drugs. From the descriptions of early adolescents in the last chapter, you know that one of the things they value above all else is privacy. They resent parental prying. If your adolescent is undecided whether or not to experiment with drugs, parental prying could be the factor that pushes him over the line in the wrong direction!

Second, don't moralize, lecture, or make drugs a "heavy emotional scene" for your child. When I was a student at Yale a friend who was a minister's son, told a group of us, "You know what I'm gonna do? I'm gonna buy a quart of liquor and go to a hotel in downtown New Haven and get myself a room. I'm gonna lock myself in and I'm gonna drink that whole bottle of booze and get myself stinking drunk just to see what it feels like! All my life I've been preached to and lectured to about the evils of alcohol and I've decided I'm going to see for myself what its like!" Obviously, the lecturing and preaching about alcohol had exactly the reverse effect from what his parents had intended.

Although this incident took place before the drug scene had appeared in America, the psychological dynamics are the same for drugs. If parents "play it heavy" on drugs as their youngster is growing up, drugs become a taboo and forbidden area, which then becomes quite fascinating to the child. It's as if for years parents lectured their child that he should eat any cereal in the pantry except one particular brand. By the time he became an adolescent he would be dying to try that brand simply because it was so fascinatingly forbidden.

I remember my daughter's reaction to two programs on drugs at the school she attended as a teen-ager. The first program was a very corny movie, with lots of preaching down to the kids. She told me her reaction afterwards. She said: "Dad, I've never smoked marijuana, but all I felt after seeing that lousy movie was, 'Let's all go out and get stoned!' " However, a few weeks later, the school had a lecture on drugs by a psychiatrist from UCLA. He began by saying: "I'm not here to lecture or moralize about drugs. I'm here to give you scientific facts and answer whatever questions you want to ask." My daughter was impressed with his approach and felt his lecture was helpful, "Because he didn't preach at us."

We parents would do well to emulate the UCLA psychiatrist. Avoid preaching, moralizing, and the heavy-handed emotional treatment. Answer questions openly and honestly, and keep the communication free and genuine.

Third, avoid cracking down on your child because of his friends. Sometimes parents hear through the grapevine that some of their child's friends are using drugs. Although there is no evidence that their own child is on drugs, they immediately crack down and forbid him to see any more of these drug-using friends. I think this is a mistake. This is saying to their child: "We can't trust you to have enough judgment not to use drugs since some of your friends are." My daughter, for example, had friends who were using drugs when she was in high school, and others who used drugs when she was in college. Our communication with her was open enough to enable her to tell us this. We showed her by our attitude that we had confidence she would not become a drug abuser merely because some of her friends had done so.

Friends are important to an adolescent, very important. If you forbid a child to see certain friends anymore, chances are very good that he will then see them on the sly. Furthermore, he will probably be so angry at your punitive action that if he has not started using drugs up to that point, he will now do so as a way of expressing his angry feelings toward you.

So, even if you hear that some of your child's friends are using drugs, take no action as long as your child himself is not on drugs.

Fourth, don't accuse your child of using drugs unless you know for certain that he is doing so. Dr. Donald Louria cites a poignant example of this:

> I recently gave a lecture in Connecticut at which the sponsors had questions written on cards so that I could select those I felt were most important for the limited question-and-answer period. About half-way through the cards I came to one that took me aback. It said, "My parents think I use drugs. I do not. How can I convince them I am not a drug user?" It would be hard to formulate a more poignant or articulate expression of a major communication gap between parent and child. This young person's plea also illustrates that where there is no communication, there is likely to be no trust.[5]

Very few things are more devastating to an adolescent than to be accused of taking drugs when in fact he is not doing so. If this happens, then he will often feel: "My parents think I'm taking drugs anyway; I might as well try it!" Learn to live with your anxious feelings. Don't jump in with unfounded accusations in order to reduce your own anxiety and pin some guilt on your child.

Fifth, some authorities who have written books or articles will give you a list of "symptoms" to watch for in your adolescent which may indicate drug abuse. The list of "symptoms" varies from authority to authority, but may include such things as redness of the eyes, a drastic increase or decrease in appetite, an excessive taste for sweets, anxiety, sloppy dress, and the like.

I disagree strongly with this approach. Parents are not competent trained professionals with a great deal of experience in dealing with adolescents who have used a variety of drugs. If a parent takes seriously such a list of symptoms indicating possible drug abuse it turns him into a worried and excessively zealous parental sleuth, who is all too liable to take one of the normal weird quirks of adolescence, and turn it into proof that his youngster is on drugs.

Instead of a list of symptoms against which to check your child I offer you only *one* commonsense thing to do. By the time your child becomes an adolescent, you have known him for a good many years. You know what kind of a person he is. If this child that you have known so well suddenly begins to act weird, if his behavior becomes bizarre and strange, then you may suspect that he has begun using drugs.

For example, let's say an adolescent suddenly begins to use incense in his room. This may be on some authority's list as a symptom to look for, since many adolescents use incense to cover up the odor of marijuana. But on the other hand, many adolescents use incense just because it is an "in" thing to do. To crack down suddenly on your teen-ager and say: "Aha, I see you're using incense in your room these days: I suspect you've begun to smoke marijuana!" is a big mistake and will spoil communications between the two of you.

Basically, I use this approach with my teen-age patients. If a patient arrives for his counseling appointment obviously acting strange, bizarre, or not "with it," I say to him, "Raymond, you seem to be acting very strangely today; are you stoned?" In every case in which I have done this, the youngster has been able to admit that he was indeed high on drugs. This then opened the door for an honest communication about drugs.

I would suggest you do the same. Use your common sense. If it tells you that your adolescent is behaving in a strange, erratic, or bizarre manner, do not ignore it. Even if drugs did not exist, it is not natural for a parent to ignore strange behavior on the part of his child. Say to your adolescent something like this: "Evelyn, I'm concerned about you. You seem to be acting in ways that are just not like you. (Then specify these ways.) I put all this together and I get the feeling you are using drugs. Is that true?"

To use this simple and commonsense approach keeps you from becoming an overzealous parental sleuth, hovering over his adolescent with a checklist of symptoms. But at the same time, it means that if there is some drastic change in your child's behavior you do not ignore it or overlook the possibility that it is caused by drugs.

WHAT TO DO IF YOU DISCOVER YOUR CHILD HAS BEEN USING DRUGS

It is appropriate at this point to quickly list the main classifications of drugs on the current drug scene.

1. "Uppers" or psychic energizers. These are the amphetamines. They lift the mood of the user, speed up his thought processes and his speech, and heighten his sensory awareness. They are used by many adults as "diet pills," but are not consciously relied upon to give a psychic lift to the person. They are to be found in the medicine cabinets of many homes. Methedrine or "speed" is the strongest of the psychic energizers. Speed may come in several forms: Benzedrine or "bennies," Dexedrine, and many others. The word is out among adolescents that "speed kills" and many adolescents know that the drug depression following an excessive dose can kill a person.

Cocaine, or "coke," is another psychic energizer. This is often sniffed or "snorted."

2. Barbiturates or "downers." These are drugs such as Seconal, Tuinal, Nembutal, also called "goofballs." They are sleeping pills, and are also found in the medicine cabinets of many homes. Such sedatives may become physically addicting and are especially dangerous when mixed with alcohol.

Adolescents may try different mixtures of "uppers" and "downers" for kicks in an effort to put themselves into a continuous "high" or euphoric state.

3. Tranquilizers. The use of meprobamates and related tranquilizers has increased rapidly among the adult population. These, too, will be found in many family medicine cabinets. Tranquilizers

are less susceptible to misuse than other drugs in that their effect is to reduce excessive anxiety which, at best is a specific unpleasant feeling and, at worst, a life-paralyzing ailment. Tranquilizers don't, in normal doses, pick you up, slow you down, or expand your mind. However, adolescents may concoct their own custom-made mix of energizers and tranquilizers to achieve a specific euphoric state pleasing to them.

4. Hallucinogenic drugs. These drugs alter the consciousness of the mind, causing the user to see, feel, or taste things that are not there. These drugs in one form or another distort reality.

Marijuana is the most commonly used hallucinogenic drug. The psychological effects of marijuana are variable, and may include distortions of hearing, vision, and sense of time. Thought becomes dreamlike. The usual feeling is a passive state of euphoria or being "high."

Although there is no physical dependence on marijuana, heavy chronic use by adolescents has been associated with what has been named the "amotivational syndrome." This is the term used for an adolescent who has lost his desire to work, to compete, and to face challenges. Instead he retreats into a passive state in which his whole life appears centered around the compulsive use of marijuana and getting "stoned."

Other hallucinogenic drugs are LSD, mescaline from the peyote cactus, psilocybin from the Mexican mushroom, morning-glory seeds which contain lysergic acid amides that are hallucinogenically active, but far less powerful than LSD.

The LSD state will vary greatly according to the personality of the user, the setting in which the drug is taken, and the dosage. In general, it will drastically alter a person's perception of reality. Changes in vision are striking. Thinking may become pictorial. The sense of time and self are dramatically altered. Illusions and hallucinations may occur.

Under the influence of LSD a person usually has what he calls a "good trip" or a "bad trip," also known as a "bummer." The good trip consists of pleasant imagery and pleasant feelings to accompany it. The bad trip is the reverse: the images perceived under LSD are deeply terrifying and the feelings are those of dread and enormous anxiety. What can happen in a bad trip is that the LSD brings out deeply repressed feelings. The sudden emergence of these feelings puts the person into a panic state. A sixteen-year-old boy sought treatment from me as a result of a bad LSD trip which brought out previously repressed homosexual feelings. He was in a panic for fear that he was a homosexual. Unpleasant trips known as "flashbacks" may also recur months or even years later.

At present, there is no way of knowing whether an individual will have a good trip or a bad trip under LSD. And there is no doubt that LSD is the most potent of all of the hallucinogenic drugs. In view of the various harmful things that can occur as a result of a bad trip under LSD, it must be classed as one of the most dangerous drugs. Word of this has spread through the adolescent culture and use of LSD or "acid" has markedly decreased.

5. Narcotics. A narcotic is a drug that relieves pain and induces sleep. Most narcotic drugs are derivatives of the opium poppy. Morthine is one such derivative, as is heroin, which is morphine chemically altered to make it about six times stronger. Heroin is the strongest illegal narcotic on the drug black market, and accounts for approximately 90 percent of the narcotic addiction problem. Heroin goes by various slang names such as "junk," "snow," "horse," "stuff," and "H."

With a shot of heroin a person feels relaxed, high, and in a pleasant, dreamlike state. However, as the body develops a tolerance to heroin the high is lost. Gradually increasing amounts of heroin are required to maintain a high and to avoid the extremely unpleasant symptoms of withdrawal. In other words, heroin is both a physically and psychologically addictive drug. The body tissues crave the drug. Like an alcoholic, whose life centers around obtaining alcohol to keep him going through the day, the heroin addict centers his daily life around getting hold of an adequate supply of heroin.

Fortunately for heroin addicts, the number and kind of synthetic narcotic substitutes is increasing. For example, a physician can withdraw heroin addicts from their habit by giving a narcotic substitute such as methadone for heroin and slowly reducing the dosage. During the time the addict is maintained on methadone, psychotherapy can help him to work through the emotional problems that caused him to become addicted in the first place.

From this brief survey of the main drugs on the current drug scene, you can understand their appeal, especially to an adolescent who suffers from an emotional hole in his personality. The drug puts him on a temporary high which, for the moment, fills the emotional hole. The drug offers "instant happiness." *All* adolescents have a number of difficult emotional tasks to work through and master during this stage of development. Is it any wonder that in our general pill-taking culture many adolescents are tempted to turn to the "instant happiness" offered by drugs, rather than work their way along the slower and harder road of facing and overcoming their problems?

All right, let's suppose you discover that your youngster has succumbed to the lure of drugs and is definitely a user. What should you do? How should you handle the situation?

First, try not to panic. To many parents, the fact that their child has used drugs (no matter what the drug) is an immediate sign that he has taken the first step on an irreversible road to the hell of drug addiction. This is simply not true. It is, nevertheless, the unfortunate mental picture that many parents have of the situation. Viewing it this way, they panic. They say things and do things they would never do in a more mature and sober mood.

My first rule of thumb is that when you discover positively that your child has been using drugs, *do not do anything about it that day.* Wait a day before you confront your child. Sleep on the problem. Talk it over with your wife. Or the two of you may want to talk it over with a professional third party: your family doctor, your minister, a psychologist or psychiatrist. Don't rush into panicky action which will only make things worse. Take your time. Make sure that your child's problem receives the best of your thinking rather than the worst.

Second, don't land on your adolescent like a ton of bricks, expecting harsh and punitive treatment to clear up the unfortunate situation. Here is one such instance of this kind of reaction by parents to their discovery that their adolescent has been using drugs:

> When Tracy, at age fifteen, came home one night, he was faced with two irate parents. Before he could ask what was wrong, his father threw a packet of marijuana at him and screamed, "You don't care what you do to us, do you?" Then his mother burst into tears. In between her sobs, she said, "I've given you everything you ever wanted. How can you destroy me this way?" In the tirade that followed, Tracy did not hear one word from his parents that indicated concern for what his drug abuse might mean in terms of Tracy himself. His parents were concerned only about themselves, but Tracy could not make them understand that.[6]

This type of reaction is typical of all too many parents. They do not take the time or effort to find out what led their teen-ager to use drugs. They give him no chance to express or explore his feelings. They do nothing to initiate a two-way communication between themselves and their teen-ager about the problem. No, it is all one-way communication, with their adolescent on the receiving end of a tirade and harsh punishment. The parents may "ground" him for a month. They may attempt to cut him off from all his friends. They may restrict him to his room. There seems to be no limit to the harsh and punitive things parents can think of in such a situation.

All measures of this type are self-defeating. Oftentimes, an adolescent, particularly a young adolescent, feels guilty about using drugs and will gladly make an honest effort to give it up. Harsh and punitive measures dissolve his guilt feelings and turn them into anger. He then loses any incentive he had to change his behavior for the better. Instead, he will probably be filled with great hostility toward his parents and a desire for revenge. Whatever his original motivation, he now has an intense desire added to continue to use drugs just to spite his parents.

One of the ways you can help prevent yourself from taking this harsh and self-defeating tack with your adolescent is to plan ahead what you will do if you discover he is taking drugs; in the same way that it is wise to plan what you would do in the case of a fire, or some other emergency, it can be very helpful to plan what you would do if you were to discover your adolescent has been taking drugs.

Third, don't try the "geographic cure." Some parents send their adolescent off to boarding school or to live with faraway relatives for a while. I have even known of cases where the parents seriously considered packing up and relocating as a family, in order to get their child away from what they considered "undesirable influences." Here is an example of one family's attempt at the "geographic cure."

Norman, at age fifteen, had a number of friends whose reputation as drug users was fully warranted. Norman's parents refused to believe Norman when he denied taking drugs with his friends. On the day that one of these children was arrested for dealing in drugs, Norman's father enrolled him in a parochial boarding school many miles from home, where, according to the school administrator, Norman would be protected from drugs. Because of the excessively harsh discipline at the school (which Norman's father never bothered to investigate) Norman ran away to California, where he subsequently died from an overdose of heroin.[7]

Attempts at a geographic cure are doomed to failure, for one very simple reason. The reason for drug abuse lies within the feelings and emotions of the adolescent. Moving him from on geographic environment to another supposedly "safer" one, does absolutely nothing to help the adolescent change the inner feelings which led him to drug abuse.

Fourth, evaluate the seriousness of the problem. A fourteen-year-old who has experimented two or three times with marijuana is obviously very different from a sixteen-year-old who has been on heroin for six months. It is quite possible you need professional help to evaluate the situation. Parents are often much too close to the problem and too involved emotionally to be able to evaluate the problem clearly. Here is an example where professional help proved invaluable:

Parents from a suburban community asked a psychiatrist to talk with their son. He was a heroin addict who was stealing from them and in trouble with the law. These were the psychiatrist's conclusions after talking with the young man:

> When I asked him what drugs he took he said sedatives, marijuana, and heroin. Now each of these has the capacity to alleviate anxiety. After further dialogue it became very apparent that he suffered from an overwhelming identity crisis that had led to severe depression, and this was turned into tension and anxiety. He took drugs to relieve the anxiety. He was indeed addicted to heroin, but in a sense he had no heroin problem. To focus on the heroin without treating the depression would have been a tremendous mistake.[8]

In speaking of professional help, I mean a psychologist or psychiatrist who by profession is trained in the psychological evaluation and counseling of adolescents as well as adults. Such a person may not be available in your community. You may have to drive a hundred miles or more to consult a professional person. In many cases it would be worth it. For one thing, by spending this time and effort (and money) you are saying to your adolescent: "We really care about you. It is worth it to us to go to all of this effort to help you with this problem."

If there is no professionally trained psychologist or psychiatrist in your community or within reasonable driving range, it may help to talk things over with an understanding family doctor or minister. I cannot make the blanket recommendation that it will help to talk things over with *all* family doctors or ministers. If the doctor or minister is harsh and punitive in his attitudes, and some are, it will only make the situation worse.

If there is no one in your community with whom you can discuss the situation in confidence, then you and your wife will have to evaluate the seriousness of the problem yourselves. To do this, you need some basic information. Has your adolescent only been experimenting with drugs, or is he deeply involved and a chronic user? Are the drugs he is involved with (whether on a brief experimental basis or on a deep level) "mild" drugs or "serious" drugs? I put "mild" and "serious" in quotation marks because in one sense the use of any drug is "serious," since it indicates a personality problem in the adolescent or he would not have turned to the drug as a chemical crutch. On the other hand, it is equally true that it is nowhere nearly as dangerous to an adolescent to use marijuana as it is for him to use LSD or heroin. So, understanding the semantic problems involved, we could class the following as "mild" drugs: marijuana, cough medicines, codeine, nutmeg, and small amounts of stimulants, sedatives, or tranquilizers taken by mouth. Classify as "serious" drugs: LSD, cocaine, opium, morphine, mescaline, methedrine, heroin, or any other drug administered by needle.

In evaluating the seriousness of the problem there are a few principal mistakes parents make: They may react to a youngster who has briefly experimented with a mild drug such as marijuana as if he had been shooting heroin for a year, thus blowing the problem totally out of proportion. This would be akin to putting their youngster in an oxygen tent of the intensive-care unit of a hospital for coming down with a common cold. And, more rarely, discovering an adolescent deeply involved with a serious drug such as LSD or heroin, the parents react as if this were only a minor problem and that if they give the boy a "good talking to" he will straighten out.

Fifth, remember that *feelings are more important than facts.* I cannot stress this too strongly, because it is the most important thing in handling a youngster with a drug problem Too many parents are overconcerned with finding out the "facts" of the situation. In doing so they ignore the feelings of the adolescent. In evaluating the problem, for example, they use the courtroom approach and fire a series of questions at their teen-ager: "How long have you been smoking marijuana? Where did you get it? What friends of yours are using it? Where have you been getting the money to buy it?" And so on and on. Such a fact-oriented approach only puts the adolescent on the defensive and makes him feel as if he is on the witness stand. It does not help him open up and tell you his feelings. But if you patiently encourage him to tell you his feelings, sooner or later the "facts" will emerge.

Once again, in this crisis situation of a drug confrontation, as in any other parent-child interaction, the most important thing you can do is to encourage your child to tell you his feelings, and then use the feedback technique to let him know you understand. One way to initiate such a communication would be to say something like this to your adolescent: "Son, could you think back to when you first tried marijuana? What were your feelings that day? What led you to try it? What feelings did you have when you were high? What feelings did you have afterward?" Such an approach is nonaccusatory. It does not put your adolescent on the defensive. Communicate on the level where it should be: the level of feelings rather than facts.

Here is an example of the kind of communication between parents and teen-ager that pays off in such a situation:

> When fourteen-year-old Melissa was asked if she would ever take drugs, she told her parents that she would never even consider it. Yet Melissa's grades had shown a significant decline, and her friends seemed suddenly reluctant to talk to Melissa's parents. These circumstances led Melissa's parents to think that she was taking drugs. One Sunday, Melissa and her parents had gone upstate to ski for the day. On the way home after a truly delightful day, Melissa's father asked how she thought they would react if she told them she had begun experimenting with drugs. She hesitated in silence for a long time, and then she said she thought they would scream at her and forbid her to see her friends. Her parents assured her that this was not so; they promised her that there would be no retribution.

With tears in her eyes, Melissa told them that she had indeed been experimenting with marijuana. Her parents fulfilled their promise in a very emotion-filled discussion, which ended with Melissa and her parents feeling closer than ever. Even when Melissa tried marijuana a year later, they still kept their word. She felt that, as a result, she was fortunate to be able to think the drug problem through with the help of her parents, whereas all of her friends had to do it alone.[9]

I have tried to point out that drug abuse is always the result of some emotional need in the adolescent and some difficulty in the parent-child relationship. Therefore, the most important thing you can do if you discover your youngster has been using drugs is to work to improve the emotional relationship between you. You do this mainly by encouraging him to tell you his feelings and by using the feedback technique to let him know you understand. If you do this, you will keep the channels of communication open and strengthen your emotional relationship with your adolescent child. Do not hesitate to express your own feelings: tell your adolescent how deeply concerned you are about him, how much you care, cry if you are moved to tears, put your arms around him. *Feelings* is the name of the game. Anything that enables each of you to express your feelings and become emotionally closer to one another is going to strengthen your adolescent's ability to withstand the lure of drugs.

Too many parents believe that information about the potential disastrous consequences of drugs will deter an adolescent from using them. This is simply not true. Information alone will not produce a change in behavior. *Changes in feelings produce changes in behavior.* Too many parents rely on a strictly rational approach. The underlying assumption of this strictly rational approach is: "If my youngster understands the possible dangers of speed or acid or heroin he will leave them alone." An adult example should serve to show the fallacy of the strictly rational approach. A definite link was established between cigarette smoking and lung cancer and heart attacks. If adults were purely rational beings, one would expect the consumption of cigarettes to go down to zero. Obviously, no such thing has happened. The reason is that mere information on the dangers of cigarette smoking is not sufficient to enable an adult to stop smoking. Smoking fills an emotional need. That need must be dealt with in order for the person to be able to stop smoking.

Here is an example on the adolescent level, of the fallacy that information on the dangers of a drug will deter a teen-ager from using it. A number of years ago, when LSD first appeared on the drug scene, I acquired a sixteen-year-old patient who had tried LSD once and had an exceedingly "bum trip" which terrified him. An article in *Life* magazine had recently come out on LSD and I asked him if he had read it. He had. I then said, "Well, if you read the article then you knew about all of the potential dangers of using LSD. Why did you try it?" He answered, "I guess I didn't think it would happen to me."

So information, even if it is scientific and accurate, will not necessarily discourage your youngster from trying drugs. The most powerful deterrent to his use of drugs is to deepen the emotional relationship between you and to keep open the channels of communication.

In the same way that you may need professional help in evaluating the seriousness of the problem, you may need professional help in opening up communication and strengthening the emotional relationship between you. If you discover your adolescent is seriously involved with a dangerous drug such as LSD or speed or heroin, I definitely recommend that a good rule to follow is for you to consult a professional—a psychologist or psychiatrist.

Sixth, use community resources if they are available. Communities vary widely across the United States as to what kinds of resources are available. Some communities have "hot lines" to deal with drug problems or any other problems teen-agers may encounter. Either parents or teen-agers may call on the hot line at any time and be referred to some community person or resource to help with the problem. A community may also have adolescent encounter groups, sponsored by a church or school, to deal with the problem. Large cities will have outpatient drug clinics, or inpatient programs for the rehabilitation of seriously involved drug users. Once again, don't wait for disaster to strike. Find out ahead of time what resources are available in your community should your adolescent turn out to have a mild or serious drug problem. Usually your family doctor or your minister will be able to give you this information.

Seventh, don't give up if it proves difficult to wean your youngster away from drugs. Drug abuse is not the kind of problem that grows up overnight, and you should not expect it to be cured overnight. If drug abuse if rooted in personality problems in the adolescent or problems in the parent-child relationship, then it will not be resolved in two or three days. It is going to take time, hard work, and patience to get at the personality problems that are causing the drug abuse and to overcome the kinks in the parent-child relationship, so that a mutually satisfying relationship can develop.

Eighth, you may have to deal with backsliding. Even after intensive work and effort on your part, and after your adolescent has supposedly given up drugs, he may revert to drugs. Again I emphasize, adolescence is no easy time to live through, and the stresses of daily living or the pressures of drug-using friends may cause your adolescent to backslide. At such a time you will be tested to the utmost. How tempting it will be to fly off the handle and lash out: "After all we've done to try to help you, and here you are back on drugs!" Resist this temptation and "keep your cool." A time of backsliding is when your youngster has the greatest need of your emotional support. You do not need to berate him for it; believe me, he is berating himself plenty. What he needs is the opportunity to pour out his feelings: his temptations to revert back to drugs, his disappointment in himself, his fears that you will censure and condemn him for slipping back. With your help and your emotional support he can start over again.

I have outlined the various things a father can do to prevent his adolescent from turning to drugs, and what he can do if he discovers that his youngster has. Many of you who read this will think I have painted a depressing picture of adolescents and the drug scene. And in many ways the picture is depressing. The death of even one teen-ager from an overdose of drugs is one too many. I am sure that all of us would like to turn the clock back to the days when there was no adolescent drug culture. Adolescence was still a difficult time for parents and children to live through, but at least parents did not have to contend with the fear that their youngsters might get involved with drugs. However, we cannot turn back the clock. The drug scene is real and parents need to know how to handle it.

I have dealt with drugs in this chapter on early adolescence because this is a time when many youngsters begin to experiment. Your youngster may not. If he does not do so now, he may, as some teen-agers do, begin to experiment with drugs in later adolescence—the years between sixteen and twenty-one. But whether a teen-ager starts to experiment with drugs in early or late adolescence, the same basic principles of how to handle the situation apply. These are the principles I have set forth here.

Before closing this chapter I want to say a few words about alcohol. It is strange that many parents today are terribly frightened and uptight with the fear that their teen-ager might be using drugs, but relatively indifferent to the possibility that their teen-ager might be abusing alcohol. I know of one family, for example, that discovered their sixteen-year-old had been smoking marijuana. In their panicky reaction, they forbade him ever to smoke marijuana again, but said that he could drink whatever he wanted from their liquor closet instead! Incredible but true.

Liquor and teenagers are a dangerous combination, particularly when the automobile is involved. I know one family whose teen-age son was driving home from a party dead-drunk. He drove off the side of the road on a steep downhill curve and totaled his car. It was a miracle he wasn't killed.

The misuse of alcohol is fully as serious a problem for a teen-ager as the misuse of drugs. And it is a fact that at many teen-age parties *both,* liquor and drugs, are used together. Whether you drink or not, I think you can make a valid case to your teen-ager that the reason the law prohibits adolescents from drinking until they have reached a certain age is that most adolescents are not sufficiently mature psychologically to handle liquor well. My personal opinion is that it is wisest not to allow your adolescent to drink until he has reached college age. If you find that your adolescent has been misusing alcohol, all the things I suggested to do for misusing drugs apply here also.

I want to close by reminding you that your best insurance against abuse of either drugs or alcohol by your youngster is to concentrate on developing a strong and close emotional relationship between you. Don't be fooled by the pseudo-independent facade of your teen-ager in early adolescence. He still needs you. Find things to do with your adolescent son or daughter on a one-to-one basis that will mean a great deal to both of you emotionally. In plain and simple terms I'm talking about love; about concern and caring and respect. If you show your teen-ager you deeply respect and love and care for him, it is highly unlikely that he will become heavily involved in the drug scene or the misuse of liquor. For drugs and liquor, after all, are only a pitiful chemical substitute for your love.

13
Late Adolescence (Ages Sixteen to Young Adulthood)

It is difficult to say with any finality where the watershed which separates "early" adolescence from "late" adolescence is and, of course, there will be enormous individual differences in this respect among specific boys and girls. However, the sixteenth birthday seems to be the most convenient line of demarcation, at least in American society.

Sixteen is the age when teen-agers are eligible to hold jobs. For many adolescents, this is a much looked-forward-to event: their first job, and, of course, their first paycheck. I can recall how delighted I was when I was sixteen to get my first summer job clerking in an architect's office, and my first part-time job during the school year working in a printshop. It is a real thrill to get pay from *outside*, from a real employer, and not from the family for doing work at home.

But perhaps the most significant psychological trait of your sixteen-year-old is that he has largely worked his way through the fierce emotional struggles for independence which were characteristic of him at ages thirteen, fourteen, and fifteen. At fifteen for example, he feels he must prove his independence to everybody by flaunting it. He feels the need to rebel against whatever parental restrictions are placed upon him. If he is supposed to be in by a certain hour, he comes home later than the time he promised. If he is not supposed to smoke, he does it on the sly, or perhaps leaves telltale cigarette butts in his room as evidences of his ability to defy his parents. If he is not supposed to drink or use drugs, he will have a fling at them. When his parents expect him to reply in a reasonable and courteous manner to questions they ask, he will reply in grunts and monosyllables. In general, it almost seems as if he spends hours thinking up ways to defy his parents, the school, and even in some cases, the neighbors.

What is going on psychologically, of course, is that the early adolescent is fighting his own need to be *dependent* on his parents as he was when he was a little child. That is why he overcompensates in his drive for independence. He is like the lecturer who wrote in his notes: "Weak point—yell like hell and pound the table!"

In contrast to what he was like as an early adolescent, your sixteen-year-old feels that he has finally made it with respect to his psychological independence, and he can therefore afford to relax. He is much more self-assured than he was at fifteen. The withdrawn moods and sullenness of fifteen are replaced by a more even and equable disposition, much to the relief of his parents.

In fact, the typical sixteen shows more sense of equality in relation to both his parents and to other adults. He is more relaxed with his parents about a number of issues which were subjects of conflict in earlier years. Since he feels he has achieved the independence he was seeking, he no longer has to defy his parents to prove it. His new equilibrium within himself gives rise to a new and better equilibrium with his parents.

You will recall, I pointed out in chapter eight that ten was an age of equilibrium which in many ways summed up middle childhood, but it was also an age which stood on the brink of the new growth forces of preadolescence. Sixteen is like ten in this respect. Sixteen is also an age at which your teen-ager has usually attained an equilibrium among the physical and emotional growth forces with which he has been struggling. The main struggle is between his desire to be independent of his parents, and his desire to cling to his dependent childhood status. Now that he has reached a reasonable balance in this inner struggle, he is on the threshold of the new and more sophisticated growth struggles that usually take place between the ages of seventeen and twenty-one.

So sixteen is a pivotal year, standing between early and late adolescence. Dr. Gesell describes the sixteen-year-old as being "at mid-adolescence a sort of prototype of a pre-adult."[1]

Whereas at fifteen he was often uncertain, dissatisfied, and a cantankerous stranger around the house, at sixteen he has developed a new sense of self-assurance. His emotional life has more balance and moderation. He is more outgoing, sociable, and affable. His emotions are generally on an even keel, and he is not as bristly and touchy as he was in early adolescence. Parents generally report that their sixteen-year-old is friendly, outgoing, and well adjusted.

Sixteen, like ten, lives in the "here and now." He tends to take himself, other people, and life for granted. As Dr. Gesell comments, "When asked what age he thinks is best, his satisfied response, 'right about now' shows that he is meeting life as it is."[2]

Sixteen's newfound maturity can be seen in his poise and self-assurance when meeting people. He no longer needs to shrink back into a corner because he feels that "Those are adults and I don't like adults." Now he feels, "Those are adults but I'm practically an adult too, so I can meet them on their own level now." Sometimes sixteen's new rapport with guests and friends of the family will astound his parents.

Although relationships within the family are much improved over early adolescence, sixteen still spends more time outside the home than with his family. He thinks of his home as a sort of background setting for his many and varied activities. Gesell phrases it well when he says that sixteen "seems remote from his family in a happy way."[3]

His friendships with both sexes are becoming deeper than at previous ages. Both boys and girls like parties and gatherings where the music is loud, the beat insistent, and activities such as dancing, talking, or just "messing around" can all go on at once. Sixteen is the age for informal parties and get-togethers. He builds up multiple friendships as part of his social development. Boys pick their friends chiefly on the basis of common interests in sports or hobbies or special activities. Girls choose friends on a more personal basis, even though they may not have common hobbies or interests. They spend time talking about personal relationships and confiding intimate secrets to one another. Discussing the traits and personalities of boyfriends may form much of the conversation of girl friends. Boys and girls choose each other for all the innumerable reasons that men and women are attracted to one another. Typically, boys and girls get involved with each other emotionally and sexually at sixteen, much more than many parents are aware. We will discuss the various ways parents can handle this later in the chapter.

A time and motion study of a sixteen-year-old would show that he spends by far the greatest amount of his time socializing with his friends.

In general, due to his newfound sense of independence sixteen acts like an adult and goes cheerfully about his own business. He is reasonably successful in keeping himself clean, taking care of his clothes, looking after his room, and doing his homework. Regarding bedtime, for example, he now thinks of himself as a semi-adult who knows he needs his sleep and realizes that it's up to him to get it. This eliminates a great number of conflicts over bedtime that occurred when he was still overcompensating to prove his independence. He is now more reasonable about many issues, where he had previously felt the need to prove himself by defying his parents.

Sixteen is often ready and eager to take on a full-time job during the summer or work part-time during the school year. A job is a symbol to him, along with the use of the car, that he is an adult or close to becoming one. Sixteen wants a "real" job outside the home, such as working in a grocery store, ushering in a movie theater, serving behind the counter at a doughnut shop, or working in a filling station or bicycle shop. Such activities give him great pride in himself and strengthen his self-concept. In the past, baby-sitting has generally been the preferred job for girls, although more and more boys are also interested in doing it, as the old sexual stereotypes that "only girls baby-sit" break down. Personally I think it is excellent training for future fathering for a teen-age boy to baby-sit.

Boys and many girls also enjoy the adult status which comes from holding down a full- or part-time job. Some boys and girls who have reasonably well-paid jobs buy their own clothes and take great pride in doing so.

For most sixteen-year-olds, this is the turning point in their education. At this age the direction in which the adolescent is heading becomes more apparent, both educationally and vocationally. Some sixteens are definitely interested in college, and are planning toward that goal. Others are beginning to realize that they are not really interested in subjects of an academic nature, but are drawn to the commercial or skilled trades. Unfortunately, many parents and schools look down on this and push the youngster whose real bent is

"DAD, I'M 16 NOW, CAN I GET MY LICENCE?"

"WELL, I WAS THINKING ABOUT IT, BUT WE'LL HAVE TO BUY YOU A LEASH, TOO!"

auto mechanics, or electronics, or some other skilled trade into an academic or college course which bores him.

Another group of sixteen-year-olds have not found themselves academically or vocationally. These are the slow maturers, the "late bloomers," or those with emotional problems which prevent them from finding a clear-cut direction for themselves at this time. Slow maturers need patience and understanding on the part of both parents and school and, perhaps, even professional help.

For these reasons it is impossible to sketch a clear-cut picture of a "typical sixteen" at school, any more than one could describe a "typical adult" at work. As he becomes more adult psychologically, sixteen shows more of the range of individual differences that our adult society displays, from the auto mechanic to the schoolteacher, from the computer programmer to the beautician, and from the naval officer to the lawyer.

This ends our brief sketch of the sixteen-year-old—who is at the beginning of late adolescence and who forms a bridge between early and late adolescence. One of my principal debts in the psychological aspects of the writing of this book is to the pioneering research work of Dr. Arnold Gesell and his associates. In their massive research effort, they have followed a group of children from birth through sixteen years of age and have given profiles for each year of the life of a growing child. Their research stops, however, at age sixteen and, as one parent put it, half humorously and half seriously, "Dr. Gesell stopped at sixteen and left me up the parental creek without a paddle! How am I going to understand my seventeen- and eighteen-year-old?"

It would be intellectually dishonest to say that we have the same kind of *detailed* information on ages seventeen to twenty-one as we have on youngsters from birth to sixteen. This does not mean that considerable research has not been done on these ages, but rather that research was not categorized on a year-to-year basis, as was accomplished by Dr. Gesell and his associates on the earlier ages.

A subdivision of late adolescence into ages sixteen and seventeen corresponds roughly to the high-school years, and ages eighteen, nineteen, and twenty, corresponds roughly to the college, trade-school, or starting-to-work years.

What is the developmental task that confronts your adolescent in these late-adolescent years? As pointed out in chapter twelve, the central developmental task of adolescence is to form a separate ego identity. In early adolescence the teen-ager is trying to answer the question: "Who am I?" pretty much within the framework of his family. At this stage he is wrestling with the question in terms of: "Am I an independent person, or am I still a dependent child tied to my family's apron strings?" In reading the last two chapters you have seen that for an early adolescent to come to terms with himself as an independent person involves considerable overcompensation and rebellion against even the most reasonable parental rules and restrictions.

By late adolescence your teen-ager begins to realize he has "made it" with respect to the issue of independence and, therefore, his self-concept changes to that of a semi-adult. Now, and only now, can he struggle with other aspects of the central developmental task of adolescence, that of his ego identity. He must (1) decide upon and prepare for a vocation; (2) work out a satisfactory relationship with the opposite sex and establish stable patterns of a heterosexual love life; and (3) complete his emancipation from parents and family.

In early adolescence the teen-ager is attempting to answer the question "Who am I?" and achieve his ego identity pretty much within the arena of the family. But in late adolescence the arena has broadened out to the larger framework of our whole society. In early adolescence your teen-ager's views on vocational choice were very much of a fantasy nature. Between sixteen and twenty-one they lose their fantasy character and become very real, involving such realistic choices as what curriculum to choose in high school, whether to go to college or go to work after graduation, whether to go to trade or technical school, what to major in at college, etc. Whereas in early adolescence your teen-ager's relations with the opposite sex were awkward and fumbling, between sixteen and twenty-one he develops strong and positive relationships with the opposite sex—or he may shy away from heterosexuality and turn to homosexuality, or rush into an early marriage (he may even be forced into marriage by an unexpected pregnancy).

Let's start with the developmental task of vocational choice. Vocational choice is a two-edged sword: on the one hand, and aside from its economic aspects, one's personality structure determines what type of vocation he chooses. It may dictate that the needs of one would be satisfied as an architect, of another as an auto mechanic, another as an engineer, another as a teacher. If you transplanted the engineer to a college faculty, making him trade places with the professor of English literature, both of them would be very unhappy because their vocation would not fill their psychological needs.

On the other hand, the vocation a person chooses will have a major effect on the kind of adult he becomes. The occupation provides the person with certain kinds of associates and colleagues, with roles he is expected to play as part of his work, with goals, ideals, mores, and a life-style that is associated with a particular vocation.

All of which underlines the fact that vocational choice is an important part of the developmental problem that needs to be solved in late adolescence. Many fathers are not the help to their adolescent sons and daughters that they could be. My own observation is that many fathers today were pushed by *their* fathers into certain occupations, and they are determined not to do the same to their sons or daughters. I think this attitude is a mistake when carried to an extreme.

As our technological society becomes increasingly complex, the problem of vocational choice becomes increasingly complicated. The *least* a father can do for his son or daughter is to continue to keep the lines of communication open. He can be a sounding board via the feedback technique for his adolescent's views concerning the problems, uncertainties, and difficulties in making his vocational choice and obtaining the requisite training. Unfortunately, few fathers do even this much. Vocational choice may hardly *ever* be talked about in a serious vein between father and late adolescent during these crucial years. If so, the girl or boy may discuss the problems of occupational choice only with their peers, a process remarkably like the blind leading the blind.

Often fathers do not discuss vocational choice with their adolescents because they fear that they will be considered being dictatorial and high-handed or because they feel inadequate to guide them in this very important decision. Many fathers do not realize that scientific help is available to them. One of the best investments you can make for sixteen-year-olds is to have them take vocational testing from a college or university or a psychologist in private practice. Many fathers do not realize that such vocational testing is available. This testing, in my opinion, should include the following four aspects of the adolescent's intelligence and personality structure: (1) his intelligence, evaluated by means of an individual rather than a group intelligence test; (2) his interests; (3) his aptitudes; and (4) his personality, evaluated by such personality tests as the Rorschach inkblot test, the Thematic Apperception Test (TAT) and the sentence-completion test.

It is necessary to evaluate a youngster's intelligence level, because if he is not intelligent enough for the occupation he envisages he obviously will not make it. If he is more intelligent than the job level he has chosen he will soon become bored and restless. I remember, for example, an adolescent I tested whose father was a physician. He wanted to become a doctor himself, but his intelligence level was not high enough. His aptitudes suggested that being a medical technician would satisfy his vocational aspirations and yet be realistic in terms of his intelligence level. It amazes me sometimes, how unrealistic are the parents' views of an adolescent's intelligence. Individual intelligence testing, in the hands of a trained psychologist, is not only something that can aid the adolescent in his choice of vocation, but in his choice of college. Once again, adolescents and parents are often highly unrealistic about which kind of college the adolescent should apply to.

The interests of an adolescent should be evaluated as part of his vocational testing. Obviously a person should be interested in the areas he will be involved with in his chosen occupation. Yet, we can be interested in things we have no aptitude for. I remember on a particular interest test I answered a question by saying that I would love to be the conductor of a symphony orchestra. But I was behind the door when musical aptitudes were passed out.

The aptitudes of an adolescent are certainly crucial in determining his success or failure. One of the problems is that many adolescents may have aptitudes for occupations they never knew existed. One adolescent girl I tested declared that she had thought about becoming a nurse. Yet she tested highest as an occupational therapist. She had never heard of occupational therapy and did not know what an occupational therapist is. I gave her a general description of the field, and suggested she contact the school of occupational therapy of a large nearby university to find out more about it. I pointed out that occupational therapy would fulfill many of the social-service interests which had led her to think of nursing as a career, but that her aptitudes for occupational therapy were higher than those for nursing.

The same type of thing happened to me personally. I have always had a strong interest in the social-service fields which were concerned with helping others. I have had contacts with ministers since I was a little boy, and so I was quite familiar with the ministry as a social-service vocation. When I was a late adolescent I had never seen a clinical psychologist and could not have told you what a psychologist did. Therefore, it was not surprising that in adolescence I made the vocational choice to become a minister rather than a psychologist. It was not until I had trained for the ministry and worked for several years as a minister that I began to have thoughts about shifting my profession to psychology. (And, incidentally, a number of psychologists are former ministers.) While in the midst of graduate work leading to my PhD in psychology, vocational testing confirmed that, in reality, my interests and aptitudes were much higher in the field of psychology than the ministry. Had I taken vocational testing when I was a late adolescent it is possible I would have chosen psychology as a profession at that time, instead of shifting, with considerable difficulty, in mid career.

Personality testing is another important part of vocational testing. But adolescents have stereotyped pictures of the personality needed for success in various vocations, so use caution. An adolescent boy I tested turned out to have a superior intelligence, plus interests and aptitudes which were high in the field of law. However, he was quite shy and introverted. Although quite attracted to law, he had become discouraged because, as he put it, "I guess I just don't have the personality for it." He was operating on the stereotype that every lawyer must be the brilliant, outgoing, verbal Perry Mason type, able to excel in public speaking and charm a jury with his words. I explained that this was only one aspect of the law, that there were other lawyers whose specialty was legal research who never made a speech before a jury. This provided him with a whole new outlook on the field and gave him the green light to push ahead to become a lawyer, which was what he basically wanted.

Another advantage of personality testing as a part of vocational testing is that it may turn up certain emotional blocks which, unless dealt with then, would interfere with success in the chosen occupational field. If such things can be tactfully but forthrightly presented, the adolescent may be motivated to get professional help to deal with these emotional blockages to occupational success. Otherwise, you might find a young man with the intelligence, interest, and aptitude to become a physician, who is dropped from medical school because of emotional problems in getting along with colleagues or patients. Such emotional difficulties might have been prevented had they been foreseen years earlier through vocational testing.

Vocational testing is not some magic panacea which will deal with all your youngster's difficulties and ambivalences in the choice of a vocation. Nor will vocational testing, as a rule, announce to your adolescent: *This specific field* (medicine or dentistry or law or teaching or whatever) is the one you should choose. Rather, the vocational testing will reveal, through the interpretations of a skilled psychologist: *These are your areas of strength,* vocationally, and it appears that these are the occupations in which you would most likely be both happy and successful.

One by-product of vocational testing and counseling is that it may be very helpful to the adolescent in his choice of college or trade school, and even in his attitude toward high school or college itself. For example, I tested one adolescent boy who wanted to be an architect. His testing confirmed that this desire was realistic. He had the intelligence, interest, aptitude, and the personality traits that would make him happy and successful as an architect. He was also very open and candid about his attitudes and actions. I inquired how he was doing in his studies and he answered, "Pretty good, except for math." I asked what was the matter with math and he said, "Well, I don't want my studies to interfere with my social life, you know, and I can bluff my way through pretty much everything else except math."

This initiated a conversation in which I pointed out that math played an important part as a foundation for architecture. He had not thought of it that way before. A few months later his father called me and said: "I don't know what you said to Anthony, but it must have been pretty potent, because his math grade is up tremendously." What had happened, of course, was that before vocational testing Anthony had thought of math only as another stupid course required by his high school. After vocational testing he saw it in quite a different light. Now math was something he needed to take seriously in order to become the new Frank Lloyd Wright of his generation.

Vocational testing can help prevent the kind of occupational tragedy I saw some years ago, when I tested a forty-two-year-old man who was unhappy in his work. He had been pressured by his father, a lawyer, into going to law school. He graduated, but never practiced law. Instead he drifted into working for a large insurance company, where he was employed when he came to me for vocational guidance. It turned out that he had always had a secret yen to be an engineer. I gave him the usual battery of vocational tests and it turned out that he would have probably been quite happy and successful had he chosen engineering in college years ago. However, he had a wife and three children and did not have the funds to go back to school full-time. It would take him approximately eight years to get his engineering degree going to school at night and, as he very realistically put it, "Who's going to want to hire a fifty-year-old engineer?" This kind of occupational tragedy could have been prevented by vocational testing in late adolescence.

However, vocational testing is not the whole answer. As part of my own vocational counseling of adolescents I encourage them to make a job description of the vocations that interest them. They should list such things as future demand for this vocation, potential salary or economic compensation, working hours, vacations and fringe benefits, education or training required and length of time this will take, etc. I also encourage adolescents to interview people already working in the field, first by writing a letter and then phoning for a personal appointment. Say, for example, a boy wants to be a dentist. I encourage him to interview dentists in the area, asking them what things they enjoy about their work and what things they dislike. I tell him to ask them specifically how their actual work as a dentist differs from their fantasies as adolescents of what it would be like. For, in many ways, it is true that almost everyone's vocational choice is partly colored and distorted by fantasy. You can only *really* know what it is like in an occupation in the same way you can only really know what a marriage is like: by being in it.

I want to emphasize again that vocational testing and guidance should only be done by a person or group professionally trained for it. This usually means the counseling and guidance center of a college or university, which may offer vocational testing—and many do not—or a trained PhD psychologist in private practice. You may not have such facilities near you but it is worth the money and time involved to drive a hundred miles or so to a place where your adolescent can obtain vocational testing and guidance. If such professional testing is totally out of the question for one reason or another, you can act as an informal vocational counselor to your son or daughter, helping them draw up a job description of the vocations they are considering, encouraging them to interview people in those occupations, etc. And even if you did nothing else but keep the lines of communication open about vocational choice and serve as a sounding board for changing feelings and perplexities, you would be rendering your adolescent a tremendous service.

The problem of vocational choice is quite different for a girl than a boy. In general, a male adolescent needs to decide on his vocation, get the required education or training, and if he has made a wise choice, work in that occupation for the rest of his life. With a girl, the situation, in the past, has been considerably different. Although she may have trained for a certain occupation, usually she married and started to raise a family. While it is possible for a woman with a preschool child or children to continue with her occupation, it is certainly not easy. She usually has to make difficult psychological demands on herself to do both.

While I am aware that my views on the differences between men's and women's occupational choices may seem hopelessly old-fashioned to some people, I still feel that psychologically the most satisfying occupational choice for most women will involve three phases: first, deciding on a vocation and becoming educated for it; second, getting married and starting a family (which may occur during the time she is training for a vocation, during the early practice of that vocation, or whenever); and third, at some later time in life returning to the practice of the vocation she has chosen (or perhaps to some other occupation). This third phase may occur at different times for different women. For some it will occur only after the last child has left the nest; for others, when the children are all in school. She can then work full-time or part-time without feeling too much psychological pressure, both as a full-time mother and as a full- or part-time worker in business and industry. It is certainly true that a larger and larger proportion of the working force in the United States consists of women. Our old patterns of who works and who takes care of the children in the family are changing rapidly.

Helping your daughter with her vocational choice is a more compli-cated task than helping your son. For example, assuming your daughter wants to get married and raise a family, you must consider that choosing a vocation which is easy to reenter after raising a family (such as teaching) is to be preferred to one which is difficult to reenter (such as medicine). I repeat: I am talking about a daughter who definitely wants to marry and raise a family. If your daughter has no such wishes (but women have been known to change their minds in this respect!), helping her to choose her vocation is no different from helping your son choose his.

I cannot leave the subject of vocational choice without noting that most of us construe its meaning too narrowly. We think of vocational choice as practically synonymous with the occupation by which we earn our living. I think the vocation of parenthood is one that is the most neglected, and the one for which we receive little or no preparation or training. Apart from economic considerations, that is one of the reasons many women seek outside employment even while their children are very little, and why so many men and women feel inadequate as parents. A woman will have been trained for the vocation of schoolteacher or secretary or doctor or lawyer, but nobody has considered the job of sufficient importance to train her for the vocation of raising babies and small children. A man may have been trained to be a plumber or a writer or an accountant, but not how to be a father.

For this reason, I hope you will include the need for this training in your communication with your sons and daughters. One natural way to do this arises when they tell you about their baby-sitting jobs (and complain about that "brat" they have to take care of). This is a good time to point out that no one should be expected to handle a "brat" without a little training in child psychology and the vocation of parenthood. You might suggest helpful books for them to read in handling children, such as *Improving Your Child's Behavior* by Madeline Hunter and Paul Carlson.

The second developmental task of late adolescence is to work out a satisfactory relationship with the opposite sex and establish some of the stable patterns of a heterosexual love life. In the chapters on early adolescence, I pointed out that your teen-ager has to master the tremendous impact of his newfound sexual impulses at puberty, and that his first efforts at this are usually fumbling and uncertain. A boy may typically have two completely different types of "sex life": a solitary one consisting of masturbation with fantasies of Playboy playmates and erotic women, and a reality-based situation, in which he feels attracted to a girl in his class but is too shy and fearful to talk to her. In addition, in early adolescence, each boy and girl finds the "family romance" reactivated and must work this through (though usually not in his conscious mind) with the parent of the opposite sex. Until the revived "family romance" of early adolescence is worked through, for example, the boy may still be too strongly tied to his mother's apron strings to date girls of his own age. Normally, these things are worked through in the three years of early adolescence. By late adolescence the young boy or girl is ready to begin dating the opposite sex in earnest.

There are great individual variations, but the movement toward the opposite sex usually begins with group gatherings and group parties. The next step is often double-dating, leading up finally to single-dating. Of course, there are many variations in this pattern. A sixteen-year-old boy, for example, may show absolutely no interest in parties or double-dating, and the next thing his parents know he has suddenly established a relationship with a girl and is seeing a great deal of her.

What is taking place in this gradual movement from group parties to double-dating to single-dating is that adolescents are overcoming their fears and inhibitions. This general pattern has not changed for many years. What *has* changed in recent years is the rapidity with which fears and inhibitions about sex are being cast off by today's adolescents. This is made startlingly evident in a recent scientific study about adolescent sexuality by Dr. Robert Sorensen, a social psychologist, entitled *Adolescent Sexuality in Contemporary America.* This is the most comprehensive national study ever made of the sexual behavior of American teen-agers. Information in the study was based upon more than 600 interviews with adolescents, who were carefully chosen to be a representative sample of teen-agers from 13 to 20 in the United States. Careful precautions were taken to make sure that the sample was representative of the teen-age population of the United States as a whole, and to make sure that the information gained from questionnaires and interviews was reliable. The confidentiality of each participant was carefully protected. The 600 adolescents interviewed were broken down into two groups: 200 in-depth interviews and a national probability sample of more than 400.

Incidentally, the information found in this national study agrees generally with my own experience and that of other therapists who talk confidentially with teen-agers.

The study is well worth reading, although no doubt many parents will be shaken by it. It abounds in statistics, but don't get lost among the statistical trees so that you can't see the total forest the study is talking about. What the study is saying could be put in the form of an analogy between the United States and Sweden. In past times, United States adolescents were not supposed to have full and complete sexual relations until after marriage. (Many did, as Kinsey's study pointed out in the late 1940s, but according to the cultural mores they weren't supposed to.) In the past, men and women were supposed to fall in love (whatever that meant) and then get married. After that they were allowed to have full and complete sexual relations. In Sweden, they did things differently. Late adolescents formed heterosexual relationships which included sexual intimacy as well as emotional intimacy. On the basis of a much wider range of sexual experience than their counterparts in America, young adults chose their marital partners.

This study says, in broad terms, that patterns of adolescent sexual relationships in the United States have moved startlingly in the direction of the patterns of Sweden. For example, 52 percent of all 13 to 19 year olds in the United States have had sexual intercourse before they are twenty. Nearly 40 percent of the first intercourse experience took place in the home of the boy or girl involved. An automobile was the location for only 20 percent. Among nonvirgin adolescents, 71 percent of the boys and 56 percent of the girls had had sexual intercourse by the age of 15. Only 5 percent of the nonvirgin boys and 17 percent of the nonvirgin girls waited until they were 18 or 19 to have intercourse for the first time.

The attitude toward sex among today's adolescents shows a striking change from that of previous decades. According to one of the questions in the questionnaire, for example, 85 percent of all adolescents believe that their sex life is "pretty normal for a person my age." Eighty-four percent believe that they have come to definite conclusions about what they think is right and wrong. In contrast to previous decades when it was widely believed that a boy wanted to marry a virgin and would lose respect for a girl who had lost her virginity, 65 percent of male adolescents disagree with the statement, "I wouldn't want to marry a girl who isn't a virgin at marriage." Seventy-one percent of boys disagree with the statement, "A girl who goes to bed with a boy before marriage will lose his respect."

The study also shows that a staunch minority of adolescents still cling to older sex ways and attitudes. Twenty-one percent of all adolescents have neither engaged in beginning sex activities nor had

"I'M AT MY WIT'S END...
THIRTEEN AND I'M STILL A VIRGIN!"

sexual intercourse. The study defined "sexual inexperience" as "the total absence of any sexual contact with another person, other than kissing, that either aimed at or resulted in pleasurable physical reactions."[4] It should be noted that according to this definition, an adolescent who masturbates would still be classified as sexually inexperienced, since he had not had intimate sexual relations with another person. Sexual inexperience declines as the adolescent grows older. The percentage of adolescents having sexual experience rises from 68 percent at age 15 to approximately 90 percent at age 16. At age 19, only about 5 percent of all adolescents remain sexually inexperienced.

The author sums up many of the findings of his study as follows: "It can be seen that a new kind of love is being worked out by American adolescents in a strongly sexual context. Mutuality and belonging are emphasized by many young people in describing what love means to them. One result of this has been a lessening need to require sex as a fundamental condition of a love relationship. Fully 82 percent of all adolescents denied that the most important thing in a love relationship is sex, with the intercourse-experienced no less firm in their conviction about this than the virgins."[5]

What do these findings mean? First, as a psychologist I cannot tell you what ethical or moral or religious stand to take on this situation. We live in a society of pluralistic moral and religious values. Even within the same church group, for example, you will find wide variations among the parents of adolescents as to what standards of sexual behavior they wish for their teen-agers. Consequently, you have to make up your mind from the standpoint of your religious background or lack of it, or your own moral and ethical value system, as to what sexual standards you hope for from your adolescent. What I can do is furnish you with psychological facts; facts such as the results of this survey, and facts such as the attitudes of different parents toward the sexual behavior of their teen-agers.

We might classify parents of late adolescents into four groups, according to their sexual attitudes and standards. First is the group holding the view of past decades that sex and sexual intercourse is to be reserved for marriage. I know parents who hold this view and communicate it clearly to their adolescents. But, as a psychologist, I also know that many such parents are in total ignorance when it comes to the sexual activities of their adolescents. In my clinical practice I have often had parents say to me, "Of course my Tommy or Jane or Suzy has had no sexual experience yet." But Tommy or Jane or Suzy have told me confidentially in therapy that they have, in fact, had considerable sexual experience which their parents know nothing about. Of course, there are other parents who have made this view clear and their adolescents have accepted it and reserved their sexual experiences for marriage.

Second, there are what I call the "head in the sand" parents. These parents have a pretty good suspicion of what is going on sexually with their adolescent, but they hide this knowledge from themselves. As one father said to me in the course of therapy, "If Betty is having sex relations with this boy I don't want to know about it!" Of course, the fact that he brought it up at all strongly suggests that at some level of consciousness he already *did* know and care about it! The message from the first group of parents is clear-cut: we want you to reserve sex for marriage. The message adolescents receive from the second group of parents is ambiguous and indecisive: "We haven't decided ourselves what kind of sexual standards we want you to have, so we will engage in a mutual pretense society that you are not engaging in any sexual activities. That way we won't have to face the issue."

There is a third group of parents who send a message like this to their adolescent. "We think it's best if you wait until later when you are more mature to have sexual intercourse and full sexual relations. But we also think an unwanted pregnancy is a pretty bad thing. And so we want you to have full information about contraceptives, which ones are reliable and which are not." Furthermore, to a girl they may say, "We may not approve of your having sex relations at this age, but if you feel you need the pill, we would much rather give our approval than take the chance of an unwanted pregnancy."

The statistics from Dr. Sorensen's study (and also the evidence from psychologists and psychiatrists who see adolescents in counseling as part of their regular practice) suggest that unwanted pregnancies are indeed a problem for many adolescents. Eleven percent of all nonvirgin girls, aged 13 to 15, and 28 percent of all nonvirgin girls, aged 16 to 19, report having been pregnant at least once.

There is a widespread belief that today's teen-agers are making intensive use of the Pill as a method of contraception. This study, and the experience of those of us in clinical practice, do not support this belief. For example, 55 percent of all nonvirgin adolescents report that at the time of first sexual intercourse, neither they nor their partners used any birth-control method or did anything to cut down on the risk of the girl becoming pregnant. The birth-control method that girls most frequently report using is birth-control pills (33%). The second method most frequently reported by girls is coitus interruptus, or withdrawal of the boy's penis before ejaculation (17%). In my own clinical experience I have seen the most incredible naiveté about contraceptive methods as teen-agers tell me about their sexual relationships. I think of one girl who used absolutely no contraceptives for over a year and by some fantastic stroke of luck did not get pregnant. I think of many who have used coitus interruptus, not knowing how unreliable that method is. A number of girls have used vaginal foam because they heard about it and can buy it easily in the drugstore, not knowing how unreliable that contraceptive method can be. My clinical experience as well as that of others, and of Dr. Sorensen's study, indicate that far from being sophisticated about birth-control techniques, today's adolescents are grossly ignorant.

And how could they be otherwise? Where are they going to get the scientific information about different birth-contol techniques? Such information is usually deliberately left out of so-called sex education courses in schools. And most adolescents do not get this information from their parents. Sixty-eight percent of all girls and 80 percent of all boys studied by Dr. Sorensen said that their parents had given them no facts about birth control. So this third group of parents I described, while indicating to their adolescents a "go slow" approach on sex and sexual intercourse, are at the same time being forthright and open sources of information on birth control to their teen-agers when compared to the norm.

Then there is a fourth group of parents. The attitude of this group can be summed up as follows. They believe there are two things that are really dangerous to their adolescent as he makes his way toward a stable heterosexual adjustment: one is an unwanted pregnancy, and the other is an early marriage. They convey this sort of attitude toward their adolescent: "Times have changed. When I was a teen-ager there was a lot of hypocrisy about sex. I got zero sex education at home. I did a lot of things my parents didn't know about and felt terribly guilty. I feel differently now, and I don't want you to go through the same things I did as a teen-ager.

"I want you to marry a person with whom you will have a happy and satisfying marriage, including a good sex life. I know that your way of arriving at this will be different from the way I arrived at it when I was an adolescent.

"One of the dangers I want you to avoid is an unwanted pregnancy. That's why I'm going to give you adequate birth-control information, and give you my permission to use contraceptives when you are at that point in your relationship with another person. I trust you and believe that you're not going to have intercourse promiscuously with just any person. I know you would have to have a deep love relationship with a person in order to want to be physically intimate.

"Also, I don't want you to rush into early marriage. Current statistics show that one out of every three marriages today ends in divorce, and if the couple are teen-agers, the odds are reduced to one out of two. I know that some couples rush into early marriage so that they can have 'legal sex.' I know that other couples rush into early marriage because the girl is pregnant and they feel they have to get married. I know, and statistics back me up, that if you are older and more mature when you are married, your chances of success are much greater. I want you to have considerable experience with the opposite sex before you get married. Drs. Masters and Johnson estimate that 50 percent of American married couples have serious sexual problems. Maybe more and deeper experiences of intimacy among couples before marriage, including sexual intimacy, will help to prevent that. At any rate, I don't want you to believe that sex is available to you only through marriage and therefore you have to rush into an early marriage to satisfy your sexual desires.

"Also, I feel I do have something to offer you about sexual information and attitudes that you may not be able to get anywhere else. I want to keep our lines of communication open so that you feel free to ask me questions or come to me with any problem involving sex without feeling that I'm going to condemn you."

Of course, none of these four groups of parents conveys the attitudes and standards I have described in a set speech to their adolescent, delivered on some specific occasion. Rather, these attitudes and standards are conveyed in a thousand different ways, some verbal and some non-verbal.

I have observed over the years how abysmally few parents have given their adolescents *any* sex education at home, and how few have been able to keep open the lines of communication about sex. Most often this is because the adolescent believes, rightly or wrongly, that if he dared to talk with his parent about the things he has really done sexually the parent would condemn him.

It is not up to me as a scientist to say which of these groups of parents you "should" belong to or what sexual standards you "should" espouse for your adolescent son or daughter. That is a matter of your own ethical, moral, and religious values. What I emphasize is that regardless of what your value standards are, *it is important that you communicate them to your adolescent.* And in the area of sex there is the largest communication gap between parent and adolescent. One of the striking findings of Dr. Sorensen's study is that 80 percent of all adolescents have a great deal of respect for their parent's ideas and opinions. So let your ideas and opinions be known to your adolescent! Even though he may later rebel against your ideas and sexual standards *he wants to know where you stand.*

Many parents feel that they do not count for much in their adolescent's lives and that their teen-agers will not really listen to what they have to say. Such parents are usually wrong. I had a father in therapy some years back whose eighteen-year-old girl informed him she was going to marry a particular young man. He said that he told her "blessings on both of you and good luck." Something in the tone of his voice made me inquire if that was how he really felt about the situation. "Hell no!" he replied. "I think she's too young to get married—at eighteen—and furthermore I think it would be a mistake for her to marry this particular guy. I think they would be divorced in a couple of years." I asked him why he had concealed his real feelings from his daughter and he said, "Because I don't think she would listen to what I have to say."

I encouraged him to tell his daughter his real feelings. To his immense surprise, she took what he had to say very seriously. She also had doubts about the wisdom of marrying this particular young man, and her father's views were exactly the outside brake she needed to put a halt to an impulsive action. She wound up deciding not to marry this particular boy. Four years later, when she was 22, she decided to get married, after much more mature consideration. If I had not happened to encourage him, that father might never have told his daughter his real feelings. He was like so many parents today who despair, quite wrongly, of having any meaningful impact at all on the thinking of their adolescents. Again I want to emphasize, don't be deceived by external appearances. Even though you may be in the psychological background of your adolescent's life, you are still a very important person to him. He needs to know where you stand on key issues, without your condemning him if he sees things differently. And he needs you to speak directly about anything where you feel he may be making a serious mistake.

For some fathers the findings of Dr. Sorensen's study and the new attitudes and sexual behavior among late adolescents may be deeply shocking and disturbing. You may fervently wish things were as they were "in the good old days" when parents did not have to cope with the new sexual freedom of their late adolescents. But wishing will not turn the psychological clock back. This is the way today's adolescents are behaving. You will probably have to wrestle with the psychological hangups left over from your own adolescence. Above all, try to keep the channels of communication open so that your adolescent will not feel that sex is a taboo subject to talk about with you.

Late adolescents are struggling to attain the capacity for *intimacy* with a member of the opposite sex, and sexuality is only a part of that struggle. Remember that a high-school junior or senior has had very little experience with the opposite sex in any deep and intimate form. His first "loves" are meaningful experiences for him. Whereas in past decades these first loves did not include intimate sexual experiences, they are likely to now. But the problem is bigger than sex. Your adolescent is very new at learning the give and take of love, learning to be close and open and genuine in his relationships, building self-confidence that he can love and be loved as an individual.

Whatever sexual experiences your youngster may have had in early adolescence have probably been highly self-centered and narcissistic. He has not been ready psychologically to tackle the problem of intimacy until late adolescence. Now he gradually begins to have a less self-centered orientation to his affectionate and sexual needs. He is beginning to learn that the welfare of the other is also important. For the first time in his life an intense emotional attachment, which combines both the affectional and the erotic, replaces the intense attachment to a parent.

When this happens, many parents, whether they are aware of it or not, become jealous. You will hear them say things like: "Well, you saw Betty all day Saturday, why do you need to see her again today?" In my clinical practice, numerous adolescents have told me, "I've got my homework and my chores done for Monday, so what reason is there for my folks not to want me to see Betty so much over the weekend?" And the answer, of course, is that his folks are jealous and don't know it. They find it deeply disturbing that this "stranger" now seems to occupy the central position in their adolescent's life.

Even though these early loves of high school rarely last, they form important learnings for the future. These early heterosexual relationships are an important maturity step, a sort of role rehearsal of how to relate to a being of the opposite sex on intimate terms. They should be taken seriously by parents and never ridiculed or belittled. Your high-school senior may be convinced that Sally is his one and true love, forever and ever, and it is best to accept his definition of the relationship until such a time as it changes!

Now we come to the third and final developmental task of late adolescence, that of completing the emancipation from parents and family.

The difference between an early and late adolescent, with regard to the way in which he strives to emancipate himself from parents and family, is that the early adolescent is still close to childhood, and fighting his dependency urges; so he tried to emancipate himself with a "crash program" and does it in an obnoxious manner. Hopefully, your adolescent will work these feelings out of his system early so he can emancipate himself from his family in a quieter manner during late adolescence.

He will be off on his own, working at his studies and extra-curricular activities in school. He will be making tentative occupational choices and experimenting with them. He will be spending enormous amounts of time with his friends, both male and female. He will be experiencing his first loves and intimate relationships with the opposite sex. In all these activities, the family is a stable psychological background he needs to know is there. Parents are now a comfortable support, rather than the prying monsters he has had to fight and continually rebel against.

On the other hand, your teen-ager might have been a conformist in early adolescence and have postponed his active and hostile rebellion until late adolescence. Each teen-ager is an individual and each is going to make his own unique way through the adolescent years. But generally, by late adolescence your teen-ager is beginning to act like a semi-adult, someone on the verge of full adult status. He is losing his child-centered perspective of the world. Hopefully, he is beginning to see you and his mother as persons with lives of their own, rather than merely as "someone who is trying to hold me down and whom I have to fight against."

If your adolescent is revolting during his late high-school years, it means that it is not until now that he has been able to tackle the task of freeing himself from his emotional dependency on you. He has spent years studying your flaws and weak points and now he begins to press on them. Welcome to the Parent's "Ouch!" Club. None of us enjoy having our behavior criticized, and a late adolescent has lots of emotional and intellectual weapons to do this job. Unfortunately, many parents return these attacks and bitterly criticize the adolescent who is attacking them. This only widens the generation gap, escalates the war, and makes things immeasurably worse. It is often hard to realize that an adolescent only wants to become emotionally free and be able to stand on his own two feet. His aim is not really to demolish you, only to become emancipated from his emotional dependence.

This is an extraordinarily difficult time for parents. You have spent years doing things for and with him, guiding and directing his behavior, investing a great deal of love and affection in him. No matter how much you try to understand this on an intellectual level, he is an ingrate on an emotional level. He is moving away from you emotionally and leaving you. How can he do this after all you have done for him? Since you cannot see and cannot *feel* into the future, you don't realize that after he has emotionally moved away from you through adolescence, the two of you can establish a new satisfying relationship of an older adult to a younger adult.

Late adolescence is doubly hard on many parents in that it coincides with a very difficult period in their own life-span, that of middle age, with its attendant middle-age crisis. I think that all middle-aged parents of adolescents should read *The Middle-Age Crisis* by Barbara Fried (Harper and Row). Sooner or later, every middle-aged person must come to terms with the realities of his accomplishments and lack of accomplishments. For the man, this will concern, in large measure, his attitude toward his work. For many men the job at which they have labored for so many years has lost its savor. They have to face the fact that their earlier fantasies of success are not going to work out. On the other hand, if the man has been successful at his job, even this may pall and he may begin to ask himself: Is this occupational carrot I chased and finally caught, so good to eat after all?

For a mother, her middle-age crisis usually centers more around the end of her children's dependency on her, and may coincide with her menopause. At any event, she must face and overcome an emptiness in her life. It is as if an inner voice is crying out: "My children used to need me and now they don't; what use am I now?"

In the years up through early adolescence much of the emotional balance of the marriage depended upon both husband and wife working together to raise the children. Now that they are no longer children but late adolescents, the parents' marriage must inevitably go through some readjustments and realignments.

Faced with the difficult emotional tasks of mid-life at the very same time they are trying to cope with the emotional flak sent up by their adolescent, is it any wonder that parents of late adolescents have a difficult time? But remember that parents have faced and overcome these twin problems for ages. Though there will be times when you will be discouraged and disheartened at the problems of trying to raise an adolescent successfully, you can do it, too.

Perhaps, I have painted too grim a picture of the late high-school years of sixteen, seventeen, and eighteen with its new sexual standards, its threat of drugs, its emotional moving away from parents so characteristic of this age, and the readjustments in the parent's own middle age, which often occur at the same time their youngsters become late adolescents.

So let's not forget the brighter side of the picture. A large number of late adolescents are not involved with drugs and not at emotional loggerheads with their parents. While they are definitely into their own activities, they can still maintain friendly and warm relationships with their parents.

Seventeen (or eighteen for some teen-agers) is the senior year of high school, and your youngster is enjoying the good things that being a senior brings: the status of being top man on the totem pole, a senior, to whom the underclassmen look up. At the same time, he feels somewhat insecure about the decisions he needs to make. Whether to go on to college, and if so, which one? Will he be accepted by the college he wants? Should he go away to college or live at home and go to a local school? Should he go to trade school instead of college? Or should he go to work? All these questions plague him and he is liable to reach out to you for help in talking these things over on a more adult basis.

Whichever decision he makes, his high-school graduation means a great deal to him emotionally. It is important for you, as his father, to give it the meaning it deserves. I have had patients in therapy, for example, who felt resentful many years later because their father did not rearrange some business trip or appointment to attend their high-school graduation. They told me with great bitterness: "I didn't even mean enough to my father for him to come and see me graduate!" Be sure to be there for your adolescent's graduation and celebrate it accordingly with gifts and a family party.

Once their youngster has graduated from high school, many parents think that he is completely on his own and has no further need for parenting. I do not agree. True, he does not need the same kind of close parenting with firmly set limits and restrictions as he did in high school. But, inside, he feels more insecure about the wide, wide world than he lets on. And so he still needs what I call *background parenting*. In the main, he is off doing his own thing, but you are there in the background to give him a feeling of security. And you are available if some emergency should arise.

Suppose your youngster decides to go away to college; he will need your help in choosing the school. You would be amazed at how many colleges are picked by students on a purely haphazard basis. He should arrange to visit the colleges from which he is making his choice so that he will have some first-hand experience with the one he ultimately does choose. If a visit is possible, I think you should insist upon it, even if your adolescent is not in favor of it.

If you can afford it, I believe it is immeasurably better for your late adolescent to go away to college rather than live at home. He will go through enormous emotional and psychological changes during his college years. If he is living at home, it will be rather difficult for a late adolescent and his parents to get along amicably in the same house. Even if your adolescent *wants* to live at home and go to college, I think parents should *insist* he go away to school as a growth experience.

Once your adolescent is away at college, you will get used to certain unpleasant realities. One is that unless your adolescent is most unusual, he will write to you very seldom. As my daughter said in her first letter home after she had been away at college two and a half months, "Everybody jokes about only writing home when you need money, so here I am writing because I need money!"

Like most parents, you may feel neglected or resentful, but remember: the fact that your son or daughter doesn't write very often doesn't mean they have ceased to love you. They are just wrapped up in their own affairs. Although they write very seldom, they do appreciate your writing to them. Especially if you clip an article out of a newspaper or magazine you think may interest them. Your college student, probably on his own for the first time in his life, needs to know he still has a secure home base, that you are still there and that you still care about him. It is a kind of one-sided parenting, where you are giving to him, but he is not giving much in return. It's helpful if you can get together with other parents of college students and commiserate with each other about the situation! What is important is that you realize that not writing very frequently is typical behavior for a student away at college. Then you will not think you have failed miserably as a parent and that's why he is acting in this way.

When your son comes home on a weekend or at Christmas or Easter, it's important to know what to expect. If he brings friends with him, please try to treat them with respect. Don't bug him or his friends about their hair or clothing or other things that were different when you were his age. Chances are he will not want to spend much time with his parents; he will want to spend it with his friends.

Parents tend to nurse hurt feelings because their son or daughter doesn't want to spend much time with them. Once again, this is typical behavior for a college student. And yet, it is as if a voice deep inside the parent is saying: "Look at all the money I'm laying out so that he can go away to college, and when he comes home at Christmas he acts like a stranger in the family! So this is my reward for being a good parent!" Cheer up, dad—he's not an adult yet. And when late adolescence is finally over, when he's graduated from college and at work on his first job, then you and he will be able to enjoy each other as adults. In fact, you will see a definite progression between his freshman and senior year as he is able to relate to you more like an adult.

There is one special circumstance you can hope you will be spared during his college years and that is being called about some emergency. The emergency can be of any sort: a warning notice that he is flunking out, an unwanted pregnancy, drunk driving, or drug problems. But if you do get that unpleasant phone call, I hope you will not land on your college student with all four feet. Instead, I hope you will hear him out. Give him a chance to tell you what happened and use the feeback technique to let him know you understand how he feels. Above all, whatever kind of crisis it is, keep your lines of communication open. How you react to your college student in some crisis situation may determine the whole course of his life.

Now suppose your adolescent son or daughter lives at home while attending college. I do not recommend this from a psychological standpoint, but it may be necessary economically. Your adolescent will be going through enormous intellectual and emotional changes during his college years. These changes may be difficult for parents to cope with if he is living at home. I myself lived at home during college and it did not help my relationship with my parents. I can still remember some of the conflicts that raged around the dinner table as I espoused some of my new found "isms" to my harassed parents. I remember responding to one of my father's political diatribes by cooly announcing to the family: "Well, as a matter of fact I'm pretty much of a Communist, myself!" Not that I really was a Communist, of course. But that flat announcement served its purpose: it put my father on the ceiling and, as I recall he didn't come down for about three days!

So a live-at-home college student may choose to issue a number of rabble-rousing statements to you, ranging from, "Marriage is on its way out; group sex is the wave of the future" to "Most of the kids at Downtown College are on drugs of some kind." Resist the temptation to rise to the bait of such provocative statements. If you can manage to carry on a reasonably calm discussion on the topic, fine; if not, stay off of the subject.

Another common phenomenon of the live-at-home college student is that his room becomes his fortress, and that's where he spends his time at home apart from mealtime. In some cases he hardly speaks to his parents and acts more like a stranger, temporarily living in your house than a member of your family. Once again, this is because the late adolescent's "bag" is elsewhere. It doesn't mean that he hates or rejects you, but he is in the final phase of emotionally separating himself from you. This final phase may be a painful one emotionally and if you can at all afford it, allow your late adolescent to have his own apartment rather than have him live at home. You and he will appreciate each other much more.

Incidentally, to his friends his parents may appear to be wonderful people, but the adolescent himself cannot stand them. The reason for this is that he still has psychological work to do emancipating himself. Sometimes the only way that can be done is to work up a number of psychological grievances against them.

Of course, none of these things may apply at all to your late-adolescent son or daughter. He may be able to live at home, attend college, and still maintain a reasonable and friendly relationship with you. If so, fine! Count your blessings and let him live at home.

Suppose your late adolescent has chosen the option of trade school. Many parents, unfortunately, discourage their high-school students from making such a choice because to them it is somehow mystically important for their son to go to college. College is not the be-all and end-all of existence and is not for all high-school kids. I think of one youngster with whom I did vocational testing. He was miserable in the academic courses in high school: history and English and foreign languages, etc., but he loved automobiles and motor-cycles, and wanted to be an auto mechanic. Fortunately, his parents did not try to force him into their mold or that of the other children in the family. They stood behind him and supported his decision to become an auto mechanic (and someday to open his own shop). After graduation from high school he entered trade school where he is now happily studying auto mechanics and doing very well.

If your youngster does go to trade school, he will either live at home or get an apartment, so the same psychological things about living at home and going to college hold true.

I want to say a good word about a growing practice among high-school graduates: deferred entrance to college. In this plan, the adolescent applies to and is accepted by the college of his choice. Then he writes and explains that he would like to be accepted under their deferred plan, in which he postpones his entrance for one year. That year between high school and college he takes out and works. Or perhaps he may get a job abroad for a year. There is much psychological merit in such an idea, because working for a year after graduation from high school is a maturing experience, probably more so than simply moving right into college.

Possibly your late adolescent has no plans for any further education and wants to begin work immediately. Fine; that's his decision and I think you should support him in it. If he works, then he should support himself financially. In such a situation it is best if he gets an apartment and lives away from home, but if he does live at home he should pay room and board for the privilege.

The one mistake you should *not* make is to allow your late adolescent the privilege of choosing not to go to college or trade school, but to continue living at home *without* working. If that is what he wants, I think you should take a stand with him, lovingly but firmly: "If you want to go to college or trade school or art school or music school or have any further education beyond high school, then your mother and I will continue to support you financially as we have in the past. We think that's part of our job as parents: to help you finish your education. But if you feel that your education is completed, fine; then it's up to you to go to work and support yourself. When your education is completed, our obligation to support you financially is completed also. So off on your own, and good luck!"

I mention this particularly because I know of many late adolescents who are bumming around the country or living in communes while they are supposedly trying to "discover their identities" and "find themselves." The only way they are able to survive financially is because of the arrival of checks from home. I think this is a mistake, and that the parents are really subsidizing *not* "finding themselves" under the guise of "finding themselves." One of the best ways parents can help these late adolescents mature is to cut off the money from home. Then the young people would have to learn to stand on their own two feet financially.

I have painted a picture of the relationship between you and your late adolescent which is not by any means one of unalloyed bliss and harmony. So once again I want to reiterate that you may find your relationship with your late adolescent son or daughter a peaceful, stable, and emotionally rewarding one. On the other hand the relationship may be one of strain, difficulty, and hurt and angry feelings on both sides. But I prefer to end with this positive note. The basic reason for the difficulties in the relationships with a late adolescent of eighteen, nineteen, or twenty, is that he is in his final stage of severing his childhood dependency, finding his identity, and standing on his own two feet as an adult. Some late adolescents, depending on their own benign temperament and a very good relationship with you beginning in their preschool years, may be able to sever the remaining parental ties in late adolescence rather gracefully and gently. Other late adolescents, with a more stormy temperament and not such a good relationship with you throughout the years, are going to sever the last remaining parental ties with pain, storm, and stress.

However, no matter how difficult your relationship with your late adolescent, if you hang in there and keep the lines of communication open, things will change drastically as he moves from late adolescence to young adulthood. As he casts off the last parental ties, your late adolescent finally makes it into young adulthood. He no longer has to fight you emotionally to be free. He *is* free, and his and your relationship can change accordingly. Now, all of the love, hard work, and patience you put into being a parent and guiding him through the different stages of development should pay off. Your relationship can take on a completely new aspect: no longer that of parent and child or parent and late adolescent, but a new relationship of young adult to older adult. Hopefully, this new and positive relationship will continue for the rest of your lives.

If you happen to have a stormy relationship with your late adolescent, remember that in the same way that the "terrible two's" passed and "preadolescence" passed, this too will pass and be succeeded by a happier and more positive relationship when your late adolescent enters young adulthood.

14

Divorce and Remarriage and Blended Families

In today's society, with its high divorce rate, it would be amiss not to cover the topic of the special problems faced by the divorced father, the stepfather, and the blended family.

This chapter is for the father in the process of divorce or who is already divorced. Other fathers may not be at that stage, but are nevertheless seriously thinking about divorce. If so, I strongly recommend that you and your wife get professional help from a psychologist, psychiatrist, or marriage counselor. You have everything to gain and nothing to lose.

Professional counseling may enable you and your wife to straighten out your personal problems and achieve sufficiently genuine communication between you so that your marriage is strengthened. On the other hand, after a period of professional counseling you may decide that the marriage had best come to an end for the benefit of all concerned. But to come to this decision after a period of professional counseling is very different from making such a decision hastily or on a trial and error basis on your own. You will at least know that you did the best you could to work out the problems and make the marriage satisfactory for both partners. You will not have to torture yourself later wondering: "If only I had tried this or that, maybe my marriage could have been saved."

Let me make it clear that I believe it is a mistake to continue in a profoundly unhappy marriage "for the sake of the children." It is not necessarily true that a child from a broken home will be more neurotic or delinquent than that same child would have been if his parents had maintained an intact home—but one torn by strife, hostility, and unhappiness.

Suppose you were unable to work out your marriage and you are now either divorced, or in the process. It may surprise you, but I still recommend that the most important thing you can do to help both yourself and your children is to get professional counseling for yourself during this period. We have the term "marriage counseling"; we should have the term "divorce counseling" as well. By "divorce counseling" I mean professional counseling with a psychologist, psychiatrist, or marriage counselor which a man or woman obtains when in the process of divorce or the first year following it.

In almost all cases, divorce is an emotionally shattering experience for both the husband and wife. No matter who takes the initiative to end the marriage, the astounding psychological fact is that *both* husband and wife end up feeling rejected! Divorce is an immense body blow to your self-concept and your self-esteem. Furthermore, even though you think your marriage was a "bad" one, divorce brings with it a great sense of loss: loss of an intact family circle where you once belonged, loss of a wife, loss of the children on a full-time basis. In many ways, the period of separation and the first year or two following divorce are the closest thing to a hell on earth that any father goes through. One man writes about his private hell in these terms:

> . . . the night I walked out of our family home was the loneliest night of my life. And it was followed by many other lonely days and nights as I tried desperately to adjust and find myself and my new position in what appeared to me to be a cruel and hostile world.[1]

The extent to which you can give your children the support and understanding they need during this difficult period depends upon how satisfactorily you are able to weather the emotional storms yourself. You could not possibly invest money more wisely during this time than in getting emotional help and guidance from a trained professional. If you live remote from this type of professional help, then perhaps a minister or family doctor can aid you. At least, find one friend you can trust to keep what you tell him confidential and talk out your problems as you go through this rough time.

In other words, there is important psychological "work" you have to do during this difficult period, whether with professional help or alone. What does this psychological work consist of? When we lose something or someone important to us, there is what psychologists call "grief work" to be done. However it happened, you have lost a marriage and family, you have lost a wife, and you have partially lost your children. The grief-work you have to do is similar to the grief-work you have to do if someone you love dies. You go through a period of psychological mourning. You mourn the death of a marriage and a family. Memories of happy times with your wife and children will come into your mind and will be very painful. At times, it will be agonizing to think of them. You need to talk out these excruciatingly painful feelings with somebody, whether it is a professional person or a trusted friend. This is the most helpful way to accomplish your grief-work, rather than keeping feelings bottled up inside. Grief-work takes time; it cannot be hurried. No definite length of time can be cited, but many divorced fathers have reported that it took them at least a year to work their way through these feelings about the death of their marriage.

One of the best ways to accomplish your grief-work is to talk to other divorced persons, both male and female. Ask them how it was with them in their first years of divorce. Parents Without Partners, a non-profit organization with chapters throughout the United States, is a good group. I recommend joining this group for many reasons, but right now I'm stressing it as a place to find other divorced parents to whom you can talk. Generally speaking, the person who understands your situation best is another divorced father or mother. Once you become a single parent, you enter a completely new psychological world. You will probably find other similar groups of divorced people you can join, Solo Parents, Singletarians, singles groups sponsored by a church, YMCA, or YWCA. It is particularly important for you to find such a group in the early stages of separation and divorce when the feelings you have to contend with are at their most difficult. In addition, a book called *The World of the Formerly Married* by Morton Hunt, will help you greatly in understanding your new psychological situation as a single person.

After working your way through a period of psychological "death" you go through a period of "rebirth." In your marriage relationship, only part of the person you really are was brought to the surface. Now other parts of you must be discovered. In other words, your concept of yourself was to a greater or lesser extent limited by your marriage. Now you go through a period in which a new self-concept is born. This isn't any easier than the grief-work. You need to break old psychological molds, experiment with new hobbies or sports or activities that you may have considered in the past but never tried.

Psychological rebirth of the self is necessary though difficult because during divorce you develop a case of low self-esteem. The woman you were married to has conveyed the message: "You are no longer desirable to me as a man." Even if you took the initiative in dissolving the marriage, you still received this message. That's why I said before that, amazingly enough, in any divorce, no matter who initiates the action, both parties have to deal with feelings of rejection. You must rediscover that you can still be lovable and desirable to the opposite sex. This is not easy. Once rejected, the natural tendency of most of us is to avoid any possible further rejection. Many fathers do this in the early period after a divorce and become psychological hermits for a while. I believe this is a mistake. Put yourself into circulation again. One of the fastest ways to recover your self-esteem is to find that other women feel differently about you than your ex-wife does.

Since divorce means the breakup of a vast web of psychological relationships, you must devise methods of countering loneliness and isolation. You can do this in a variety of ways. Join some singles groups. Keep up your relationships with your married friends wherever possible. I know one divorced father who asked a married couple with children if he could eat dinner with them one night a week. They agreed to this arrangement and then, every so often, he took the whole family out to dinner. He thought them as his "new family" and it was very helpful psychologically. There are many, many ways you can build a new framework of emotional relationships to replace the old. As one of my patients, a divorced father said to me: "Never again will I take for granted what it means to come home to a family at night: to eat dinner together, to be with the kids, to go to sleep with a wife next to you and wake up in the morning with her there." Often we do not realize how much these things mean until we lose them. So part of your task as a divorced father is to find new people and new relationships to replace the old.

Many magazine articles on divorce give well-meaning advice to fathers: "You should do such and so in relation to your children," but they forget the father's lonely feelings and his psychological situation. That's why I emphasize what you need to do *for yourself* before I say anything about the best ways to handle children in relation to the divorce.

Of course each divorce is unique. The couple, married twenty years with children eighteen and sixteen years old, are in quite a different situation from the couple with an eight-month-old baby who divorce after a year of marriage. But in every divorce, regardless of how long the marriage lasted, who initiated the divorce, how many children there are, what their ages are, whether another man or woman is involved ... in every divorce, both father and mother have grief-work to do and must work their way through the rebirth of their self-esteem.

HOW TO TELL CHILDREN ABOUT THE DIVORCE

Since divorces and divorce situations are so enormously varied, there is, of course, no single psychologically correct way to tell children. Sometimes children are expecting the news because of tension and discord within the home. Other times it will come as a complete shock (particularly if another man or woman is involved).

When telling children about the divorce, remember the legal oath, "To tell the truth, the whole truth, and nothing but the truth." Adopt part of this oath as a guideline for what you tell the children. Be sure to tell the truth and nothing but the truth. Children can take the truth much better than we think, but lies will only cause them to lose faith in you. And children are very quick to detect when they are being lied to. However, this doesn't mean you must tell a child "the whole truth." The gruesome details of what caused your marriage to break up are irrelevant.

If the children are in the preteen years, and it is psychologically possible for you and your wife, tell the children about the impending divorce together. You can do it in this fashion:

"We have something to tell you and it is unhappy news. When we were first married we were happy together, but we're not happy anymore. Probably you've noticed that we haven't been getting along very well together lately. We have decided that it will be best if we don't live together anymore and so we are getting a divorce. That means we won't be husband and wife. But we want you to know that this divorce has nothing to do with you children. You did not cause it. It is entirely due to the fact that your father and mother are unhappy together and we've decided we don't want to be married to one another. Your father will live somewhere else, but you will visit him often. You will stay with your mother, and your father will send her money each month to help take care of you.

"Although we will no longer be married, one thing will never change. Your father will always be your father and he will always love you. Your mother will always be your mother and she will always love you. That's one thing you can always count on. Now if you have any questions about the divorce and what it will mean to you, you can ask us now or any time you want to."

It is certainly better if you and your wife tell the children together in some such fashion as I have indicated. However, that may not be possible due to the strained relationship between you. In such cases, it is still important for each of you individually to tell the children about the divorce along the lines indicated. In some cases it may be better to tell each child separately, but, generally it is better to tell all the children at the same time. Then no one worries and about what might have been said to another.

When should you tell the children? I would counsel against telling them the day father moves out. Some parents select this time in order to deliver the painful news as quickly as possible and get it over with. I suggest you tell the children about a week before father moves out. There are many reasons for this.

First, your children will have many questions or feelings about the divorce which they are afraid to bring out into the open. If you tell them the same day father moves out, you make it much harder for them to ask these questions or explore their feelings. But in a more-or-less normal routine of family living for a week there should be a number of opportunities for a child to question you or your wife.

One feeling which almost all children seem to have, irrational though it may be, is that somehow the divorce was their fault. The child feels guilty about the divorce as if he had caused it. This is particularly true with a boy between the ages of three and six who is in the middle of the "family romance." In the family romance the little boy wishes that daddy would go away so that he can have mother all to himself. When this actually happens, and daddy leaves, the child feels it was his wish that caused it. We call this "magical thinking" on the part of the child, but it is very powerful thinking nevertheless.

Of course this is going on in the child's *unconscious* rather than his conscious mind. Don't expect him to tell you openly: "I feel guilty because I wanted you to go away and now I see you're going!" But be alert for subtle clues your child may give you. Reassure him that it was entirely because you and your wife were unhappy with each other that you decided to get the divorce. One reassurance may not do it; it may take several over a period of time. On the other hand, don't make a big issue of it or he will surely come to feel the opposite. After you have said it once, leave it alone unless he gives you some clue to his feelings.

THE IMMEDIATE IMPACT OF SEPARATION

The immediate impact on a child when his father moves out is psychological—he has been abandoned. Tragically enough, this comes at the same time that you are psychologically feeling abandoned and alone. Again, I emphasize your need for sources of emotional support and people and groups where you feel a sense of acceptance and belonging. Otherwise, it will be very difficult to give your child the support and understanding he needs in this difficult period of readjustment.

Assuming then, that you are arranging for sources for emotional support for yourself, what can you do to counteract your child's feelings of abandonment, particularly in the early stages of the separation and divorce?

First you can reassure him that you love him and will never stop. There are many ways to do this, of course. One is by phoning him. A phone call takes only a few minutes, but it will mean to him: "Daddy still loves me even though he's not living here anymore." Don't expect him to be very verbal or talkative on the phone; many children are not. Sometimes when a father doesn't get much verbal response he thinks the call didn't mean much to the child and stops phoning. This is wrong. You can safely conclude that every single phone call you make his meaning and gives your child the message: Dad still loves me. The importance of your phone calls to your child is much deeper than his surface response.

Another good way of communicating with your child is through short notes or letters. I have already suggested this method of keeping in communication with your child for fathers in an intact family; it is even more valuable for fathers in a divorce situation. You have no idea how important such notes and letters can be. A child will read them over and over, as a means of reassuring himself he is not abandoned. For example, shortly after the separation you could send your child, depending on his age, a short note something like this:

Dear Jimmy,
I know this is a tough time for you now that Daddy has moved out of the house. You miss me and I miss you. It's hard on both of us not seeing each other in the same house every day as we used to. But I want you to know one thing that will never be changed by the divorce between your mother and me, and that is my love for you. I will always be your father. I will always love you. That's something you can count on. I look forward to our times together, and I'll be seeing you next Saturday morning.
Love,
Dad

This is the type of love and support your child needs from you. Of course you will adapt the writing of the note to his age and individual situation. But don't assume that older children, teen-agers for example, are above such things. Not at all. A sixteen-year-old boy or girl will also treasure and read over and over a more sophisticated version of these expressions of love and caring.

In addition to being reassured that you still love him, you need to be *reachable* for your child. If you have the type of job where he can phone you at work, then let him know he can call you anytime about anything. If you have the type of job where this is more difficult, you may need to make other arrangements. But do whatever you can to help your child feel that you are not "far away" psychologically speaking. He may phone you about something that seems trivial to you, but what he is probably saying in code is: "I need to talk to you, Dad, just to make sure you and I are still emotionally connected." It is not only important that you reach out to your child through phone calls and notes, but that he be able to reach out to you.

Of course the most reassuring thing of all to a child, particularly in the first weeks and months of separation, is your visitation with him.

There are two kinds of visitations: regularly scheduled, and spontaneous. Regularly scheduled visitation periods with a child are very important. They give a certain order and routine to his life and help overcome his feelings of abandonment. How often should they be? That depends entirely on the individual situation. I know one father who arranged to take his children out for dinner one specific night each week, took them out to a movie or sports event every Friday night, and then had them stay over at his apartment every other weekend. For him this worked out well. Another father might not like to take his children on a Friday night because it would interfere with social engagements. But the important thing is that once you have worked out a regular schedule of visitation, stick with it unless unusual circumstances, business or otherwise, prevent it. In such cases, be sure you let your child know why you can't be with him.

Second, don't feel bound by the regular schedule of visits. If something comes up and you feel like taking your kids out for an ice-cream cone some evening, arrange with your ex-wife to make it possible for you to call and do this kind of spontaneous thing. In the divorce agreement, it is best if there is not only the regularly spelled-out period of visitation (every other weekend, every other Thanksgiving, Christmas, Easter, etc.), but also provision for the kind of spontaneous visitation I have mentioned. Of course, there may be such bitterness between ex-spouses that this type of spontaneous visitation is not possible. But if it is, I think it is a very helpful thing for the child.

VISITING YOUR CHILD

In the first few months of separation and divorce, shorter and more frequent visits may be better for both father and child. As I mentioned previously, this is a very difficult time emotionally for a father, and he may not be up to an extended visit such as taking the children for a weekend. It often comes as a rude psychological shock to a father on his first weekend alone with his children that caring for them and being with them continuously for two days is not all pleasure, particularly when he is feeling lonely and rotten himself.

The father may realize, for the first time in his life, that previously he was never alone with the children for an extended period of time where he was entirely responsible for them. He may suddenly feel: "Good grief, what am I going to do to entertain them?" Such a father is letting himself be trapped by the idea that the *quantity* of time spent with his children is more important than the *quality*.

For some fathers shorter and more structured visits are preferable at first: taking the children out for dinner, an ice-cream cone, to a movie, or sports event, or amusement park. All these things are psychologically easier on the father than having the children visit him for two solid days. In other words, the father should not just take it for granted, since he has been interacting with his children happily for a number of years, that he will be able to do the same thing as a separated or divorced father. The kind of interaction he had with them in the day-to-day living of an intact home is vastly different psychologically from the kind of interaction he will have with them at visitation times as a divorced father. The divorced father should think of the visitation relationship as a *learning* situation for both the children and him.

Of course this does not apply to all father-child relationships. A divorced father who formerly took his school-age children camping or backpacking will probably have little difficulty taking the children camping or backpacking on a visitation weekend. But most fathers should plan ahead of time what they will be doing with their children, especially on their first weekend visitation. Have alternate plans ready in case inclement weather forces you to change your original plans. And don't feel that you have to spend *every* minute of a weekend together. After all, when you were in an intact family you didn't spend every minute of the weekend together, did you? Of course not: the children were out playing, or inside watching TV or doing other things. And so it will be quite natural for this kind of situation to exist during their visitation weekend. Don't feel you have to keep them amused every single minute. On the other hand, your children will hardly appreciate it if their visitation with you consists of being plunked in front of a television set most of the time.

"LET'S SEE—WE WENT TO THE ZOO, TO THE ICE CREAM PARLOR, TO A BASEBALL GAME, AND IT'S ONLY 2:30—WHAT ARE WE GOING TO DO FOR THE REST OF THE AFTER-NOON?"

A divorced father must *learn* to make the visits with his children a rewarding experience. Don't expect it just to happen naturally. It takes planning, time, and patience. All this, of course, will depend upon how close a relationship you had with your children in the intact home and how well you got along then. Many fathers in intact homes saw very little of their children, actually interacted very little with them as human beings. When a divorce occurs, it is these men who have the most difficult time learning how to visit successfully with their children.

In the immediate months after the separation, a divorced father needs to guard against his own guilt feelings about the divorce. He often feels, unconsciously, that he has to make up to the children for the divorce. He does this by being afraid to discipline his children or say no to them, or by showering them with gifts every time he sees them. In general, he acts more like a "sugar daddy" than a father.

On the other hand, a number of men who were actively interested fathers before the divorce, have relatively little to do with their children in the months immediately following the separation. Friends and neighbors are often surprised by this. The cause of such behavior is often that seeing his children in this changed capacity as a part-time father awakens such painful and agonizing memories of the past that he cannot face them yet. So he occupies himself feverishly with other things and stays away from his children. Such a father is avoiding part of his task of mourning. If you find that business activities or other things are interfering with regular visits to your children, ask yourself if you are unconsciously avoiding them to eliminate painful memories.

If more than one child is involved, should you visit them separately or together? What held true for the intact family holds true for the divorced family: sometimes it is good for the father to see the children together, and sometimes it is good to see one child only, on a one-to-one relationship. Unfortunately, court decisions on visitation are not usually arrived at that way. In most cases, the father is the one who leaves and will be visiting all the children at the same time. Also, it is by no means easy for a mother to act as a single parent and raise children by herself. When father has the children for a whole weekend it is soon clear to him that raising children as a single parent is no picnic. A divorced mother needs some time away from the children, and she cannot have this if the father has only one child at a time. The most practical arrangement to suit the psychological needs of all concerned is for the father to take all the children on regularly scheduled visitations, but to be able to take one child with him from time to time in spontaneous, additional visitations. I realize, of course, that such an ideal kind of visitation program will be dependent upon the maturity of the divorced father and mother and their ability to handle the children cooperatively even though they may have bitterness toward each other.

The father (or mother) should pick up the children where they live and take them on an outing or to his (or her) own house or apartment. Unfortunately, some fathers and mothers insist on having the children seen at home with the parent around. This is a bad psychological environment in which to visit the children. Youngsters are very much aware of *both* mother and father and of the feelings between them. This makes the children feel uncomfortable. If your ex-spouse refuses to let you visit your children except at her house in her presence, you may need legal help to make it possible—because this is not "reasonable visitation."

If you were giving your children an allowance before the divorce, you should definitely continue. If you were not, this is a good time to start. An allowance means a certain amount of money per week which a child gets, not for doing any work, but just because he is your child and you love him. If he wants to earn extra money by doing chores such as washing the car, that's fine. But I don't think a child should have to earn his allowance. That is a symbol of your love for him.

Also, as their father, I believe you should tell your children that each month you send money to their mother for their support. Explain that you send their mother this money because you love them and that this helps her buy food and clothes and other things for them. Very few divorced fathers do this, and they are over-looking a very powerful way of showing their children that they continue to love and care for them.

When you visit your children try to have them stay overnight whenever possible. This has a great deal of meaning because it tells them, "I am a part of Daddy's house or apartment just as I am a part of Mother's house." If he never stays overnight with you he will soon feel that you are more like a visitor who takes him on outings than his father. If you have a house with an extra room which can be the permanent room where your children sleep when they visit you, that is ideal. But even if you only have a one-bedroom apartment, you can buy inexpensive sleeping bags and they can bed down in the living room.

It is a good idea to keep special toys and games and books for your children. This helps them feel, "I have a special place in Daddy's house because I have my toys and books and games there." They are familiar objects that your child will use again and again when he comes to visit you.

Try to keep your dating separate from your visits with your child until you become strongly involved with another woman. Particularly in the early stages of divorce, it is hard enough on children to feel they have lost you. It becomes doubly hard it they have to share you with someone else—in this case, another woman. As time goes on and your children become more comfortable in the divorce situation, then you and another woman or another family can go on a joint outing during your visitation time.

All the things suggested keep you a permanent part of your child's psychological world. Many fathers in intact families are so obsessed with their work and careers that they have little time left over to spend with their children. In that case, the father is really more like a guest in the house and is not a part of the youngster's psychological world. So even though you are a divorced father, you may actually end up spending more time with your children and be a more important part of their "psychological world" than many fathers in intact families.

It is especially important for a divorced father to be thoroughly familiar with the psychological stages of development from birth through adolescence. Otherwise, he may misinterpret some behavior as due to the divorce (and so feel guilty about it) when his child would have shown the same traits at that stage of development anyway.

A divorced father I counseled was telling how belligerent and cantankerous and negative his eleven-year-old boy had become. The father was quite upset by this. He said: "If only my wife and I had been able to make it and we hadn't had that terrible divorce I know he wouldn't be acting this way. He must hate me because I divorced his mother." I pointed out that the behavior the father described was very typical of an eleven-year-old in the stage of preadolescence. His boy would probably be acting that way had the divorce never occurred. It was a great relief to the father to learn this. Many divorced fathers already have a great deal of unconscious guilt about their children. They certainly do not need to heap any extra guilt upon their heads by misinterpreting their child's negative behavior or uncommunicative attitude as due to the divorce rather than his psychological stage of development.

As you know, during the adolescent years teen-agers are turning away from their parents to seek their own identity with their peer group. This is still true when you visit with your children during adolescence. However, in late adolescence your children, surprisingly enough, may seek you out for discussions and help in making such basic decisions as what college to attend and what occupation to choose. Be prepared for this when your son or daughter reaches late adolescence, sixteen, seventeen, eighteen or over. This is a good time to invite them out on a one-to-one basis for lunch or dinner. Such a situation gives them a chance to open up and talk with you about important decisions they must make and things that really concern them.

Sooner or later you will find that one or more of your children will not want to come to see you. The child may have something special he wants to do with a friend that evening or weekend. His reasons may be clear or obscure. It is important at these times that you do not take this act personally (unless, of course, you have done something directly to cause the child not to want to see you). Naturally your feelings will be hurt by your child's refusal to see you, but you need to be mature enough not to respond in the martyred manner of: "Well, that's a fine attitude, Jimmy, when I haven't seen you for some time and was really looking forward to it." Instead, you need to use the feedback technique, and say something like this: "You feel you want to go to the movie with Bryan tonight instead of coming to visit with me. I can understand that you feel that way, so I'll see you next week."

If you are able to take such an attitude, in which you offer your child the psychological gift of a visit with you, but give him the freedom to refuse it, it is one of the greatest gifts you can give him. You are showing him your love, but giving him the freedom to receive it or not that particular week.

HOW TO HELP YOUR CHILD ADJUST IN A HEALTHY WAY

We can assume that regardless of age, all children whose parents get a divorce are going to have some unpleasant negative feelings of anger, guilt, fear, and grief. Many children are confused and do not understand what is going on, particularly if the parents do not speak truthfully. Most children in a divorce situation wish their parents would be reunited so they can have their old family back again. In addition, there are deeper feelings the child probably has great difficulty putting into words, such as: "I hate both of you for messing up my life." "Have I done something real bad and is that why you two are getting a divorce?" "Who's going to take care of me now? Daddy's already left; is Mommy going to leave me too?"

Divorced parents need guidance in dealing with these feelings. They need to help their children understand the divorce, and make a psychologically healthy adjustment.

Fortunately for children of divorced parents there is now a book written especially for them, called *The Boys and Girls Book about Divorce* by Richard A. Gardner, MD. This is a marvelously helpful book for any children of divorced parents who are five years or older. You can buy the book (it is in paperback) and read it to a young child who has not yet learned to read, or give it to an older child to read himself. You discuss together some of the topics in the book.

At a child's level, the book covers the feelings children have after a divorce, such as your parents did not get divorced because you were bad, the fear of being left alone, how to get along better with your divorced father, how to get along better with your divorced mother, the problem of how much time to spend with your father, how to get along better with your stepfather and stepmother, what to do if parents are using you as a tool or a weapon.

For each problem the author gives sound, down-to-earth advice as to what a child can do to make himself feel better about the situation or solve the problem.

As Dr. Gardner points out, the primary purpose of his book is to help children get along better with their divorced parents. He believes, as I do, that children need to be told the truth with regard to the divorce and its aftermath. He and I also agree that children are much more capable of accepting painful realities than most adults give them credit for. What is much more difficult for them to cope with are "the anxieties associated with ignorance and parental furtiveness, for then fantasy runs free and their worst anticipations can neither be confirmed nor refuted."[2] When the child knows the truth about a situation, no matter how unpleasant, then he has the security of knowing where he stands. He also has the security of knowing that he can trust what you say.

This book deals with a lot of potentially sticky situations and you will find it an invaluable aid. Whether you read the book to your child or he reads it himself, it is best not to cover the whole book at one time. Read sections (not necessarily in order) and use these readings as a basis for discussion.

Of course, no book is going to take the place of parents. Your child needs to be able to express his unhappy feelings to both of you. Oftentimes, he will not express these feelings directly in words. But you can see by the expression on his face, or his listless attitude, or his inability to have fun while playing that something is wrong. Then you can say to him, "Rick, I get the feeling you're unhappy about something. Can you tell Daddy what it is?" If he is able to put his feelings in words, use the feedback technique to let him know you understand. It may take some time and much encouragement for him to be able to verbalize the feelings that are bothering him. Be patient. Don't expect your child's negative feelings about the divorce to vanish in a month or two, any more than *your own* negative feelings will vanish in a few months!

Your child may need professional help in coping with his feelings about the divorce. If so, it is a wise investment for you to send him to a child psychologist or child psychiatrist.

Not only does your child have negative feelings he needs to get out of his system about the divorce, but much more important, he needs to continue to build the security that you are still his father who loves him and that he can always count on you.

FIGHTING YOUR WIFE THROUGH THE CHILDREN

The temptation for every divorced parent is to fight the other one through the children. Let us not forget that the experience of divorce for a man and woman is a searing emotional shock of explosive intensity. Very powerful emotions—rejection, rage, failure, grief, deep hurt, self-pity, spite—any and all of these may be expected to erupt during the divorce process, and especially during the legal wrangles prior to the final settlement. There is no such thing as a "friendly" divorce. Therefore, once the divorce is final, and even before that time, one or both parties may be tempted to try to hurt the other through the children. Much of this is unconscious rather than conscious. But things like this happen. The father is late with child support payment, so the mother withholds visiting privileges or she may "forget" that the father was coming over to see the children that night. When the mother does this, the father may retaliate by withholding a month's child support. And so the war escalates.

In other words, though the parents are divorced, they still have not resolved their hostilities to each other. They "bad mouth" the other, sometimes blatantly, sometimes subtly.

Of course, all of this places a great emotional stress on the children, because generally they love both their father and their mother. But now mother and father, by their actions, are conveying this message to the children: "If you love the other parent, then you can't love me and I don't like that." The children are pulled in two directions and feel: "If I continue to love Daddy then Mother won't love me, and if I continue to love Mother then Daddy won't love me."

I hope that you will be able to resist the temptation (and believe me, you will be tempted) to use your children in this way. I hope you will not "bad mouth" your ex-wife, for unless she is a truly despicable character, she is, after all, your children's mother and they love her. If you find that you cannot help getting the children involved in an emotional vendetta against your ex-wife, then you may need professional help.

IF YOU GET CUSTODY

In approximately ten percent of divorce settlements, the father, rather than the mother, gets custody. This happens when the court decides that the mother is not fit to care for her children. Or the mother may voluntarily relinquish custody to the father, realizing that for one reason or another she is not able to cope with the children. For example, I know of a mother with a severe alcohol problem who was wise enough to let the father have custody.

If you are awarded custody you should hire a housekeeper who will function as a substitute mother while you are at work. If you are lucky enough to find a good live-in housekeeper, so much the better. Generally, there is no trouble in finding someone to keep house. But finding a woman who is warm and cares about children and can be a good substitute mother is usually rather difficult.

I suggest that you interview a number of women and be guided by what your own feelings tell you. If you have narrowed the choice down to two or three, try to observe them in action with your children. Don't arbitrarily say "An older woman is better," or "A younger woman is better," or anything like that. And I don't think references do that much good either. There is no substitute for your own first-hand observation, asking yourself such questions as: is she a warm and genuine person? Does she really seem to enjoy being around children or do they get on her nerves? Does her philosophy of raising children seem reasonably congruent with mine? Frankly, if I found a woman who seemed to be a good substitute mother I wouldn't worry too much about her abilities as a housekeeper.

Of course, the real test is how she and the children interact once you have hired her. If things do not work out well, be flexible enough to admit you made a mistake and hire another person.

What kind of a housekeeper and substitute mother you get will also depend upon the ages, sexes, and stages of development of your children. A woman who is ideal for very young children may not work out well for older ones. (In the same way that all of us are better parents with children at one age than we are at another.)

In general it is better to leave young preschool children with a warm and caring substitute mother-housekeeper than to send them to a day-care center where you leave them at 6:30 a.m. and pick them up at 5:30 or 6:00 at night. The day-care center is not to be confused with a good nursery school, which usually runs from 9 to 12, and which I enthusiastically recommend for three- and four-year-olds. The substitute mother-housekeeper can take a child to nursery school at 9 and pick him up at 12. But a school day lasting from 6:30 a.m. to 5:30 p.m. is much too long for a preschooler.

If you are a father who has custody, you quickly learn what makes mothers get cabin fever and feel like climbing the walls. You will soon discover that sole and exclusive management of children every night and every weekend is a harrowing experience until you get adjusted to it. That's one reason I recommend a live-in housekeeper if you can afford it. You can get away more easily for an evening or part of a weekend. Especially in the early months of being a father with full-time custody it is most important for you to get away from your children for adult experiences and fun. If you should feel somewhat overwhelmed by caring for your children all alone, at least you can console yourself that you are not suffering from the horrible loneliness of the father separated from his children and living in a bachelor apartment.

HOW TO MAKE A SUCCESS OF YOUR DIVORCE FOR YOUR CHILDREN

You and your ex-wife did not make a success of your marriage. But paradoxical as it may sound, you can make a success of the divorce for your children. There is no reason why your children need to be psychologically wrecked, become neurotic, or delinquent simply because your marriage failed.

Popular myths exist to the effect that a child from a "broken home" is psychologically doomed. Nonsense! Admittedly, I have heard schoolteachers and educators say about a child with a behavior problem, "Well, of course he comes from a broken home," as if that one single fact explained everything. At such times, I have considered saying about other children as their behavior problems were discussed: "Well, of course he comes from an intact home!"

Many people, for example, believe that a broken home is a major cause of juvenile delinquency. Scientific research shows otherwise. A study of approximately 18,000 delinquent children by M. C. Elmer demonstrated that only one-tenth of delinquent boys and about one-fifth of delinquent girls came from families broken by divorce.[3] From what kind of homes did the other nine-tenths of the boys and four-fifths of the girls come? They came from *intact but unhappy* homes.

We can generally say that most children are better off in a broken home than in an unhappy home. Often it is better for children to have what Dr. Louise Despert, a well-known authority on divorce, calls "the cleansing surgery of divorce by law."[4] As Dr. Despert points out, "Not legal divorce but *emotional divorce* is the destroyer of children."[5]

Rid your mind of these old myths that divorce, in itself, is going to cause your children to become neurotic or delinquent or psychologically maladjusted. Of course, divorce is an unhappy experience for your children at first. But as time goes on, what will determine the psychological adjustment of your children is not divorce per se, but the level of psychological maturity with which you and your ex-wife handle the situation. As the initial bitterness of the court hassle fades away, the two of you, if you truly care about your children, will learn *to work together* to bring them up.

Regardless of the divorce, she will always be their mother, and you will always be their father. If the two of you are truly loving parents, sooner or later you will lay aside the bitterness and hostility you harbored and work together as a *team* of mother and father, helping and supporting one another with the children. If you take this mature approach, your children may well turn out to be psychologically healthier than many children of intact homes where there has been emotional divorce but no legal divorce.

This is not an easy task for a divorced mother and father. The two of you may want to call in the help of a trained professional, a psychologist, psychiatrist, or marriage counselor. The money spent for even a few joint consultations may be the best money you ever invested in your children's welfare.

WHEN YOU MARRY AGAIN

Chances are six out of seven that you will marry again. And if you do, the odds are fairly good that the woman you marry will have children of her own. At this point you will face the psychological problems of becoming a stepfather and dealing with a "blended" family situation.

The first and most important thing about becoming a stepfather is that there is no reason why a stepfather cannot be a better, more involved and loving father than the natural father was. In fact, as indicated previously in this book, there are millions of natural fathers who are so obsessed by work and career that they pay very little attention to their children, and end up being very poor fathers.

Becoming a stepfather will vary enormously depending on the family situation you marry into. For example, you may become a stepfather to a two-year-old girl whose father lives far away in another state. You find out that he is not really interested in the child, and quite willing to let you adopt her in order to save child support. Obviously this is quite a different situation than if you marry a woman with **three** boys, ages 9, 11, and 14, whose father lives a half hour away and likes to take them camping or skiing every other weekend.

In spite of the wide variation in ages, sexes, and stages of development of children, certain basic psychological feelings will exist when they acquire you as their stepfather. Depending upon how long their mother has been divorced or widowed, the children will have weaker or stronger feelings when their mother finds a father to replace the one they lost. But these feelings about getting a new father are mixed. As Dr. Despert puts it "the child both wants a new father and fears that he may get one."[6] On the one hand, the child wants a new father so that he will again be a part of a family with a mother-and-father unit. On the other hand, he enjoys having mother all to himself. As a new stepfather you should be aware of these mixed feelings.

What this means to you is that you should go slowly in building a relationship with your wife's children. Many stepfathers make the mistake of pushing too hard and being too zealous in courting their new stepchildren. Be careful not to overwhelm the children with attention and gifts.

Expect the children to draw back a bit at first. Remember that to them you are new and untried. They are naturally cautious. Internally, they are asking themselves: "Can this man be trusted to take care of me? Or will he desert me as my first father did? Can I really rely on him? Will he really be good to me?"

Don't be surprised if the children do hostile or aggressive things to test you. This will not be done consciously but unconsciously. A child may say or do things that are rude or hostile as an unconscious way of trying you out as a new father. If he discovers that his aggression or hostility is met with patient good nature instead of harsh punishment, he will gain confidence that he can risk giving you his love.

If the natural father has lost interest in the children or has moved away, especially if he will give permission for you to adopt them, then in one sense you have a much easier job as a stepfather. You have no one with whom to compete. But if the natural father is very much around, taking the children with him every other weekend, sending them child support, phoning them, etc. (all the things that hopefully you are doing with the children of your first marriage) then this is quite a different situation. In such a case it is important to remember this: you cannot supplant the natural father, *so do not try.* If the stepchildren in such a situation feel you are attempting to take their father's place they will resent you. So be yourself. You are not their natural father who lived with them since they were born. You are their mother's new husband and their new friend and father-surrogate. And, incidentally, it is usually best for your new children to call you by your first name. Don't insist on their calling you "father" or "Dad." They will probably feel they are betraying their natural father if they do, since they may have called him "father" for a number of years.

Above all, remember that it is going to take time to establish rapport and a good relationship with your new wife's children. One of your best assets here is your ability to draw out a child's feelings and use the feedback technique. This is invaluable in the rapport-building process. But with psychological understanding, with tolerance and acceptance of the children's mixed feelings—that they both want you as a new father and do not want you—with feeding back their feelings so they know you truly understand . . . you will be able to build a solid and loving relationship with your new stepchildren.

THE BLENDED FAMILY

Not only do you need to build a relationship with your new wife's children, but you need to work together with your new wife, your ex-wife, and probably her new husband, to blend the two families at certain times, such as weekends or vacations. This is no easy task because, of course, you run into all of the multiple jealousies of the different children involved.

Here again, how successfully this is accomplished depends in large part on how psychologically mature the four adults are. If they are still fighting old marital battles, it is going to be awfully difficult for the children to get along. (Of course the ages, sexes, and stage of development of the children is very pertinent.) But if the four adults concerned have worked their way through the old marital hassles and can truly pull together for the common good of the children, then on weekends and vacations it can become a "blended" family, where the children concerned learn to like and appreciate one another.

We've talked about many things since we first began this chapter on divorce. And I want to leave you with this main point. Divorce is painful to both father and mother. Divorce is painful to children, no matter what age. But divorce does not have to be a psychological disaster. Depending on how you and your ex-wife handle it, your children can get over the psychological scars of the divorce and grow up to be normal, healthy, and happy human beings. Remarrying and becoming a stepfather is not easy at first. You need to proceed slowly and gently in building the relationship to your stepchildren. But being a stepfather can be an emotionally rich and rewarding experience.

Natural father, divorced father, stepfather . . . our society gives very little in the way of training for any of these roles. That's why I have written this book. I hope that it is helpful to all fathers.

As with any book, it is, unfortunately, a one-way conversation of author to reader. You do not have a chance to ask a question, to challenge a point, to disagree, or to say: "You left this out!" If you do wish to make comments, positive or negative, or raise questions which you feel I have not covered fully in this book, I would be happy to have you write to me in care of my publisher: Nash Publishing Company, 9255 Sunset Boulevard, Los Angeles, California 90069. I assure you that your questions or comments will receive attention in the revision of this book as well as in a future book, *Questions Parents Ask*.

Whether you are a natural father, a divorced father, a stepfather, or possibly all three, I hope this book will enable you to understand your children better and to find more joy in your role as a father.

Appendix A

A Father's Guide to Toys and Play Equipment

I. The Stage of Infancy (from birth until creeping and walking begins, usually around the end of the first year)

Many fathers are not aware of it, but the first year of life is a powerful year for learning. The young child is doing basic research on the sensory qualities of his world. He spends all his waking hours seeing, hearing, tasting, smelling, touching everything he can manage to make contact with. Years before he acquires the language ability to name objects, he is busy creating models of all these objects in his mind. He manipulates the hardness, softness, and shape of each object. He compares it mentally with other objects. He measures it in his own primitive way, matches it, puts it in his mouth, or smells it. He is endlessly manipulating his environment.

Because of the nature of the young baby, this is the time he needs *sensory toys*. Here are toys which will help him in this all-important sensory exploration of his early environment:

    1. Crib mobiles, bought or homemade
    2. Cradle gym
    3. Rattles

4. Rubber squeeze toys, such as the Hedgehogs by Creative Playthings
5. Teething toys
6. Playtentials is a particularly fine series of infant toys created and tested by Dr. Burton White, director of the Harvard University Preschool Project.

    Playtentials Series I is designed for babies three weeks to four months and consists of a Dura-stand for the crib, find-me mitts, bat-and-feel toys, faces and forms mobile, animal grabbie, and baby's image mirror.

    Playtentials Series II is for babies three and one-half months to six and one-half months and consists of play chimes, color play wind-mill, Handi-Pal, trapeze teether and exerciser, and pull-me-up.

    I recommend Playtentials enthusiastically. They will not only aid your baby in his sensory exploration of his environment, but reward him for his active exploration and stimulate cause-effect discoveries. Playtentials are made by Kenner Toys.
7. Texture pad: different textures of cloth sewn on a two-foot-square piece of rubber matting
8. Musical carrousel or musical mobile
9. Musical pull-toys which hang from the crib (Fisher-Price has some nice ones, such as Pull-a-Tune Bluebird Music Box and Pull-a-Tune Pony Music Box)
10. Small, soft texture ball, such as Creative Playthings Texture Ball
11. Soft cuddly animals or dolls, such as Creative Playthings bear and dog or Snuggler or Bruna Dolls

    Creative Playthings, Childcraft, and Playskool all have excellent groups of infant toys. From Creative Playthings you can obtain (items 12-17)
12. Five-finger exerciser: freely moving balls with which the baby creates sounds
13. Activator: cords for the baby to pull for different sounds
14. Baby mirror: for self-image development
15. Wobbly Balls and Tray: balls which are weighted so they wobble about without rolling out of reach. Encourages the baby to reach, touch, and explore.
16. Jingle-Rattle-Clunk Blocks: each block makes a different sound.
17. See-Me-Whirly: an interestingly designed crib toy, with a large ring to pull to make multiple mirrors whirl, which stimulates and rewards eye-hand coordination

    Playskool's infant toy series includes (items 18 through 21)
18. Baby Chimes
19. Baby Action Ball
20. Baby Drum Drop

21. Shapes and Sounds: for squeezing, biting, chewing, clutching, and placing

   Water (items 22, 23)

22. Bath boys, plastic and rubber

23. Sponges for bath play

24. Busy Box: a manipulation toy for infants and toddlers by Kenner

25. Games to Grow On: an inexpensive Monthly Activity Kit, which begins in babyhood and follows through the crucial preschool years. Each month's kit includes games, toys, books, records, or posters that teach your child through play, plus an Activity Enrichment Card which suggests how you can enrich each game experience with objects found around the home, plus a copy of *Open Home,* a monthly newsletter for parents. This superbly designed set of toys and instructions for parents was created by Carter Smith and Sara Stein, two people very knowledgeable in the field of early childhood. The kits are available by mail only from Grolier Enterprises, Sherman Turnpike, Danbury, Connecticut 06816. They will even send you the first Activity Kit for fourteen days' free trial; if you don't like it, return it and pay nothing. I have a feeling you'll be so delighted with the kit (and especially its inexpensive price) that you will not return it!

26. Let's not forget that by far the best toy you can provide for your baby cannot be bought in any store. The most interesting and emotionally satisfying toy you can provide for your baby is you! So be sure to get the book I recommend in Appendix E to guide you in stimulating your baby through play: *Baby Learning Through Baby Play* by Dr. Ira Gordon. This book is terrific in showing you specifically what to do to teach your baby and develop a close emotional relationship with him.

II. The Stage of Toddlerhood (approximately from onset of walking to second birthday)

The basic developmental task of this stage is the *active motor exploration of his environment.* The child can now get around on his own two feet, and he's "into everything." He is either developing self-confidence and assertiveness as he tries to explore his environment, or he is developing self-doubt and learning to fear his own eager curiosity. What kind of toys and play equipment will help him to develop self-confidence?

A. Play Equipment For Large-Muscle Development (mostly outdoor play equipment)

   1. Playdome (Childcraft): this is the best single item of play equipment for a toddler. Based on the geodesic dome concept of Buckminster

Fuller, the Playdome can safely support the weight of as many children as can climb on it. It is great for your toddler's large-muscle development, and with a piece of canvas or cloth over it, it can also serve as a tent, playhouse, submarine or anything else your child's imagination can dream up. It will last throughout the preschool years.

2. Slide
3. Tyke Bike (Playskool)
4. Wee Wagon (AMF)
5. Wee Wheeler (AMF)
6. Wee Buggy (AMF)
7. Hollow wooden blocks
8. Boards, small but sturdy
9. Sandbox and sand toys: cups, spoons, pie pans, sifters
10. Small metal cars and trucks for sand play
11. Hard plastic animals and people for sand play
12. Dirt
13. Water toys for outside water play: plastic boats, coffee cans, measuring spoons, etc.
14. Old coffee percolator
15. Small but sturdy shovel for dirt digging and sand play
16. Large wooden or metal outdoor trucks and cars (Princeton Playthings, Creative Playthings, Childcraft, Tonka Toys)
17. Outside playhouse: bought or preferably homemade by father
18. Large cardboard boxes big enough for child to get inside
19. Pets: a dog, not a cat (At this age a child does not know how to play gently with a cat and will usually end up getting scratched.)

B. Indoor Play Equipment
1. Toddler's Gym (Childcraft) or Indoor Gym House (Creative Playthings): the same piece of play equipment, under different names. I think this is the outstanding piece of indoor play equipment for a toddler. It has a ladder, a slide, and a tunnel for crawling through. Marvelous for large-muscle development inside the house.
2. Open shelves (rather than toy chests) for toys and books
3. Hollow cardboard blocks (Creative Playthings, Childcraft)
4. Modular blocks twelve inches square, with one side open: for building and for toy storage (You can make them.)
5. Pull-toys of various sorts (Fisher-Price and Playskool)
6. Cardboard boxes of various sizes
7. Beanbags
8. Stacking toys of various sorts (Playskool and Fisher-Price)

9. Hammering and pounding toys, such as a Pounding Bench (Play-skool)

10. Large beads to string

11. Balloons

12. Soft, cuddly animals

13. Form boards (Playskool, Creative Playthings)

14. Nesting Bowls, Nesting Eggs, Stacking Barrels (Playskool)

15. Very simple puzzles (Playskool, Fisher-Price, Simplex)

16. Rubber animals, domestic and jungle (Creative Playthings, Child-craft)

17. Rubber beach ball

18. Small rubber ball

19. Tiny metal cars and trucks (Tootsietoy)

20. Large wooden or metal cars and trucks (Creative Playthings, Princeton Playthings, Tonka, Mattel)

21. Dolls: Playskool's Hug-a-Book dolls are good. Four favorite characters each have their stories on twelve-page full-color books securely fastened to their tummies: *Jack and the Beanstalk, The Three Little Pigs, Little Red Riding Hood,* and *The Three Bears.*

22. Dress-up clothes (Goodwill, Salvation Army)

23. Gumby and Pokey

24. Water and water play toys: soap flakes, floating objects of many kinds

25. Playtentials' Touch 'n' Teach: another educational toy developed by Dr. Burton White, director of the Harvard Preschool Project. This toy fosters language development through play, with records and matching pictures. Exposes the infant and young child to virtually every word and grammatical pattern he is capable of learning as his language abilities begin to take form. The words, phrases, and grammatical structure conform to a baby's usage during this period. The first series is for children from seven to eighteen months, and there are two supplemental series for children from eighteen to twenty-four months.

26. Walker Wagon of Blocks (Playskool): a push-wagon filled with blocks which helps a child in learning to walk

27. Walker Chair (Playskool): encourages the coordination and confidence of the beginning walker, but can also be used as a chair

28. First Blocks (Creative Playthings)

29. Peg Bus (Creative Playthings)

30. Cloth Cubes (Creative Playthings): four sides with basic pictures, hand washable

31. First Rider (Creative Playthings)

32. Walker Wagon (Creative Playthings): for first walking and carrying things

C. Books

1. Hardboard or cloth books (The child will probably explore these first by putting them in his mouth.)
2. Sears or Montgomery Ward catalogs
3. Trading stamp catalogs
4. Toy catalogs
5. *Best Word Book Ever* by Richard Scarry
6. *Cat in the Hat Dictionary* by Dr. Seuss
7. Other books which have large pictures of objects or people, with a word naming the object or person, to help the child label his environment and stimulate his language development
8. *Mother Goose*
9. Very simple picture story books, such as *Goodnight Moon* by Margaret Wise Brown

III. The Stage of First Adolescence (approximately second to third birthday)

The basic developmental task of this stage is *self-identity* versus *social conformity*. In his ladder of "play maturity" your child has now reached the stage of *parallel play.*

The toys and play equipment you provided for him in the previous stage of toddlerhood will continue to be used with eagerness and gusto. But he is now ready for new types of play equipment. For example, you didn't provide crayons and chalk and paint in the stage of toddlerhood because he might eat them. He has now reached a new developmental level and can handle these media. He is also now ready for a whole new group of unstructured creative play equipment which he could not handle in the previous stage of development.

A. Play Equipment For Large-Muscle Development

The same toys and play equipment of the toddlerhood stage will continue to be enthusiastically used by your child for his large-muscle development. In addition, he is capable of handling some new toys:

1. ATV Explorer (Fisher-Price): a rugged indoor-outdoor six-wheel riding toy
2. Ladder Exerciser (Creative Playthings): an outdoor toy, ladder on top, rungs on all sides

B. Indoor Play Equipment

1. Blackboard, four feet by four feet (or as large as you can get it), white and colored chalk: this is the most basic item of play equip-

ment you can get for your child at this stage of development. He will continue to use his blackboard throughout the preschool years and into grade school.

2. Small desk or table for him to draw and paint on (this will also be used for many years)
3. Small, sturdy chair
4. Bulletin board (Celotex) to pin up his scribblings, drawing, and printing
5. Painting easel (wall-type is best)

C. Unstructured Creative Play Materials
1. Paper: various shapes, sizes, textures, including newsprint and newspaper (Let your child paint directly over your ordinary newspaper.)
2. Crayons, wax and pastel
3. Watercolor felt pens
4. Paint, liquid or dry
5. Finger paints
6. Play-Do, bought or homemade (See the recipe for homemade Play-Do in *How to Parent*.)
7. Clay
8. Plasticene
9. Outside easel for painting (Make one that will go on a fence in your yard; use cut-down milk cartons for paint containers.)
10. Hardwood or softwood blocks (Get a small set, since at this stage your child will not do much more than stack them and become familiar with them. In the next stage you can add a much larger set, since he will then be ready for more elaborate block building. Playskool, Creative Playthings, and Childcraft have very good sets of blocks.)
11. Lego beginner set

D. Toys Dealing with Sounds and Music
1. Rhythm instruments: drums, pans, cigar boxes, cymbals, triangles, etc., bought or homemade
2. Special sounds: toy xylophone, accordion, etc.
3. Inexpensive "push-in" type of record player, where the records cannot be scratched, such as the Close 'n' Play Phonograph (Kenner) or the Music Box Record Player (Fisher-Price)
4. Inexpensive records your child can play by himself
5. Good family record player
6. Good records you play for him (See Appendix D for a list of good children's records.)

E. Miscellaneous Toys and Play Equipment
    1. Picture Lotto
    2. Puzzles (Playskool, Fisher-Price, Simplex)
    3. Hard plastic animals: domestic and jungle animals, dinosaurs
    4. Hard plastic people: astronauts, cowboys and Indians, soldiers
    5. Tumble Tower (Fisher-Price): trains the child in coordination and planning; requires a variety of small-muscle movements
    6. Igloo (Creative Playthings) made of inflatable plastic, fifty inches high. Your youngster will love to "hole up" in this.
    7. Creative Playthings makes splendid wooden toys for children of this age: a bus, auto, helicopter, airplane, dump truck, steam roller, fire engine, train, tug, barge, blockmobile, and gas station.
    8. Mattel has an excellent line of wood and plastic toys called the Putt-Putt series. It includes a steam shovel, bulldozer, cement mixer, dump truck, tow truck, car, van, tanker, biplane, jet, helicopter, and blimp.
    9. Mattel has another fine preschool series called Tuff Stuff, made of hard, durable plastic to take the pounding a child of this age will give it. This series includes the Play Truck, Pound-a-Truck, Alpha Truck, and Numbers Truck.
    10. Stuffed animals. Creative Playthings has some excellent ones: owl, walrus, sheep, tortoise, chicken, hedgehog, mouse.
        Creative Playthings also has a line of rugged wooden toys which are designed to hold your child's weight. He can actually ride on these durable toys and will get enormous play value out of them. They are expensive, but since they should last throughout the preschool years, they are a wise investment (items 11-13)
    11. Giant Ride 'em Bus
    12. Riding Truck
    13. Ride 'em Tractor and Trailer

IV. The Preschool Stage (ages three through five)

These are years of enormous development for your child, both emotionally and intellectually. He has now reached the stage of truly cooperative play with other children. He is particularly responsive to intellectual stimulation. The closer your home comes to having the kind of indoor and outdoor play equipment that is found in a good nursery school, the richer an environment, both emotionally and intellectually, it will provide for your preschooler.

If there is a good nursery school nearby, it would actually pay you to take a morning off from work and visit it. Pay particular attention to both the inside and outside play equipment and see how you can duplicate it in your own home. Much of this equipment you can make yourself, with a little ingenuity.

A. Play Equipment for Large-Muscle Development
1. Abstract tree house, built low to the ground, with ladder and slide. Why not make it yourself?
2. Tricycles
3. Wagons
4. Rope ladders or cargo netting
5. Large hollow blocks
6. Boards
7. Balancing boards
8. Walking and balancing board: a two-by-four with wooden supports which will allow it to be used either flat or on edge (See Appendix B.)
9. Tunnel of Fun (Childcraft, F.A.O. Schwarz): a crawl-through play tunnel
10. "The" Machine (Samsonite): a wheeled toy, with a reversible body, four wheels, and fifteen interchangable parts, so that it is really many toys in one
11. Jumpin' Jiminy (Childcraft): can be used indoors or outdoors as a non-tip bouncing exerciser
12. Irish Mail (Childcraft): great fun for kids and wonderful for large-muscle development. Chain-drive completely enclosed for safety. Seat can be brought forward for younger children.
13. Play-All (Childcraft): three curved sections of unbreakable poly-ethylene can be combined to form a circle, a reclining seat, or whatever your child's imagination decrees. Can be used as rockers, balancing toys, play walls, etc. A remarkably versatile toy.

B. Play Equipment For Small-Muscle Development
1. Crayons, pencils, felt pens, and paper
2. Scissors (including left-handed scissors for left-handed children)
3. Glue and paste
4. Pounding toys
5. Hardware tools: hammer, nails, saw, etc.—not make-believe, but real tools which a child can use under supervision
6. Make-a-Toy (Playskool): wooden parts for making a toy with screwdriver, plastic nuts and screws
7. Nesting Nuts and Bolts (Playskool)

C. Construction Toys
1. Put-together construction toys
   a) Lego
   b) Tinkertoy

c) Bilofix
d) Baufix
e) Brio
f) Playplax
g) Star Blocks
h) Crystal Climbers (Pressman)
i) Ziva (Pressman)

2. A large number of wooden blocks which can be used for elaborate block building by an individual child, extension of field trips through block building, or cooperative block play by several children

3. Wooden cars and trucks for play in the block cities children will create

4. Tiny, hard plastic people and animals for use in connection with block play or sand play

5. Rubber animals for use in connection with block play or sand play (Creative Playthings, Childcraft)

6. Metal cars and trucks, bulldozers, cranes, etc. (Tonka)

7. Very small metal cars and trucks (Tootsietoy, Matchbox, Corgi)

8. Items from Mattel's Putt-Putt series
   a) Wooden cars and trucks and airplanes
   b) Construction Yard
   c) Airport
   d) Railroad
   e) City: this can also be used in a car or as a carrying case on trips

9. Playskool Village: a city with ninety-seven colored wood parts; excellent

10. Skaneatles Transportation Sets (Playskool): this unique set of railroad cars and interlocking track, all made of the finest hard northern maple, carefully sanded and impregnated with wax, is one of the most useful preschool toys in existence. There are many kinds of track you can buy and many different railroad cars. These Skaneatles sets offer enormous play value for your child.

11. Princeton Playthings Preschool Modular Toys

These preschool toys (trucks, trailers, bulldozers, trains, tug, barge, etc.), superbly designed by Eugene DeChristopher, are so excellent they deserve a section all by themselves. They are hardwood toys and are called "modular" because they are designed so that parts of one toy will fit onto another toy, enchancing the play value of both toys. You will never go wrong buying one of these excellent Princeton Playthings for your preschooler. The total line of toys includes

a) Mod Mobile Truck

b) Mod Mobile Fire Truck

c) Mod Mobile

d) Mod Mobile Dump Truck

e) Mod Mobile Timber Trailer

f) Mod Mobile Bulldozer

g) Mod Mobile Steam Locomotive and Tender

h) Ladder Unit

i) Timber Trailer Truck

j) Mod Mobile Crane

k) Tug 'n' Barge

12. Arkitek Blocks: another excellent preschool toy designed by Eugene DeChristopher for Princeton Playthings. These unique interlocking architectural blocks are made of durable hardwood and offer unlimited play possibilities for your child.

13. Miniature Toys By The Pound (Creative Playthings): this toy is a real bargain. You get about 150 parts (houses, churches, trees, etc.) for building miniature cities. Since preschoolers all have "normal" inferiority complexes comparing themselves to the giant adult world they encounter, they take great delight in playing with miniature toys. This toy is particularly good for a sick child to play with in bed.

14. Clip-on Wheels and Block (Creative Playthings): a marvelous invention which allows your child to clip these plastic wheels on any of his blocks and create his own cars and trucks

15. Giant Blocks (Rotadyne): a unique set of eight giant polyethylene blocks of different geometric shapes

D. Role-Playing and Creative Fantasy Development (especially for four- and five-year-olds)

1. Puppet stage, bought or handmade (Try using one side of a homemade playhouse as an outside, open puppet stage.)

2. Hand puppets (Creative Playthings)

3. Finger puppets (Creative Playthings)

4. Bendable family doll set (Childcraft)

5. Costume box: dress-up clothes (Salvation Army, Goodwill)

6. Doctor kit, hospital kit

7. Flannel cutouts and flannel board

8. Play store (It is expensive to buy, but you can make a simple one yourself.)

9. Playsacks (Creative Playthings): flame-retardant paper, king-size masks of lion, leopard, bear, rabbit, owl, zebra, etc. The idea is a

great one, so why not make your own for your child out of large
brown paper bags, colored with crayons or felt pens?

10. Fisher-Price has a line of well-designed, sturdy toys with which
children can act out roles through the little people in the different
miniature environments. An additional value of these toys is that
they are good for taking along on trips for a child to play with in the
car.

    a) Play Family House
    b) Play Family Farm
    c) Play Family School
    d) Play Family School Bus
    e) Play Family Garage
    f) Play Family Airport
    g) Play Family Fun Jet

11. Fort Apache (Louis Marx)

12. Battleground (Louis Marx): both Battleground and Fort Apache are
prized by preschool (and even slightly older) children. Each set is
complete in itself, with the background and all of the people needed
to stage the battles. Both come in a case so that they can be carried
easily on a trip.

13. Lock-up Zoo (Playskool): an excellent toy for role playing and
fantasy. Comes complete with a large cage, a traveling cage, six
animals, a family of four play people, two cars, and a folding
set-the-scene board.

E. Homemaking Corner and Dollhouse Play for Girls

1. Stove, sink, refrigerator, bought or homemade

2. Child-size pots and pans, tea set, silverware (Creative Playthings,
Childcraft)

3. Dolls: I think the best dolls are those in which the play is in the child
rather than in the doll. Creative Playthings has some good dolls,
including black dolls. Playskool's Dressy Bessy and Dapper Dan are
nice. Childcraft has the old reliable Raggedy Ann and Raggedy Andy
dolls. Mattel's Newborn Baby Tender Love is excellent, as is their
Mrs. Beasley rag doll. Mattel's Bean Puppets are like a doll and a
puppet combined.

4. Dollhouses: Childcraft has an excellent open-top dollhouse of modern design. This allows even a very young child to manipulate the
furniture and dolls easily. Creative Playthings has an open-walled
eight-room dollhouse which is also very good. Both Creative Playthings and Childcraft have complete and well-made sets of doll
furniture: living room, dining room, kitchen, bedroom, bathroom.

5. Small dolls: Childcraft has a set of small flexible dolls to go with the dollhouse. The dolls include father, mother with infant, brother, and sister; the adult dolls are about four and one-half inches high. The dolls can be bent to assume various postures for dramatic dollhouse play.

F. Creative Arts and Crafts
   1. Play-Do
   2. Plasticene
   3. Clay
   4. Large crayons
   5. Paint
   6. Large paintbrushes (Avoid small ones for children of this age.)
   7. Colored tissue paper for collage
   8. Glue and collage (Don't throw anything away; put it in the collage box for your child to use!)
   9. Gummed paper cutouts for abstract collage
   10. Wood-block print set: Design Stamps by Creative Playthings are good. You can also make your own for your child. (See Appendix D.)
   11. Various materials for block printing: lemons, oranges, cutout potato, key, wire, leaf, etc.
   12. Etch-a-Sketch (Ohio Art Company)
   13. Magic Rainbow Drawing Board (Multi-Marketing Corp.): "finger painting" without mess
   14. Playtiles (Playskool): 224 plastic tiles in 3 basic shapes and 4 colors, plus a plastic pegboard. An art toy which does not limit your child's imagination.
   15. Inexpensive prints for your child's room to expose him to good art
   16. Mobiles for your child's room (You and he can make them.)

G. Cognitive Stimulation Toys and Equipment
   1. Reading and Language Development
      a) Plastic alphabet letters and numerals (Mattel, Child Guidance)
      b) Magnetic letters and numerals
      c) Sandpaper letters and numerals
      d) Fit-A-Space and Alph-A-Space (Lauri Toys)
      e) Rubber stamps you can make of letters and numerals
      f) Cardboard signs with familiar words you print on them
      g) Materials to make your child's own picture book by gluing cutout pictures from magazines (He dictates to you, and you print what he says.)
      h) Puzzles of all sorts (Playskool, Simplex)

i) Matching games: matching colors, shapes, etc. Creative Playthings has a number of these games and Lottos listed in the Ponder Play section of their catalog.

j) Play and Learn Computer (Playskool): an excellent and interesting toy. Your child will learn to match words to objects; to recognize beginning sounds, rhyming words, matching letters; to use numbers; and to measure.

k) Listen and Learn With Phonics: an excellent way for your preschooler to begin learning to read at home. Records and instruction booklet. For information on it, write Americana Corporation, Mundelein, Illinois.

2. Mathematics and Numbers

a) Cuisenaire Rods Parents' Kit: the best thing you could do for your preschooler to help him get off to a good start in math. Buy this parents' kit and work with him at home. He will enjoy it and so will you. It's easy and fun. For information on it, write to Cuisenaire Company of America, 12 Church Street, New Rochelle, New York 10805.

b) Sum Stick (Childcraft): a simple, tangible introduction to math for young children. Weights placed in either direction of this balance scale demonstrate the processes of addition, subtraction, multiplication, and division.

c) Clocks for learning to tell time (Mattel)

d) Dial-To-Learn Math (Ohio Art)

3. Science

a) Magnets

b) Super Magnet (Creative Playthings)

c) Big I, little i Lenses (Creative Playthings): lens set with a concave reducing lens and a convex magnifying lens

d) Giant Magnifier (Creative Playthings, Childcraft): lens, specially mounted so it will not break, on heavy, three-legged wood framework. It introduces your child dramatically to the phenomenon of magnification.

e) Giant Ant Farm (Childcraft)

f) Phonograph records on science: the Motivation Science Records series (See Appendix D for more elaborate description.)

g) Book series on science to be read to preschoolers (See Appendix C for a further description of these three excellent series of science books.)

(1) *Let's Read and Find Out Science Book* series, Crowell

(2) *True Book* series, Children's Press

(3) *Science Is What and Why* series, Coward-McCann

      4. Foreign Language
        a) Various phonograph records for teaching foreign language to young children (See Appendix D.)
        b) Berlitz Books: *Spanish For Children, French For Children,* etc.
        c) *Cat In The Hat Beginner Dictionary* in Spanish and French

H. Music and Dance Toys
    1. Rhythm instruments (Creative Playthings or make your own.)
    2. Activity and participation records (See Appendix D.)

I. Field Trips to Local Places of Interest
    1. Fire station
    2. Police station
    3. Newspaper
    4. Dairy
    5. Bank
    6. Bakery, etc.

J. Secret Toys You Carry inside Your Head
    1. Stories you make up
    2. Stories your preschooler makes up
    3. Round Robin family stories
    4. "Wouldn't It Be Funny If . . ."
    5. "What Would Happen If . . ."
    6. Solid, Liquid, or Gas (One person names something, and the other has to guess whether it's a solid, liquid, or gas.)
    7. Person, Place, or Thing (One person names something, and the other must guess whether it's a person, place, or thing.)
    8. Twenty Questions (Instead of "animal, vegetable, or mineral" with preschoolers, leave off the vegetable and mineral because those terms will probably confuse them. One person picks some kind of animal— it could be a human animal, and the other tries to guess it by using only twenty yes-or-no questions.)

V. The Stage of Middle Childhood (ages six through ten)

In the stage of middle childhood, your child is leaving the security of home and family and venturing out into a much larger universe. He is now relating to three "worlds" at the same time: the world of school, the world of his peer group, and the world of his family. His self-identity is now forged in terms of how well he masters the specific skills and accomplishments that are demanded of him in school, in his group, and at home. The developmental task of this stage is that of *mastery* versus *inadequacy.* If your child feels secure that he can do what is demanded of him at school, with his peers, and at home, then he will develop a sense of mastery. If he is not able to master the tasks demanded of him, then he will feel a sense of inadequacy.

What are the toys that will help your child develop a sense of mastery? What are the toys that exert a particular fascination for a child of this age?

First of all, remember that your middle-childhood youngster has by no means outgrown all of those wonderful toys he delighted in as a preschooler. He will still love to dig in the sand, build cities of blocks, play with puppets, play with cars and trucks and boats, play with dolls and dollhouses, etc. But, in addition, he is now ready for a new set of toys and games and play materials for which he was not mature enough as a preschooler.

A. Games

The child at this stage loves to play games—with you, with his friends, with the whole family. Since he is intellectually much advanced over the preschool stage, he is capable of playing much more sophisticated games.

1. A pack of playing cards
2. *Fifty Card Games for Children* by Vernon Quinn. An investment in a pack of cards and this book will result in hours of happy play for your youngster. Many of the card games can be played by only two people, and these are particularly handy for your youngster to know.
3. Checkers
4. Chess
5. Pick Up Sticks
6. Dominoes
7. Parcheesi
8. Monopoly
9. Roulette
10. Bridge for Juniors (Selchow and Righter)
11. Three-Dimensional Tic-Tac-Toe
12. Bridg-It (Hassenfeld)
13. Blockhead (Saalfield)
14. Conflict (Parker Brothers): a war game, much prized by boys, but not particularly by girls
15. Don't Break the Ice (Schafer)
16. Rug Croquet (Creative Playthings): miniature croquet, played inside the house on the rug
17. Talking Football (Mattel)
18. Talking Baseball (Mattel): these two games are real favorites with boys. They include an automatic sportscaster, a number of records, and a spin-dial scoreboard.
19. Big Five Sports (Childcraft): magnetic baseball, football, basketball, grand prix racing, and spin bowling. A special advantage of these games is that they can be played while traveling.

20. Cross-Fire (Ideal): an exciting two-man game with particular appeal for boys

B. Sports
1. Nerf ball: the ball that can be safely thrown around the house. Helps a six- to eight-year-old learn proficiency in throwing and catching a ball.
2. Whiffle Ball: another special kind of ball your youngster can use in learning to throw and catch
3. Baseball: fathers often underestimate how long it takes for their middle-childhood youngster to develop true proficiency in throwing and catching a baseball.
4. Bat
5. Football: this takes a lot of time and practice also.
6. Bicycle: some six-year-olds may be ready to learn to ride a bike; others will not be ready until they are seven.
7. Roller skates
8. Jump rope
9. Marbles
10. Tops
11. Basketball: you may want to start by using a volleyball or similar-sized ball which is easier for your middle-childhood youngster to handle. Then, when he is really comfortable shooting and dribbling the smaller ball, he will be ready for a full-fledged basketball.
12. Wood Hi-Sticks (Creative Playthings): five-foot-long stilts, just the right size for middle childhood

C. Dolls for Girls and Boys
That title may jar you—what, dolls for girls *and boys!* Yes, boys of this age have always had the need to play with dolls, which they use for fantasy role playing, for models of what they will become later, and for dramatic play. Unfortunately, for years nobody provided boys with suitable dolls until GI Joe, with his various changes of costume and settings, arrived on the toy scene. Then toy manufacturers began to get the idea and realized they didn't need to limit themselves to male dolls in war settings. So now we have male dolls in peacetime settings.
1. Big Jim, Big Josh, and Big Jack (Mattel): excellent dolls for boys this age. Made of sturdy plastic, they can be posed in any position. Big Jim can be dressed for going camping, as a cowboy, baseball player, football player, basketball player, skin diver, fire fighter, karate expert, etc. There are also a variety of settings you can buy to go with him, such as a fishing trip, rescue rig, camper, etc.
2. GI Joe still remains a favorite of many boys.
3. Barbie and Ken (Mattel): who could forget these two dolls, which

have been the favorites of many, many girls? We parents may object to having to hock the family jewels to pay for Barbie's various wardrobes, but middle-childhood girls continue to love these dolls.

D. Crafts
   1. Model making: it may not be particularly creative, but children of this age, particularly boys, go ape over putting together models of airplanes, prehistoric scenes, cars, dinosaurs, horror characters, and you-name-it. Some of the models simply snap together; others are put together with plastic glue. Don't believe all the claims that the model will simply snap together; buy some plastic glue to be safe.
   2. Clay modeling
   3. Papier mâché
   4. Weaving
   5. Woodworking
   6. Leather work
   7. Instant Papier Mâché (Creative Playthings)
   8. Geo-D-Stix (Childcraft)
   9. Flexagons (Creative Playthings)
   10. Sew Magic (Mattel): makes sewing simple enough for a child of this age. Miracle Stitch, an innovative liquid sewing formula, joins the fabric fast.

E. Intellectual Stimulation Toys
   1. Scrabble for Juniors (Selchow and Righter)
   2. Scrabble
   3. On Sets (Childcraft): deals with the set theory of math
   4. Wiff 'N Proof: math and logic games (You will have to read the directions and teach your child these math games. He cannot learn to play them by himself.)
   5. Ends 'n' Blends (Childcraft): stimulates interest in and understanding of words
   6. Tuf (Childcraft): a game based on math equations. Middle-childhood youngsters can play the earlier games in the series, which goes all the way up to college.
   7. Kalah (Childcraft): an ancient game which teaches arithmetic in a painless way
   8. Numble (Childcraft): covers addition, subtraction, multiplication, and division. The game develops the math aptitude it requires.
   9. Scribbage (Lowe): aids in learning words and spelling
   10. Probe (Parker Brothers): a game of words
   11. Skunk (Schaper): teaches counting in a most interesting and painless fashion

F. Science Toys
  1. Biology Lab (Skilcraft)
  2. Chemistry Lab (Skilcraft)
  3. Geology Lab (Skilcraft)
  4. Learning Labs (Childcraft): a unique home learning program in science from one of America's finest science museums, the Franklin Institute of Philadelphia. Each Learning Lab contains six experiments. There are three series of labs: Explorer Series (ages six to eight), Discoverer Series (ages eight to ten), and Inventor Series (ages ten to twelve).
  5. A microscope (You will need to be sure your child is mature enough to handle it wisely.)
  6. *Experiments in Science* by Franklin Branley and Nelson Beeler and *Fun With Chemistry* by Mae and Ira Freeman: two books of science experiences just right for the stage of middle childhood

G. Musical Toys
  An interest in playing a musical instrument or having music lessons usually begins to develop when the child is around eight or nine (unless he has a true and deep gift for music, in which case the interest may well develop earlier). What kinds of instruments can he begin to play at this age?
  1. Piano
  2. Recorder
  3. Autoharp
  4. Ukelele
  5. Toy clarinet
  6. Flute
  7. Xylophone (Creative Playthings)
  8. Melodica (Childcraft): a unique musical instrument, so easy to play that many educators use it to teach beginners the basics of harmony, chord formation, and musical theory. You can play chords and single notes, sharps, and flats.

H. Miscellaneous Toys
  1. Electric trains (It's not wise to give these to your child until he's nine or ten.)
  2. Cassette tape recorder: your child will find hundreds of uses for this; a gift with great play value
  3. Magic Set (Creative Playthings)
  4. Bolt-Tight (Creative Playthings)
  5. Real tools: hammer, pliers, brace and bit, crosscut saw, coping saw, screwdriver, hand plane, wood file and rasp, hand drills. I suggest you

provide a pegboard for your youngster to hang these on, rather than a toolbox to stuff them in

6. Pets that reproduce easily: white mice, guinea pigs, gerbils
7. Hot Wheels (Mattel): a perennial favorite with boys of this age
8. Sizzlers (Mattel): power-charged electric cars, using the Juice Machine, the battery-powered recharger. Another favorite of boys.
9. Chopcycles (Mattel): motorcycles power-charged the same as Sizzler cars
10. Technik (Childcraft): a sophisticated construction toy
11. Disguise Kit (Childcraft)
12. Cub Printing Press (Childcraft)

VI. The Stages of Preadolescence and Adolescence (sources for toys and play equipment)

I will not give any recommended list of toys for the stages of preadolescence and adolescence for several reasons: preadolescents and adolescents are quite individual and unique in their choice of toys and games. Therefore, you need to know your adolescent's particular likes and dislikes in order to buy a game for him that he will like. Second, when a youngster reaches the stage of pre-adolescence or adolescence, he is oversensitive to anything that reminds him of being younger. So consult with your preadolescent or adolescent before buying him a Christmas or birthday present to make sure you are on his wave length.

Many parents are limited by the toys in their local toy stores and are not familiar with these sources of excellent toys and play equipment:

1. Childcraft, 52 Hook Road, Bayonne, New Jersey 07002
2. Creative Playthings, P.O. Box 1100, Princeton, New Jersey 09540
3. F.A.O. Schwarz, Fifth Avenue at 58th Street, New York, New York 10022
4. Community Playthings, Rifton, New York 12471
5. Childplay, 43 East 19th Street, New York, New York 10003
6. Novo Education Toy and Equipment Company, 585 6th Avenue New York, New York 10011
7. Cuisenaire Company of America, 12 Church Street, New Rochelle, New York 10805
8. Musicon Inc., 42-00 Vernon Boulevard, Long Island City, New York 11101

You can get a free catalog by writing to these companies, and it would be well worth your while to do so. You will quickly see the difference between the excellent selection of educational toys in these catalogs and the toys in many local toy stores. You can also make your own version of many of the items you see in these catalogs.

Appendix B
Inexpensive Toys and Play Equipment a Father Can Make

In Appendix A I furnished you with a guide to the best toys you can buy for your child at each stage of his development. Now I want to point out that your child may get the most play value out of toys which you can make for him yourself out of free or inexpensive materials. Your child will often cherish these toys much more than store-bought ones simply because you have made them. A toy is very special when your own father makes it for you. And no other kid in the neighborhood can have a toy like that, because you can't buy it in a store. It is unique!

These toys I am going to describe can be made out of cardboard, wood, old plastic bottles, or old tin cans. I want to make it clear that you do not need to be an expert in woodworking or an artist, or have an elaborate home workshop in order to make these toys. All you need to be able to do is to cut cardboard with a sharp knife, saw wood, nail or glue pieces of wood together, paint plastic bottles or tin cans, or glue pictures on cardboard, wood, or tin cans.

All of these toys can be used by preschoolers from the age of three on up. Many can still be used with great enjoyment by children in the stage of middle childhood, up to age ten.

TOYS YOU CAN MAKE FROM CARDBOARD

The average father overlooks the fact that empty cardboard boxes are a gold mine for toy making. Let's start with the smaller sizes. You can find them everywhere. But if you have trouble, go to a drugstore, a shoe store, or any store which has things sent to it or sends things out in small packages.

You can delight your preschooler by using small cardboard boxes to construct buildings of different shapes and sizes which will make a little city for him. Cut doors in the boxes this way

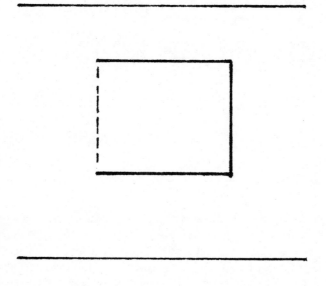

so that they can open. You can cut windows the same way. Or you can paint the windows, without having them open. The fastest way to paint the windows, put handles on the doors, or decorate the buildings is to use a marking pen. These come in different bright colors, and you can work very quickly with them. You can also use crayons—either wax crayons, the kind most people are familiar with, or pastel crayons, which produce brilliant colors, but which smudge easily. If you use pastel crayons, it would be best to spray the finished result with a clear acrylic paint or varnish. You can also decorate your buildings with acrylic paints.

They come in brilliant colors and are a water-base paint, very easy to use. When you have painted a building with acrylic paint and it has dried, use clear acrylic gloss as a covering paint to bring out the brilliance of the color.

I suggest you experiment with all four of these media for coloring the toys you make for your child. You may discover that you prefer one media to color one kind of toy and another media to color another. Marking pens are the fastest way to go, so if you have a limited time, use them. You can find colored marking pens in any stationery store, and wax crayons, pastel crayons, and acrylic paints in any art store.

Besides the media to color your buildings, you will need a sharp knife to cut the cardboard. An X-acto knife or its equivalent, which you can buy in any hardware store, will do the job nicely for you. When you finish, you'll have a group of buildings of different shapes and sizes which may look something like this:

Of course the same kinds of buildings you make from small cardboard boxes can also be made from larger cardboard boxes. It all depends on the room you have in your house for the toy city you make for your youngster.

Shifting to a different kind of project, you can also make a dollhouse out of cardboard for a little girl. In the long run it is probably better to make a dollhouse out of wood because it is more durable. But you can try a cardboard dollhouse and see how well it lasts. The cardboard box should be large enough to contain the size of dolls and doll furniture your little girl likes.

There are two basic designs in dollhouses: the more traditional type with one side open and the more modern type, which is open completely from the top and easier for a child to play with. For the more traditional type, get a cardboard box which is sturdy and large enough. Cut one side open; then cut floors out of cardboard to fit the house. Anchor them in place with either glue or package sealing tape which you can buy at a stationery store. Then color the house brightly. When you finish, you will have something like this:

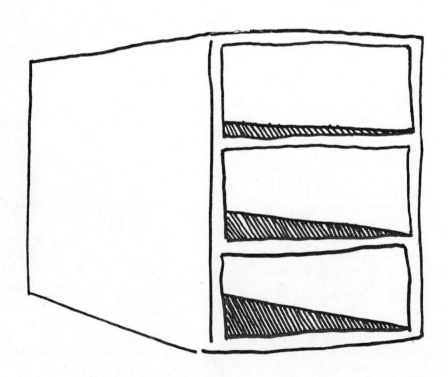

For the open-top dollhouse, get a large cardboard box and cut the sides down so that they are an appropriate height. Then cut out cardboard walls, with doors that open in each wall. Attach the walls with glue or package sealing tape. When you finish, you will have something like this:

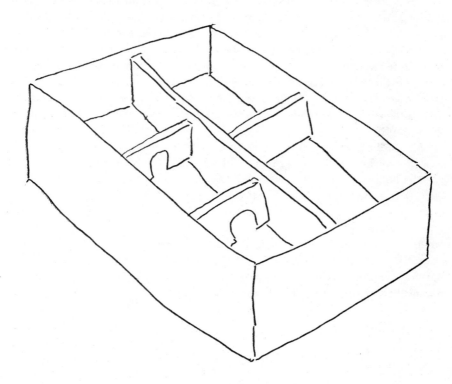

Let's move still further up the scale of large cardboard boxes. One of the finest toys you can ever provide for your child is a huge cardboard box itself (the kind a refrigerator comes in, for example). Basically, there are two ways you can make a toy for your child out of such a huge box. You can decide what you want to make, such as a house, a robot, a boat, or whatever. Cut appropriate holes at the appropriate places, color it, and present it as a surprise to your youngster. Or you can work with him as the two of you decide what to make out of it: "Jenny, here's a big box I got for you. Let's decide what to make out of it." She will come up with ideas, and you and she can make it together. You will be doing the cutting, and she can do the coloring with a marking pen.

Or you can just present the empty box to your youngster without any suggestions at all. I guarantee he will find uses for it you never dreamed of!

Dolls can be easily and quickly made from cardboard. When I say *dolls*, don't jump to the conclusion that I mean something only for a little girl. I mean different kinds of dolls for either sex. The easiest way to make a doll out of cardboard is to find a complete, or almost complete, figure of a person from a magazine, cut it out, and glue it to a piece of cardboard.

The best glue for this purpose is Wilhold glue or Elmer's glue. The easiest way to glue any kind of paper, cardboard, or wood is to begin by pouring some glue into an empty coffee can. Then get a small, very cheap brush from an art store and use it to apply the glue. If the figure you cut out from the magazine isn't quite complete, that's all right; just take a colored marking pen and complete the job. It doesn't matter how rough or how finished it looks; your preschooler isn't finicky about such things. Once you have glued the figure to the cardboard, then cut out the cardboard figure very carefully with a sharp X-acto knife.

All sorts of figures can be used to make dolls: mothers, fathers, children, teen-agers, babies, policeman, firemen, artists, sports figures, etc.

The dolls can simply be cut out of the cardboard the way they are. Or you may want to make them a little more elaborate by giving them a base, so they can stand upright. Bases can be made out of small scraps of wood. Cut a notch across the top of the block of wood so that the cardboard doll will fit into the notch. If you happen to be a sophisticated home workshop owner with an electric saw, then you simply make what is known as a "dado" cut in the wood. But you can do the same thing with an ordinary fret saw. The finished result on the small block of wood will look something like this:

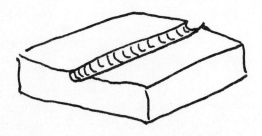

You can also make animals out of cardboard for your child in two different ways. First, as with the dolls, you simply find pictures of animals in magazines, cut them out, and glue them on the cardboard. Cut around the cardboard with your X-acto knife. Then make wood blocks with grooves so that the animals can stand up.

I also want to encourage you to cut your own animals out of cardboard. Don't worry about their looking like real animals; these can all be fantasy animals. Your preschooler should be especially delighted by this kind of fantasy zoo, for no other child will have anything like it. He will really prize this, and may announce proudly to his friends, "My Daddy made this for me!" Be sure to draw an eye on each fantasy animal. This makes them come alive. Color them different bright colors with marking pens, crayons, or acrylic paint. Here, for example, are some of the fantasy shapes you might make:

Cardboard is such a versatile medium and so easy to use. Please don't feel limited by the suggestions I have made here. You may think of all sorts of things you can make out of cardboard that I haven't discussed here: airplanes, trucks, cars, ships, submarines, and many, many more. Cardboard also has the virtue that no matter where you are, you can always find some to make toys for your child. (For example, if it suddenly starts raining on your vacation trip and the family is marooned in a cabin or motel, you can always make some cardboard toys for your child!)

TOYS YOU CAN MAKE FROM WOOD

Many of the same toys that you can make from cardboard you can also make from wood: dolls, animals (which you cut out with a coping saw), people, dollhouses, and buildings. Naturally, if you make these things out of wood, they will be more durable.

Let's start our section on wooden toys with something your preschooler is sure to derive many hours of play value from: a toy city. Playskool has an excellent one you can buy in a toy store. But your child will get more enjoyment from one that has been made by you. Here's how you do it. First get a large enough piece of half-inch plywood as the base for the toy city. Decide how large you want to make it: 2' x 3', 3' x 3', or whatever. I don't think I would make it any larger than 3' x 3'. Then, with a colored marking pen, mark out streets, with residential and commercial sections in between, which you can color green. You'll end up with something like this:

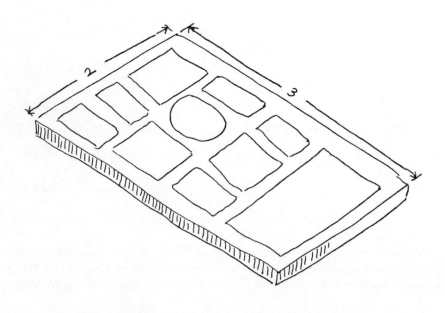

You will need to find tiny wood scraps out of which to make the buildings. A nearby cabinet shop is often an excellent source of wood scraps, many of which can be used as is. Sometimes you may find some business near you which will have a load of wood scraps they throw away. You need small chunky scraps 2" x 1", 2" x 2", 2" x 3", or something like that. If all else fails, you can have your local lumber store cut you a number of such sizes. Also get some old broomsticks as well as some 3/4- or 1-inch dowels and cut them into 1- or 2-inch sections. You can glue the dowel or broomstick pieces on top of the other pieces for different kinds of buildings. If you find some odd-shaped scraps, so much the better. They will make more interesting buildings. Use a marking pen, crayons, or paint to put doors and windows on your buildings. You may end up with a bunch of quite different-looking buildings, something like this:

Preschool children like to play with a tiny town with tiny buildings. The reason for this is that they feel inferior because they are so small in comparison to the world of giants (the adults). Playing with tiny buildings and tiny people gives them a sense of being big and powerful. But children also like to play with buildings which are larger. You can use the same basic principles to build larger buildings out of larger wood scraps, such as you would find on the scrap heap where a new house or apartment house is being constructed.

You can also make boats and cars out of wood. These are quite simple to do. Let's start with boats. They need not be elaborate at all. The basic structure, in its simplest form, is merely two different pieces of wood, cut to shape and nailed or glued together, topped by a piece of broomstick or dowel on top. Something like this:

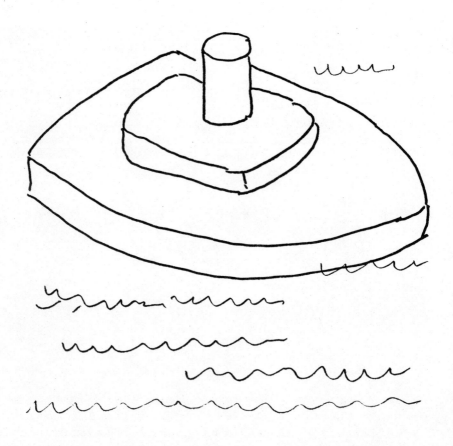

Here's a slightly more elaborate boat:

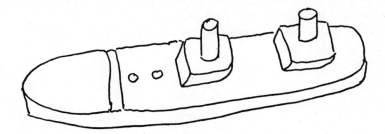

And here's a side view of a different kind of boat:

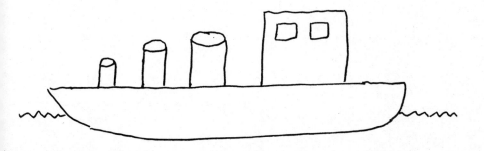

Cars and trucks are "naturals" to make out of wood. You make the body out of chunky wood pieces, nailed or glued together. The wheels are made out of circular wooden pieces or large dowels sawed thin. The wheels are joined to one another by thin dowels underneath the car. The thin dowels are attached to the underside of the car by steel brads which are big enough so the dowels can turn freely. There is infinite variety in the types of cars you can make. But they are all variations on the theme of a single piece of chunky wood with four round wheels attached to one another by dowels underneath the car, like this:

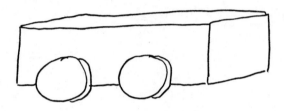

You can make many different varieties of cars and trucks by using differently shaped wood bodies, nailing or gluing differently shaped pieces on top, etc. You can also make cars by cutting out unique shapes in two pieces of two-by-four and nailing them together. Here are some examples of differently shaped cars and trucks you can make:

If you decide to make a dollhouse out of wood instead of cardboard, follow the same directions I gave for making dollhouses out of cardboard. Why not make some doll furniture as well? The furniture can be chunky and modernistic, with simple lines. Use a marking pen (this time, one with a fine line) to draw in the details of drawers, drawer pulls, dials on the TV set, electric coils on the stove, etc. Here are some examples of simple dollhouse furniture:

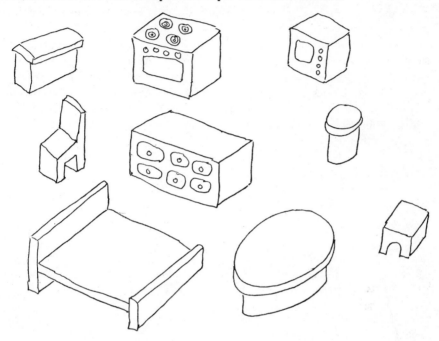

You can also make two personalized types of games for your child out of wood. The first is a Parcheesi-type game where you get a piece of 1/4-inch plywood about 2′ x 2′, or 2½′ x 2½′. Mark out the path the players will take around the board and divide it up into squares. You can personalize the game in many ways. For instance, you could have the squares represent favorite places your child likes to go in your community: the ice cream store, the library, the swimming pool, etc. You could include places you have gone on vacation. You could include special interests of your child: sports, animals, TV shows, etc. Every once in a while write things on some of the squares such as "Go back three spaces" or "Advance to Disneyland." You need a set of markers so that each player can have one. You could use small colored blocks of wood, small Tootsietoy metal cars, or something like that. Now all you need is a pair of dice and you're ready to play!

Another type of game your child will like is a marble game. Get a suitably sized piece of 1/4-inch plywood, about 2′ x 3′. Bore holes near one end, with different scores for the different holes. Nail an endpiece and two sidepieces to the plywood so the marbles will not roll all over the floor.

Wooden puzzles will also be appreciated by your preschool child. Get a simple picture from a magazine and glue it to a piece of 1/4-inch plywood. I prefer to use acrylic gloss paint, which acts as a glue, but gives a more beautiful finish to the picture. Put it on the back side of the picture first as you would glue, and then on the front side. Leave about a 2-inch margin around your picture.

After the picture has dried and is glued fast to the wood, cut it up into simple shapes, being sure to leave your 2-inch margin uncut. You can do the cutting with a jigsaw in a jiffy, or more slowly with a coping saw. After you have cut the simple shapes out, then put them all back together in the picture. Then nail or glue the 2-inch frame to a back-up piece of 1/2-inch plywood, the same size as your first one, including the margin. When you finish you will have something that will look like this:

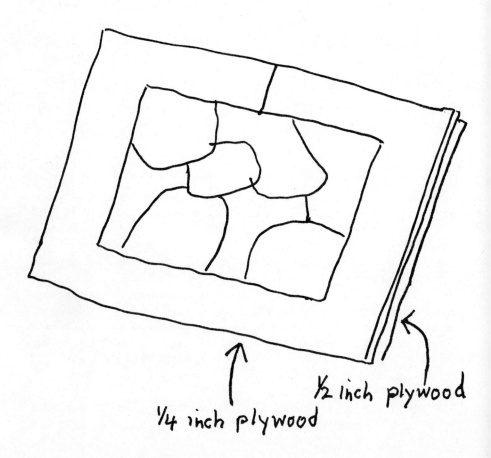

½ inch plywood

¼ inch plywood

A puppet stage, which might be used either inside or outside, can also be made of wood. It should be constructed so that your child can stand upright next to the lower part of the stage and not have to crouch down in order to show his puppets. If you make it out of a frame of two-by-fours with 1/2- or 3/4-inch plywood nailed to the frame, it should be very sturdy. It will look something like this:

There are also many wooden toys for outdoor play you can make for your youngster. Children usually have scoops or large wooden spoons for digging in the sand. But why not make your child some unusual wooden sand scrapers for playing in the sand or making designs in it, such as these:

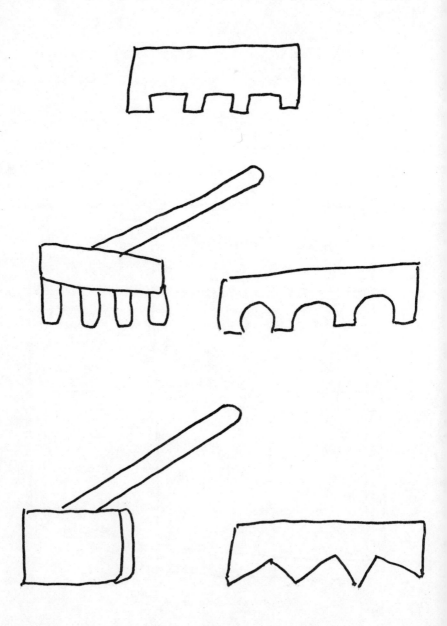

These sand scrapers can be made of plywood and wooden dowels, glued or nailed together.

If there is room in your backyard for tricycle riding, your youngster might like a set of realistic traffic signs, which you can make out of wood. Here are some examples:

One of the finest toys you could make for your preschooler is his own set of large hollow blocks. Every good nursery school has a set of these, and children delight in playing with them. Sad to say, very few homes have them, possibly because they are so expensive to buy. But they're not expensive if you make them yourself. You don't have to be a topnotch carpenter to nail six boards together!

It helps the child to grip the hollow block if you leave an open space between two boards on one side of the block. Sand the block down to remove splintery surfaces. You can varnish or shellac the blocks if you want, but it's not absolutely necessary. Half-inch plywood is probably the best wood to use. Make them in different sizes, such as 1' x 2', 1' x 3', etc.

Another outdoor plaything your child will enjoy, and which will help his coordination as well, is a coordination walking board. You make this by using a two-by-four, so that it will fit both sideways and edgeways into two supporting side pieces. Cut the side pieces like this:

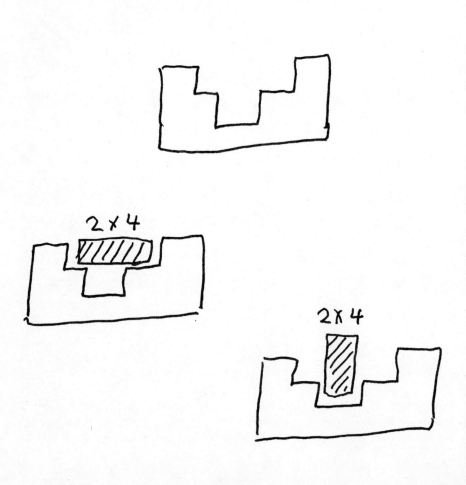

When your preschooler first begins to balance himself on the two-by-four, you place it sideways in the two supporting side pieces, so that he is balancing himself on the 4-inch side. When he has mastered that, you can place it edgeways into the supporting side pieces, so that he is now balancing himself on the 2-inch side. The finished piece of equipment will look like this:

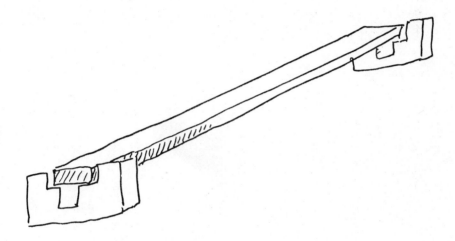

One piece of outdoor equipment your youngster will cherish beginning in his preschool years and continuing through middle childhood is a treehouse not in a tree. (If you want to build it in a tree, fine, but I found it simpler not to when I built this for my kids.) The base for the treehouse can be made of four redwood four-by-fours. Sink these into the ground for about three feet and pour concrete around them. Let them extend up as high as you would like the treehouse to be

Once you have your four supporting posts anchored solidly, then the secret of success in building this treehouse, as far as I'm concerned, is to know absolutely nothing about carpentry. Just get yourself boards and heavy nails and nail a floor and four walls and a roof on it. Then add on extra boards going in any old direction your fancy pleases. Be sure to put a hole in the roof, with a cover on it and a makeshift ladder leading up to it so that your youngster can climb up on the roof. And be sure that there is a rope securely attached to the roof so he can shinny down if he so desires.

You will end up with something absolutely out of this world which can be used by your child as a clubhouse, a fort (be sure to cut out lookout holes in the walls), a submarine, a space module, or whatever. It might look something like this:

This last toy I'm going to mention is not made completely of wood. The wood is used only for backing. This is a set of abstract rubber stamps. Your child can use these with different color stamp pads to print interesting abstract designs. You could also cut out the letters of the alphabet from rubber, and he could print with these. An old inner tube is perfect material to use for these shapes or letters.

Cut out the shapes or letters from the rubber with a sharp knife. Glue them to a piece of wood big enough for your child to grasp easily. You can glue a dowel to the piece of wood for a handle. The shapes can be as abstract as you want to make them, or you can use the simple shapes of square, triangle, circle, etc. Something like this for the rubber shapes:

The completed hand stamp will look like this:

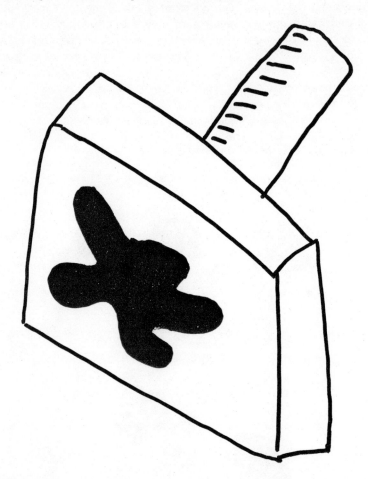

As with cardboard, once you discover the joy of making toys and playthings out of wood for your child, I am sure you will end up making many toys that I have not even mentioned, but which will occur to you.

TOYS MADE FROM PLASTIC BOTTLES OR TIN CANS

You can add variety to your toy towns by making other toy buildings for your child out of cylindrical plastic bottles (the same ones that drugstores use to fill prescriptions, for example) and tin cans of various sizes. Again, you can paint on windows and doors with colored marking pens or acrylic paints, or paint the whole can or bottle some vivid color.

I have described in this appendix toys which are easy to make and can be done relatively quickly. Once you get hooked on making homemade toys for your child, you will probably wonder why you missed all the fun of making your own special toys for him during the years when the only toys you got him came from a store!

Appendix C

A Father's Guide to Children's Books

You can furnish your child with an enormous amount of intellectual stimulation (especially during the all-important preschool years) simply by taking him to the library once a week, getting several of the books listed in this appendix, and reading them to him during the following week. If you follow up your trip to the library with a visit to the ice-cream store or doughnut shop or some other place where your child can have a special treat, it will not be long before he'll look forward to his weekly visits to the library with considerable anticipation! (Remember what we discussed in chapter five: any behavior that is followed by a reinforcer or reward is likely to be repeated.)

I read a large number of the books on this list to my three children when they were preschoolers. They learned a great deal from the books and so did I! My children not only learned valuable information from the books, but in the process of their trips to the library with me they learned that Daddy likes and values books—so they learned to like and value books also.

However, please don't make the mistake of confining all the books your child reads to library books, merely because it saves you money that way. The same parents who "save money" by not buying books for their child will buy toys for him at Christmas and throughout the year. If a parent does this, whether he is aware of it or not, he is transmitting this message to his child: "Toys are more important than books, because we buy you toys to keep but we never buy you books to keep." But a child *needs* books to keep—books he feels are his very own.

It is difficult for a child to grow up really valuing books if he never has any books of his own, never enjoys the thrill of building up his own personal library as he adds to it book by book over the years. Even if you can only afford to buy your child five paperback books a year, buy him those books and let them become part of his growing little library. If you bought him only five books a year and continued this habit until he graduated from high school, at that time he would have eighty-five books in his personal library. And that would be eighty-five more books than a lot of American children have in their own libraries when they graduate from high school.

One factor that will help you keep the cost of children's books down is the growing number of high-quality paperback books for children. If you do not happen to live near a bookstore which carries a good selection of children's paperbacks, your solution may be to buy books by mail. You can deal with Scholastic Book Services, 904 Sylvan Avenue, Englewood Cliffs, New Jersey, or 5675 Sunol Boulevard, Pleasanton, California. Ask for their free Reader's Choice catalog, which lists more than 500 good paperbacks for children.

I want to emphasize that you should not use my list of recommended books or any other list, in a blind fashion. Before you buy any book on this list for your child or even before you get one of these books out of the library for him, look it over yourself first. Probably the single most important criterion of selecting a book for a child, particularly a book you are going to read to a child when he is a preschooler, is that you should like the book yourself. If the book "speaks" to you, it will "speak" to your child. But if you don't enjoy it, chances are that your child won't enjoy having you read it to him. This principle that you yourself should like the book becomes less important, of course, as your child grows older and develops his own taste in books (which may be quite different from yours).

This list of books is arranged according to ages and stages of development.

I. **The Stage of Toddlerhood** (approximately from first to second birthday)
   A. Books for "Labeling the Environment"
      At this age a "book" is not something that contains a continuous narrative story, but something with pictures of people or objects, and words labeling those people or objects. Books are useful devices at this age to help your child play the "label the environment" game we discussed in the chapter on toddlerhood.

      Books for this age should be sturdy affairs, of cardboard or cloth, because the first thing your toddler will probably do with these beginning books is put them in his mouth.

1. Sears or Montgomery Ward catalog, trading stamp catalogs, or toy catalogs. Although ordinarily not thought of as books, these catalogs are ideal for playing the "label the environment" game. And who cares if a few pages get torn out here and there?

2. *Best Word Book Ever,* Richard Scarry (Western Publishing). This book is one of the best investments a parent could ever make for a toddler. When you have finished playing the "label the environment" game with this book, with its 1,400 gaily illustrated objects with words to match, your child will have a vocabulary of 1,400 words. A terrific boost to his language development! Uniquely appealing animals are pictured in all kinds of activities related to a young child's experience and interest. This book can be used for several years with a young child.

3. *The Cat in the Hat Beginner Book Dictionary,* Dr. Seuss (Random House). Another excellent picture dictionary to play "label the environment." Funny pictures and a phrase show the meaning of 1,000 words in Dr. Seuss's inimitable style. You can read it to your child when he is a toddler. And he can read it himself in the first three grades of school.

4. *My First Book* and *My First Toys* (Platt and Munk). Extra sturdy, vividly colored books. Each page clearly pictures three objects you can point to and teach your toddler to name.

B. Mother Goose Books

There is a tremendous number of Mother Goose books on the market. You should browse and find one most suited to your own taste. I recommend three for special consideration.

1. *Mother Goose,* Brian Wildsmith (Franklin Watts). I must confess I am a dyed-in-the-wool fan of this wonderful British artist. That's why I would personally choose his book, with the authentic nursery rhymes illustrated in vivid and striking colors.

2. *The Puffin Book of Nursery Rhymes,* Iona and Peter Opie (Penguin [paperback]). Two hundred rhymes in related sequence.

3. *Hi Diddle Diddle* (Scholastic). Contains very simple rhymes. There is also a small 33-1/3 rpm record, *Hi Diddle Diddle,* which parallels the book and will aid in introducing your child to Mother Goose.

Incidentally, a father often does not need to wait until his child's first birthday to start reading Mother Goose, but may begin when the baby is nine or ten months old. A baby this age will delight in the rhythmic repetition of sounds in simple nursery rhymes.

C. Other Books for the Toddler

1. *Pat the Bunny,* Dorothy Kunhardt (Western Publishing). On each

small page there is something for baby to do: look in the mirror, play peek-a-boo, smell the flowers, or pat the felt-lined bunny. A delightful book for a toddler.

2. *The Giant Nursery Book of Things That Go,* George Zaffo (Doubleday). Boys especially love this book. Large action pictures of boats, trains, trucks, planes . . . things that go.

3. *Baby's First Book,* Garth Williams (Western Publishing). A picture book on cardboard pages. Excellent for baby to begin with, as are Garth Williams' *Baby Animals* and *Baby Farm Animals.*

4. *First Things,* George Adams and Paul Henning (Platt and Munk). A stunning picture book of things that are familiar. Done in beautiful, natural color.

5. *Anybody at Home?* H. A. Rey (Houghton Mifflin). Toddlers will delight in finding the surprise picture under the flap of each page.

6. *Farm Animals,* Irma Wilde (Grosset and Dunlap). Young children love to look at books about animals. This book of farm animals will exert a great appeal.

7. *Things to See,* Thomas Matthiesen (Platt and Munk). Beautiful color photographs depict things a little baby will recognize.

8. *Who Lives Here?* Pat and Eve Witte (Western Publishing). Peek under the flap and see who lives here. A charming book. Little ones love it.

9. *The Touch Me Book,* Pat and Eve Witte (Western Publishing). This touch and feel book will fascinate toddlers. With a flick of a finger they can work a seesaw, turn a bicycle wheel, move a giraffe's head, and operate many other objects.

D. Bedtime Books for the Toddler

1. *Goodnight Moon,* Margaret Wise Brown (Harper and Row). A toddler's classic. All of my children loved it. Old-fashioned illustrations of a little bunny saying goodnight to everybody and especially to "nobody."

2. *A Child's Goodnight Book,* Margaret Wise Brown (W. R. Scott). This delightful book, geared to a toddler's level, describes bedtime.

3. *Bedtime for Frances,* Russel Hoban (Harper and Row). Russel Hoban is one of our best writers for young children, and his series of books about Frances, the irresistible little badger, is particularly fine. This one tells of Frances' clever ways to stay up past her bedtime. If you should find this a little too advanced for your toddler, wait a bit and try it out on him in the next stage of first adolescence, when he will be sure to like it.

II. **The Stage of First Adolescence** (approximately second to third birthday)
The age ranges in this book list are not to be taken rigidly and absolutely. A

book that hits one two-year-old "just right" may be too advanced for another two-year-old or too babyish for another. Your child is unique, and the book must meet him "where he is." Some of the books that were his favorites in the stage of toddlerhood will continue to be his favorites in this stage. Some of the books that are listed in this booklist under the preschool stage would be too advanced for many first adolescents. Other first adolescents will be delighted by them and beg you to read them again and again. This or any other booklist is only a rough-and-ready guide to selecting books for children of different ages. *Your child is the final arbiter of what book is appropriate for him. Be guided by his response.*

A child in this stage is fascinated by words and word play. And so he will continue to love nursery rhymes, with their rhythm and repetition sounds. The child of this age loves to repeat something until he feels he has mastered it. He likes the repetition in familiar nursery tales such as *The Three Little Pigs* or *Chicken Little.* He likes to recognize what is coming next in the story and chant it with you as you read it to him. He also loves sounds of all sorts, particularly unusual or funny sounds. When you read books of sounds to him, emphasize the sound.

He also enjoys stories about the "here and now" of his everyday world: going to the market with mother, riding in a car or bus, playing in a park, going to a zoo. Animal stories are especially popular at this age.

Reading to a first adolescent should be a cooperative affair. He likes to look at the book and touch it. He likes to be asked to find things in the illustrations. Sometimes he likes to join in the chant of a familiar repetition from a well-loved book.

He often has favorite books he will want you to read him day after day. Woe betide you if you dare to change a phrase in a familiar book! Sometimes it is difficult to get him to listen to a new book.

A. ABC and Counting Books
   1. *Brian Wildsmith's ABC,* Brian Wildsmith (Watts). An Animal ABC book done in Wildsmith's usual stunning colors.
   2. *ABC of Cars and Trucks,* Anne Alexander (Doubleday). Instructs a child in his ABC's by using cars and trucks.
   3. *ABC of Buses,* Dorothy Shuttlesworth (Doubleday). Another ABC book with a definite appeal to boys.
   4. *Bruno Munari's ABC,* Bruno Munari (World). A highly original alphabet book with beautiful illustrations.
   5. *Richard Scarry's ABC Word Book;* Richard Scarry (Random House). A unique way of showing the capital and lower-case letters by printing each one he is focusing on in red.
   6. *Dr. Seuss's ABC,* Dr. Seuss (Random House). A wonderful ABC book done in Dr. Seuss's inimitable style.

7. *Brian Wildsmith's 1 2 3's,* Brian Wildsmith (Watts). A unique counting book for young children. A visual delight.
8. *One Snail and Me,* Emily McLeod (Little Brown). A child learns to
   count in a most delightful way—in a bathtub.
9. *Counting Carnival,* Feenie Ziner and Paul Galdone (Coward-
   McCann). A clever way to stimulate number awareness.
10. *Brown Cow Farm,* Dahlov Ipcar (Doubleday). A thoroughly enjoy-
    able book about counting up to 100. Excellent illustrations.
11. *The Nutshell Library,* Maurice Sendak (Harpers). Young children are
    fascinated by miniature things, and these tiny, tiny books have an
    irresistible appeal. This nutshell library includes a counting book, an
    alphabet book, a book about the months.

B. Books About Sounds, Which Help to Develop a Child's Perceptual
   Acuity
   As I mentioned above, a child of this age is fascinated by sounds, and
   particularly the repetition of sounds. Margaret Wise Brown has probably
   done more books of this nature than anybody. Here is a selection
   including several of her books which will appeal to the first adolescent.
   1. *The Noisy Book,* Margaret Wise Brown (Harper and Row).
   2. *The Indoor Noisy Book,* Margaret Wise Brown (Harper and Row).
   3. *The City Noisy Book,* Margaret Wise Brown (Harper and Row).
   4. *The Country Noisy Book,* Margaret Wise Brown (Harper and Row).
   5. *The Seashore Noisy Book,* Margaret Wise Brown (Harper and Row).
   6. *The Summer Noisy Book,* Margaret Wise Brown (Harper and Row).
   7. *The Winter Noisy Book,* Margaret Wise Brown (Harper and Row).
   8. *Bow Wow! Meow! A First Book of Sounds,* Melanie Bellah (Western
      Publishing). A good introduction to sounds for the first adolescent.
   9. *Listen to My Seashell,* Charlotte Steiner (Knopf). Another good
      book of sounds for the young child.

C. Nursery Tales
   Tall Book of Nursery Tales. Illustrated by Feodor Rojankovsky
   (Harper and Row). Twenty-four of the most popular nursery tales, with
   superb illustrations. Children particularly like the repetition found in
   tales such as *The Little Red Hen, The Three Little Pigs,* and *The Three
   Bears.*

D. Animal Stories
   Animal stories are popular with this age when the child often identi-
   fies more closely with animals than he does with children.
   1. *The Tale of Peter Rabbit,* Beatrix Potter (Warne). This classic tale has
      been going strong since it was first published in 1903. It is doubtful

that children will ever get tired of the story of Peter, who set out to do precisely what his mother told him not to do: go into Mr. McGregor's garden. Has a particular appeal to the negative nature of the first adolescent!

2. *Millions of Cats,* Wanda Gag (Coward-McCann). A very old man and woman wanted a cat—just one cat—but soon they had "millions and billions and trillions of cats." Your child will soon be chiming in as you read: "hundreds of cats, thousands of cats, millions and billions and trillions of cats!" Wood-block illustrations of great distinction by the author.

3. *Make Way for Ducklings,* Robert McCloskey (Viking). Another animal story that has become a children's classic. A family of mallard ducks in Boston finds a home and are befriended by a policeman. The bold illustrations by the author are excellent.

4. *Little Bear,* Else Minarik (Harper and Row). The delightful adventures of a little bear and his many antics. Depicts the warmth of feeling and the special companionship that exists between a small child and his mother.

5. *The Duck,* Margaret Wise Brown (Harper and Row). Gorgeous photographs by Ylla and a simple text by the author tell the story of a duck that visits the zoo and sees many animals.

6. *Harry the Dirty Dog,* Gene Zion (Harper and Row). A white dog with black spots gets himself so dirty his owners don't know him. Finally he has an amusing struggle to get clean again. Distinctly appealing to the love-to-get-messy nature of the first adolescent.

7. *The Story about Ping,* Marjorie Flack (Viking). The story of a fluffy yellow duck who lives on a Chinese riverboat.

8. *Swimmy,* Leo Lionni (Pantheon). Swimmy, a black fish, decides to explore the unknown depths of the ocean. The full-color illustrations are stunning. This book will introduce a young child to good art.

9. Speaking of books to introduce a young child to good art, here is a marvelous threesome by Brian Wildsmith. Animal books with spectacular full-color illustrations.
   a) *Brian Wildsmith's Birds* (Watts)
   b) *Brian Wildsmith's Fishes* (Watts)
   c) *Brian Wildsmith's Wild Animals* (Watts)

10. *Johnny Crow's Garden,* Leslie Brooke (Warne). A delightful story of Johnny Crow and the growth of his garden.

11. *Bread and Jam for Frances,* Russel Hoban (Harper and Row).

12. *A Birthday for Frances,* Russel Hoban (Harper and Row). Two more amusing adventures of Frances, the lovable badger.

13. *The Runaway Bunny,* Margaret Wise Brown (Harper and Row). A nice story of a naughty little bunny and his understanding mother.

14. *Whatever Happens to Puppies?* Bill Hall (Western Publishing).
15. *Whatever Happens to Kittens?* Bill Hall (Western Publishing).
16. *Whatever Happens to Bear Cubs?* Bill Hall (Western Publishing).
17. *Where Have You Been?* Margaret Wise Brown (Hastings; Scholastic, paperback). Fourteen animals answer the same question. Children love the repetition.
18. *The Cat in the Hat,* Dr. Seuss (Random House). A nonsense story in verse about an unusual cat and his tricks. A modern classic for children. Also by the same author: *The Cat in the Hat Comes Back.*

E. Books about the Child and His Everyday World
   1. *This Is the Way Animals Walk,* Louise Woodcock (Scott). The author of *The Life and Ways of the Two-Year-Old* really knows this age. A simple repetitious text which children of this age will like, together with humorous pictures.
   2. *All Falling Down,* Gene Zion (Harper and Row). Young children like this because of its repetition and also its reassuring surprise ending. Various things are falling down: leaves, snow, the block house. But then comes the ending: "Daddy lifts him up and tosses him in the air. *He doesn't fall.* . . . (Italics added) Daddy catches him."
   3. *Play With Me,* Marie Ets (Viking). A little girl needs someone to play with and tries to get a grasshopper, frog, turtle, chipmunk, and other animals to play with her.
   4. *Just Like Me,* Marie Ets (Viking). A little boy can walk like a cat, hop like a rabbit, and wriggle like a snake. However, his greatest joy is in running "just like me," when his daddy calls.
   5. *Umbrella,* Taro Yashima (Viking). A young Japanese girl in New York wants it to rain so she can use her new umbrella and red rubber boots. Gorgeous illustrations by the author.
   6. *Big Red Bus,* Ethel Kessler (Doubleday). The everyday story of what the big red bus does. Boys will especially like this.
   7. *A Friend Is Someone Who Likes You,* Joan Walsh Anglund (Harcourt Brace and World). A modern classic—a book of friendship and kindly feelings, with delicate illustrations by the author.
   8. *While Susie Sleeps,* Nina Schneider (Scott). "What happens when I sleep?" is a question asked by young children. Nice story about what goes on at night.
   9. *Daddies: What They Do All Day,* Helen Puner (Lothrop). A wonderful book. Children need to know and understand what daddies do.
   10. *The Carrot Seed,* Crockett Johnson (Harper and Row). Charming story of a little boy with faith.
   11. *Where's Andy?* Jane Thayer (Morrow). Mother and Andy play hide-and-seek.

12. *The Day Daddy Stayed Home*, Ethel and Leonard Kessler (Double-day). A delightful story about things a daddy can do when he has to stay home.
13. *When You Were a Little Baby*, Rhoda Berman (Lothrop). Children at this stage love to hear about what they were like when they were tiny babies. This book has great appeal for that reason.
14. *Here Comes Night*, Miriam Schlein (Whitman). A bedtime book that tells about the night.
15. *Saturday Walk*, Ethel Wright and Richard Rose (Scott). Large, vivid pictures of cars, ships, and trains. Especially appealing to boys.
16. *Everybody Eats and Everybody Has a House*, Mary McBurnery Green (Scott). An illustrated book showing what animals do and eat.
17. *The Night when Mother Was Away*, Charlotte Zolotow (Lothrop). Daddy takes care of his little girl, who doesn't want to sleep.
18. *The Hole Book*, Peter Newell (Harper and Row). An old book which never loses its fascination. Small children love to look through the hole and see where it leads to next.

III. The Preschool Stage (approximately third to sixth birthday)

These are years of enormous intellectual potential for your youngster. Research studies have shown that how much a child is read to during these years correlates highly with how successful he is in school. We need to read both nonfiction and fiction to the preschooler. Nonfiction provides him with key concepts which help him understand his world; fiction enlarges his imagination and his creative thinking.

A. Nonfiction: "Double-Duty" Beginning to Read Books

These books do double duty for both the child who has not yet learned to read and the child who is just learning to read. You can read the book to your child in his preschool years before he has learned to read. Later, as he is learning to read in kindergarten or first grade, these books will aid him. He will regard them as old familiar friends, rather than frightening "newcomers" full of unfamiliar words. His familiarity with the book will build confidence in his ability to master this strange new task of learning to read.

Rather than break these books down into specific categories of subject matter, I have listed each of the twenty series by publisher to make it easy for you to become familiar with the beginning reader series of each publisher. Although I have listed them under nonfiction, in actuality the beginning reader books contain both nonfiction and fiction.

If you read only a small number of these books to your preschooler, he (and you!) will absorb an amazing amount of information about science and the world in which we live.

a) Harper: I Can Read Books
  1. *Doctors and Nurses: What Do They Do?* Carla Greene
  2. *Soldiers and Sailors: What Do They Do?* Carla Greene
  3. *Railroad Engineers and Airplane Pilots: What Do They Do?* Carla Greene
  4. *Policemen and Firemen: What Do They Do?* Carla Greene
  5. *Truck Drivers: What Do They Do?* Carla Greene
  6. *Animal Doctors: What Do They Do?* Carla Greene
  7. *Little Bear*, Else Minarik
  8. *A Kiss for Little Bear*, Else Minarik
  9. *Little Bear's Visit*, Else Minarik
  10. *Little Bear's Friend*, Else Minarik
  11. *Father Bear Comes Home*, Else Minarik
  12. *No Fighting, No Biting!* Else Minarik
  13. *Danny and the Dinosaur*, Syd Hoff
  14. *Sammy the Seal*, Syd Hoff
  15. *Julius*, Syd Hoff
  16. *Chester*, Syd Hoff
  17. *Oliver*, Syd Hoff
  18. *Little Chief*, Syd Hoff
  19. *Stanley*, Syd Hoff
  20. *Last One Home Is a Green Pig*, Edith Hurd
  21. *Hurry Hurry*, Edith Hurd
  22. *Stop Stop*, Edith Hurd
  23. *No Funny Business*, Edith Hurd
  24. *Emmet's Pig*, Mary Stolz
  25. *Harry and the Lady Next Door*, Gene Zion
  26. *The Fire Cat*, Ester Averill
  27. *David and the Giant*, Mike McClintock
  28. *Morris Is a Cowboy, a Policeman, and a Baby-Sitter*, B. Wiseman
  29. *A Picture for Harold's Room*, Crockett Johnson
  30. *Tell Me Some More*, Crosby Bonsall
  31. *Who's a Pest?* Crosby Bonsall
  32. *The Happy Birthday Present*, Joan Heilbroner
  33. *This Is the House where Jack Lives*, Joan Heilbroner
  34. *Little Runner of the Longhouse*, Betty Baker
  35. *What Spot?* Crosby Bonsall
  36. *The Secret Three*, Mildred Myrick
  37. *Grizzwold*, Syd Hoff
  38. *Lucille*, Arnold Lobel
  39. *Red Fox and His Canoe*, Nathaniel Benchley
  40. *Tom and the Two Hands*, Russel Hoban
  41. *Three to Get Ready*, Betty Boegehold

42. *Johnny Lion's Book*, Edith Hurd
43. *Oscar Otter*, Nathaniel Benchley
44. *Amelia Bedelia and the Surprise Shower*, Peggy Parish
45. *Magic Secrets*, Rose Wyler and Gerald Ames
46. *Spooky Tricks*, Rose Wyler and Gerald Ames
47. *I Am Better Than You!* Robert Lopshire
48. *Small Pig*, Arnold Lobel

b) Harper: I Can Read Science Books
   1. *Seeds and More Seeds*, Millicent Selsam
   2. *Plenty of Fish*, Millicent Selsam
   3. *Tony's Birds*, Millicent Selsam
   4. *Terry and the Caterpillars*, Millicent Selsam
   5. *Greg's Microscope*, Millicent Selsam
   6. *Let's Get Turtles*, Millicent Selsam
   7. *Benny's Animals and How He Put Them in Order*, Millicent Selsam
   8. *When an Animal Grows*, Millicent Selsam
   9. *The Bug That Laid the Golden Eggs*, Millicent Selsam
   10. *Hidden Animals*, Millicent Selsam
   11. *Red Tag Comes Back*, Fred Phleger
   12. *Prove It!* Rose Wyler and Gerald Ames
   13. *The Toad Hunt*, Janet Chenery
   14. *Ants Are Fun*, Mildred Myrick
   15. *Wolfie*, Janet Chenery
   16. *Catch a Whale by the Tail*, Edward Ricciuti
   17. *The Penguins Are Coming*, R. L. Penney

c) Harper: I Can Read History Books
   1. *The Pig War*, Betty Baker
   2. *Indian Summer*, F. N. Monjo
   3. *Sam the Minuteman*, Nathaniel Benchley

d) Harper: I Can Read Sports Books
   1. *Here Comes the Strikeout*, Leonard Kessler
   2. *Kick, Pass, and Run*, Leonard Kessler
   3. *Last One In Is a Rotten Egg*, Leonard Kessler

e) Harper: I Can Read Mystery Books
   1. *The Case of the Hungry Stranger*, Crosby Bonsall
   2. *The Case of the Cat's Meow*, Crosby Bonsall
   3. *The Case of the Dumb Bells*, Crosby Bonsall
   4. *The Strange Disappearance of Arthur Cluck*, Nathaniel Benchley
   5. *A Ghost Named Fred*, Nathaniel Benchley

6. *The Homework Caper*, Joan Lexau
7. *The Rooftop Mystery*, Joan Lexau
8. *Big Max*, Ken Platt
9. *Binky Brothers, Detectives*, James Lawrence

f) Harper: Early I Can Read Books
   1. *Albert the Albatross*, Syd Hoff
   2. *Who Will Be My Friends?* Syd Hoff
   3. *Cat and Dog*, Else Minarik
   4. *What Have I Got?* Mike McClintock
   5. *Come and Have Fun*, Edith Hurd

g) Crowell: Let's Read and Find Out Science Book Series
   It is difficult to praise this series of books too highly. The scientific information is accurate and up-to-date, for the editor of the series is Dr. Franklin Branley, coordinator of educational services for the American Museum of Natural History-Hayden Planetarium. In addition, Dr. Branley himself has written a number of books for the series. Educationally, the books are superb and meet the child on his level, for the special adviser of the series is Dr. Roma Gans, Professor Emeritus of Childhood Education at Teachers College, Columbia University. The format of the books is splendid, and the illustrations are eye-catching. A father will thoroughly enjoy reading any book in this series to his child.
   1. *Before You Were a Baby*, Paul Showers and Kay Showers
   2. *A Baby Starts to Grow*, Paul Showers
   3. *Your Skin and Mine*, Paul Showers
   4. *The Wonder of Stones*, Roma Gans
   5. *Why Frogs Are Wet*, Judy Hawes
   6. *What the Moon Is Like*, Franklyn Branley
   7. *What Makes Day and Night?* Franklyn Branley
   8. *What Makes a Shadow?* Clyde Bulla
   9. *Watch Honeybees with Me*, Judy Hawes
   10. *Upstairs and Downstairs*, Ryerson Johnson
   11. *A Tree Is a Plant*, Clyde Bulla
   12. *The Sun: Our Nearest Star*, Franklyn Branley
   13. *The Sunlit Sea*, Augusta Goldin
   14. *Where Does Your Garden Grow?* Augusta Goldin
   15. *Starfish*, Edith Hurd
   16. *Straight Hair, Curly Hair*, Augusta Goldin
   17. *Spider Silk*, Augusta Goldin
   18. *Snow Is Falling*, Franklyn Branley
   19. *Shrimps*, Judy Hawes
   20. *Seeds by Wind and Water*, Helene Jordan

21. *Sandpipers*, Edith Hurd
22. *Salt*, Augusta Goldin
23. *Rockets and Satellites*, Franklyn Branley
24. *Rain and Hail*, Franklyn Branley
25. *North, South, East, and West*, Franklyn Branley
26. *My Hands*, Aliki
27. *My Five Senses*, Aliki
28. *The Moon Seems to Change*, Franklyn Branley
29. *A Map Is a Picture*, Barbara Rinkoff
30. *Look at Your Eyes*, Paul Showers
31. *The Listening Walk*, Paul Showers
32. *Ladybug, Ladybug*, Judy Hawes
33. *It's Nesting Time*, Roma Gans
34. *In the Night*, Paul Showers
35. *Icebergs*, Roma Gans
36. *Hummingbirds in the Garden*, Roma Gans
37. *How You Talk*, Paul Showers
38. *How Many Teeth*, Paul Showers
39. *How a Seed Grows*, Helene Jordan
40. *High Sounds, Low Sounds*, Franklyn Branley
41. *Hear Your Heart*, Paul Showers
42. *Glaciers*, Wendell Tangborn
43. *Follow Your Nose*, Paul Showers
44. *Floating and Sinking*, Franklyn Branley
45. *Flash, Crash, Rumble and Roll*, Franklyn Branley
46. *Fireflies in the Night*, Judy Hawes
47. *Find Out by Touching*, Paul Showers
48. *The Emperor Penguins*, Kazue Mizumura
49. *Ducks Don't Get Wet*, Augusta Goldin
50. *Down Come the Leaves*, Henrietta Bancroft
51. *The Clean Brook*, Margaret Bartlett
52. *Where the Brook Begins*, Margaret Bartlett
53. *The Bottom of the Sea*, Augusta Goldin
54. *Birds Eat and Eat and Eat*, Roma Gans
55. *Birds at Night*, Roma Gans
56. *Big Tracks, Little Tracks*, Franklyn Branley
57. *The Big Dipper*, Franklyn Branley
58. *Bees and Beelines*, Judy Hawes
59. *Animals in Winter*, Henrietta Bancroft and Richard Van Gelder
60. *Air Is All Around You*, Franklyn Branley

h) Follett: Beginning Science Books Series
1. *Air*, John Feilen

2. *Airplanes,* Edward Victor
3. *Animals without Backbones,* Robin Pfadt
4. *Ants,* Charles Schoenknecht
5. *Astronautics,* Julian May
6. *Bats,* Richard Van Gelder
7. *Birds,* Isabel Wasson
8. *Butterflies,* Jeanne Brouillette
9. *Climate,* Julian May
10. *Deer,* John Feilen
11. *Earth through the Ages,* Philip Carona
12. *Electricity,* Edward Victor
13. *Fishes,* Hubert Woods
14. *Friction,* Edward Victor
15. *Frogs and Toads,* Charles Schoenknecht
16. *Grasshoppers,* Robin Pfadt
17. *Heat,* Edward Victor
18. *Hummingbirds,* Betty John
19. *Insects,* Jeanne Brouillette
20. *Machines,* Edward Victor
21. *Magnets,* Edward Victor
22. *Mammals,* Esther Meeks
23. *Mars,* Isaac Asimov
24. *Molecules and Atoms,* Edward Victor
25. *The Moon,* Isaac Asimov
26. *Moths,* Jeanne Brouillette
27. *Oceans,* Sy Barlowe
28. *Our Planet Earth,* Philip Carona
29. *Plants With Seeds,* Dorothy Wood
30. *Reptiles,* Robert Inger
31. *Robins,* Edwin Mason
32. *Rockets,* Julian May
33. *Rocks and Minerals,* Lou Page
34. *Salmon,* Wallace Dillon
35. *Snakes,* Esther Meeks
36. *Soil,* Richard Cromer
37. *Sound,* Charles Neal
38. *Space,* Marian Tellander
39. *Spiders,* Ramona Dupre
40. *Squirrels,* John Feilen
41. *Stars,* Isaac Asimov
42. *Water,* Philip Carona
43. *Weather,* Julian May
44. *Your Wonderful Body,* Robert Follett

i) Coward-McCann: Science Is What and Why Books Series
   1. *Rain and the Valley*, Edith Hurd
   2. *Magnets*, Raymond Sacks
   3. *Telephones*, Bernice Kohn
   4. *Echoes*, Bernice Kohn
   5. *Wheels*, Lisa Miller
   6. *Sound*, Lisa Miller
   7. *Atoms*, Melvin Berger
   8. *Seashell Towns*, Peter Sauer
   9. *Friction*, Howard Liss
   10. *Levers*, Bernice Kohn
   11. *Electricity*, Ben Kerner
   12. *Heat*, Howard Liss
   13. *Light*, Bernice Kohn
   14. *Motion*, Seymour Simon

j) Children's Press: The True Book Series
   This fine series of books will provide your child with valuable information about science and his world. Each book is scientifically accurate,
well written, and illustrated to appeal to a small child. The series has
been prepared under the general direction of Illa Podendorf of the
Laboratory School of the University of Chicago. She has done an
outstanding job.
   1. *African Animals*, John Purcell
   2. *Air Around Us*, Margaret Friskey
   3. *Airports and Airplanes*, John Lewellen
   4. *Animal Homes*, Illa Podendorf
   5. *Animal Babies*, Illa Podendorf
   6. *Animals of Sea and Shore*, Illa Podendorf
   7. *Animals of Small Pond*, Phoebe Erickson
   8. *Automobiles*, Norman and Mary Carlisle
   9. *Bacteria*, Anne Frahm
   10. *Birds We Know*, Margaret Friskey
   11. *Bridges*, Norman and Mary Carlisle
   12. *Chemistry*, Philip Carona
   13. *Circus*, Mabel Harmer
   14. *Cloth*, Esther Nighbert
   15. *Communication*, Opal Miner
   16. *Conservation*, Richard Gates
   17. *Cowboys*, Teri Martini
   18. *Deserts*, Elsa Posell
   19. *Dinosaurs*, Mary Lou Clark
   20. *Dogs*, Elsa Posell

21. *Energy*, Illa Podendorf
22. *Farm Animals*, John Lewellen
23. *Flight*, E. Blandford
24. *Freedom and Our U.S. Family*, Paul Witty
25. *Health*, Olive Haynes
26. *Holidays*, John Purcell
27. *Honeybees*, John Lewellen
28. *Horses*, Elsa Posell
29. *Houses*, Katherine Carter
30. *Indians*, Teri Martini
31. *Insects*, Illa Podendorf
32. *Jungles*, Illa Podendorf
33. *Knights*, John Lewellen
34. *Little Eskimos*, Donald Copeland
35. *Maps*, Norman and Mary Carlisle
36. *Magnets and Electricity*, Illa Podendorf
37. *Money*, Benjamin Elkin
38. *Moon, Sun and Stars*, Illa Podendorf
39. *Science Experiments*, Illa Podendorf
40. *More Science Experiments*, Illa Podendorf
41. *Numbers*, Philip Carona
42. *Oceans*, Katherine Carter
43. *Our Post Office*, Opal Miner
44. *Pebbles and Shells*, Illa Podendorf
45. *Pets*, Illa Podendorf
46. *Pioneers*, Mabel Harmer
47. *Plant Experiments*, Illa Podendorf
48. *Plants We Know*, Opal Miner
49. *Policemen and Firemen*, Opal Miner
50. *Reptiles*, Lois Ballard
51. *Rivers*, Norman and Mary Carlisle
52. *Rocks and Minerals*, Illa Podendorf
53. *Schools*, Benjamin Elkin
54. *Seasons*, Illa Podendorf
55. *Ships and Seaports*, Katherine Carter
56. *Sounds We Hear*, Illa Podendorf
57. *Space*, Illa Podendorf
58. *Spiders*, Illa Podendorf
59. *Time*, Elizabeth Thompson and Feenie Ziner
60. *Tools for Building*, Jerome Leavitt
61. *Toys at Work*, John Lewellen
62. *Transportation*, Elsa Posell
63. *Trees*, Illa Podendorf

64. *Tropical Fishes,* Ray Broekel
65. *Travel by Land,* Joan Beales
66. *Travel by Water,* John Hornby
67. *Weather Experiments,* Illa Podendorf
68. *Weeds and Wild Flowers,* Illa Podendorf
69. *Whales,* Elsa Posell
70. *Your Body and You,* Alice Hinshaw

k) Random House: The Beginner Book Series
1. *Dr. Seuss's ABC,* Dr. Seuss
2. *My Book about Me,* Dr. Seuss and Roy McKie
3. *The Cat in the Hat,* Dr. Seuss
4. *The Cat in the Hat Comes Back,* Dr. Seuss
5. *Hop on Pop,* Dr. Seuss
6. *Green Eggs and Ham,* Dr. Seuss
7. *One Fish, Two Fish, Red Fish, Blue Fish,* Dr. Seuss
8. *Dr. Seuss's Sleep Book,* Dr. Seuss
9. *Foot Book,* Dr. Seuss
10. *Ear Book,* Dr. Seuss
11. *Fox in Socks,* Dr. Seuss (This is an especially good book for a child just learning to read. With it, he can practice his phonics in the most painless way possible. Read it to your youngster in his preschool years, and let him read it to you as he is learning how.)
12. *Go Dog Go!* P. D. Eastman
13. *Don and Donna Go to Bat,* Al Perkins
14. *A Fish out of Water,* Helen Palmer
15. *Do You Know What I'm Going to Do Next Saturday?* Helen Palmer
16. *The Digging-est Dog,* Al Perkins
17. *Cowboy Andy,* Edna Chandler
18. *Book of Riddles,* Bennett Cerf
19. *Book of Laughs,* Bennett Cerf
20. *Animal Riddles,* Bennett Cerf
21. *The Big Jump,* Benjamin Elkin
22. *The Big Honey Hunt,* Stanley and Janice Berenstain
23. *The Best Nest,* P. D. Eastman
24. *The Bear's Picnic,* Stanley and Janice Berenstain
25. *The Bear's Vacation,* Stanley and Janice Berenstain
26. *The Bear Scouts,* Stanley and Janice Berenstain
27. *Are You My Mother?* P. D. Eastman
28. *Ann Can Fly,* Fred Phleger
29. *Inside Outside Upside Down,* Stanley and Janice Berenstain
30. *The Whales Go By,* Fred Phleger
31. *Summer,* Alice Low

32. *Snow*, Roy McKie and P. D. Eastman
33. *Sam and the Firefly*, P. D. Eastman
34. *Robert the Rose Horse*, Joan Heilbroner
35. *Put Me in the Zoo*, Robert Lopshire
36. *Off to the Races*, Fred and Marjorie Phleger
37. *The King's Wish and Other Stories*, Benjamin Elkin
38. *King Midas and the Golden Touch*, Al Perkins
39. *The King, the Mice, and the Cheese*, Nancy and Eric Gurney
40. *I Was Kissed by a Seal at the Zoo*, Helen Palmer
41. *Hugh Lofting's Travels of Doctor Doolittle*, Al Perkins
42. *Hugh Lofting's Doctor Doolittle and the Pirates*, Al Perkins
43. *How To Make Flibbers, etc.*, Robert Lopshire
44. *Why I Built the Boogle House*, Helen Palmer

l) Grosset and Dunlap: Living Science Books
   1. *Air and Water*, Woods Palmer
   2. *Plants*, Leslie Waller
   3. *Mountains*, Leslie Waller
   4. *Light*, Leslie Waller
   5. *Gems and Rare Metals*, Leslie Waller
   6. *Energy*, Jordan Moore
   7. *Continents and Islands*, Leslie Waller
   8. *Plains and Prairies*, Woods Palmer
   9. *Birds*, Woods Palmer
   10. *Animals*, Leslie Waller

m) Grosset and Dunlap: Early Start Preschool Reader Series
   A particularly good series of books to use to teach your youngster to
read in the preschool years. They have the smallest vocabulary of any of
the early reader books, ranging from sixteen words to thirty-nine words
for an entire book. They are definitely on the level of a preschooler, and
young children like them.
   1. *Happy Day*, Anne DeCaprio
   2. *Dinosaur Ben*, Anne DeCaprio
   3. *Willy and the Whale*, Anne DeCaprio
   4. *The Tent*, Dorothy Seymour
   5. *The Sandwich*, Dorothy Seymour
   6. *The Rabbit*, Dorothy Seymour
   7. *The Pond*, Dorothy Seymour
   8. *Poems*, Tony Lazzaro
   9. *On the Ranch*, Dorothy Seymour
   10. *One, Two*, Anne DeCaprio
   11. *New Bugle*, Anne DeCaprio

12. *Lion and the Deer*, Anne DeCaprio
13. *Jumping*, Karen Stephens
14. *Crate Train*, Dorothy Seymour
15. *Bus from Chicago*, Anne DeCaprio
16. *Bill and the Fish*, Dorothy Seymour
17. *Big Beds and Little Beds*, Dorothy Seymour
18. *Ballerina Bess*, Dorothy Seymour
19. *Ann Likes Red*, Dorothy Seymour

n) Grosset and Dunlap: Easy Reader Series
1. *Will You Come to My Party?* Sara Asheron
2. *When I Grow Up*, Jean Bethell
3. *What's Going On Here?* Mary Elting
4. *A Train for Tommy*, Edith Tarcov
5. *The Three Coats of Benny Bunny*, Sara Asheron
6. *The Surprising Pets of Billy Brown*, Tamara Kitt
7. *A Surprise in the Tree*, Sara Asheron
8. *The Surprise in the Storybook*, Sara Asheron
9. *The Secret Cat*, Tamara Kitt
10. *Question and Answer Book*, Mary Elting
11. *Petey the Peanut Man*, Jean Bethell
12. *Old Man and the Tiger*, Alvin Tresselt
13. *Mr. Pine's Purple House*, Leonard Kessler
14. *Mr. Pine's Mixed Up Signs*, Leonard Kessler
15. *The Monkey in the Rocket*, Jean Bethell
16. *Miss Polly's Animal School*, Mary Elting
17. *Little Popcorn*, Sara Asheron
18. *Little Gray Mouse Goes Sailing*, Sara Asheron
19. *Little Gray Mouse and the Train*, Sara Asheron
20. *Laurie and the Yellow Curtains*, Sara Asheron
21. *I Made a Line*, Leonard Kessler
22. *Hurry Up Slowpoke*, Crosby Newell
23. *How to Find a Friend*, Sara Asheron
24. *How the Animals Get in the Zoo*, Mary Elting
25. *Hooray for Henry*, Jean Bethell
26. *The Fox Who Traveled*, Alvin Tresselt
27. *The Duck on the Truck*, Leonard Kessler
28. *The Clumsy Cowboy*, Jean Bethell
29. *The Boy Who Fooled the Giant*, Tamara Kitt
30. *The Boy, the Cat, and the Magic Fiddle*, Tamara Kitt
31. *Billy Brown Makes Something Grand*, Tamara Kitt
32. *Billy Brown, the Baby-Sitter*, Tamara Kitt
33. *The Big Green Thing*, Miriam Schlein

34. *Barney Beagle Plays Baseball,* Jean Bethell
35. *Barney Beagle and the Cat,* Jean Bethell
36. *Barney Beagle,* Jean Bethell
37. *Adventures of Silly Billy,* Tamara Kitt

o) Grosset and Dunlap: Easy to Read Books
    1. *The Dinosaur and the Dodo,* Anne DeCaprio
    2. *The Hippopotamus,* Bobbi Herne
    3. *The Train,* Jean Fritz
    4. *The Dog and the Wolf,* Anne DeCaprio

p) G. P. Putnam's Sons: See and Read Biography Book Series
    A most unusual series of biographies of persons important in the
history of our country. These books can be read to a preschooler, and a
first grader can read them himself.
    1. *Christopher Columbus,* Helen Olds
    2. *George Washington,* Vivian Thompson
    3. *Nathan Hale,* Virginia Voight
    4. *Daniel Boone,* Patricia Martin
    5. *Andrew Jackson,* Patricia Martin
    6. *Abraham Lincoln,* Patricia Martin
    7. *Jefferson Davis,* Patricia Martin
    8. *John Fitzgerald Kennedy,* Patricia Martin

q) Follett: Beginning to Read Book Series
    1. *Abraham Lincoln,* Clara Judson
    2. *All Kinds of Cows,* Madeline Dodd
    3. *Animal Hat Shop,* Sara Murphey
    4. *Barefoot Boy,* Gloria Miklowitz
    5. *Benny and the Bear,* Barbee Carleton
    6. *Big Bad Bear,* Zula Todd
    7. *Big Bug, Little Bug,* Jean Berg
    8. *Big New School,* Evelyn Hastings
    9. *Bing-Bang Pig,* Sara Murphey
    10. *Birthday Car,* Margaret Hillert
    11. *Boy Who Wouldn't Say His Name,* Elizabeth Vreeken
    12. *Christopher Columbus,* Clara Judson
    13. *Come to the Circus,* Margaret Hillert
    14. *The Curious Cow,* Esther Meeks
    15. *Danny's Glider Ride,* Don Snyder
    16. *A Day on Big O,* Helen Cresswell
    17. *The Dog Who Came to Dinner,* Sydney Taylor
    18. *The Elf in the Singing Tree,* Sara Bulette

19. *The First Thanksgiving*, Lou Rogers
20. *Funny Baby*, Margaret Hillert
21. *George Washington*, Clara Judson
22. *Gertie the Duck*, Nicholas Georgiady and Louis Romano
23. *Grandfather Dear*, Celentha Finfer, Esther Wasserberg, and Florence Weinberg
24. *Grandmother Dear*, Celentha Finfer, Esther Wasserberg, and Florence Weinberg
25. *Have You Seen My Brother?* Elizabeth Guilfoile
26. *Henry*, Elizabeth Vreeken
27. *The Hole in the Hill*, Marion Leyton
28. *In John's Back Yard*, Esther Meeks
29. *Jiffy, Miss Boo and Mrs. Roo*, Aileen Brothers
30. *Kittens and More Kittens*, Marci Ridlon
31. *Let's Ride in the Caboose*, David Burleigh
32. *Linda's Airmail Letter*, Norman Bell
33. *Little Quack*, Ruth Woods
34. *Little Red Hen*, Jean Berg
35. *Little Runaway*, Margaret Hillert
36. *Mabel the Whale*, Patricia King
37. *The Magic Beans*, Margaret Hillert
38. *Mr. Barney's Beard*, Sydney Taylor
39. *My Own Little House*, Merriman Kaune
40. *The No-Bark Dog*, Stanford Williamson
41. *Nobody Listens to Andrew*, Elizabeth Guilfoile
42. *No Lights for Brightville*, Letta Schatz
43. *One Day Everything Went Wrong*, Elizabeth Vreeken
44. *Our Country's Flag*, Nicholas Georgiady and Louis Romano
45. *Our National Anthem*, Nicholas Georgiady and Louis Romano
46. *This Is a Department Store*, Nicholas Georgiady and Louis Romano
47. *Our Statue of Liberty*, Thelma Nason
48. *Peter's Policeman*, Anne Lattin
49. *Picture Dictionary*, Alta McIntire
50. *Piggyback*, David Burleigh
51. *Beginning to Read Poetry*, Sally Clithero
52. *Beginning to Read Riddles and Jokes*, Alice Gilbreath
53. *Shoes for Angela*, Ellen Snavely
54. *Shoofly*, David Burleigh
55. *Snow Baby*, Margaret Hillert
56. *Something New at the Zoo*, Esther Meeks
57. *Spark's Fireman*, Anne Lattin
58. *This Is a Newspaper*, Lawrence Feigenbaum and Kalman Siegel
59. *This Is an Airport*, Richard Bagwell and Elizabeth Bagwell

60. *Three Bears*, Margaret Hillert
61. *Three Little Pigs*, Margaret Hillert
62. *Three Goats*, Margaret Hillert
63. *Too Many Dogs*, Ramona Dupre
64. *Uniform for Harry*, Caary Jackson
65. *Wee Little Man*, Jean Berg
66. *Who Will Milk My Cow?* Janet Jackson
67. *Yellow Boat*, Margaret Hillert
68. *This Is a Town*, Polly Curren
69. *This Is a Road*, Polly Curren

r)   The Bowmar Early Childhood Series
      A unique series of beautifully illustrated picture books with only a few sentences per page. With each book there is a record, so that your child will be able to hear again and again the stories from the picture books. These books are ordinarily sold to schools and libraries and are not available in the average bookstore. Your bookstore would have to special-order them for you.
      1. *Father Is Big*, Ruth and Ed Radlauer
      2. *Watch Me Outdoors*, Ruth Jaynes
      3. *Follow the Leader*, Marion Crume
      4. *Benny's Four Hats*, Ruth Jaynes
      5. *My Friend Is Mrs. Jones*, Nancy Curry
      6. *Friends! Friends! Friends!* Ruth Jaynes
      7. *Where Is Whiffen?* Ruth Jaynes
      8. *What Is a Birthday Child?* Ruth Jaynes
      9. *Funny Mr. Clown*, Marion Crume
      10. *Watch Me Indoors*, Ruth Jaynes
      11. *That's What It Is!* Ruth Jaynes
      12. *How Many Sounds*, Marion Crume
      13. *An Apple Is Red*, Nancy Curry
      14. *Do You Know What . . .* Ruth Jaynes
      15. *The Biggest House*, Ruth Jaynes
      16. *A Beautiful Day for a Picnic*, Nancy Curry
      17. *Let Me See You Try*, Marion Crume
      18. *Three Baby Chicks*, Ruth Jaynes
      19. *A Cowboy Can*, Beth Clure and Helen Rumsey
      20. *The Littlest House*, Nancy Curry
      21. *Colors*, Ruth and Ed Radlauer
      22. *I Like Cats*, Marion Crume
      23. *A Box Tied with a Red Ribbon*, Ruth Jaynes
      24. *What Do You Say?* Marion Crume
      25. *Do You Suppose Miss Riley Knows?* Nancy Curry

26. *Furry Boy,* Marion Crume
27. *Melinda's Christmas Stocking,* Ruth Jaynes
28. *My Tricycle and I,* Ruth Jaynes
29. *Tell Me, Please! What's That?* Ruth Jaynes
30. *Morning,* Marion Crume
31. *Evening,* Ruth and Ed Radlauer
32. *Listen!* Marion Crume

s) McGraw-Hill: Science Books by Tillie Pine and Joseph Levine
1. *Air All Around*
2. *Friction All Around*
3. *Gravity All Around*
4. *Heat All Around*
5. *Light All Around*
6. *Sounds All Around*
7. *Water All Around*
8. *Weather All Around*
9. *Electricity and How We Use It*
10. *Magnets and How to Use Them*
11. *Rocks and How We Use Them*
12. *Simple Machines and How We Use Them*
13. *The Egyptians Knew*
14. *The Chinese Knew*
15. *The Eskimos Knew*
16. *The Incas Knew*
17. *The Indians Knew*
18. *The Pilgrims Knew*

t) Franklin Watts: The Let's Find Out Books
1. *Bread,* Olive Burt
2. *Weather,* David Knight
3. *Air,* Martha and Charles Shapp
4. *What Electricity Does,* Martha and Charles Shapp
5. *What's in the Sky,* Martha and Charles Shapp
6. *Water,* Martha and Charles Shapp
7. *Wheels,* Martha and Charles Shapp
8. *The Moon,* Martha and Charles Shapp
9. *Snakes,* Martha and Charles Shapp
10. *The Sun,* Martha and Charles Shapp
11. *Fishes,* Martha and Charles Shapp
12. *Winter,* Martha and Charles Shapp
13. *Fall,* Martha and Charles Shapp
14. *Summer,* Martha and Charles Shapp

15. *Spring*, Martha and Charles Shapp
16. *Wheels*, Martha and Charles Shapp
17. *What the Signs Say*, Martha and Charles Shapp
18. *Birds*, Martha and Charles Shapp
19. *Animals of Long Ago*, Martha and Charles Shapp
20. *Animal Homes*, Martha and Charles Shapp
21. *What's Big and Small*, Martha and Charles Shapp
22. *What's Light and What's Heavy*, Martha and Charles Shapp
23. *Houses*, Martha and Charles Shapp
24. *Firemen*, Martha and Charles Shapp
25. *Policemen*, Martha and Charles Shapp
26. *Cowboys*, Martha and Charles Shapp
27. *Indians*, Martha and Charles Shapp
28. *The United Nations*, Martha and Charles Shapp
29. *Abraham Lincoln*, Martha and Charles Shapp
30. *Daniel Boone*, Martha and Charles Shapp
31. *Mars*, David Knight
32. *Magnets*, David Knight
33. *Telephones*, David Knight
34. *Earth*, David Knight
35. *Insects*, David Knight
36. *Addition*, David Whitney
37. *Subtraction*, David Whitney
38. *The President of the United States*, David Whitney
39. *Milk*, David Whitney
40. *Color*, Ann Campbell
41. *Boats*, Ann Campbell
42. *Farms*, Ann Campbell
43. *The Red Cross*, Valerie Pitt
44. *The City*, Valerie Pitt
45. *The Clinic*, Robert Froman
46. *Eskimos*, Eleanor and Ted Wiesenthal

B. Books that Deal with Intellectual or Emotional Development

These books can be read to your preschool child to stimulate his intellectual development. They are listed under different categories, according to what aspect of development the book deals with. Since some books cannot be categorized precisely, you may find a particular book listed in more than one place.

a) Sensory Awareness and Perceptual Acuity

1. *The Silly Listening Book*, Jan Slepian and Ann Seidler (Follett)
2. *An Ear Is to Hear*, Jan Slepian and Ann Seidler (Follett)

3. *Bendemolena*, Jan Slepian and Ann Seidler (Follett)
4. *The Hungry Thing*, Jan Slepian and Ann Seidler (Follett)
5. *Ding-Dong, Bing-Bang*, Jan Slepian and Ann Seidler (Follett)
6. *Do You Hear What I Hear?* Helen Borten (Abelard-Schuman)
7. *Do You See What I see?* Helen Borten (Abelard-Schuman)
8. *Do You Move As I Do?* Helen Borten (Abelard-Schuman)
9. *A Picture Has a Special Look*, Helen Borten (Abelard-Schuman)
10. *Bow Wow! Meow! A First Book of Sounds*, Melanie Bellah (Western Publishing)
11. *Of Course, You're a Horse!* Ruth Radlauer (Abelard-Schuman)
12. *Good Times Drawing Lines*, Ruth Radlauer (Melmont)
13. *The Headstart Book of Looking and Listening*, Shari Lewis and Jacqueline Reinach (McGraw-Hill)

b) Concept Formation: Relationships
   1. *Let's Find Out What's Light and What's Heavy*, Charles and Martha Shapp (Franklin Watts)
   2. *Let's Find Out What's Big and What's Small*, Charles and Martha Shapp (Franklin Watts)
   3. *The Very Little Boy*, Phyllis Krasilovsky (Doubleday)
   4. *The Very Little Girl*, Phyllis Krasilovsky (Doubleday)
   5. *So Big*, Eloise Wilkin (Western Publishing)
   6. *The Up and Down Book*, Mary Blair (Western Publishing)
   7. *Nothing But Cats*, and *All About Dogs: Two Very Young Stories*, Grace Skaar (William R. Scott)
   8. *Hi Daddy, Here I Am*, Grete Hertz (Lerner Publications)
   9. *High Sounds, Low Sounds*, Franklyn Branley (Crowell)
   10. *Fast Is Not a Ladybug*, Miriam Schlein (Scott)
   11. *It Looks Like This*, Irma Webber (Scott)

c) Concept Formation: Classification
   1. Classification by Color
      a) *All the Colors*, Saint Justh (Grosset and Dunlap)
      b) *Let's Find Out about Color*, Ann Campbell (Franklin Watts)
      c) *Colors*, Ruth and Ed Radlauer (Bowmar)
      d) *Ann Likes Red*, Dorothy Seymour (Grosset and Dunlap)
      e) *The Color Kittens*, Margaret Wise Brown (Western Publishing)
      f) *What Is Red?* Susanne Gottlieb (Lothrop, Lee and Shepard)
      g) *Is It Blue as a Butterfly?* Rebecca Kalusky (Prentice-Hall)
      h) *Let's Imagine Colors*, Janet Wolff (E. P. Dutton)
      i) *My Slippers Are Red*, Charlotte Steiner (Knopf)
      j) *I Like Red*, Robert Bright (Doubleday)

2. Classification by Shape
   a) *Round and Round and Square,* Fredun Shapur (Abelard-Schuman)
   b) *Square as a House,* Karla Kuskin (Harper and Row)
   c) *Shapes,* Miriam Schlein (William R. Scott)
   d) *A Kiss Is Round,* Blossom Budney (Lothrop)
   e) *Squares Are Not Bad,* Violet Salazar (Western Publishing)
   f) *Hello! Do You Know My Name?* Cecile Jeruchim (Putnams)
   g) *The Wing on a Flea,* Ed Emberley (Little, Brown)
   h) *Round and Square,* Janet Martin (Platt and Munk)
   i) *On My Beach There Are Many Pebbles,* Leo Lionni (Ivan Obolensky)
3. Classification by Time
   a) *It's about Time,* Miriam Schlein (Scott)
   b) *Let's Think about Time,* Jane Hart (Hart)
4. Classification by Number
   a) *One Is No Fun, But Twenty Is Plenty!* Ilse-Margret Vogel (Atheneum)
   b) *One, Two, Three: A Little Book of Counting Rhymes,* pictures by Norah Montgomerie (Abelard-Schuman)
   c) *Ten Black Dots,* Donald Crews (Scribners)
   d) *Over in the Meadow,* John Langstaff (Harcourt Brace)
   e) *Counting Carnival,* Feenie Ziner and Paul Galdone (Coward-McCann)
   f) *I Can Count,* Carl Memling (Western Publishing)
   g) *Brian Wildsmith's 1, 2, 3's,* Brian Wildsmith (Franklin Watts)
   h) *Little 1,* Ann and Paul Rand (Harcourt, Brace and World)
   i) *Now I Can Count,* Dean Hay (Lion Press)
5. Classification by Seasons of the Year
   a) *Let's Find Out about Fall,* Charles and Martha Shapp (Franklin Watts)
   b) *Let's Find Out about Winter,* Charles and Martha Shapp (Franklin Watts)
   c) *Let's Find Out about Spring,* Charles and Martha Shapp (Franklin Watts)
   d) *Let's Find Out about Summer,* Charles and Martha Shapp (Franklin Watts)
   e) *The Year Around Book,* Helen Fletcher (McGraw-Hill)

d) Concept Formation: Basic Scientific Concepts Which Tie Together a Large Number of Events in One Basic Concept
   1. *Friction All Around,* Tillie Pine and Joseph Levine (McGraw-Hill)
   2. *Gravity All Around,* Tillie Pine and Joseph Levine (McGraw-Hill)

3. *Heat All Around*, Tillie Pine and Joseph Levine (McGraw-Hill)
4. *Friction*, Howard Liss (Coward-McCann)
5. *Heat*, Howard Liss (Coward-McCann)
6. *Motion*, Seymour Simon (Coward-McCann)
7. *Atoms*, Melvin Berger (Coward-McCann)
8. *Molecules and Atoms*, Edward Victor (Follett)
9. *Friction*, Edward Victor (Follett)
10. *Heat*, Edward Victor (Follett)

e) Problem Solving
1. *What Makes Day and Night?* Franklyn Branley (Crowell)
2. *What Makes a Shadow?* Clyde Bulla (Crowell)
3. *Why I Built the Boogle House*, Helen Palmer (Random House)
4. *How Do You Get from Here to There?* Nicholas Charles (Macmillan)
5. *How Do I Go?* Mary Hoberman (Little, Brown)
6. *Are You My Mother?* P. D. Eastman (Random House)
7. *The Shadow Book*, Beatrice DeRegniers (Harcourt, Brace and World)
8. *What Can You Do with a Shoe?* Beatrice DeRegniers (Harper and Row)
9. *The Upside-Down Day*, Julian Scheer (Holiday House)
10. *Why Can't I?* Jeanne Bendick (McGraw-Hill)

f) Scientific Method for Preschoolers
1. *Prove It!* Rose Wyler and Gerald Ames (Harpers)
2. *Benny's Animals and How He Put Them in Order*, Millicent Selsam (Harpers)
3. *Greg's Microscope*, Millicent Selsam (Harpers)
4. *How Can I Find Out?* Mary Bongiorno and Mable Gee (Children's Press)
5. *The Learning Book*, Susan Dorritt (Abelard-Schuman)
6. *What Could You See?* Jeanne Bendick (McGraw-Hill)
7. *The Headstart Book of Thinking and Imagining*, Shari Lewis and Jacqueline Reinach (McGraw-Hill)

g) Alphabet and Learning to Read
1. *Curious George Learns the Alphabet*, H. A. Rey (Houghton Mifflin)
2. *Don Freeman's Add a Line Alphabet*, Don Freeman (Golden Gate)
3. *We Read: A to Z*, Donald Crews (Scribners)
4. *Richard Scarry's Great Big Schoolhouse*, Richard Scarry (Random House)
5. *Picture Dictionary*, Alta McIntire (Follett)
6. *Cat in the Hat Picture Dictionary*, Dr. Seuss (Random House)
7. *The Headstart Book of Knowing and Naming*, Shari Lewis and Jacqueline Reinach (McGraw-Hill)

h) Richard Scarry

Richard Scarry is so unique and wonderful, he deserves a category all by himself. He has a series of absolutely enchanting books which teach children what happens in school, what people do all day, and the occupations of people all over the world. I would advise buying all of these books for your preschooler. He will use them for years and receive enormous intellectual stimulation from them.

1. *Richard Scarry's Great Big Schoolhouse*, (Random House). Getting ready for school, the routine of school, the alphabet, counting, measuring, shapes, the hours of the day, colors, the months of the year, and learning to print and write. A marvelous book!
2. *What Do People Do All Day?* (Random House). All of the various activities that go on inside a city: the different workers in the city, building houses, the postal system, the work of mothers, ships, the police department, the fire department, the hospital, building a new road, and many other aspects of the city of Busytown.
3. *Busy, Busy World* (Random House). Amusements and occupations of people all over the world: Paris policemen, Norwegian fishermen, Greek painters, New York firemen, and many more. The most painless lessons in geography your child could ever have.
4. *Hop Aboard, Here We Go!* (Western Publishing). Deals with all the various means of transportation, in great and interesting detail: cars, trucks, buses, airplanes, spacecraft, trains and locomotives, ships and boats.
5. *Richard Scarry's Great Big Air Book* (Random House). In the form of an interesting story, covers such topics as how airplanes fly, rescue by air, how an airport functions, and air pollution.

i) Mathematics

1. *Let's Find Out about Addition*, David Whitney (Franklin Watts)
2. *Let's Find Out about Subtraction*, David Whitney (Franklin Watts)

j) The Self-Concept

1. *My Book about Me*, Dr. Seuss and Roy McKie (Random House)
2. *My Hands*, Aliki (Crowell)
3. *My Five Senses*, Aliki (Crowell)
4. *Who Am I?* June Behrens (Elk Grove Press)
5. *Umbrellas, Hats and Wheels*, Ann Rand (Harcourt, Brace and World)
6. *Look at Me*, Marguerita Rudolph (McGraw-Hill)
7. *Just Like Everyone Else*, Karla Kuskin (Harper and Row)
8. *Inside You and Me*, Eloise Turner and Carroll Fenton (John Day)
9. *Your Body and How It Works*, Patricia Lauber (Random House)
10. *What's Inside of Me?* Herbert Zim (Morrow)

11. *A Boy and His Room*, Ogden Nash (Franklin Watts)
12. *Jack Is Glad, Jack Is Sad*, Charlotte Steiner (Knopf)
13. *Katie's Magic Glasses*, Jane Goodsell (Houghton Mifflin). For a child who wears glasses.

k) Relationships within the Family and with Peers
1. *My Family*, Miriam Schlein (Abelard-Schuman)
2. *The Don't Be Scared Book*, Ilse-Margret Vogel (Atheneum)
3. *It's Not Your Birthday*, Berthe Amoss (Harper and Row)
4. *It's Mine—A Greedy Book*, Crosby Bonsall (Harper and Row)
5. *If It Weren't for You*, Charlotte Zolotov (Harper and Row)
6. *When I Have a Little Girl*, Charlotte Zolotov (Harper and Row)
7. *When I Have a Son*, Charlotte Zolotov (Harper and Row)
8. *Stevie*, John Steptoe (Harper and Row)
9. *Mommies Are for Loving*, Ruth Penn (Putnams)
10. *Mommies*, L. C. Carton (Random House)
11. *Mommies at Work*, Eve Merriam (Knopf)
12. *Daddies*, L. Carton (Random House)
13. *Daddies—What They Do All Day*, Helen Puner (Lothrop)
14. *My Sister and I*, Helen Buckley (Lothrop)
15. *My Grandfather and I*, Helen Buckley (Lothrop)
16. *My Grandmother and I*, Helen Buckley (Lothrop)
17. *Animal Daddies and My Daddy*, Barbara Hazen (Western Publishing)
18. *When I Grow Up*, Lois Lenski (Henry Z. Walck)
19. *Animal Babies*, Tony Palazzo (Doubleday)
20. *When You Were a Little Baby*, Rhoda Berman (Lothrop)
21. *Everybody Has a House and Everybody Eats*, Mary Green (Wm. R. Scott)
22. *The Little Girl and Her Mother*, Beatrice DeRegniers (Vanguard)
23. *Polar Bear Brothers*, Crosby Bonsall (Harper and Row)
24. *Whose Little Bird Am I?* Leonard Weisgard (Warne)
25. *Mommies Are That Way*, Ruth Radlauer (Abelard-Schuman)
26. *My Daddy's Visiting Our School Today*, Myra Berry Brown (Watts)
27. *Grandmothers Are to Love*, Lois Wyse (Parents Magazine Press)
28. *Grandfathers Are to Love*, Lois Wyse (Parents Magazine Press)
29. *Keep It Like a Secret*, Sandol Warburg (Little, Brown)
30. *Ice Cream for Breakfast*, Myra Brown (Watts)
31. *Company's Coming for Dinner*, Myra Brown (Watts)

l) The Community and Community Helpers
1. *My Favorite City*, Willma Willis (Elk Grove Press)
2. *The March of the Harvest*, Irma Johnson (Elk Grove Press)
3. *What Is a Community?* Edward and Ruth Radlauer (Elk Grove Press)

4. *A Walk in the Neighborhood*, June Behrens (Elk Grove Press)
5. *I Know a Policeman*, Barbara Williams (Putnam's)
6. *I Know a Fireman*, Barbara Williams (Putnam's)
7. *I Know a Garageman*, Barbara Williams (Putnam's)
8. *I Know a Mayor*, Barbara Williams (Putnam's)
9. *I Know a Bank Teller*, Barbara Williams (Putnam's)
10. *I Know a Librarian*, Virginia Voight (Putnam's)
11. *I Know a Postman*, Lorraine Henriod (Putnam's)
12. *I Know a Teacher*, Naoma Buchheimer (Putnam's)
13. *I Know a House Builder*, Polly Bolian and Marilyn Schima (Putnam's)
14. *I Know an Airline Pilot*, Muriel Stanek (Putnam's)
15. *I Know a Zoo Keeper*, Lorraine Henriod (Putnam's)
16. *I Know a Nurse*, Marilyn Schima and Polly Bolian (Putnam's)
17. *Policeman Small*, Lois Lenski (Walck)
18. *The "Where's That?" Book*, Blair Walliser (Grosset and Dunlap)
19. *The "Who's That?" Book*, Blair Walliser (Grosset and Dunlap)
20. *How Do You Get from Here to There?* Nicholas Charles (Macmillan)
21. *The Little Fire Engine*, Lois Lenski (Walck)
22. *The Truck and Bus Book*, William Dugan (Western Publishing)
23. *Planes, Trains, Cars and Boats*, Muriel and Lionel Kalish (Western Publishing)
24. *Rides*, Virginia Parsons (Doubleday)
25. *What Do People Do All Day?* Richard Scarry (Random House)
26. *Whose Tools Are These?* Ed and Ruth Radlauer (Elk Grove Press)
27. *Get Ready for School*, Ruth Radlauer (Elk Grove Press)
28. *Airports U.S.A.*, Lou Jacobs, Jr. (Elk Grove Press)

m) The Larger Community: The World
1. *People around the World*, Rozella Donan and Jane Hefflefinger (Elk Grove Press)
2. *Where in the World Do You Live?* Al Hine and John Alcorn (Harcourt, Brace and World)
3. *Money around the World*, Al Hine and John Alcorn (Harcourt, Brace and World)
4. *You Will Go to the Moon*, Mae and Ira Freeman (Random House)
5. *A Book of Astronauts for You*, Franklyn Branley (Crowell)

n) Children's Emotions or Special Problems
1. *Timid Timothy*, Gweneira Williams (Scott). It's a mother's job to help her child enjoy new experiences, and mother cat does a good job with Timothy.
2. *Lost and Found*, Kathryn Hitte (Abingdon). Getting lost is often a

frightening experience. This is a reassuring book to read to a child about this subject.

3. *Will I Have a Friend?* Miriam Cohen (Macmillan). "Will I have a friend?" is a silent question children often ask on their first day in school. Though they are afraid to ask this question out loud, they nevertheless want to have it answered. This charming story will help your child ask this question.

4. *Curious George Goes to the Hospital*, Margret and H. A. Rey (Houghton Mifflin). Curious George always has high adventures, and this time the adventures are in a hospital.

5. *The Really Real Family*, Helen Doss (Little, Brown). A special book about adoption which covers the topic as a child would see it.

6. *Where Is Daddy? The Story of a Divorce*, Beth Goff (Beacon). This book will help a child understand what it is like when parents get divorced. Excellent.

7. *Benjy's Blanket*, Myra Berry Brown (Watts). Benjy's blanket is a security item. This is the delightful story of how he learns to give it up.

8. *First Night Away From Home*, Myra Berry Brown (Watts). Sleeping away from home for the first time always has both good and bad features. This is a delightful story which covers both sides of the experience.

9. *The Dead Bird*, Margaret Wise Brown (Scott). A very sensitive story which deals with death and how a group of children experience the problems of death.

10. *Dumb Stupid David*, Dorothy Aldis (Putnam's). Big brother's jealous reaction to a new baby and how it is overcome.

11. *This Room Is Mine*, Betty Wright (Whitman). It is always hard for brothers and sisters to share. This delightful book describes how two sisters work out their problems of sharing.

12. *Big Sister and Little Sister*, Charlotte Zolotov (Harper and Row). A picture book of love between sisters.

13. *The Quarreling Book*, Charlotte Zolotov (Harper and Row). An authentic picture of sibling relations in most families—a book greatly enjoyed by preschool children.

14. *Amy and the New Baby*, Myra Berry Brown (Watts). A warm and understanding story of how Amy's jealousy of the new baby eventually is overcome.

15. *Love Is a Special Way of Feeling*, Joan Walsh Anglund (Harcourt, Brace). All of Mrs. Anglund's books are beautifully done, and this one is no exception.

16. *Judy's Baby*, Sally Scott (Harcourt, Brace). Happiness is not always a new baby, and this little girl has problems with the "intruder" who

comes into her family. This is the story of how she struggles through
these problems.

17. *The Man of the House,* Joan Fassler (Behavioral Publications). Four-
year-old David tried to become the grown-up protector of the house
while his father is on a business trip.

18. *All Alone with Daddy,* Joan Fassler (Behavioral Publications). A
little girl tries to take her mother's place when her mother is away.

19. *My Grandpa Died Today,* Joan Fassler (Behavioral Publications). A
little boy learns about death for the first time.

20. *The Boy with a Problem,* Joan Fassler (Behavioral Publications). A
little boy discovers that the best way to cope with a problem is to
talk about it to someone who really listens.

21. *Don't Worry, Dear,* Joan Fassler (Behavioral Publications). A very
little girl with an understanding mother grows out of her thumb-
sucking and bed-wetting habits.

22. *One Little Girl,* Joan Fassler (Behavioral Publications). Because she is
somewhat retarded, Laurie has been called a "slow child." Laurie
learns that she is only slow in doing some things and that there are
other things she can do quite well.

23. *The Angry Book: My ABC of Mean Things,* Robin King (Norton)

24. *The Thinking Book,* Sandol Warburg (Little Brown)

o) The Magic of Words and the Magic of Books

1. *Books!* Murray McCain and John Alcorn (Simon and Schuster)

2. *Ounce, Dice, Trice,* Alastair Reid (Little, Brown). This book is so
unique it deserves a special mention. It will help your child to love
words. Although written for older children or adults, you can still
use it with a preschooler. Begin when your child is four, because he is
so fascinated by language at that age. Read parts of this book to him
in small doses. Do not attempt to read the whole book to him at
once. It can be read to your child throughout grade school. A book
designed to be read aloud, it particularly lends itself to family
reading. I dare you to check this book out of the library and not
become so fascinated by it that you end up buying it!

3. Nonsense Poems

These are a good way to get a preschooler fascinated by words and
language at an early age. When your child is four is an especially good
time to begin reading him nonsense poems. Here are some particularly fine books of nonsense poems.

a) *The Pobble Who Has No Toes and Other Nonsense,* Edward Lear
(Follett)

b) *Calico Pie and Other Nonsense,* Edward Lear (Follett)

     c) *The Scroobious Pip*, Edward Lear, completed by Ogden Nash (Harper and Row)

     d) *Silly Songs and Sad*, Ellen Raskin (Crowell)

     e) *Lear's Nonsense Verses*, Edward Lear (Grosset and Dunlap)

p) Painless Etiquette and Manners for the Preschooler

  1. *What Do You Say, Dear?* Seslye Joslin (Scott). For the preschooler, but with a delightful touch of whimsy.

  2. *What Do You Do, Dear?* Seslye Joslin (Scott). More painless manners for your preschooler.

q) Books about Religion for Preschoolers

    Sad to confess, good books about religion for preschoolers are mighty scarce. Here are a few. There should be more.

  1. *A Book about God*, Florence Fitch (Lothrop). The mathematicians use the word *simple* to mean elegant. In this sense, this religious book for preschoolers is simple. Gorgeous illustrations by Leonard Weisgard enhance its value even more.

  2. *Once There Was a Little Boy*, Dorothy Kunhardt (Viking). A lovely and charming story of the Christ Child.

  3. *Told under the Christmas Tree*, Association for Childhood Education International (Macmillan). All you need to know about Christmas, and Hanukkah—beautifully and simply done.

  4. *A Child's Grace*, Ernest Claxton (Cutton). A child's prayer simply and beautifully written and easy for a preschooler to learn by heart.

  5. *Children's Prayers for Every Day*, Jessie Moore (Abingdon). Everyday prayers on a preschool level for both Christians and Jews.

  6. Mary Alice Jones

    Mrs. Jones has written a series of excellent books on religion for children. Highly recommended.

     a) *God Is Good* (Rand McNally)

     b) *My First Book about Jesus* (Rand McNally)

     c) *Tell Me about God* (Rand McNally)

     d) *Tell Me about Jesus* (Rand McNally)

     e) *Tell Me about the Bible* (Rand McNally)

     f) *Tell Me about Christmas* (Rand McNally)

     g) *Prayers and Graces for a Small Child* (Rand McNally)

r) Other General Books on Science Not Previously Listed

  1. *Science in the Bathtub*, Rebecca Marcus (Watts)

  2. *Let's Look inside Your House*, Herman and Nina Schneider (Scott)

  3. *Let's Go to the Brook*, Harriet Huntington (Doubleday)

4. *Let's Go to the Seashore,* Harriet Huntington (Doubleday)
5. *Let's Go to the Woods,* Harriet Huntington (Doubleday)
6. *Let's Go to the Desert,* Harriet Huntington (Doubleday)
7. *Let's Go Outdoors,* Harriet Huntington (Doubleday)
8. *Sound,* Solveig Russell (Bobbs Merrill)
9. *A Book of Astronauts for You,* Franklyn Branley (Crowell)
10. *A Book of Planets for You,* Franklyn Branley (Crowell)
11. *The Honeybees,* Franklin Russell (Knopf)
12. *In the Days of the Dinosaurs,* Roy Chapman Andrews (Random House)
13. *To Be a Bee,* Ellsworth Rosen (Houghton Mifflin)
14. *Insects Do the Strangest Things,* Leonara and Arthur Hornblow (Random House)
15. *Finding Out about the Past,* Mae Freeman (Random House)
16. *Mammals and How They Live,* Robert McClung (Random House)
17. *A Book of Stars for You,* Franklyn Branley (Crowell)
18. *A Book of Moon Rockets for You,* Franklyn Branley (Crowell)
19. *Catch a Cricket,* Carla Stevens (Scott)
20. *Animal Habits,* George Mason (Morrow)
21. *The First People in the World,* Gerald Ames and Rose Wyler (Harper and Row)
22. *Nabob and the Geranium,* Judith Miller (Golden Gate)
23. *There Was a Time,* Susan Morrow (Dutton)

s) "Open Books" for Parents and Children by Sara Stein
(Educational Press, Inc., Multimedia Publishing Corp., New York)

These books have a story that can be read aloud to a child, with a text running beside the story for the parents. The text explains the childhood fears that are being dealt with in the story, the questions a child might have at a given point, and how the parent can further explore this part of the story with his child through questions and discussion. An excellent series. Really "tells it like it is" about the fears of children.

1. *A Hospital Story.* A child is prepared to deal with both the actual events during a stay in the hospital and his own feelings about those events.
2. *Making Babies.* A child learns to accept in a natural way ideas about his own body and how babies are made.
3. *About Dying.* The death of a bird encourages a child and his parents to handle painful feelings, ideas and questions about dying.
4. *Who'll Take Care of Me?* About how fights, separation, or even a divorce can be handled without endangering a child's sense of security.
5. *That New Baby.* Talking over his feelings helps a child handle the inevitable difficulties of a new baby in the family.

C. Fiction and Fantasy

If you have skimmed this appendix thus far, you have definitely gathered the impression that there is an enormous number of good nonfiction books for a preschooler. Unfortunately, the number of really excellent books of fiction for preschoolers is far, far fewer. But here are a selected number of excellent works of fiction and fantasy for pre-schoolers, with the cream of the crop starred.

1. *The Story of Babar,* Jean De Brunhoff (Random House). Everyone knows and loves Babar, the wonderful elephant. This book could easily be called a classic.

2. *Madeline,* Ludwig Bemelmans (Viking). Madeline always has a good time. This time it's in Paris.

3. *The Five Chinese Brothers,* Claire Bishop (Coward-McCann). Once upon a time there were five Chinese brothers, and they looked exactly alike. Around these remarkable characteristics is woven a most ingenious tale.

4. *The Little House,* Virginia Burton (Houghton Mifflin). Urban development as told on the preschool level. A delightful story.

5. *Springtime for Jeanne-Marie,* Francoise (Scribners). Gay and stylized illustrations will delight a young child's eye as he enjoys the adventures of a little French girl and her white sheep.

6. *Corduroy,* Don Freeman (Viking). The illustrations and the story are direct and just right for the very young who like bears and escalators.

7. *The Biggest House in the World,* Leo Lionni (Pantheon). In this gorgeously illustrated picture book, a small snail has a very large wish. He wants the largest house in the world.

8. *Little Leo,* Leo Politi (Scribners). Soft colors and lovely double-page pictures of villages and children enhance this delightful story.

9. *Spectacles,* Ellen Raskin (Atheneum). A picture book done with imagination and humor. May be useful with a child who is resisting glasses which he needs.

10. *Rain Makes Applesauce,* Julian Schneer (Holiday). A really unique picture book which a young child will want to look at again and again.

11. *Caps for Sale,* Esther Slobodkina (Scott). A tale of a peddler, his caps, and some monkeys who combine to produce a bit of delightful monkey business.

12. *The Biggest Bear,* Lynd Ward (Houghton Mifflin). A story of a boy and his pet bear and the masterful task this boy must perform.

13. *Theodore Turtle,* Ellen MacGregor (McGraw-Hill). The amusing story of a turtle who forgets where he leaves things. Any similarity to children you know is more than coincidental.

14. *The Little Family,* Lois Lenski (Doubleday). Lois Lenski writes of a little family—especially for small children.

15. *The Little Auto,* Lois Lenski (Walck). All of Miss Lenski's books are simple and appealing to young children.

16. *Gwendolyn the Miracle Hen,* Nancy Sherman (Western Publishing). Gwendolyn can lay Easter eggs. A modern story with a folk tale flavor.

17. *Where the Wild Things Are,* Maurice Sendak (Harper and Row). Great pictures of wild things by Maurice Sendak, with a story to match. A little boy's dreams help other children to deal with their fears on a child's level and thus overcome them. An enormous favorite with little children.

18. *A Little House of Your Own,* Beatrice Schenk DeRegniers (Harcourt, Brace and World). Every child likes to have a small and secret place of his very own. This book is a great favorite with little children.

19. *Mike Mulligan and His Steam Shovel,* Virginia Burton (Houghton Mifflin). Boys love the story of Mike and his steam shovel. A charming modern classic.

20. *The Little Red Computer,* Ralph Steadman (McGraw-Hill). A modern-day story of a dunce at computer school.

21. *Little Toot,* Hardie Gramatky (Putnam's). An old, old favorite describes the adventures of a small tugboat in New York harbor.

22. *A Rainbow of My Own,* Don Freeman (Viking). A small boy looks for a rainbow to own.

23. *The House on East 88th Street,* Bernard Weber (Houghton Mifflin). The funny adventures of Lyle the Crocodile.

24. *Crictor,* Tomi Ungerer (Harper and Row). Such fantasy. Would you believe a boa constrictor with his own bed and a sweater for the snow? Just great!

25. *And to Think That I Saw It on Mulberry Street,* Dr. Seuss (Vanguard). One of Dr. Seuss' first and best—a classic.

26. *The 500 Hats of Bartholomew Cubbins,* Dr. Seuss (Vanguard). A fun fantasy with never-ending hats. A great favorite of small children, not to mention their parents.

27. *Crow Boy,* Taro Yashima (Viking). The tender story of a shy Japanese boy.

28. *Ferdinand,* Munro Leaf (Viking). Who does not know of this venerable children's classic of the bull who preferred to smell flowers rather than fight in the bull ring? Your preschool child probably does not, so read him the book and let him discover Ferdinand also.

29. *Inch by Inch,* Leo Lionni (Obolensky). All of Leo Lionni's books are beautiful. This one teaches the concept of measuring.

30. *Lentil,* Robert McCloskey (Viking). Charming—like all of McCloskey's. A small boy, Lentil, plays music on his harmonica and becomes a hero.

31. *Make Way for Ducklings,* Robert McCloskey (Viking). Another children's classic about a family of ducks on Beacon Street in Boston.
32. *One Morning in Maine,* Robert McCloskey (Viking). A wonderful story about the loss of the first tooth. Homey illustrations of leisurely family life.
33. *Timothy Turtle,* Alice Davis (Harcourt, Brace and World). A delightful picture story of what happens to a turtle who gets turned on his back and how his friends manage to rescue him from his plight.
34. *The Alligator Case,* William Pene DuBois (Viking). Mr. DuBois writes fun and fantasy for young children. A little boy plays detective.
35. *Burt Dow, Deep Water Man,* Robert McCloskey (Viking). More of Mr. McCloskey's imaginative work. You have heard of adult "fisherman's tales"—well, here is a preschool fish "tail."
36. *Horton Hatches the Egg,* Dr. Seuss (Random House). Poor Horton sits on an egg while a silly bird goes away.
37. *The Snowy Day,* Ezra Keats (Viking). Beautiful illustrations. A charming, very simple story of a small boy in the snow.
38. *Staying Home Alone on a Rainy Day,* Chihiro Iwasaki (McGraw-Hill). What to do on a rainy day? Answer: Daydream!
39. *Switch on the Night,* Ray Bradbury (Pantheon). The famous science-fiction writer turns his hand to a child's book with delightful results.
40. *A Tree Is Nice,* Janice Udry (Harper and Row). A charming story of a tree.
41. *Where Have You Been?* Margaret Wise Brown (Hastings). Fourteen different animals answer the same question. Your child will enjoy joining in and repeating the gay poetic lines of this book as you read to him.
42. *Anatole,* Eve Titus (McGraw-Hill). The wonderful adventures of a mouse who decides to work for a living and becomes head taster for a cheese factory in Paris.
43. *Frederick,* Leo Lionni (Pantheon). A field mouse rescues his friends from the long, cold winter by his word pictures of sunshine and colors. The usual vivid illustrations we have come to expect from Mr. Lionni.
44. *Casey, the Utterly Impossible Horse,* Anita Feagles (Scott). The amusing tale of a talking horse who expects much from his pet boy—as many children expect much from their parents.
45. *The Happy Lion,* Louise Fatio (McGraw-Hill). A happy lion manages to escape from the zoo in a French town, only to find that people run away from him.
46. *Space Cat,* Ruthven Todd (Scribners). A cat goes by rocketship to outer space.
47. *Pedro, the Angel of Olvera Street,* Leo Politi (Scribners). A lovely

story of a small Mexican boy who celebrates Christmas on Olvera Street.

48. *Gilberto and the Wind,* Marie Ets (Viking). A charming picture book about a little Mexican boy who has trouble with the wind.

49. *Little Pear,* Eleanor Lattimore (Harcourt). A modern classic about a little Chinese boy.

50. *May I Bring a Friend?* Beatrice Schenk DeRegniers (Atheneum). The fantasy adventure of a little boy who visits the king.

51. *Angus and the Ducks,* Marjorie Flack (Doubleday). Angus, a feisty Scottish terrier, has trouble with some smart ducks.

52. *Harold and the Purple Crayon,* Crockett Johnson (Harper and Row). A great favorite with small children. Harold is a most unusual artist.

53. *Emile,* Tomi Ungerer (Harper and Row). The story of an octopus who can do great things.

54. *A Hole Is to Dig,* Ruth Krauss (Harper and Row). A delightful story of words and what they mean as viewed by a small child.

55. *Olaf Reads,* Joan Lexau (Dial). Learning to read can be funny, as you will discover with Olaf.

56. *The Brave Cowboy,* Joan Walsh Anglund (Harcourt, Brace). Another marvelous story of a preschool cowboy.

57. *The Lively Adventures of a Burly Woodcutter, A Pint-Sized Inventor, Two Pretty Pastry Cooks, and a Gang of Desperate Criminals,* Hilde Jenzarik (Harper and Row). Does any parent really need to do more than read the title of this book to know that it is a wonderful book of fantasy for children? (And parents!)

58. *Blueberries For Sale,* Robert McCloskey (Viking). More of wonderful Mr. McCloskey. A little girl helps her mother pick berries.

59. *Old MacDonald Had an Apartment House,* Judith Barrett (Atheneum). A delightful fantasy of a modern-day four-story farm.

60. *From Ambledee to Zumbledee,* Sandol Warburg (Houghton Mifflin). Bugs from A to Z.

D. Collections of Stories, Tales, or Folk Tales

1. *Told under the Green Umbrella,* by the Association for Childhood Education International (Macmillan). Folk tales for young children.

2. *Castles and Dragons: Read-to-Yourself Fairy Tales for Boys and Girls,* compiled by the Child Study Association of America (Crowell).

3. *Read-to-Me Storybook,* compiled by the Child Study Association of America (Crowell). Modern stories and verses.

4. *Fables From Aesop,* retold by James Reeves (Walck). Famous fables told with modern-day language.

5. *The Book of Greek Myths,* Edgar and Ingri D'Aulaire (Doubleday). Outstanding book and a must for children.

E. Poetry for Preschoolers
  1. *Something Special*, Beatrice Schenk DeRegniers (Harcourt, Brace and World). Begin reading poetry to your preschooler with this book and he will love poetry. And if you are not much for poetry yourself, begin reading poetry to your preschooler with this book, and *you* will learn to love poetry! Free verse, rhymed verse, and a chanting game: "What Did You Put in Your Pocket?" Begin with the chanting game and work forward and backward from there, at your pleasure.
  2. *I Can't, Said the Ant*, Polly Cameron (Coward-McCann). The scene: the kitchen. The hero: an ant. The time: now.

> "Teapot fell," said the dinner bell.
> "Broke her spout," said the trout.
> "Push her up," said the cup.
> "I can't," said the ant.
> "Please try," said the pie.

  Your preschooler will be delighted with this tale in verse.
  3. *I Met a Man*, John Ciardi (Houghton Mifflin). One of America's foremost poets proves that a poetry book written in a limited vocabulary for beginning readers doesn't have to be dull or trite. These verses sparkle. Your preschooler will love to have you read him "The Man That Lived in a Box," "The Man from Nowhere," and other poems in this wonderful book.
  4. *Cricket Songs*, Harry Behn (Harcourt, Brace and World). A group of Japanese haiku, poems of nature.
  5. *Sung under the Silver Umbrella*, Association for Childhood Education International (Macmillan). Good selection of poems for children from preschool through third grade.
  6. *Whispers and Other Poems*, Myra Cohn Livingston (Harcourt, Brace and World). A small book of poems which gives a child's view of such things as riding on a train and going to the zoo.
  7. *Poems to Read to the Very Young*, Josette Frank (Random House). A well-chosen collection of poems, with charming illustrations.
  8. *Hailstones and Halibut Bones*, Mary O'Neill (Doubleday). A stunning collection of poems about colors, with beautiful illustrations by Leonard Weisgard.
  9. *People I'd Like to Keep*, Mary O'Neill (Doubleday). Gay verse about nice people.
  10. *Nibble Nibble*, Margaret Wise Brown (Scott). A lovely book. Poems about nature and things that fly, crawl, and swim.
  11. *You Read to Me, I'll Read to You*, John Ciardi (Lippincott). A unique poetry book in which poems for adults to read aloud to children alternate with those which children can read aloud to adults.
  12. *Cricket in a Thicket*, Aileen Fisher (Scribners). Nature study is a

fond love of young children. These poems will delight the young child.

13. *All around the Town,* Phyllis McGinley (Lippincott). Happy poems for the city child.

14. *Don't Ever Cross a Crocodile,* Kaye Starbird (Lippincott). Poems filled with humor and a delightful appreciation of a small child's experiences.

15. *A Child's Garden of Verses,* Robert Louis Stevenson. There are several versions, but I strongly suggest you get the one illustrated by Brian Wildsmith (Watts). Some of these poems seem a little dated, but others will never grow old. A classic.

16. *The First Book of Poetry,* Isabel Peterson (Watts). A first-rate selection of poems for young children, but the illustrations could be considerably improved. If Brian Wildsmith or Leo Lionni did the illustrations for this book, it would be superb!

17. *When We Were Very Young* and *Now We Are Six,* A. A. Milne (Dutton). These classic poems for children, written in the 1920s, will never grow old. Thus it seems only fitting to close our section on poetry for young children with them. They are my favorite poems to read to preschoolers. Children particularly love Milne's use of nonsense words like "wheezles and sneezles." And who could resist the wonderful rhythm of:

> James James
> Morrison Morrison
> Weatherby George Dupree
> Took great
> Care of his Mother,
> Though he was only three!

If you have not yet discovered these wonderful poems which Milne wrote to amuse his own son Christopher Robin, rush right out to a bookstore or library! Get the books and read them to your child. After you have put your child to bed, read them over once again to yourself just for the sheer delight of it!

IV. The Stage of Middle Childhood (approximately sixth to eleventh birthday)

This stage corresponds to the elementary grades in school. However, it is particularly important that you not take the suggested year levels for a book too literally. When a publisher puts year levels or grade levels on a book (or when I do the same in this bibliography), these represent only our best guesses for the "average child" and his ability to read the book. But in reality there is no such thing as an average child. For one thing, each child will be much more highly motivated to read a book on some subjects than on others. A girl who loves horses will be able, because of her high motivation, to read more advanced books on horses than on other subjects.

So try to use this as your guide: *Let your child read anything he likes.* If he likes to read it, it will develop his reading ability. If you go to the library and get a book which is too advanced for him or in which he is not interested, wait a year or so and try it again.

Many youngsters spend the first three grades of elementary school not only learning the mechanics of reading, but learning to feel comfortable about reading so that they can truly enjoy it. Probably most children do not really "explode" into reading for enjoyment until the fourth or fifth grade. So as a general rule don't expect your child to become an avid and voracious reader in his first three grades at school. This is particularly true with the irresistable pull of television on the six-, seven-, and eight-year-old. But be patient: if you keep taking your youngster to the library and the bookstore as I have suggested, the appeal of television will gradually lessen, and an interest in reading will take over. (Not that there is anything inherently bad about television. As I've pointed out earlier in this book, even with all of its obvious deficiencies, TV is still a good educational influence on our young children.)

A. Nonfiction

"Double-Duty" Beginning to Read Books

The first list of good nonfiction books for the six-year-old, and in some cases for the seven- or eight-year-old as well, consists of these same books I gave you for the preschool stage. Remember that I listed twenty different series of books designed for beginning readers and suggested you read as many of these books as you could to your preschool child. Then when he learns to read in kindergarten or first grade, reading these books will build his confidence in his ability to master the new and possibly difficult task of learning to read. For he will think of these books you have read to him as "old friends," not new and possibly frightening books full of strange words.

At any rate, whether you have read these double-duty books to your child when he was a preschooler or not, they are excellent books to get for him as he is learning to read, and in general, during the first three grades in school. So in this stage of middle childhood you will want to refer back again and again to the twenty series of double-duty books I listed for the preschool stage.

a) The Franklin Watts "First Book" Series (ages eight to eleven)
   1. *The First Book of How to Make a Speech*, David Powers (For the rest of this list, I will not repeat the words "The First Book of.")
   2. *Facts and How to Find Them*, David Whitney
   3. *How To Run a Meeting*, David Powers
   4. *Codes and Ciphers*, Sam and Beryl Epstein
   5. *News*, Sam and Beryl Epstein
   6. *Words*, Sam and Beryl Epstein
   7. *Creative Writing*, Julia Mahon

8. *Acting*, Karl Schuon
9. *How to Write a Report*, Sue Brandt
10. *Letter Writing*, Helen Jacobson and Florence Mischel
11. *Language and How to Use It*, Mauree Applegate
12. *How to Improve Your Written English*, Sue Brandt
13. *The Aztecs*, Barbara Beck
14. *The Incas*, Barbara Beck
15. *The Ancient Maya*, Barbara Beck
16. *Stone Age Man*, Alice Dickinson
17. *The Cliff Dwellers*, Rebecca Marcus
18. *Ancient Bible Lands*, Charles Robinson
19. *The Vikings*, Louise Rich
20. *Ancient Egypt*, Charles Robinson
21. *Ancient Greece*, Charles Robinson
22. *Ancient Rome*, Charles Robinson
23. *Medieval Man*, Donald Sobol
24. *The Founding of the Republic*, Richard Morris
25. *The Early Settlers*, Louise Rich
26. *Indians*, Benjamin Brewster
27. *Pioneers*, Walter Havighurst
28. *The Civil War*, Dorothy Levenson
29. *Women of the West*, Dorothy Levenson
30. *New World Explorers*, Louise Rich
31. *Women's Rights*, Janet Stevenson
32. *American Negroes*, Margaret Young
33. *Politics*, Patricia Markun
34. *Ethics*, Richard Morris
35. *The United Nations*, Edna Epstein
36. *Eskimos*, Mary Bringle

b) The Franklin Watts "First Book" Science Series

These are advanced versions (for ages eight to eleven) of the Franklin Watts First Book Series I listed under the preschool "double-duty" books. Once again, in this list, I will not bother to repeat "The First Book of" for the title of each book.

1. *Flower Gardening*, Alizabeth Abell
2. *The Seashore*, Wyatt Blassingame
3. *Wildflowers*, Betty Cavanna
4. *Gases*, Vicki Cobb
5. *Stones*, Maribelle Cormack
6. *Trees*, Maribelle Cormack
7. *Plants*, Alice Dickinson
8. *Glass*, Sam and Beryl Epstein

9. *The Ocean*, Sam and Beryl Epstein
10. *The Elements*, Gail Haines
11. *Caves*, Elizabeth Hamilton
12. *Ecology*, John Hoke
13. *The Jungle*, John Hoke
14. *Terrariums*, John Hoke
15. *Gardening*, Virginia Kirkus
16. *Air*, David Knight
17. *Deserts*, David Knight
18. *Glaciers*, Rebecca Marcus
19. *Volcanoes and Earthquakes*, Rebecca Marcus
20. *The Earth's Crust*, William Matthews
21. *Soils*, William Matthews
22. *Rivers*, Corinne Naden
23. *The Earth*, Irene Sevrey
24. *Mountains*, Frances Smith
25. *Conservation*, Frances Smith
26. *Water*, Frances Smith
27. *Weather*, Rose Wyler
28. *Fishes*, Jeanne Bendick
29. *Living Things*, Jeanne Bendick
30. *Animal Signs*, C. B. Colby
31. *Prehistoric Animals*, Alice Dickinson
32. *Snakes*, John Hoke
33. *Horses*, Isabel McMeekin
34. *The Spider World*, Penelope Naylor
35. *Zoos*, John Perry
36. *Bees*, Albert Tibbets
37. *Birds*, Margaret Williamson
38. *Bugs*, Margaret Williamson
39. *Mammals*, Margaret Williamson
40. *Space Travel*, Jeanne Bendick
41. *Space Base*, Mae Freeman
42. *Solar Energy*, John Hoke
43. *The Sun*, David Knight
44. *The Universe*, Colin Ronan
45. *Machines*, Walter Buehr
46. *Heat*, Vicki Cobb
47. *Electricity*, Sam and Beryl Epstein
48. *Engines*, Peter Limburg
49. *Television*, Edward Stoddard
50. *Automobiles*, Jeanne Bendick
51. *Time*, Jeanne Bendick
52. *Science Experiments*, Rose Wyler

c) The Franklin Watts Human Body Series (ages eight to eleven)
 1. *The Brain,* Kathleen Elgin
 2. *The Ear,* Kathleen Elgin
 3. *The Eye,* Kathleen Elgin
 4. *The Female Reproductive System,* Kathleen Elgin
 5. *The Glands,* Kathleen Elgin
 6. *The Hand,* Kathleen Elgin
 7. *The Heart,* Kathleen Elgin
 8. *The Male Reproductive System,* Kathleen Elgin
 9. *The Muscles,* Kathleen Elgin
10. *The Skeleton,* Kathleen Elgin
11. *The Skin,* Kathleen Elgin
12. *Your Health: Nutrition,* Francine Klagsbrun and Samuel Klagsbrun
13. *The Human Senses,* Gene Liberty

d) The Franklin Watts "They Lived Like This" Series (ages eight to eleven)
   This excellent series, by Marie Neurath, introduces young readers to cultural anthropology in a fascinating way. In each book your child will get to glimpse into the everyday life of a particular ancient culture, as the author describes homes, clothing, beliefs and ceremonies, farming and manufacturing techniques, and ways of communicating. I recommend this series highly. And by the way, you will probably enjoy reading it yourself and discussing it with your youngster.
 1. *Ancient Africa*
 2. *Ancient Britain*
 3. *Ancient Crete*
 4. *Ancient China*
 5. *Ancient Egypt*
 6. *Ancient Greece*
 7. *Ancient India*
 8. *Ancient Mesopotamia*
 9. *Ancient Mexico*
10. *Ancient Palestine*
11. *Ancient Persia*
12. *Ancient Peru*
13. *Ancient Rome*
14. *Chaucer's England*
15. *Old Japan*
16. *The Old Stone Age*
17. *The Roman Empire*
18. *Shakespeare's England*
19. *The Ancient Maya*
20. *The Vikings*

e) The Franklin Watts "Colonial Americans" Series (ages eight to eleven)
   Leonard Fisher both writes and illustrates a series dealing with the tools, techniques, and extraordinary skill of pioneer American craftsmen.
   1. *The Architects*
   2. *The Cabinetmakers*
   3. *The Doctors*
   4. *The Glassmakers*
   5. *The Hatters*
   6. *The Limners* (portrait painters)
   7. *The Papermakers*
   8. *The Peddlers*
   9. *The Potters*
   10. *The Printers*
   11. *The Schoolmasters*
   12. *The Shipbuilders*
   13. *The Shoemakers*
   14. *The Silversmiths*
   15. *The Tanners*
   16. *The Weavers*
   17. *The Wigmakers*

f) The Grosset and Dunlap How and Why Wonder Books (ages eight to eleven)
   1. *Air and Water*, Claire Cuniff
   2. *Airplanes and the Story of Flight*, Joseph Highland
   3. *Ants and Bees*, Ronald Rodd
   4. *Atomic Energy*, Donald Barr
   5. *Birds*, Robert Mathewson
   6. *Sound*, Martin Keen
   7. *Chemistry*, Martin Keen
   8. *Dinosaurs*, Darlene Geis
   9. *Basic Inventions*, Irving Robbin
   10. *The Human Body*, Martin Keen
   11. *Machines*, Jerome Notkin
   12. *Electronics*, Martin Keen

g) The John Day "Reason Why" Book Series (ages eight to twelve)
   Written by two splendid science writers, Irving Adler and his wife Ruth, these books provide "in-depth" explanations of science fundamentals.
   1. *Atomic Energy*
   2. *Atoms and Molecules*
   3. *Calendar*
   4. *Communication*

5. *Directions and Angles*
6. *Earth's Crust*
7. *Fibers*
8. *Heat*
9. *Houses: From Cave to Skyscraper*
10. *Language and Man*
11. *Machines*
12. *Magnets*
13. *Oceans*
14. *Rivers*
15. *Sets*
16. *Taste, Touch, and Smell*
17. *Tree Products*
18. *Why, A Book of Reasons*
19. *Your Ears*
20. *Your Eyes*

h) William Morrow Science Books by Herbert Zim (ages eight to eleven)
   Zim, a distinguished scientist, is one of our most gifted writers on science for children. I recommend his books most enthusiastically.

1. *What's Inside of Animals?*
2. *What's Inside of Engines?*
3. *What's Inside of Plants?*
4. *What's Inside the Earth?*
5. *Your Heart and How It Works*
6. *Blood*
7. *Bones*
8. *Our Senses and How They Work*
9. *Alligators and Crocodiles*
10. *Big Cats*
11. *Comets*
12. *Corals*
13. *Dinosaurs*
14. *Golden Hamsters*
15. *Goldfish*
16. *Lightning and Thunder*
17. *Monkeys*
18. *Ostriches*
19. *Sharks*
20. *Shooting Stars*
21. *Snakes*
22. *Sun*
23. *Waves*

24. *Universe*

i) G. P. Putnam's Science Explorer Series (ages eight to twelve)
1. *Bridges,* Morton Golding
2. *The Deepest Hole in the World,* Louis Wolfe
3. *Finding the Forgotten,* Steven Frimmer
4. *The Stone That Spoke,* Steven Frimmer
5. *The Brain of Man,* John McNeel
6. *Captive Rivers,* Doris Faber
7. *Digging into Yesterday,* Estelle Friedman
8. *Four Men Who Changed the Universe,* Robert Silverberg
9. *The Great Tree of Life,* L. J. Ludovici
10. *How the Indians Really Lived,* Gordon Baldwin
11. *Hurricans, Storms, Tornadoes,* James Winchester
12. *Know Your Skin,* John Woodburn
13. *Man in the Making,* Estelle Friedman
14. *Mechanical Man,* Beril Becker
15. *Miracle Fabrics,* Hugh Kenny and Ellsworth Newcomb
16. *Miracle Glass,* Hugh Kenny and Ellsworth Newcomb
17. *Miracle Metals,* Hugh Kenny and Ellsworth Newcomb
18. *The Miracle of Vitamins,* Doris Faber
19. *The Origins of Language,* L. J. Ludovici
20. *Race against Time,* Gordon Baldwin
21. *The Right Size,* Hal Hellman
22. *Robots in Space,* Michael Chester
23. *Seeing Near and Seeing Far,* L. J. Ludovici
24. *The World of Cryogenics,* Waldo Boyd
25. *The World of Prehistory,* Gordon Baldwin
26. *The World of the Microscope,* L. J. Ludovici

j) Children's Press Stepping into Science Books Series (ages six to ten)
All of these books have been written by Illa Podendorf, whom I referred to previously for having done such an outstanding job in editing the True Book Series for Children's Press. Her science series are also excellent and highly recommended.
1. *Animals and More Animals*
2. *Change and Time*
3. *Color*
4. *Every Day Is Earth Day*
5. *Food Is for Eating*
6. *How Big Is a Stick?*
7. *Living Things Change*
8. *Magnets*
9. *Many Is How Many?*

10. *Predicting with Plants*
11. *Shadows and More Shadows*
12. *Shapes: Sides, Curves, and Corners*
13. *Sounds All About*
14. *Things Alike and Different*
15. *Things Are Made to Move*
16. *Things to Do with Water*
17. *Toby on the Move*
18. *Tools for Observing*
19. *Touching for Telling*
20. *Who, What and When?*

k) Children's Press Adventures in Nature and Science (ages eight to twelve)
1. *Animals of the Sea*, M. Verte
2. *The Ants*, E. Ross
3. *Atomic Submarines*, W. Anderson
4. *The Bees*, E. Teale
5. *Camouflage in Nature*, E. S. Ross
6. *Digging for Dinosaurs*, E. Colbert
7. *Life in the Desert*, P. Larson
8. *Rocket to the Moon*, C. Bonestell
9. *The Solar System*, C. Bonestell
10. *Young Animals*, J. Saunders

l) Children's Press Frontiers of America, (ages nine to twelve)
1. *Wagons over the Mountains*, E. McCall
2. *Steamboats to the West*, E. McCall
3. *Stalwart Men of Early Texas*, E. McCall
4. *Settlers on a Strange Shore*, E. McCall
5. *Pirates and Privateers*, E. McCall
6. *Pioneers on Early Waterways*, E. McCall
7. *Pioneering on the Plains*, E. McCall
8. *Pioneer Traders*, E. McCall
9. *Pioneer Show Folk*, E. McCall
10. *Over the Mormon Trail*, H. Jones
11. *Men on Iron Horses*, E. McCall
12. *Mail Riders: Paul Revere to the Pony Express*, E. McCall
13. *Log Fort Adventures*, E. McCall
14. *Hunters Blaze the Trails*, E. McCall
15. *Heroes of the Western Outposts*, E. McCall
16. *Grizzly Adams*, H. James
17. *Gold Rush Adventures*, E. McCall
18. *Forts in the Wilderness*, E. McCall

19. *Explorers in a New World*, E. McCall
20. *Cumberland Gap and Trails West*, E. McCall
21. *Cowboys and Cattle Drives*, E. McCall

Although these twelve series of nonfiction books have been listed for the stage of middle childhood, some of them may also continue to be enjoyed by older children. In spite of the fact that your youngster will be able to read these books himself, he will still enjoy having you read them to him as bedtime stories, or when he is sick, perhaps up to the age of eight or nine. Don't assume that just because your child has learned to read, he no longer wants to have you read to him. A bedtime story read to a youngster of middle childhood is still an important emotional ritual between father and child.

m) Books of Activities and Experiments for Children of Six to Ten Years
   1. *Fossils Tell of Long Ago,* Aliki (Thomas Y. Crowell). The stories told in fossils will delight readers who are interested in finding out more about the evolution of life on our planet.
   2. *Masks,* Chester Jay Alkema (Sterling). Instructions, accompanied by clear black-and-white photographs and colored illustrations, help the child master the "how-to" of mask making.
   3. *The Complete Crayon Book,* Chester Jay Alkema (Sterling). Ideas for the use of crayons are explored in detail.
   4. *Puppet Party,* Goldie T. Chernoff (Walker). Illustrated instructions for making puppets from such easily accessible things as paper cups and kitchen utensils make this book a source of interest and help for all would-be puppeteers.
   5. *Perplexing Puzzles and Tantalizing Teasers,* Martin Gardner (Simon and Shuster). A good book of puzzles for this age group.
   6. *Look Again!* Tana Hoban (Macmillan). Beautiful photographs, first seen through a small square "peep hole" and then viewed in their entirety, lead to interesting analysis and discussion.
   7. *Eric Plants a Garden,* Jean Hudlow (Whitman). The planning, planting, cultivating, and harvesting of crops by young gardeners are depicted in clear photographs.
   8. *Fingerprint Owls and Other Fantasies,* Marjorie P. Katz (M. Evans). An interesting book with all kinds of suggestions for using paper, a stamp pad, a felt-tipped pen, and one's own fingers for making designs.
   9. *Illustrated Chess for Children,* Harvey Kidder (Doubleday). A really good guide, with diagrams and illustrations, for the beginning chess player.
   10. *Yarn: The Things It Makes and How to Make Them,* Carolyn Meyer

(Harcourt, Brace, Jovanovich). Knitting, weaving, macrame, and crocheting are explained carefully and clearly. Even the left-handed child will find explicit instructions.

11. *Model Car Building*, Bill Neumann (Putnam)
12. *Kids Cooking*, Aileen Paul and Arthur Hawkins (Doubleday)
13. *You're a Good Dog, Joe: Knowing and Training Your Puppy*, Kurt Unkelback (Prentice)
14. *Lens and Shutter: An Introduction to Photography*, Harvey Weiss (Young Scott Books). For the young, inexperienced photographer, this book offers information and helpful suggestions.

n) Biography for Children of Six to Ten Years
1. *Sebastian Bach: The Boy from Thuringia*, Opal Wheeler and Sybil Deucher (Dutton)
2. *Beethoven: Master Musician*, Madeliene Goss (Holt)
3. *Buffalo Bill*, Ingri and Edgar P. D'Aulaire (Doubleday)
4. *Christopher Columbus*, Clara Ingram (Follett)
5. *The Story of Ben Franklin*, Eve Merriam (Four Winds)
6. *Meet Andrew Jackson*, Ormonde DeKay (Random House)
7. *Meet Martin Luther King, Jr.*, James T. DeKay (Random House)
8. *Lincoln's Birthday*, Clyde Bulla, (Crowell)
9. *Squanto: Friend of the Pilgrims*, Clyde Bulla (Crowell)
10. *George Washington*, Ingri and Edgar P. D'Aulaire (Doubleday)

o) Books on Religion for Children of Six to Twelve Years
One God: The Ways We Worship Him, Florence Fitch (Lothrop). This book is outstanding for this age group. Describes the religious beliefs of Protestants, Catholics, and Jews, and the ways they worship. It is an excellent book for any family to have in its home library, for it will answer many questions your child may ask about the three major religious faiths in America. Highly recommended.

B. Fiction and Fantasy
As you can see, there are many, many good books of nonfiction for the youngster of middle childhood. But, as with the preschooler, the number of fine nonfiction books far surpasses the number of excellent books of fiction and fantasy. Nevertheless, here are a selected number of excellent works of fiction and fantasy for middle childhood. First, some series of fiction books for this age group.

a) Grosset and Dunlap Illustrated Junior Library of Classics for Children (ages nine to eleven)
1. *The Adventures of Huckleberry Finn*, Mark Twain
2. *Adventures of Tom Sawyer*, Mark Twain

3. *Aesop's Fables*
4. *Alice in Wonderland and Through the Looking Glass*, Lewis Carroll
5. *Andersen's Fairy Tales*, Hans C. Andersen
6. *The Arabian Nights*, illustrated by Earle Goodenow
7. *Black Beauty*, Anna Sewell
8. *Call of the Wild and Other Stories*, Jack London
9. *Five Little Peppers and How They Grew*, Margaret Sidney
10. *Grimm's Fairy Tales*, Grimm Brothers
11. *Gulliver's Travels*, Jonathan Swift
12. *Hans Brinker, or The Silver Skates*, Mary M. Dodge
13. *Heidi*, Johanna Spyri
14. *The Jungle Book*, Rudyard Kipling
15. *Kidnapped*, Robert Louis Stevenson
16. *King Arthur and His Knights*, Sidney Lanier and Howard Pyle
17. *Little Women*, Louisa Alcott
18. *Pinocchio*, Carlo Collodi
19. *Robin Hood*, Howard Pyle
20. *Robinson Crusoe*, Daniel Defoe
21. *Swiss Family Robinson*, Johann D. Wyss
22. *A Tale of Two Cities*, Charles Dickens
23. *Treasure Island*, Robert Louis Stevenson
24. *The Wind in the Willows*, Kenneth Grahame
25. *The Wizard of Oz*, Frank Baum

b) Newberry Medal Winners

The Newberry Medal is awarded annually by the Children's Services Division of the American Library Association to the book which in their opinion is the outstanding contribution to children's literature that year. Here is the complete list of Newberry winners. Not all of these can be read by a youngster of middle childhood, but the list can be a guide for your book-giving to an older child as well.

1973 *Julie of the Wolves*, Cooper (Harper and Row)
1972 *Mrs. Frisby and the Rats of NIMH*, O'Brien (Atheneum)
1971 *Summer of the Swans*, Byers (Viking)
1970 *Sounder*, Armstrong (Harper)
1969 *The High King*, Alexander (Holt)
1968 *From the Mixed-Up Files of Mrs. Basil E. Frankweiler*, Konigsburg (Atheneum)
1967 *Up a Road Slowly*, Hunt (Follett)
1966 *I, Juan de Pareja*, Trevino (Farrar)
1965 *Shadow of a Bull*, Wojciechowska (Atheneum)

1964 *It's Like This, Cat*, Neville (Harper)
1963 *A Wrinkle in Time*, L'Engle (Farrar)
1962 *The Bronze Bow*, Speare (Houghton Mifflin)
1961 *Island of the Blue Dolphins*, O'Dell (Houghton Mifflin)
1960 *Onion John*, Krumgold (Crowell)
1959 *The Witch of Blackbird Pond*, Speare (Houghton Mifflin)
1958 *Rifles for Watie*, Keith (Crowell)
1957 *Miracles on Maple Hill*, Sorensen (Harcourt)
1956 *Carry On, Mr. Bowditch*, Latham (Houghton Mifflin)
1955 *The Wheel on the School*, De Jong (Harper)
1954 *And Now Miguel*, Krumgold (Crowell)
1953 *Secret of the Andes*, Clark (Viking)
1952 *Ginger Pye*, Estes (Harcourt)
1951 *Amos Fortune, Free Man*, Yates (Dutton)
1950 *The Door in the Wall*, de Angeli (Doubleday)
1949 *King of the Wind*, Henry (Rand McNally)
1948 *The Twenty-One Balloons*, du Bois (Viking)
1947 *Miss Hickory*, Bailey (Viking)
1946 *Strawberry Girl*, Lenski (Lippincott)
1945 *Rabbit Hill*, Lawson (Viking)
1944 *Johnny Tremain*, Forbes (Houghton Mifflin)
1943 *Adam of the Road*, Gray (Viking)
1942 *The Matchlock Gun*, Edmonds (Dodd, Mead)
1941 *Call it Courage*, Sperry (Macmillan)
1940 *Daniel Boone*, Daugherty (Viking)
1939 *Thimble Summer*, Enright (Holt)
1938 *The White Stag*, Seredy (Viking)
1937 *Roller Skates*, Sawyer (Viking)
1936 *Caddie Woodlawn*, Brink (Macmillan)
1935 *Dobry*, Shannon (Viking)
1934 *Invincible Louisa*, Meigs (Little, Brown)
1933 *Young Fu of the Upper Yangtze*, Lewis (Holt)
1932 *Waterless Mountain*, Armer (McKay)
1931 *The Cat Who Went to Heaven*, Coatsworth (Macmillan)
1930 *Hitty, Her First Hundred Years*, Coatsworth (Macmillan)
1929 *The Trumpeter of Krakow*, Kelly (Macmillan)
1928 *Gay-Neck*, Mukerji (Dutton)
1927 *Smoky, The Cowhorse*, James (Scribner)
1926 *Shen of the Sea*, Chrisman (Dutton)
1925 *Tales from Silver Lands*, Finger (Doubleday)
1924 *The Dark Frigate*, Hawes (Little, Brown)
1923 *The Voyages of Doctor Dolittle*, Lofting (Lippincott)
1922 *The Story of Mankind*, Van Loon (Liveright)

c) Caldecott Medal Winners

This medal is awarded annually by the Children's Service Division of the American Library Association to the artist of the most distinguished American picture book for children published during the preceding year. Here is the complete list of Caldecott winners (the books and their illustrators).

1973 *The Funny Little Woman*, Mosel and Lent (Dutton)

1972 *One Fine Day*, Hogrogian (Macmillan)

1971 *A Story—A Story*, Haley (Atheneum)

1970 *Sylvester and the Magic Pebble*, Steig (Windmill/Simon and Schuster)

1969 *The Fool of the World and the Flying Ship*, Shulevitz (Farrar)

1968 *Drummer Hoff*, Emberley (Prentice-Hall)

1967 *Sam, Bangs, and Moonshine*, Ness (Holt)

1966 *Always Room for One More*, Hogrogian (Holt)

1965 *May I Bring a Friend?* Montresor (Atheneum)

1964 *Where the Wild Things Are*, Sendak (Harper)

1963 *The Snowy Day*, Keats (Viking)

1962 *Once a Mouse*, Brown (Scribner)

1961 *Baboushka and the Three Kings*, Sidjakov (Parnassus)

1960 *Nine Days to Christmas*, Ets (Viking)

1959 *Chanticleer and the Fox*, Cooney (Crowell)

1958 *Time of Wonder*, McCloskey (Viking)

1957 *A Tree Is Nice*, Simont (Harper)

1956 *Frog Went A-Courtin'*, Rojankovsky (Harcourt)

1955 *Cinderella*, Brown (Scribner)

1954 *Madeline's Rescue*, Bemelmans (Viking)

1953 *The Biggest Bear*, Ward (Houghton Mifflin)

1952 *Finders Keepers*, Mordvinoff (Harcourt)

1951 *The Egg Tree*, Milhous (Scribner)

1950 *Song of the Swallows*, Politi (Scribner)

1949 *The Big Snow*, Hader (Macmillan)

1948 *White Snow, Bright Snow*, Duvoisin (Lothrop)

1947 *The Little Island*, Weisgard (Doubleday)

1946 *The Rooster Crows*, Petersham (Macmillan)

1945 *Prayer for a Child*, Jones (Macmillan)

1944 *Many Moons*, Slobodkin (Harcourt, Brace)

1943 *The Little House*, Burton (Houghton Mifflin)

1942 *Make Way for the Ducklings*, McCloskey (Viking)

1941 *They Were Strong and Good*, Lawson (Viking)

1940 *Abraham Lincoln*, d'Aulaire (Doubleday)

1939   *Mei Li,* Handforth (Doubleday)
1938   *Animals of the Bible,* Lathrop (Lippincott)

d)   Personalized Books

Every once in a while a truly original idea hits the field of children's books. Such an idea is that of the personalized book. This is a book about the child who is reading it; it uses the child's own name, his address, the names of his brothers or sisters or friends, and his pet dog and cat. The bookplate is also personalized, for it says, "This book was written especially for (whatever the child's name is) with love and kisses from (whoever is giving the book)." The actual contents of the book are personalized in over seventy places through the use of computer print-outs.

Research findings by reading consultants at the University of Southern California show that the personalized book—"a book written all about me!"—has a tremendous impact on a young child reading it. Mediocre readers have been found to do as well as excellent readers with the personalized book.

The wave of the future is the introduction of an even greater number of personalized items into books: the color of a youngster's eyes and hair, his favorite foods, his school and church, a nearby park or playground, etc.

These personalized books are called "Me-Books," and at present there are four available: *My Friendly Giraffe, My Jungle Holiday, My Birthday Land Adventure,* and *My Special Christmas.* The parent buying the book fills out the child's name and address, the first names of up to three brothers, sisters, or friends, the names of the child's pets, the child's birthdate, and hometown. If your local bookstore does not have Me-Books, you can get them by mail from Me-Books Publishing Company, 11633 Victory Blvd., North Hollywood, California 91609. These books are for children reading at the kindergarten or first grade level. Wait until your child has acquired enough reading ability to read the book without a great deal of difficulty. Be sure to give it to him yourself, because you wouldn't want to miss the expressions on his face when he discovers that the book is about him!

e)   Shufflebooks

Here is another breakthrough in books for children. A shufflebook consists of a box of over 100 durable, wipe-clean pages with words and pictures from which a child can literally compose over a million stories. For ages six to eight. Great to develop your child's imagination.

1. *A Shufflebook,* Richard Hefter and Martin Moskof (Western Publishing)

      2. *An Animal Shufflebook,* Richard Hefter and Martin Moskof (Western Publishing)

f) Children's Press's Tizz Books (ages seven to ten)
    This is a series by Elisa Bialk dealing with the adventures of a mischievous cream-colored pony, Tizz, a "member" of the Hill family. With the Hills, Tizz travels the country from Canada through Mexico, stumbling into trouble. Authentic regional backgrounds enable young readers to learn about other parts of North America while they enjoy reading about Tizz. This series has a special appeal for girls.
    1. *Tizz*
    2. *Tizz and Company*
    3. *Tizz at the Fiesta*
    4. *Tizz at the Stampede*
    5. *Tizz in Cactus Country*
    6. *Tizz in Texas*
    7. *Tizz in the Canadian Rockies*
    8. *Tizz is a Cow Pony*
    9. *Tizz on a Horse Farm*
    10. *Tizz on a Pack Trip*
    11. *Tizz on a Trail Ride*
    12. *Tizz Plays Santa Claus*
    13. *Tizz South of the Border*
    14. *Tizz Takes a Trip*

g) Children's Press's Rally Books Series (ages nine to twelve)
    These books by Ed Radlauer are a delight to a boy's heart if he is at all interested in motorcycles or racing cars.
    1. *Dragstrip Challenge*
    2. *Karting Challenge*
    3. *Minibike Challenge*
    4. *Quarter Midget Challenge*
    5. *Motorcycle Challenge*

h) Children's Press's Secret Seven Adventures (ages nine to eleven)
    The Secret Seven is a secret society of three girls and four boys who solve mysteries. A small toolshed is their meeting place, and only the secret password and a badge will allow anyone beyond the door marked "S7." These stories by Enid Blyton are designed to appeal to the "secret club" interest so characteristic of the middle childhood youngster.
    1. *The Secret Seven and the Bonfire Adventure*
    2. *The Secret Seven and the Case of the Dog Lover*
    3. *The Secret Seven and the Case of the Music Lover*

4. *The Secret Seven and the Case of the Missing Medals*
5. *The Secret Seven and the Case of the Old Horse*
6. *The Secret Seven and the Case of the Stolen Car*
7. *The Secret Seven and the Circus Adventure*
8. *The Secret Seven Get Their Man*
9. *The Secret Seven and the Grim Secret*
10. *The Secret Seven and the Hidden Cave Adventure*
11. *The Secret Seven and the Mystery of the Empty House*
12. *The Secret Seven and the Old Fort Adventure*
13. *The Secret Seven and the Railroad Mystery*
14. *The Secret Seven and the Tree House Adventure*

i) G. P. Putnam's See and Read Storybook Series (ages eight to ten)
1. *Adventures of Mole and Troll,* Tony Johnson
2. *Amish Boy,* Florence Rowland
3. *Amish Wedding,* Florence Rowland
4. *Andrew's Amazing Boxes,* Unada
5. *Bottles of Pop,* James Holding
6. *The Boy Who Lived in a Cave,* Estelle Friedman
7. *Brave Betsy,* Miriam Dreifus
8. *Chipper the Beaver,* Ed Dodd
9. *Cindy Lou,* Sonia Fox
10. *The Cowboy Surprise,* William Wise
11. *Cuff, A Baby Bear,* Virginia Voight
12. *The Horse That Liked Sandwiches,* Vivian Thompson
13. *Ida the Bearback Rider,* Syd Hoff
14. *Jeffrey at Camp,* Syd Hoff
15. *Juan Patrico,* Barbara Todd
16. *Little Brown Bat,* Virginia Wight
17. *Little Sponge Fisherman,* Florence Rowland
18. *Living in Navajoland,* Flora Hood
19. *The Lucky Little Porcupine,* Patricia Martin
20. *Mario's Mystery Machine,* Sibyl Hancock
21. *The Marshmallow Caper,* Gloria Miklowitz
22. *Mittens in May,* Maxine Kumin
23. *Night Outdoors,* Naomi Buchheimer
24. *The Luminaria for Antonio,* Flora Hood
25. *Palace Bug,* Syd Hoff
26. *The Parade Starts at Noon,* Gloria Miklowitz
27. *Peter and the Desert,* Lorraine Henridd
28. *The Raccoon and Mrs. McGinnis,* Patricia Martin
29. *Ricky's Boots,* Unada
30. *The Robber of Featherbed Lane,* James Holding
31. *School for Julia,* Florence Rowland

32. *Sir Howard the Coward*, William Wise
33. *There Goes the Tiger*, Patricia Martin
34. *Wilfred the Lion*, Syd Hoff

j) Marguerite Henry Books, Rand McNally (ages eight to eleven)
   Strictly speaking, this is not a series, but merely a number of books by a very gifted author. They are about horses and have a great appeal to girls.
   1. *Misty of Chincoteague*
   2. *Stormy, Misty's Foal*
   3. *Sea Star, Orphan of Chincoteague*
   4. *White Stallion of Lippizza*
   5. *Born to Trot*
   6. *Brighty of the Grand Canyon*
   7. *King of the Wind*
   8. *Justin Morgan Had a Horse*

k) Morrow's Henry Huggins Books (ages eight to eleven)
   These are the hilarious adventures of an irrepressible boy, written with great skill by Beverly Cleary. A real favorite in middle childhood.
   1. *Henry Huggins*
   2. *Henry and Beezus*
   3. *Henry and the Paper Route*
   4. *Henry and Ribsy*
   5. *The Mouse and the Motorcycle*
   6. *Ramona, The Pest*
   7. *Ribsy*
   8. *Runaway Ralph*

l) Fiction and Fantasy for Children of Six to Eight Years
   1. *June 7!* Aliki (Macmillan). A picture book which shows an ever-expanding crowd of relatives gathering in a city apartment to celebrate a birthday. A humorous book for youngsters from both large and small families.
   2. *Little Runner of the Longhouse*, Betty Baker (Harper). A humorous Iroquois Indian story about Little Runner, who ultimately receives the reward of maple sugar in the New Year rites. For beginning readers.
   3. *The House of Wings*, Betsy Byars (Viking). This book, best shared with an understanding adult, gives insight into a boy's adjustment to living in his grandfather's old house filled with birds.
   4. *A Pocketful of Cricket*, Rebecca Caudill (Holt). A pet cricket goes to school with Jay on his first day in the "awesome institution."
   5. *Did You Carry the Flag Today, Charley?* Rebecca Caudill (Holt).

Charley, a relentless user of the word *why*, goes to a summer preschool program in the mountainous area where he and his family live. A nonconformist, Charley tries the patience of his teachers, but eventually earns their approval.

6. *The Wanderers*, Elizabeth Coatsworth (Four Winds). An adventure story unfolds as Father Ambrosius travels through Irish villages beset by Viking raiders. Collecting a dog and two boys along the way, Father Ambrosius infects them with his gentle, kindly ways.

7. *The New Teacher*, Miriam Cohen (Macmillan). When the first-grade teacher leaves to have a baby, the members of her class speculate on the qualities of her replacement. In a bid for peer acceptance, Jim tries to encourage the class members to ridicule her but is faced with a backfiring situation.

8. *What's the Prize, Lincoln?* Dale Fife (Coward, McCann and Geoghegan). An easy-to-read story about Lincoln's attempts to enter contests for profit. When he wins twelve dozen cans of hash instead of the color TV set he planned to win, the story becomes believable.

9. *Old Woman Who Lived in a Vinegar Bottle*, Rumer Godden (Viking). A poor woman who sets a fish free is given whatever she wishes. Starting with simple wishes, she stretches the magical generosity of her benefactor until at last she is reduced to her original poverty—almost.

10. *Nobody Listens to Andrew*, Elizabeth Guilfoile (Follett). Andrew tries frantically to tell everyone that there is a bear in his bed! A funny easy-to-read book.

11. *A Bargain for Frances*, Russel Hoban (Harper). The latest book in a series about a small badger whose antics are amusing and very childlike. A story which contains a lesson but never becomes annoyingly didactic.

12. *One Fine Day*, Nonny Hogrogian (Macmillan). The interdependence of nature is depicted in this picture story of the quest of a fox.

13. *We Are Having a Baby*, Viki Holland (Scribner's). The confused reactions of a young child confronted by the appearance of a new baby in the family are examined skillfully. The "sad feeling" which persists until her father's guidance helps Dana to understand that the little stranger is also her brother is a familiar one to many children.

14. *Be Nice to Josephine*, Betty Horvath (Watts). At the insistence of his mother, Charley spends Saturday with his visiting cousin—a girl. Surprisingly to him, the encounter turns out to be a happy one!

15. *I Wonder if Herbie's Home Yet*, Mildred Kantrowitz (Parent's Magazine). It is a terrible feeling when your good friend goes off to play with someone else!

16. *Emily, the Klunky Baby and the Next-Door Dog*, Joan Lexau (Dial

Press). When mother, who is divorced and has increased chores as a result, cannot play with her, Emily sets off for Daddy's apartment.

17. *Nightmare in My Closet,* Mercer Mayer (Dial Press). The nagging suspicion that someone or something lurks in the closet of one's bedroom becomes a reality in this book of fantasy.

18. *The Funny Little Woman,* Arlene Mosel (Dutton). An accomplished cook of rice-flour dumplings, the plump little Japanese woman runs after one of her concoctions only to find it has fallen into the hands of fierce monster-like figures who lurk underground.

19. *If I Built a Village,* Kazue Mizumura (Thomas Y. Crowell). Wishing is the prerogative of the young child. Wishing is the theme of this gentle book of a child's view of environmental spoilage.

20. *Take It or Leave It,* Osmond Molarsky (Walck). Chester, a master in the art of swapping, makes a series of trades which make him the owner of a dog he knows he won't be allowed to keep.

21. *The Secret of the Sachem Tree,* F. N. Monjo (Coward, McCann and Geoghegan). A lively account of colonial life and a Connecticut legend of the Charter Oak made this easy-to-read book convincing and interesting.

22. *Theodore's Rival,* Edward Ormondroyd (Parnassus Press). Rivalry between Theodore, a lovable teddy bear, and a new musical Panda received by Lucy as a birthday present, provides some quiet fun for youngsters.

23. *Goodnight Andrew, Goodnight Craig,* Marjorie Weinman Sharmet (Harper and Row). Two boys get very noisy after going to bed. Father delivers an ultimatum. All-dialogue story.

24. *The Dead Tree,* Alvin Tresselt (Parent's Magazine Press). This book, which does not overemphasize death, but which introduces the web-of-life, is a hopeful and warm story of ecology.

25. *The Adventures of Obadiah,* Brinton Trukle (Viking). Obadiah, a Quaker boy who often resorts to tall-tale telling, becomes involved in a real adventure at the Nantucket sheep-shearing squantum.

26. *Alexander and the Terrible, Horrible, No-Good, Very Bad Day,* Judith Viorst (Atheneum). Everything goes wrong for Alexander, and he vows to move to Australia. Mother assures him, however, that "some days are like that"—even in Australia!

27. *The Tenth Good Thing about Barney,* Judith Viorst (Atheneum). When a boy's cat dies, his mother helpfully suggests that he think of ten good things to tell about Barney during the funeral.

28. *Ira Sleeps Over,* Bernard Waber (Houghton Mifflin). When Ira is invited to spend the night with his next-door neighbor, he cannot decide whether or not he should take his teddy bear. His parents are supportive and encourage him to take the beloved toy with him, but

his sister convinces him that his host might laugh. All ends well when both boys discover the need for "teddy-bear security."

29. *Nobody is Perfick,* Bernard Waber (Houghton Mifflin). A series of independent stories about everyday topics such as keeping a diary, making friends and daydreaming are sandwiched between bright red divider pages.

30. *The Girl Who Loved the Wind,* Jane Yolen (T. Y. Crowell). An overly protected princess finally escapes the loving but suffocating attention of her doting father.

31. *A Father Like That,* Charlotte Zolotow, illustrated by Ben Shecter (Harper). A fatherless boy describes the kind of father he would like to have and is reassured, by his mother, that he himself can grow up to be just that kind of man!

32. *Dr. Gardner's Stories about the Real World,* Richard Gardner, M.D. (Prentice Hall). A most unique book of fiction by a most unique child psychiatrist. These are stories about grade-school children in real-life situations, such as being shy and afraid to try new things, having other boys pick on you and not knowing what to do about it, and similar situations. Reading one of these stories to your child (or having him read it himself) may initiate a close talk between the two of you, leading to action which will solve a problem. I recommend it highly.

m) Fiction and Fantasy for Children of Nine to Ten Years

1. *Then Again, Maybe I Won't,* Judy Blume (Bradbury). A boy is upset about his family's changed attitudes when they become well-to-do, and by his first sexual stirrings.

2. *Andy's Mountain,* Bianca Bradbury (Houghton). Love and loyalty between a determined grandfather and his grandson shine through the pleasant story of an old man who refuses to sell his farm to make way for a new highway.

3. *Indian Hill,* Clyde Bulla (T. Crowell). Moving from an Indian reservation to an apartment in a big city provides trauma for a Navaho family.

4. *Surprise for a Cowboy,* Clyde Bulla (T. Crowell). A city boy wants desperately to become a cowboy who lives on a ranch.

5. *D. J.'s Worst Enemy,* Robert Burch (Viking). D. J. Madison's relationships with his family—negative and unproductive at first—begin to change as the book unfolds its story of the rural South in the 1930s.

6. *Simon and the Game of Chance,* Robert Burch (Viking). A stern and tyrannical father whose dictatorial ways affect each member of the

family figures prominently in this story of Simon's adjustment to problems within his family.

7. *The Letter on the Tree,* Natalie Carlson (Harper and Row). A believable ten-year-old boy, who wants an accordian desperately, attaches a letter to a Christmas tree shipped from his home on a Canadian farm to the United States.

8. *Beanie,* Ruth and Latrobe Carroll (Walck). The Smoky Mountains serve as the setting for a warm, happy family story.

9. *All Except Sammy,* Gladys Cretan (Little, Brown). In an otherwise musical family, Sammy Agabashian puts his passion for baseball in perspective. As the story unfolds, he reconciles his family's artistic expectations and his own love of sports.

10. *The House of Sixty Fathers,* Meindert DeJong (Harper and Row). A Chinese story about a boy looking for his lost family.

11. *Shadrach,* Meindert DeJong (Harper and Row). Father and grandfather try to help David develop physically and emotionally by giving him a job, a pet rabbit, and encouragement to grow up. A well-meaning but overprotective mother seems to want to keep Davie something of a baby.

12. *The Moffats,* Eleanor Estes (Harcourt). Episodes in the life of first one member of the Moffat family and then another make up this well-loved story of an American family.

13. *Gull 737,* Jean George (Crowell). A sea gull chick is being studied by Dr. Rivers, a scientist father who is self-centered and closed-minded. His son Luke offers logical, creative ideas of his own which eventually lead to the beginnings of true communication between father and son.

14. *The Grizzly,* Annabel and Edgar Johnson (Harper). Since his parents' separation, David has had little opportunity to get to know his father. During a fishing trip together, David tries to overcome his fear and anxieties of both his father and the natural elements.

15. *Ben and Me,* Robert Lawson (Little). The life of Benjamin Franklin is told through the eyes of a mouse who makes claim to fame in his own right.

16. *Rabbit Hill,* Robert Lawson (Viking). Little Georgie, a happy little rabbit boy, and old rabbit Uncle Analdas move engagingly through the story about a new family which moves into the nearby house.

17. *Rough Ice,* Beaman Lord (Walck). A young boy tries to equal the skill of his father, who was a champion hockey player.

18. *Onion John,* Joseph Krumgold (Crowell). A story of a father's dominance over his son Andy. This is a story of growing independence in a boy and understanding in his father.

19. *Meet the Austins,* Madeleine L'Engle (Vanguard). Including the children of the family in serious discussions, developing and cultivating respect for all people, and inculcating values are the goals of Dr. and Mrs. Austin as they share their knowledge and understanding with their children.

20. *The Lion, the Witch, and the Wardrobe,* C. S. Lewis (Macmillan). Written by a theologian and poet, this book is the first in a series about the magic land of Narnia. The children become involved in countless conflicts between good and evil, which are symbolized by a kindly lion and a wicked witch.

21. *Homer Price,* Robert McCloskey (Viking). A series of funny stories about a lively boy in contemporary life, this book was one of the first to spoof comic books.

22. *It's Like This, Cat,* Emily Neville (Harper and Row). A father's intolerance and disapproval of his son's activities (including ownership of a pet cat) make the boy unhappy and his mother physically ill. Family harmony increases, but true unity is still in the distance.

23. *The Borrowers,* Mary Norton (Harcourt). The beginning of a series of delightful books about the little people who live under the floorboards.

24. *Bed-Knob and Broomstick,* Mary Norton (Harcourt). As Miss Price is studying to become a witch, she is discovered by the Wilson children. The adventures that come from her awarding them some special magic of their own to maintain silence make for interesting reading.

25. *Hannah Elizabeth,* Elaine Rich (Harper and Row). This is the story of a ten-year-old Indiana Mennonite girl. Her father refuses to fight in the war, causing her schoolmates to tease and taunt her.

26. *Miracles on Maple Hill,* Virginia Sorenson (Harcourt). Father has been in a war prison, and the family moves to the country hoping that he will regain his health.

27. *All-of-a-Kind Family,* Sydney Taylor (Follett). The story of a Jewish family living in New York City in the early 1900s. All the children are girls until eventually Papa gets a boy! Papa is hardworking, and Mama is pretty and lovable in this story of deeply rooted Jewish religious customs.

28. *Harriet the Spy,* Louise Fitzhugh (Dell paperback). Harriet has a secret notebook which she fills with painfully honest comments about her parents, neighbors, and classmates. Every day on her "spy route" she observes and jots down anything of interest to her. A sparkling and delightful book.

29. *Little House in the Big Woods,* Laura Ingalls Wilder (Harper Trophy paperback). This book and seven others (*Little House on the Prairie, Little Town on the Prairie,* etc.) contain the author's vivid memories

of her own childhood during the days of pioneer living in the United States. An excellent series which can now be called a modern classic for children.

30. *The Wizard of Oz*, L. Frank Baum (Grosset and Dunlap). The delightful adventures of Dorothy, a little girl from Kansas, and her friends in the wonderful and magical land of Oz. Another classic.

31. *The Incredible Journey*, Sheila Burnford (Little Brown). The fantastic account of three house pets in a dangerous and lengthy trek through the wilderness to reach their former home. When the Walt Disney movie about this is reissued, this would be a good time to get the book for your child.

32. *Little Rascal*, Sterling North (Dutton). The heartening story of a raccoon and a lonely boy. Another book brought to the screen by Walt Disney.

n) And now I want to conclude this section of books of fiction and fantasy for middle childhood with thirteen of my own personal favorites for this age group:

1. *Charlie and the Chocolate Factory*, Roald Dahl (Knopf). A modern classic. Five children get to see the mysterious machinery in the marvelous chocolate factory of Mr. Willy Wonka. Mr. Wonka's fantastic inventions will delight all small children.

2. *James and the Giant Peach*, Roald Dahl (Knopf). Another delightful fantasy by Roald Dahl. "Fabulous unbelievable things" happen to James inside the giant peach.

3. *The Talking Machine*, James Kruss (Universe). Professor Prendergast and his nephew Martin have invented a fabulous Talking Machine which can make instant translations of animal languages into several human languages, and vice versa. With a beginning like that, what book could possibly go wrong?

4. *Stuart Little*, E. B. White (Harper and Row). The whimsical first sentence of this book reads, "When Mrs. Frederick C. Little's second son was born, everybody noticed that he was not much bigger than a mouse." In fact, he *was* a mouse! The rest of the book describes his fascinating adventures. A modern classic.

5. *Charlotte's Web*, E. B. White (Harper and Row). Another wonderful tale of whimsy and imagination by E. B. White. Charlotte, the spider, saves the life of her friend, a doomed pig, by spinning messages in her web. Another classic.

6. *Winnie-the-Pooh*, A. A. Milne (Dutton). Be sure to get the original edition of this and not the watered-down Walt Disney version. Originally written by A. A. Milne for his own son Christopher Robin, this is one of the most wonderful children's classics ever written.

7. *Just So Stories*, Rudyard Kipling (Grosset and Dunlap). Another children's classic that will never grow old. A delightful collection of humorous animal fantasy tales, such as "How the Leopard Got His Spots," and "How the Whale Got His Throat." One of the few books you can read simultaneously to children of all ages, from preschool through twelve. Adults enjoy these stories as much as children do.

8. *Mary Poppins*, P. L. Travers (Harcourt, Brace and World). Disney's wonderful movie Mary Poppins has spread the fame of the fabulous nursemaid of the Banks children. Wherever Mary Poppins is, magic is sure to be in the air.

9. *Mr. Popper's Penguins*, Richard and Florence Atwater (Little, Brown). Mr. Popper, a paper hanger with a passion for the Antarctic, is given a penguin by an explorer. The one penguin becomes twelve, and the twelve penguins proceed to turn upside down the lives of the entire Popper family. Hilarious whimsy.

10. *The Twenty-One Balloons*, William Pene DuBois (Viking). This is the book that I personally enjoyed reading to my children the most. Professor William Waterman Sherman goes adventuring in a flying balloon which lands on the amazing island of Krakatoa, where twenty families live in secluded luxury. The inventions of the families of Krakaoa will delight both a child and his parents.

11. *Chitty Chitty Bang Bang, The Magical Car*, Ian Fleming (Random House). Walt Disney has also popularized this one. Boys particularly will love to hear the story of Commander Crackpot and his marvelous car, which can swim, fly, and communicate with people.

12. *The Enormous Egg*, Oliver Butterworth (Little, Brown). A twelve-year-old boy finds a huge egg which hatches into a dinosaur.

13. *The Wind in the Willows*, Kenneth Grahame (Scribners). This marvelous children's classic is the story of Mole, Badger, Water Rat, and Toad, and their life along the banks of the Thames River. They have such delightfully human characteristics. I agree 100 percent with A. A. Milne, who said in his introduction to the book, "One does not argue about *The Wind in the Willows*. The young man gives it to the girl with whom he is in love, and if she does not like it, asks her to return his letters. The older man tries it on his nephew, and alters his will accordingly. The book is a test of character. We can't criticize it, because it is criticizing us."

V. Preadolescence and Adolescence

I have decided not to include any booklists for the stages of preadolescence and adolescence for several reasons. One is that many of the books listed for middle childhood will still be enjoyed by youngsters in the stage of preadolescence (ages eleven and twelve). In fact, a number of the nonfiction and fiction series listed under middle childhood are noted as appealing to children as old as eleven or twelve.

But the main reason I decided not to do a formal booklist for preadolescence and adolescence is that by these ages your youngster is no longer a child but a preteen-ager or a teen-ager. His reading taste will be quite individualistic and unique by now. In other words, his reading taste in many ways will be similar to that of an adult. So you will need to tune in on his own unique and idiosyncratic reading preferences. If he is interested in fishing, hot rods, and motorcycles, a list of excellent books of biography for adolescents will not be of much help as a guide to buying him books. Give him books that fit his reading preferences, and he will be very happy with them.

BUYING AN ENCYCLOPEDIA FOR YOUR CHILD

I believe that when your child arrives midway in the stage of middle childhood (fourth, fifth, or sixth grade, depending on the child), if you can afford it, it is a good idea to get him an encyclopedia. I say, "if you can afford it," because an encyclopedia is a major investment. I won't even attempt to specify in dollars what that means, because with today's alternately creeping and galloping inflation, the figures would probably be out of date by the time they were printed. But an encyclopedia will be costly, and you need to choose carefully. One of the best ways to do this is to visit your local library and browse through the different encyclopedias there. Look up a topic on which you are pretty well informed. Ask yourself, is the topic easy to locate? Is the writing interesting? Is it, so far as you know, accurate? Ask your librarian's help and her views as to which encyclopedias are best.

There are two encyclopedias generally recommended by librarians for the fourth through sixth grades and up:

1. *Compton's Encyclopedia,* (twenty-four volumes for grades four to twelve), published by F. E. Compton Company, a division of Encyclopedia Britannica, 425 N. Michigan Avenue, Chicago, Illinois 60611
2. *The World Book Encyclopedia,* (twenty volumes for grades four to twelve), published by Field Enterprises Educational Corporation, Merchandise Mart Plaza, Chicago, Illinois 60654

I will stick my neck out and say I personally believe *The World Book Encyclopedia* is the best for this age group.

Encyclopedias can only be bought through salesmen, not in department stores or bookstores. However, it is sometimes possible to buy used sets, or sets a few years old. Not that much information changes in an encyclopedia in two or three years, so if you happen to find a set which is a few years old, give it a careful inspection. You may have found yourself a good buy. Sometimes you may find used sets in a bookstore. Or it may be possible to buy a used set from a salesman or from a library which has replaced its old set with a newer one.

When your child has outgrown the particular junior encyclopedia you have chosen for him (which may be in junior high or high school, depending on the child), then he is ready for an adult encyclopedia. In my opinion there is one adult encyclopedia which is so superior to the others that there is no comparison. That is the *Encyclopedia Britannica.* I recommend it most enthusiastically.

In any case, don't just buy an encyclopedia and present it "cold" to your child. You will need to teach him how to use it so that it will not be a forbidding set of strange volumes to him. Choose some topic in which you know he has an interest and show him how to look it up. Show him how to use the index. Explain to him how to follow cross references to other articles. Above all, show him how to find the main points in an encyclopedia article. That way he will not be like many students, who do their homework by merely copying part or all of an article, woodenly and mechanically.

MAGAZINES FOR CHILDREN

I would be remiss if I closed this appendix without some mention of good magazines for children. Children get so little mail that it is always a thrill when a magazine arrives for them. They will beg you to read these magazines to them in the preschool years, and they will read them themselves in the years of middle childhood. They also enjoy doing the puzzles, cutouts, and other activities in the magazines. Here are the magazines I recommend, along with the age levels for each:

a) The Preschool Stage
  1. *Humpty Dumpty's Magazine* (Better Reading Foundation, 52 Vanderbilt Avenue, New York, New York 10017). Puzzles, things to do, stories you can read to your child, stories for beginners to read themselves, games. Ages three to seven.
  2. *Jack and Jill* (Curtis Publishing Company, Independence Square, Philadelphia, Pennsylvania 19105). Puzzles, things to make, stories, poems, simple science and nature articles. Ages four to ten.
  3. *Highlights for Children* (2300 W. Fifth Avenue, Columbus, Ohio 43212). Stories, puzzles, science, poetry. Ages three to eight.
  4. *Child Life* (1100 Waterway Blvd., Indianapolis, Indiana 46202). Stories, things to do, verses, riddles, science, sports, books, art, music. Ages four to twelve.

b) The Stage of Middle Childhood
  1. *Ranger Rick's Nature Magazine* (National Wildlife Federation, avail-

able only to members who pay the annual dues of $6. The membership office is Ranger Rick's Nature Magazine Membership Services, 381 W. Center Street, Marion, Ohio 43302). Activities, adventures, and information about nature. Appeals especially to boys. Ages six to ten.

2. *Children's Digest* (Better Reading Foundation, 52 Vanderbilt Avenue, New York, New York 10017). Stories, puzzles, how-to-do-it projects. Ages eight to twelve.

3. *Golden Magazine* (Golden Press Division of Western Printing Company, North Road, Poughkeepsie, New York 12601). Stories, nonfiction articles, puzzles, things to do. Ages eight to twelve.

4. *Boys' Life* (Boy Scouts of America, New Brunswick, New Jersey 08901). Stories and nonfiction articles on crafts, hobbies, outdoor life, sports, nature, science, scoutcraft. For boys ages eight to sixteen.

5. *The American Girl* (Girl Scouts of America, 830 Third Avenue, New York, New York 10022). Stories, nonfiction articles for girls on clothing etiquette, nature, party ideas, recipes. For girls ages nine to sixteen.

Appendix
D
A Father's Guide
to Children's Records

If you go into your nearest record shop or into the record section of your local department store, in all probability you will find a reasonably adequate selection of records for adults or adolescents. But if you want to find good records for a child under the age of adolescence, I daresay you will find very few. Oh, they will have a section marked "Children's Records," of course, but the quality of most of them is poor.

The records that will typically be found in the children's records section are what I call "kiddie records." The kiddie records are designed and packaged to appeal to parents, not children, since the record manufacturers know all too well that it is parents who buy these records. However, these types of "cute" records do not do much for children. Typically, they are too fast, trite, and over-orchestrated, with a large orchestra or chorus.

In the average record shop you will probably not find a single record in the children's section by the record company that in my opinion makes the best records, overall, for children: Folkways Records. If you live in Los Angeles, you will have no trouble buying Folkways records. In fact you will have no trouble buying literally thousands of good children's records because you can simply drive over to the Children's Music Center at 5373 West Pico Boulevard, talk with

Mrs. Sherman, and browse through the extensive collection of children's records. Every once in a while I take the time and trouble to drive over there just for the privilege of doing exactly that. Mrs. Sherman and her entire staff are very knowledgeable about children's records, and they have always been helpful to me when I wanted to buy a record. As a matter of fact, Mrs. Sherman and her staff were very helpful to me in preparing this appendix. I spent several days browsing through their entire stock of records before I compiled this appendix.

If you are not satisfied with the selection of children's records at your local music store or record shop, at least you have one other option. Children's Music Center does sell both to parents and schools by mail order. They put out a free catalog, and have a number of records that space prevented me from listing in this appendix. Or if you want a particular kind of record for a particular child, you can describe your needs in a letter, and they will suggest a record to do the job.

It is a pity that many fathers think of a child's record as something you buy purely for entertainment, instead of a valuable learning device. Any good record can be used for training the memory, developing listening skills, training the ear, teaching thinking, building the vocabulary, and providing a child with information.

When you play a record for your child, ask him leading questions about the story or song. Suppose, for example, you play him a good record of *The Three Little Pigs*. After he has heard the record, ask him: If the three pigs had neighbors, who do you think they would be? What kind of a home would they live in? Do you think they would live in a big city or a small town? What kind of voice did the big bad wolf use when he first knocked on the door? Which pig was the best architect? Questions such as these will give your child experience in all of the above-mentioned skills.

I. Very Young Children (up to the age of two)

1. *Music for for Ones and Twos*, Tom Glazer (CMS records)
2. *Child's First Record*, Frank Luther (Vocalion)
3. *Train to the Zoo, Train to the Farm* (Young People's Records)
4. *Songs to Grow on for Mother and Child*, Woody Guthrie (Folkways)
5. *Little White Duck*, Burl Ives (Harmony Records)
6. *Lullabies for Sleepy Heads*, Dorothy Olsen (RCA Camden)
7. *Lullabies from Round the World*, Marilyn Horne and Richard Robinson (Rhythm Production)
8. *Golden Slumbers: Lullabies from Near and Far* (Caedmon)
9. *Lullabies and Other Children's Songs*, Nancy Raven (Pacific Cascade Records)
10. *Songs for the Quiet Time*, Dorothy Olsen (Camden)

II. Preschool Children (ages two to six)

I have said that these records are for children between the ages of two and six. However, that is a general statement, and your child might be too young (or too old) to like a particular record. The problem is more likely to be that the child will be too young, if he is between two and three, to like a particular record. Some two-year-olds, who may be more verbal than the average, will like almost all of the records here. Other two-year-olds may not like a certain record at two or two and one-half, but will like it at three. So you have to know your own child pretty well to know what records he will tend to like between the ages of two and three. But if you buy him a record and find he is uninterested at two or two and one-half, wait until three or three and one-half or four and try it again. Never force a record on a child who shows he does not care for it.

Regardless of any problems you might encounter between two and three, almost all children aged three to six will like the records listed here.

A. Young People's Records

This is a terrific, but little-known "double value" series for children. One side is a delightful story and song. The second side contains classical music. Young People's Records publishes a catalog which is broken down by age groups. Therefore, I have listed only a few of their best.

1. *Carrot Seed*
2. *The Little Fireman*
3. *Aladdin*
4. *My Friend*
5. *Funniest Song in the World*
6. *Me, Myself and I*
7. *The Waltzing Elephant*
8. *Drummer Boy*
9. *Little Indian Drum*
10. *Build Me a House*
11. *Clock That Went Backwards*

B. Dance, Body Movement, and Rhythm

Most young children move freely to rhythm and music. It is only later that they become self-conscious and inhibited. These records give an opportunity for young children to experience that wonderful feeling of movement.

1. *Dance-A-Story* by Ann Barlin (RCA Victor) is a unique type of dance record series. Each title is a storybook-record combination for creative rhythms, pantomime, dramatizations, and storytelling. Each album contains a record and a storybook. One side of the record is narrated, with possible movements to go with the melody. The

reverse side has music alone, and your child is free to interpret the music as he feels it. An excellent series, with eight different titles:
a) *Little Duck*
b) *Noah's Ark*
c) *Magic Mountain*
d) *Balloons*
e) *Brave Hunter*
f) *Flappy and Floppy*
g) *The Toy Tree*
h) *At the Beach*

2. *Rhythmic Songs,* Grette Agatz (Peripole Records)
3. *Come Dance with Me,* Anne Landry (James H. Heineman, Publishers)
4. *Marching across the Green Grass and Other American Children Game Songs,* Jean Ritchie (Asch Records)
5. *Activity Songs,* Marcia Berman (Tom Thumb Records)
6. *Activity Songs for Kids,* Marcia Berman (Folkways)
7. *Drummer Boy* (Young People's Records)
8. *This Is Rhythm,* Ella Jenkins (Folkways)
9. *Rhythms of Childhood,* Ella Jenkins (Folkways)
10. *Songs and Rhythms from Near and Far,* Ella Jenkins (Folkways)
11. *You Sing a Song and I'll Sing a Song,* Ella Jenkins (Folkways)
12. *Rhythm and Game Songs for the Little Ones,* Ella Jenkins (Folkways)
13. *Counting Games and Rhythms for the Little Ones,* Ella Jenkins (Folkways)
14. *Rhythms for Today,* Album No. 29, Carrie Rasmussen and Violette Stewart (Activity Records)
15. *Dance, Sing and Listen Again and Again,* Miss Nelson and Bruce, Volume 3 (Dimension 5 Records)
16. *Dance Music for Preschool Children,* arranged by Bruce King (S&R Records)
17. *OLATUNJI, Drums of Passion* (Columbia)
18. *More Drums of Passion* (Columbia)
19. *Strictly Percussion,* Daniel Barrajanos and his drummer (Hoctor Dance Records)
20. *Creative Movement and Rhythmic Exploration,* Hap Palmer (Educational Activities Records)
21. *Modern Tunes and Rhythms and Instruments,* Hap Palmer (Educational Activities Records)
22. *Together* (A participation musical concept record from Dimension Five Records)
23. *Dance to the Music* (Dimension Five Records)

24. *Play Your Instruments and Make a Pretty Sound*, Ella Jenkins (Folkways)
25. *Early Early Childhood*, Ella Jenkins (Folkways)
26. *Little Johnny Brown*, Ella Jenkins (Folkways)
27. *My Street Begins at My House*, Ella Jenkins (Folkways)
28. *And One and Two*, Ella Jenkins (Folkways)

C. Misterogers

Misterogers is a well-known television personality who runs a wonderful program for children. He has some delightful and unique records dealing with the feelings of children. For example, he sings about how frightened a child feels when it thunders; what he should do when he feels angry; how he can control himself if he feels like biting. Here are some of Misterogers' records.

1. *You Are Special* (Small World Records)
2. *Won't You Be My Neighbor* (Small World Records)
3. *Misterogers Tells the Story of Josephine the Short-Neck Giraffe* (Small World Records)
4. *Let's Be Together Today* (Small World Enterprises)
5. *Come On and Wake Up* (Small World Records)
6. *A Place of Our Own* (Small World Records)

D. Self and Body Image

Although these records were designed for slow-learning children of grade-school age, they are also valuable learning aids to the normal young child. What will help a slow-learning child of eight or nine to learn self and body image is often just right for a normal child of preschool age.

1. *More Learning as We Play*, selected and arranged by Winifred Stiles and David Ginglend (Folkways)

E. Story Records

A story record is a child's equivalent of reading or being read a book. Television leaves no room for a child's imagination; it gives the child little opportunity for make-believe. A story record, however, gives him the opportunity to imagine things for himself.

Some of these records may be a little too advanced for your preschooler; others may be just right. If a record seems too advanced for your child, save it and try it a year or two later. You won't be wasting your money. All of the records are first rate.

a) Caedmon Recordings of the Spoken Word (Leading modern poets and well-known actors and actresses have recorded children's classics.)

1. *A Gathering of Great Poetry for Children*, Volume 1

2. *Let's Listen,* four children's stories by contemporary authors
3. *Miracles: Poems Written by Children,* collected by Richard Lewis
4. *Mother Goose*
5. *Puss in Boots and Other Fairy Tales from around the World*
6. *The Three Little Pigs and Other Fairy Tales*
7. *Hans Christian Andersen's Fairy Tales*
8. *Hans Christian Andersen's The Ugly Duckling and Other Tales*
9. *Madeline and Other Bemelmans,* Ludwig Bemelmans
10. *Nonsense Verse of Carroll & Lear,* Lewis Carroll and Edward Lear
11. *Pinocchio,* Carlo Collodi
12. *Petunia, Beware!* Roger Duvoisin
13. *The Reluctant Dragon,* Kenneth Grahame
14. *The Jungle Book: Mowgli's Brothers,* Rudyard Kipling
15. *A Child's Garden of Verses,* Robert Louis Stevenson, narrated by Judith Anderson
16. *Mary Poppins,* P. L. Travers
17. *Mary Poppins Comes Back,* P. L. Travers
18. *Mary Poppins and the Banks Family,* P. L. Travers
19. *Mary Poppins Opens the Door,* P. L. Travers
20. *Mary Poppins from A to Z,* P. L. Travers

b) Other Good Stories
1. *Winnie the Pooh and Christopher Robin,* Frank Luther (Decca)
2. *The Original Sound Track of Hansel and Gretal* (RCA Camden)
3. *The Little Engine That Could* (RCA Camden)
4. *Dr. Seuss Presents Bartholemew and the Oobleck* (RCA Camden)
5. *Abiyoyo and Other Story Songs for Children,* Pete Seeger (Folkways)

c) Classroom Materials Records has a number of fine story records (thirty in all) for young children. Stories are read by Ruby Dee and other excellent narrators. Among their best records are
1. *About Ourselves*
2. *In Our Neighborhood*
3. *Sh! Listen*
4. *All about Color*
5. *Touch and Tell*
6. *Stories That Make Us Think*
7. *What Will the Weather Be*
8. *Beginning in Science*
9. *Step into Space*
10. *Prose and Poetry for the Early Years*
11. *Wheels, Wings, and Things*

12. *Halloween*
13. *Christmas Is a Special Time*
14. *American Tall Tales*
15. *Folk Tales*
16. *Fables From East and West*

F. Foreign Language for Preschoolers
    1. *Songs in Spanish for Children,* Elena Travesi (Columbia)
    2. *Songs in French for Children,* Lucierne Vernay (Columbia)
    3. *Folksongs for Children of All Ages,* sung in Spanish and English by Jerry Vincent (Cantemos Records)
    4. *Building Spanish Vocabulary through Music* (CP Records)
    5. *Spanish-American Children's Songs* (Cantemos Records)
    6. *Songs in Spanish for Children,* Jean Rojas (Columbia)

G. Folk Songs for Children
    1. *Abiyoyo and Other Story Songs for Children,* Pete Seeger (Folkways)
    2. *The Wandering Folk Song,* Sam Hinton (Folkways)
    3. *Whoever Shall Have Some Good Peanuts?* Sam Hinton (Folkways)
    4. *Through Children's Eyes,* the Limelighters (RCA Victor)
    5. *Birds, Beasts, Bugs and Little Fishes,* Pete Seeger (Folkways)
    6. *Birds, Beasts, Bugs and Bigger Fishes,* Pete Seeger (Folkways)
    7. *Songs to Grow On,* Woody Guthrie (Folkways)
    8. *Songs to Grow On for Mother and Child,* Woody Guthrie (Folkways)
    9. *Woody Guthrie Children's Songs,* Bob and Louise de Cormier (Golden Records)
    10. *On Top of Spaghetti,* Tom Glazer (CMS Records)
    11. *American Folk Songs for Children,* Pete Seeger (Folkways)
    12. *Folk Songs for Young People,* Pete Seeger (Folkways)
    13. *American Game and Activity Songs for Children,* Pete Seeger (Folkways)
    14. *Goofing Off Suite,* Pete Seeger (Folkways)
    15. *American Play Parties,* Pete Seeger (Folkways)
    16. *Songs to Grow On, Vol. 2: School Days,* Woody Guthrie (Folkways)
    17. *Songs to Grow On, Vol. 3: American Work Songs,* Woody Guthrie (Folkways)
    18. *Ladybug, Ladybug and More Children's Songs,* Johnny Richardson (Folkways)
    19. *Sing a Rainbow and Other Children's Songs,* Ginni Clemens (Folkways)
    20. *Old-Time Songs for Children,* The New Lost City Ramblers (Folkways)

21. *Marching across the Green Grass and Other American Children's Game Songs,* Jean Ritchie (Folkways)
22. *Jean Ritchie Sings Songs and Games from the Southern Mountains,* Jean Ritchie (Folkways)
23. *Songs of Camp* (Folkways)
24. *The Wagoners Sing Folk Songs for Camp,* the Wagoners (Folkways)
25. *Seasons for Singing: A Summer Music Workshop of St. Paul's Church,* Ella Jenkins (Folkways)

H. Miscellaneous Songs
    1. *Building a City* (Young People's Records)
    2. *Train to the Zoo, Ranch, Farm* (Young People's Records)
    3. *Won't You Be My Friend,* Marcia Berman and Patty Zeitlin (Educational Activities Records)
    4. *Muffin in the City, Muffin in the Country* (Young People's Records)
    5. *Our House Is Upside Down,* Marais and Miranda (Peripole Records)

I. Music of Other Cultures
    1. *Bouzoukee—The Music of Greece,* Iordanis Tsomidis, Bouzoukee, others
    2. *The Koto Music of Japan,* Master Hagiwara, Master Hatta, Master Kitagawa, Master Kukusui
    3. *Caledonia!,* the Macpherson Singers and Dancers of Scotland
    4. *The Pennywhistlers,* seven young women sing folk songs from Bulgaria, Czechoslovakia, Hungary, the U.S.A., the U.S.S.R., Yugoslavia
    5. *The Real Mexico in Music and Song,* recorded in the State of Michoacan by Henrietta Yurchenco, E. Ramos, and T. Naranjo
    6. *A Heritage of Folk Song from Old Russia,* Maria Christova
    7. *Music of Bulgaria,* soloists, chorus and orchestra of the Ensemble of the Bulgarian Republic
    8. *The Real Bahamas in Music and Song,* Peter K. Siegel and Jody Stecher
    9. *Classical Music of India,* John Levy
    10. *Tahiti: The Gauguin Years,* Francis Maziere
    11. *Favorite Songs of Japanese Children* (Bowmar)

J. Intellectual Stimulation
    If you do nothing more than just play these records for your child, he will be gaining a great deal of information. If you take the time to discuss them with him, he will be getting a wealth of information!
    1. *It's A Small World,* Disneyland Boys Choir (Disneyland Records) Can be enjoyed simply for the melody and songs, but it is also a very interesting geography lesson.
    2. *Noisy and Quiet, Big and Little,* Tom Glazer (Camden)

3. *Why Mommy?* Tom Glazer and Paul Tripp (Columbia)
4. *Listening Skills for Pre-readers,* Volume I
5. *Listening Skills for Pre-readers,* Volume II
6. *Listening Skills for Pre-readers,* Volume III
7. *Listening Skills for Pre-readers,* Volume IV (Classroom Materials Records)
8. *Sounds for Young Readers,* Volume I (Classroom Materials Records)
9. *Acting Out the ABC's—A Child's Primer of Alphabet, Counting and Acting Out Songs* (Disneyland Records) Illustrated book and LP record.
10. *Counting Song and Alphabet Song* (Peter Pan Records)
11. *Play and Learn,* Suzy Mallery (Singalong Educational Records)
12. *Singing Sounds,* Album 1 (Bowmar)
13. *Singing Sounds,* Album 2: Simplified Phonics Set to Music (Bowmar)
14. *Winter, Spring, Summer, Fall* (Columbia)
15. *Do You Know How You Grow Inside?* Isabel Abrams and Roxana Alsberg (Folkways)
16. *Do You Know How You Grow Outside?* Isabel Abrams and Roxana Alsberg (Folkways)
17. *Musical Experiences for Basic Learning Readiness: Who Am I?* Lois Raebeck (Classroom Materials Records)
18. *Finger Play Songs and Games* (Classroom Materials Records)
19. *Dance, Sing and Listen with Miss Nelson and Bruce* (Dimension Five Records)
20. *Developing Body-Space Perception Motor Skills,* Album 1 (Classroom Materials Records)
21. *Getting to Know Myself,* Hap Palmer (Educational Activities Records)
22. *Learning Basic Skills through Music,* Hap Palmer (Educational Activities Records)
23. *Learning Basic Skills through Music,* Volume 2, Hap Palmer (Educational Activities Records)
24. *Learning Basic Skills through Music,* Volume 3, Hap Palmer (Educational Activities Records)
25. *Vocabulary,* Hap Palmer (Educational Activities Records)
26. *Vocabulary and Concepts,* Hap Palmer (Educational Activities Records) All of the Hap Palmer records are excellent for teaching such things as numbers, colors, how to tell time, basic math concepts, and language development.

K. Science

All of the records listed below are Motivation Records. These records are superb. I cannot praise them too highly. They introduce a preschool child to science concepts in a delightful way that he can understand.

1. *Space Songs*, Tom Glazer and Dottie Evans
2. *Weather Songs*, Tom Glazer
3. *Nature Songs*, Marais and Miranda
4. *More Nature Songs*, Marais and Miranda
5. *Experiment Songs*, Dorothy Collins
6. *Energy and Motion Songs*, Tom Glazer and Dottie Evans

III. Middle Childhood (ages six to ten)

As I mentioned earlier, many of the records which your child liked as a preschooler he will continue to like in the early years of middle childhood. Singers like Sam Hinton, Ella Jenkins, Pete Seeger, Woody Guthrie, Hap Palmer, and Tom Glazer will still be enjoyed. Story records and the Motivation science records will continue to appeal to your child. So if you have not yet gotten any of these records for your child, don't feel that you dare not buy him one of these merely because he has turned six years old.

However, in middle childhood he is now ready for new records, new intellectual and musical concepts which were too advanced for him as a preschooler.

A. Folk Songs
1. *900 Miles and Other Railroad Songs*, Cisco Houston (Folkways)
2. *Cowboy Ballads*, Cisco Houston (Folkways)
3. *You Can Sing It Yourself*, Robin Christenson (Folkways)
4. *You Can Sing It Yourself*, Volume 2, Robin Christenson (Folkways)
5. *Frontier Ballads*, Pete Seeger (Folkways)
6. *Simplified Folk Songs*, Hap Palmer (Educational Activities Records)
7. *Pueblo Indians* (Caedmon)
8. *Navajo Skip Dance and Two-Step Songs* (Indian House Records)

B. Adventure Stories by Spoken Arts Records
In this series, which has great appeal for boys, adventure and sea stories are re-created for the ear in excellent dramatizations, with music and sound effects. Children eight years old and up should enjoy this series, which consists of ten stories:
1. *Robinson Crusoe*
2. *Captains Courageous*
3. *Treasure Island*
4. *20,000 Leagues Under the Sea*
5. *Kidnapped*
6. *The Swiss Family Robinson*
7. *Kim*
8. *Around the World in Eighty Days*
9. *The Time Machine*
10. *The Lost World*

C. Tales of Mystery and Terror by Spoken Arts Records

Again, this will appeal to children of eight years and up, particularly boys. There are four titles in the series:

1. *Dracula*
2. *Frankenstein*
3. *Dr. Jekyll and Mr. Hyde*
4. *The Monkey's Paw and a Terribly Strange Bed*

D. Folk Tales

These folk and fairy tales by Spoken Arts Records come in either records or cassettes and will appeal to children aged eight years and up.

1. *American Tall Tales,* Volume 1, Ed Begley, (Caedmon)
2. *American Tall Tales,* Volume 2, Ed Begley, (Caedmon)
3. *American Tall Tales,* Volume 3, Ed Begley, (Caedmon)
4. *Folk and Fairy Tales from Ireland* (Spoken Arts)
5. *Folk and Fairy Tales from Japan* (Spoken Arts)
6. *Folk and Fairy Tales from Russia* (Spoken Arts)
7. *Folk and Fairy Tales from Africa* (Spoken Arts)
8. *Folk and Fairy Tales from Italy* (Spoken Arts)
9. *Folk and Fairy Tales from Mexico* (Spoken Arts)

E. Record-Book Combinations by Scholastic

Each combination includes a seven-inch LP record and a Scholastic paperback book. Compared to the price of other records, the price is surely right at $1.95! Currently there are sixteen in the series, which appeal to children from six to ten.

1. *Benjamin Budge and Barnaby Ball*
2. *The Bigger Giant*
3. *Charlie the Tramp*
4. *City Mouse, Country Mouse*
5. *Clifford's Tricks*
6. *Congo Boy*
7. *The Emperor's New Clothes*
8. *Hi Diddle Diddle*
9. *Jack and the Beanstalk*
10. *Old MacDonald Had a Farm*
11. *Puss in Boots*
12. *Rich Cat, Poor Cat*
13. *Stone Soup*
14. *That's What Friends Are For*
15. *The Life and Words of Martin Luther King, Jr.*
16. *Folksong Festival Sampler*

F. The Newberry Award Book Records, by Miller-Brody Productions

These are dramatized versions of the Newberry Award-winning books.

There are thirty-two titles in the complete series at present. These will
appeal to children from eight years of age on up. Here are some examples
of the records available. (You will find a complete list of Newberry
Award winners in Appendix C.)

    1. *Call It Courage*
    2. *Ginger Pye*
    3. *The Cat Who Went to Heaven*
    4. *The Matchlock Gun*
    5. *Johnny Tremain*
    6. *It's Like This, Cat*
    7. *Sounder*
    8. *The Cricket in Times Square*

G. The Music Appreciation Series by CMS Records

    If your child is particularly interested in music, here is a series of
records with a biography of each composer in words and music. An
excellent series, which will appeal to children from eight years old on up.
At present there are twelve composers in the series:

    1. *Franz Liszt*
    2. *Wolfgang Mozart*
    3. *Franz Schubert*
    4. *Ludwig Beethoven*
    5. *Felix Mendelssohn*
    6. *Josef Haydn*
    7. *Peter Tchaikovsky*
    8. *Johann Bach*
    9. *Frederic Chopin*
    10. *Johannes Brahms*
    11. *Robert Schumann*
    12. *Claude Debussy*

H. Other Records Introducing a Child to Music
    1. *Invitation to Music,* Elie Siegmeister (Folkways). This record teaches
       music in a simple and interesting way, covering such areas as melody,
       rhythm, harmony, tone color, form, counterpoint, fugue, and jazz.
    2. *The Story of Jazz,* Langston Hughes (Folkways)

I. Intellectual Stimulation Records
    1. *Dancing Words,* Henry Glass (Educational Activities Records).
       Teaches reading and language skills in an exciting way to children
       aged five to eight.
    2. *Dancing Numerals,* Henry Glass (Educational Activities Records).
       Teaches math concepts for children of ages five to seven.

3. *Math Readiness, Addition and Subtraction,* Hap.Palmer (Educational Activities Records). Excellent.
4. *Singing Multiplication Tables,* Hap Palmer (Educational Activities Records). Another fine Hap Palmer record.
5. *The World of Man, Volume 1: His Work,* Harold Courlander, noted cultural anthropologist (Folkways)

J. Electronic Music

This is music made with materials of a purely electronic nature or natural sound sources recorded on tape with many manipulations of speed, filtering, and cutting. Electronic music seeks to express ideas and emotions by this new method.
1. *The "In" Sound from Way Out,* Perry-Kingsley (Vanguard Records)
2. *Short Circuits,* Ruth White (Angel Records). Classics such as "Flight of the Bumblebee," "Anvil Chorus," etc., "turned on" with the Moog Synthesizer and other electronics.

IV. Preadolescence and Adolescence

It is only through the stage of middle childhood that we can suggest records or tapes that will appeal to most children. When your child becomes a pre-adolescent and later an adolescent, his music and record taste becomes a highly individualistic matter. By these ages he will be into teen-age records and tapes and adult records and tapes.

If his taste is rock music, you will need to know which particular groups he likes if you are going to buy him a record as a present. If he is into folk singers, or classical music, or whatever, you will need to know his individual taste. Particularly when he is an adolescent, you may think his musical taste is horrible. But remember, one of the reasons adolescents choose their particular brand of music is that adults generally hate it—and so it becomes a socially accepted part of the adolescent rebellion!

Appendix E
A Survival Kit for Fathers

A LIST OF BASIC BOOKS TO AID FATHERS IN THE RAISING
AND EDUCATION OF THEIR CHILDREN

Many times a father will want some information to help him in the raising of his child, but he doesn't know where to get it. Suppose, for example, you wanted to teach a three-year-old to swim. Where would you turn to get this information? Or suppose you want to delve further into the subject of child discipline than what I have covered in this book. To what books would you turn?

The purpose of this annotated list of books is to help you find just about any kind of information you might need in raising your child. Some of the books on this list are for all fathers, because they deal with aspects of child raising that are universal. Others will apply only to fathers in special situations, such as a father of twins or a divorced father or a situation where there has recently been a death in the family.

I enthusiastically recommend every book on this list. That does not mean I agree 100 percent with everything in each book, but that, on the whole, I believe the book is a wise and thoughtful discussion of some aspect of child raising. I refer to the hardcover edition of each book, unless I specifically mention that it is available in paperback also.

A. Books Covering the Stages of Development in Children
1. *The Magic Years,* Selma Fraiberg (Scribners). You will gain a new understanding of the first five years of your child's life by reading this book. However, take with a grain of salt the author's belief that parents should not spank children.
2. *The Child under Six,* James Hymes (Prentice-Hall). Another clearly written, down-to-earth book which covers the development of the child through the first five years.
3. *Baby Learning through Baby Play,* Ira Gordon (St. Martin's Press, hardback and paperback). Fathers often don't know how to play with babies. This book, a guide to the first two years of life for parents, shows fathers way of playing with their babies which will enhance the child's emotional and intellectual development. I recommend it highly to help a father get off to a good start in developing a relationship with his new baby.
4. *Baby and Child Care,* Benjamin Spock (Pocket Books, paperback). I doubt that any book will ever replace Spock for an excellent and thorough coverage of the medical and physical aspects of infancy and early childhood. However, it is unwise to use Spock as a complete guide to raising children, for many significant aspects of child raising are left out. Spock is particularly deficient in discussing the intellectual development of children in the first five years and the importance of intellectual stimulation during those crucial early years. A careful glance at the index of Spock's latest revised edition will show you the general medical orientation of the book and what important subjects are left out. For example, the index contains one reference to erythroblastosis, three references to hernias, four references to hexachlorophene soap . . . but there is not one single reference to intellectual stimulation, cognitive development, or kindergarten!
5. *How to Parent,* Fitzhugh Dodson (Nash; New American Library, paperback). I think this book is the single most complete guide for parents to both the emotional and intellectual development of the child from birth to age six. But I could be biased. This book covers the material on the intellectual development of the child which Spock leaves out. The two chapters on discipline apply not only to the preschool child, but to the school-age child as well.
6. *Childhood and Adolescence,* Joseph Stone and Joseph Church (Random House). A college-level textbook covering birth through adoles-

cence. It is scientific and comprehensive, but it is also *readable*, which makes it one of the most unusual college texts in existence. You may want to skip over some of the early sections of the book. They go into considerable physiological detail which has little practical value to a parent. Once past those sections, the rest of the book is delightful reading.

B. Books on Child Discipline
1. *Improving Your Child's Behavior,* Madeline Hunter and Paul Carlson (Bowmar). This book packs into 130 pages an immense amount of clear and practical advice to parents on how to discipline their child and improve his behavior. You are not likely to find the book in your local bookstore, but it is well worth having your bookstore order it. Or if you live too far from a bookstore, you can order it by mail from the publisher, Bowmar Books, 622 Rodier Drive, Glendale, California.
2. *Between Parent and Child,* Haim Ginott (Macmillan; Avon, paperback). This book was on the New York *Times* best seller list for over a year, and deservedly so. It is particularly effective in getting across to parents that they need to learn to empathetically tune in to the "coded language" a child is speaking through his behavior as well as his words. A really splendid book; however, I disagree with the author's belief that parents should not spank their children.
3. *Between Parent and Teenager,* Haim Ginott (Macmillan; Avon, paperback). I do not believe that this book really comes to grips with today's teen-age scene. However, I still think it is well worth reading. Think of it as an expansion of *Between Parent and Child,* and you will get a great deal out of it.
4. *New Ways in Discipline,* Dorothy Baruch (McGraw-Hill). The late Dorothy Baruch has been one of the most important influences on my own thinking about parenting. She has written many books, and she has never written a poor book for parents. This is one of her best. Her writing is always informed, practical, and lively.
5. *Parent Effectiveness Training,* Thomas Gordon (Peter Wyden). If I had to buy only one book on discipline, I think I would buy this one. Gordon's book deals more effectively than any other with the thorny problem of conflict between parents and children, using the author's "no-lose" method of handling conflict.

I heartily endorse all of the methods Dr. Gordon describes. But fathers should be warned that things are not liable to work out quite so neatly in real real life as they seem to in the pages of this book! And I disagree with Dr. Gordon when he says that the use of the methods he advocates will eliminate the rebellion of adolescents against their parents. I don't care how good the parents' methods are; I regard it as a normal psychological developmental task for adolescents to rebel against their parents.

6. *Children: The Challenge,* Rudolph Dreikurs (Duell, Sloan and Pierce). This book is basically a revision of Dreikurs's earlier book, *The Challenge of Parenthood,* which is still a good book to read. *Children* is a really splendid book on discipline, full of examples which illustrate very well the points made in the book. You will see yourself and your children in this book many times.

7. *Living with Children: New Methods for Parents and Teachers,* Gerald Patterson and Elizabeth Gullion (Research Press). This is a unique book. It is a programmed book, which means it is like a teaching machine in book form. This makes it particularly easy to read. It is based on the same principles of reinforcement I discussed in my chapter on discipline.

8. *Play Therapy,* Virginia Axline (Ballantine, paperback). This book is actually not written for parents, but for child therapists. Fortunately, however, Dr. Axline writes in such a clear and interesting manner that any parent can also profit from reading her book. The book describes the "reflection of feelings" technique of Dr. Carl Rogers as applied to children in play therapy. There are many verbatim accounts of what the child said and how the therapist reflected the child's feeling. By using your imagination you can see how this same technique can be applied in the home.

C. Books Which Help Fathers Understand the World from the Child's Point of View

1. *Summerhill: A Radical Approach to Child Rearing,* A. S. Neill (Hart; hardcover and paperback). The subtitle describes the book accurately: a radical book on child raising and education, discussing the author's theories and experience with children at his school, Summerhill, in England. I do not agree with all of Mr. Neill's theories; for example, I believe he overplays the role of sex in causing neurosis. Nevertheless, I think it is a book every parent should read. It shakes up parental complacency and gives some basic insights into the way children look at the world. I make a practice of rereading it *once a year.* I feel I am more sympathetic toward my children for at least a week after I have read it!

2. *The Complete Book of Children's Play,* Ruth Hartley and Robert Goldenson (Crowell). This book is exactly what its title says it is: *the single, most complete guide to understanding children's play from*

birth through adolescence. It is a magnificent book, which all too few parents know about. The authors obviously have an immense background in the scientific literature on play, a thorough knowledge of children, and the capacity to write in a simple and interesting manner. A gold mine of practical information for fathers concerning all aspects of your child's play. You will refer to it again and again.

3. *Your Child's Play*, Arnold Arnold (Essandess Special Edition, paperback). This is a revision of Arnold's classic book, *How to Play with Your Child*, now, unfortunately, out of print. A sensitive, down-to-earth book which can help a father understand the play of his child and participate in that play. A splendid book.

4. *Child's Play: A Creative Approach to Playspace for Today's Children*, David Aaron and Bonnie P. Winawer (Harper and Row). Another excellent book, which will illuminate the meaning of children's play for adults. Includes a fine section of instructions for a father who wants to build a backyard playspace for his children.

5. *Play and Playthings for the Preschool Child*, Elizabeth Matterson (Penguin, paperback). A really excellent book. Similar to Hartley and Goldenson's book in that Mrs. Matterson stresses the importance of play for the intellectual and emotional development of children in the preschool years. She shows how natural materials and improvised playthings in the home are far superior to "gimmick" toys.

6. *Your Inner Child of the Past*, Hugh Missildine (Simon and Schuster). Written mainly as a book for adults to help them understand themselves, this book can help a father see the connection between different patterns of child raising and their effect on the adult personality.

7. *Understanding Children*, Richard Gardner (Jason Aronson, Inc.). A gold mine of information for fathers about what goes on in the minds of children and how fathers can better handle their children. Covers a wide range of topics such as parent-child love and parent-child pseudolove, self-esteem, childhood sexuality, dealing with guilt, dealing with anger, children's play, education, and television.

8. *Your Child's Sensory World*, Lise Liepmann (Dial Press). A unique book for parents, particularly in our culture, which does little or nothing to train children to the full development and use of their senses. I think the most valuable part of the book is part three, which contains games a parent can play with his child to increase his youngster's skills in hearing, seeing, touching, moving (kinesthetic perception), smelling, and tasting. These games need little or no preparation or special materials, can be incorporated into the daily life of the child with no special practice, and are fun to play. If you

find yourself getting bogged down in the more theoretical material at the beginning of the book, skip over to part three and start to use the games.

D. Books to Help Fathers in the Education of Their Children

1. *Give Your Child a Superior Mind,* Siegfried and Therese Engelmann (Simon and Schuster). An absolute must for parents interested in the intellectual development of their children in the crucial preschool years. Concentrates exclusively on the intellectual development of the child and does not deal with emotional or social development. I like especially how specific and realistic the authors are in telling parents how to go about providing a stimulating environment for their child. For example, in telling parents how to teach a preschool child to differentiate left from right, the Engelmanns point out that this is one of the most difficult concepts imaginable to teach a young child. They suggest specific ways to teach the child this important concept; but they state that it may take him a year or more to learn it. This is typical of the down-to-earth nature of the Engelmanns' advice. They give very specific teaching instructions to parents, including the amount of time to spend teaching each concept. They avoid extravagant claims and specious promises.

2. *How to Raise a Brighter Child,* Joan Beck (Trident Press). Another very fine book instructing parents in how to provide a stimulating intellectual environment for their children in the first five years of life. Packed with information for parents, it is an excellent supplement to the Engelmann book. Mrs. Beck is a journalist rather than a behavioral scientist, and for that reason at some points in the book she is a little naive. For example, in the chapter on the Montessori method, she is apparently unaware that good nursery schools in the United States have for many years been working with young children in ways which she thinks are a monopoly of Montessori schools. Nevertheless, it is still an excellent book, and I would recommend it most highly.

3. *Thinking Is Child's Play,* Evelyn Sharp (E. P. Dutton). A real educational bonanza for parents. The first part of the book is devoted to a theoretical overview of how young children learn to think, based on the work of the French psychologist Piaget and of Americans such as Jerome Bruner of Harvard, Robert Karplus of the University of California, and Patrick Suppes of Stanford. The second part of the book contains twenty-two beginning games and eighteen advanced games which will teach logical thinking to young children. These mind-stretching games can be played by a father and child using the

most ordinary materials, such as playing cards, baby-food jar tops, cellophane tape, paper plates, napkins, string, and spools. This book is on a par with the Engelmanns' book and is recommended just as enthusiastically.

4. *A Parent's Guide to Children's Education,* Nancy Larrick (Trident Press; Pocket Books, paperback). Although this book is available at lower cost in paperback, I strongly advise buying it in hardcover. This is *the* guide to the education of your child through the elementary grades. It tells you what your child will be learning in the different subject areas at school. It is also full of specific suggestions as to how you can enrich his education at home. The most basic reference book any father of a grade-school youngster could own. The only weaknesses of the book are that the section on the new math is short and inadequate, and the new English is not covered at all. Dr. Larrick writes clearly and interestingly. This book has deservedly become a classic in its field.

5. *Tested Ways to Help Your Child Learn,* Virginia Warren (Prentice-Hall). Along with Dr. Larrick's book, this is the most comprehensive and helpful book for parents that I know of. It is an encyclopedia of specific suggestions for children from preschool through high school. It is a book to which you will refer again and again for your child.

E. A Father's Guide to Children's Books

1. *A Parent's Guide to Children's Reading,* Dr. Nancy Larrick (Trident Press; Pocket Books, paperback). Absolutely indispensable for parents! The most comprehensive guide available to books for children up to twelve years of age.

2. *Your Child's Reading Today,* Josette Frank (Doubleday). Equally as good as Dr. Larrick's book. Unfortunately not available in paperback. More comprehensive than Dr. Larrick's book, in that it covers the adolescent years adequately.

3. *Best Books for Children,* Patricia Allen (R. R. Bowker, paperback). This book includes adult books for adolescents and 3,700 titles of books currently available, annotated and arranged by age and grade level. An indispensable guide for parents in buying books for their children.

F. For Fathers with a Gifted Child

1. *Helping Your Gifted Child,* Ruth Strang (Cutton). Fathers of intellectually gifted children often need special help in understanding and raising these children. Dr. Strang has had considerable experience with gifted children, and her book is jam-packed with specific and down-to-earth suggestions for parents.

2. *Your Gifted Child: A Guide for Parents,* Florence Brumbaugh (Collier, paperback). Another excellent book for the father of a gifted child.

G. A Father's Guide to Doing Things with His Child
1. *Exploring Nature with Your Child,* Dorothy Shuttlesworth (Hawthorn). If you are at all interested in the world of nature, camping or hiking, I cannot recommend this book too highly. We have used it on many camping trips with our family. I have learned a great deal by using the book to educate my children! Mrs. Shuttlesworth has a magnificent way of opening up the world of nature and living things in a clear, down-to-earth, and fascinating manner.
2. *How to Fly a Kite, Catch a Fish, Grow a Flower,* Alvin Schwartz (Pocket Books). Written by a father of four, this book covers just about everything you and your child could do together: bike riding, roller skating, swimming, boating, fishing, family camping, ice skating, skiing, baseball, football, basketball, tennis, hobbies, magic, pets . . . you name it. A book every father should own.
3. *A Parent's Guide to Children's Play and Recreation,* Alvin Schwartz (Collier Books). Another excellent book by Alvin Schwartz. His emphasis is on creative play and recreation that is absorbing, but not elaborate and expensive. Covers such areas as play materials, books, trips, parties for children, games, music, and even includes directions on how to make a simple workbench for your child.
4. *Steven Caney's Toy Book,* Steven Caney (Workman Publishers). A most unique book. Contains "recipes" for making fifty-one creative toys, some of which the child can make by himself and some of which he will need your help with. These toys can be made from everyday objects which cost little or nothing. You and your child will have a wonderful time making them!
5. *The Rainy Day Book,* Alvin Schwartz (Trident Press). Another excellent book by Mr. Schwartz. This one is designed to be a complete guide to rainy-day activities for children, as well as a survival kit for their harassed parents on such days. The book contains quiet games of all types, arts and crafts projects a child can handle by himself, science experiments, nature projects, dramatics, music, hobbies, as well as active indoor games for letting off steam.

H. When Your Child Is Ill
When a child becomes ill, fathers often tend to abdicate their responsibility and assume that "mother will take care of it," as if it is her job and hers alone to see that the child gets well. This is unfortunate in many ways. What if mother is not around and father

has to take action in some medical emergency? Or even if that does not occur, the child will still learn to perceive the situation of being sick as one in which mother takes responsibility for seeing that he is cared for, but father does not. The following books can be of great help to a father in aiding him to assume his share of the responsibility when his child is sick.

1. *When Your Child Is Ill: A Guide to Infectious Diseases in Childhood,* Samuel Karelitz (Random House). A thorough and comprehensive book. Not to be used as a substitute for a doctor, but as an aid which answers the questions parents ask both before and after the doctor's visit. More than 1,000 specific questions which parents ask repeatedly are answered in this book.

2. *Childhood Illness,* Jack Shiller (Stein and Day). A guide to children's illnesses: to indicate when a simple disease can be treated at home, to alert parents to when competent medical help should be sought, and to enable young parents to take better care of their sick children. Clear and down-to-earth advice by a competent pediatrician.

3. *Young Children in Hospitals,* James Robertson (Basic Books). A psychological analysis of the experiences of young children in hospitals, with suggestions for minimizing their anxiety and distress.

4. *Play for Convalescent Children in Hospitals and at Home,* Anne Marie Smith (A. S. Barnes). Stresses the value of play in the recovery of a convalescent child. Gives many practical suggestions for play activities suitable for convalescent children.

5. *Johnny Goes to the Hospital,* Josephine Sever (Houghton Mifflin). The story of Johnny, whose stomach hurt and who needed to go to the hospital to have it taken care of. A good book to read to preschool children to allay their fear of the strange world of a hospital.

6. *Johnny Visits His Doctor,* Josephine Sever (Children's Medical Center, 300 Longwood Avenue, Boston). A thirty-two-page booklet for parents to read to their preschool child before a visit to the doctor's office.

7. *Johnny's First Visit to His Dentist,* Josephine Sever (Children's Medical Center). Another thirty-two-page booklet to read to a preschool child before his first visit to the dentist.

I. Parties for Children

I always played an important part in the birthday parties we gave for all three of my children. Many times the mothers who brought or picked up the children would say things like, "Oh you could never get my husband involved in running a birthday party for kids." I think that's a shame, for such fathers don't realize what they are missing. However, a father does need to know how to gear the party to the age and stage of development of his child. That's exactly what this next book helps him to do.

1. *The Gesell Institute Party Book,* Frances Ilg, Louise Ames, Evelyn Goodenough Pitcher, and Irene Anderson (Harpers; Dell, paperback). Would you know the difference between planning and giving a birthday party for a two-year-old, a three-year-old, and a four-year-old? If you are not sure (and most fathers are not), this is the book for you. Discusses the planning and giving of parties for children in relation to their age and stage of development.

J. A Guide to Baby-Sitters
1. *A Parent's Guide to Better Baby-Sitting,* Faye Cobb (Pocket Books). A really excellent book, which I recommend enthusiastically to all parents. It discusses how to find a good baby-sitter and how to work with her to become a better baby-sitter. Part two of the book is a baby-sitter's manual. You can ask the baby-sitter to read this so that she can do a better job for you and your child. A "must" for all parents and a real buy at fifty cents.

K. A Father's Guide to Sex Education in the Home
1. *New Ways in Sex Education,* Dorothy Baruch (McGraw-Hill). By all odds the best book available for parents on how to handle the sex education of their children at home. Highly recommended.

The following are books for parents to read to preschool children or for grade-school children to read themselves. All of them are excellent.

2. *A Baby Is Born,* Milton Levine and Jean Seligmann (Golden Press)
3. *Before You Were a Baby,* Paul Showers and Kay Showers (Crowell)
4. *Growing Up,* Karl de Schweinitz (Macmillan)
5. *The Wonderful Story of How You Were Born,* Sidonie Gruenberg (Doubleday)
6. *Being Born,* Frances Strain (Meredith)

The group of books listed above will give your child all of the basic information he needs on sex up to the age of puberty. At puberty a whole new area of sex is going to open up, and he needs a different type of book to help him deal with it.

7. *Facts About Sex,* Sol Gordon (John Day). Dr. Gordon packs a lot of information for preadolescents and adolescents in this forty-three-page book full of practical advice and frank explanations. One of the

unusual features of the book is its definitions of sex slang. Dr. Gordon believes that once a young person knows what the slang words mean, he will not be anxious about them, and he will be less likely to use them as a means of making his parents angry.

8. *Boys and Sex,* Wardell Pomeroy (Delacorte Press). There have been numerous books on sex for puberty-age children, but in my opinion most of them have been pretty poor. Dr. Pomeroy has now changed that situation with his book, *Boys and Sex,* and its companion, *Girls and Sex.* Dr. Pomeroy pulls no punches, but "tells it like it is." I think both books are excellent, straightforward, and informative.

9. *Girls and Sex,* Wardell Pomeroy (Delacorte Press). Of the same high caliber as Dr. Pomeroy's book for boys. Both of these books are ideal for youngsters to read around the age of puberty (eleven, twelve, thirteen).

L. A Father's Guide to Children's Art

  1. A series of books by Harvey Weiss (Young Scott Co.)
     a) *Paper, Ink, and Roller*
     b) *Sticks, Spools, and Feathers*
     c) *Clay, Wood, and Wire*
     d) *Pencil, Pen, and Brush*
     e) *Ceramics from Clay to Kiln*

  These books are written for grade-school children. However, fathers can also use them for wonderful times with their children. Or fathers can use them for their own pleasure and instruction. These are the most unique how-to-do-it books on art in existence. They encourage real creativity in both children and adults, rather than prescribing rigid step-by-step formulas.

  2. *Creative Crafts for Everyone,* G. Alan Turner (Viking). Contains hundreds of ideas you can use for art projects with your child.

M. Guide to Children's Music and Dance

  1. *Children Discover Music and Dance,* Emma Sheehy (Holt, Rinehart, Winston). Thorough, comprehensive, and practical, this book covers preschool through the elementary grades. Suggests how you can introduce singing, various instruments, phonograph records, and dance forms into the day-to-day experience of children. The most basic book of its kind.

N. Teaching Young Children to Swim

  1. *Teaching an Infant to Swim,* Virginia Newman (Harcourt, Brace and World). Mrs. Newman majored in physical education and minored in psychology in college. She has been a private swimming instructor

for many years and has an ideal background to write this book. She believes it is valuable for children to learn to swim as early as possible, because of the child's safety in and around water. In addition, learning to swim early will build the child's self-confidence and open up to him a lifetime of enjoyment in the water. An excellent book.

2. *Teaching Young Children to Swim and Dive,* Virginia Newman (Harcourt, Brace and World). In this sequel to her earlier book, Mrs. Newman deals this time with the child from five to ten years old. She provides step-by-step instructions for teaching swimming and diving to children between these ages. All of her advice is psychologically sound. She starts by explaining how to get a child used to the water, then how to teach him the "dog paddle," and how to move on to the Australian crawl, the backstroke, and a simple forward dive. Excellent.

O   For Fathers of Twins

1. *Twins: Twice the Trouble, Twice the Fun,* Betsy Gehman (Lippincott). Although there are over four million twins in the United States, there is precious little available in written form to help a parent raise twins. It should be obvious that the psychological job of raising twins is *not* the same as that of raising two siblings who are not twins. Mrs. Gehman stresses the theme of individuality as the key to raising twins, asserting that individuality is what twins value above all else. I agree with her 100 percent that this idea is the key to raising twins in a psychologically healthy manner. Her book is full of practical and down-to-earth suggestions, all the way from the easiest ways to feed twins when they are infants, to the address of the National Mothers of Twins Club. No father of a twin should be without this book.

P. For Parents of a Handicapped Child

1. *Caring for Your Disabled Child,* Benjamin Spock and Marion Lerrigo (Macmillan; Fawcett, paperback). A most excellent and comprehensive book for parents with a child who is blind, deaf, crippled, or in any way handicapped. Contains a useful annotated bibliography to which parents may turn for further help in understanding their child and his particular disability. Highly recommended.

2. *The Directory for Exceptional Children: Education and Training Facilities,* Porter Sargent (Porter Sargent, publisher). A very basic aid for parents of handicapped children. Lists 2,000 programs for the training and education of exceptional children, including 1,100 clinics. Gives information on associations, societies, foundations, and

federal and state agencies which are directly concerned with handicapped children.

Q. The Child with Speech Problems
   1. *Your Child's Speech Problems,* Charles Van Riper (Harpers). Discusses home treatment of speech defects in children. Especially helpful if you live far from a speech clinic.

R. The Mentally Retarded Child
   1. *When a Child Is Different,* Maria Egg (John Day). Fathers of a mentally retarded child are often unwilling to face the physical and psychological facts about their child. Consequently they are greatly handicapped in guiding his emotional and intellectual growth. This is a splendid book, full of wise counsel and specific suggestions.
   2. *Child in the Shadows: A Manual for Parents of Retarded Children,* Edward French and Clifford Scott (Lippincott). Another excellent practical guide.

S. If You Are Planning to Adopt a Child
   1. *If You Adopt a Child,* Carl and Helen Doss (Holt, Rinehart, and Winston). A complete handbook for childless couples planning to adopt a child. The Dosses themselves are adoptive parents, and they cover just about everything a couple planning to adopt a child needs to know.
   2. *The Adopted Family,* Florence Rondell and Ruth Michaels (Crown, revised edition). Contains two books: Book I—*You and Your Child: A Guide for Adoptive Parents* gives excellent and specific advice on all phases of adoption and after. Book II—*The Family That Grew* is a picture and story book to read to the adopted child and to use in explaining the situation to him. I think all adoptive parents should buy this book.
   3. *Adoption and After,* Louise Raymond (Harper and Row). Covers all phases of adoption and its aftermath, including specific procedures for telling the child he is adopted. Excellent.

T. Books for Fathers to Help Them Understand Drugs and the Drug Scene
   1. *A Parent's Guide to the Prevention and Control of Drug Abuse,* Paul Goldhill (Henry Regnery). If you had to buy only one book which would help you prevent your youngster from turning to drug abuse or give you specific directions as to what to do if he is already on drugs, this is the one to buy. Dr. Goldhill points out that drug abuse stems from psychologically unhealthy family relationships. He goes on to show how healthy family relationships can be developed or, if

they are already fractured, how they can be repaired. The book is written simply, clearly, and interestingly.

2. *Overcoming Drugs,* Donald Louria (McGraw-Hill). Dr. Louria "knows where it's at" with respect to the drug scene. The heart of his book, as far as fathers are concerned, is the section entitled "A Program for Parents." However, the rest of the book provides valuable information on drugs and the drug scene which parents should know if they are going to discuss the subject intelligently with their adolescents.

3. *You, Your Child, and Drugs,* by the staff of the Child Study Association of America (The Child Study Press). A seventy-two-page booklet packed full of helpful information for parents. Covers such topics as why youngsters misuse drugs, specific information on various drugs, where to go for help, sources for information, counseling, and treatment. A very helpful booklet.

4. *Marijuana, A Signal of Misunderstanding: The Official Report of the National Commission on Marijuana and Drug Abuse* (New American Library, paperback). There is no questions that marijuana is the most widely used drug among American adolescents today. One of the gripes of many adolescents is that they know more of the facts about marijuana than their parents do (and many times, sad to say, it is true!). Any parent who wants to be sure of his facts about marijuana and stand on firm ground in dialogues with his adolescent should read this book. It is the report of the National Commission on Marijuana and Drug Abuse prepared for the President and Congress and is now available in paperback book form. This report deals with over fifty studies and projects conducted all over the world on every aspect of the marijuana question. The report answers such questions as, Who smokes marijuana, and why? Does it trigger crime? Is it a sexual stimulant? What is the effect of smoking marijuana on driving? What is the future of its medical and legal status? The report is a thorough and carefully documented piece of work.

U. For Divorced or Separated Fathers

1. *The Boys and Girls Book of Divorce,* Richard Gardner (Science House). In our increasingly divorce-ridden society, it seems obvious that someone should have written a book like this years ago. The author, a child psychiatrist, writes out of a sensitive and perceptive knowledge of the divorced parents and their children he has had as patients. It is an excellent book. It is written for children themselves to read, yet parents can also read it and receive great insight into how children feel about divorce. I recommend it most highly for any divorced family where the children involved are five years or older.

2. *Explaining Divorce to Children,* Earl Grollman (Beacon Press). A

most helpful book for divorced parents in explaining divorce to the children involved and helping them to accept it. It is a comforting book in that it helps divorced parents learn that all is not lost. It abounds with specific suggestions for them as to what to say and do with their children. It reports research showing that, contrary to popular opinion, there is significantly less juvenile delinquency among children of one-parent homes than among children of intact homes. Dr. Evelyn Pitcher's chapter on explaining divorce to young children is a particularly helpful one.

3. *Children of Divorce,* J. Louise Despert (Doubleday; Dolphin, paperback). This book will be very helpful to parents confronting the problem of their child's emotional adjustment during the process of divorce and afterward. Excellent psychological insight into the world of divorce as seen through the eyes of children.

4. *Parents without Partners: A Guide for Divorced, Widowed, or Separated Parents,* Jim Egleson and Janet Egleson (E. P. Dutton). One of the organizations I have been recommending for many years to friends or patients who are divorced or going through a divorce is Parents Without Partners. All parents of intact homes indulge in a kind of informal "group therapy" when we get together with other parents and "talk shop" about our children. Divorced parents need to do this also, for the world of the "parent without a partner" is different from the world of the two-parent home. A single parent needs the experience of belonging to a group of parents who will understand his unique problems. Parents who are not divorced have great difficulty truly understanding the situation of single parents. This book tells the story of the Parents Without Partners groups throughout the United States, and contains many helpful suggestions for single mothers and fathers.

5. *The World of the Formerly Married,* Morton Hunt (McGraw-Hill). A "must" for every divorced father. More than any other book I know, it helps you to understand your psychological situation as a divorced person and a single parent. I used it in a course I once taught for divorced parents and it received high praise from all the parents taking the course.

6. *The Successful Stepparent,* Helen Thomson (Harper and Row). Many divorced families are inevitably confronted with the problems of the relationship between stepparents and stepchildren, as well as between stepsiblings. Stepparents face a difficult job in defining the new roles and relationships among the divorced parents and children concerned, and in working out a satisfactory adjustment to those new roles and relationships. This book is a thoughtful and comprehensive analysis of all the many problems that arise in such a situation, such

as: Who takes care of discipline, and how? Should children be adopted by the new stepparent? How can friendly ties of affection be created between stepsiblings? Psychologically it is harder to be a stepparent than any other kind of parent. This book gives insight and guidance which will make the task of the stepparent easier.

V. What to Tell Your Child in Special Situations
    1. *What to Tell Your Child about Birth, Death, Illness, Divorce, and Other Family Crises*, Helene Arnstein (Bobbs-Merrill). A comprehensive book which discusses various crises which may arise in the life of a family and suggests how to handle these crises with your children. Covers such topics as illness and disability in the family, a divorce, when a mother needs to go to work, the remarriage of a parent, death, a family financial crisis, and when a parent is mentally ill. Happily, the book avoids pat formulas or superficial rules for meeting such critical situations. Instead, the author suggests looking at problem situations in new ways, which will stimulate the thinking of parents to face crisis situations constructively with their children.

I. Dr. Dodson's Whiz-Bang, Super-Economy Father's Survival Kit
(for $19.60, plus tax)

I am well aware that to buy all of the books I have recommended in this appendix would throw the family budget severely out of whack. And furthermore, your local library may not have some of them. So I have asked myself what books would be crucially important for a father to have in his home library to help him raise his children. I have come up with the following list of eleven books. I tried to keep the cost down by choosing only paperbacks. But I put *Parent Effectiveness Training* on the list even though it is not yet in paperback, because it is such an excellent book. Here is the list:
    1. *Baby and Child Care*, Benjamin Spock (Pocket Books), $.95
    2. *How to Parent*, Fitzhugh Dodson (New American Library), $1.25
    3. *Parent Effectiveness Training*, Thomas Gordon (Peter Wyden), $6.95
    4. *Between Parent and Child*, Haim Ginott (Avon), $1.25
    5. *The Complete Book of Children's Play*, Ruth Hartley and Robert Goldenson (Apollo paperback edition, Thomas Crowell), $3.95
    6. *Play Therapy*, Virginia Axline (Ballantine), $1.25
    7. *A Parent's Guide to Children's Reading*, Nancy Larrick (Pocket Books), $1.25
    8. *A Parent's Guide to Children's Education*, Nancy Larrick (Pocket Books), $1.25
    9. *How to Fly a Kite, Catch a Fish, Grow a Flower*, Alvin Schwartz (Pocket Books), $.75

10. *Accident Handbook,* Children's Hospital (Children's Medical Center, 300 Longwood Ave., Boston, Massachusetts), $.25
11. *A Parent's Guide to Better Baby-Sitting,* Faye Cobb (Pocket Books), $.50

A. Magazines and Newsletters for Parents

I cannot end this list of recommended reading for fathers having referred exclusively to books. I want to recommend some magazines and newsletters which also provide valuable information for fathers:

1. *Toy Review* (quarterly, $2.00 a year, 383 Elliot Street, Newton, Massachusetts 02164)
2. *Around the Neighborhood* (monthly, $2.00 a year, P.O. Box 1623, Columbus, Ohio 43216)
3. *The Open Home* (monthly, $5.95 a year, 159 West 53rd Street, New York, New York 10019)
4. *Sesame Street Magazine* (monthly, $3.50 a year, North Road, Poughkeepsie, New York 12601)
5. *Parent's Magazine* (monthly, $3.88 a year, 80 Newbridge Road, Bergenfield, New Jersey 07621)

Many of these magazines and newsletters are oriented more toward mothers than fathers, but don't let that stop you. They contain much valuable information you can make use of in raising your child, particularly in the early years. And who knows—maybe someday we will have a *Father's Newsletter,* oriented specifically to the father's role in raising children!

B. Two Organizations for Parents

Before closing this appendix, I want to call to your attention two organizations which are dedicated to helping parents (fathers as well as mothers) do a more effective job of parenting. I think it would be worth your while to know about these organizations and see if you want to make use of their services.

1. *Committee on Parenthood Education.* This is a nonprofit corporation based in San Diego, California. Every year it sponsors a one-day National Convention for Parents, usually held on the West Coast. The committee is also organizing parenting groups throughout the country; these are small (fifteen couples) groups of mothers and fathers who meet regularly, discuss books, listen to tapes, or have speakers, in order to improve the quality of their parenting. The organization also publishes a newsletter. To get on the mailing list, write COPE, P.O. Box 9533, San Diego, California.
2. *Parent Effectiveness Training.* This organization, begun by Dr.

Thomas Gordon, trains leaders who run eight-week classes, which meet once a week to teach parents to become more effective. Some of the classes are held during the day, and, of course, that usually limits them to mothers. But others are held in the evening, so that both father and mother can attend. I have recommended these classes enthusiastically to many, many fathers.

Sometimes parents balk at the expense of the classes, although I consider it quite reasonable for eight sessions. But I have discovered a good way to get reluctant fathers interested in the classes. I explain to them that not only will the class help them become better parents, but that there is no investment the father could make which would advance his business career more than to learn what Dr. Gordon calls "active listening" and what I have called in this book the "feedback technique." I tell the father to think of the people he deals with in business as basically little children encased in oversized bodies. Then he can use all of the techniques he learns in the classes with his business associates and customers. Once a father has really grasped this principle and has found it successful in dealing with difficult people in his business, then he is really motivated to use it at home with his children (sometimes with his wife, too!).

Some of you may be thinking, "Well, why not just read Dr. Gordon's book, *Parent Effectiveness Training*? Why take the class?" My answer to that is, If you're trying to learn to play golf, which is better—just reading a book on how to play golf, or taking eight lessons from the pro at the club?

If you are interested in finding out where your nearest Parent Effectiveness Training class is, you can write to P. E. T. Information, Effectiveness Training Associates, 110 South Euclid, Pasadena, California 91101.

Notes

CHAPTER FOUR
1. Fitzhugh Dodson, *How to Parent* (Nash Publishing Company, Los Angeles: 1970), p. 94.

CHAPTER FIVE
1. Thomas Gordon, *Parent Effectiveness Training* (Peter H. Wyden, Inc., New York: 1970), pp. 153-157.
2. Ibid.
3. Ibid.

CHAPTER SIX
1. Theodore Lidz, *The Person* (Basic Books, Inc., New York: 1968).
2. Arnold Gesell and Frances Ilg, *Infant and Child in the Culture of Today* (Harper & Row, New York: 1943).
3. Arnold Gesell and Frnaces Ilg, *The Child From Five To Ten,* Harper & Row, New York: 1946).
4. Ibid.
5. Dodson, *How to Parent.*

CHAPTER SEVEN
1. Dodson, *How to Parent.*
2. Lidz, *The Person.*
3. Dodson, *How to Parent.*
4. David Wechsler, *The Measurement and Appraisal of Adult Intelligence* (The Williams and Wilkins Co., Baltimore: 1958).
5. Dodson, *How to Parent.*

CHAPTER EIGHT
1. B. M. Atkinson and Whitney Darrow, *What Dr. Spock Didn't Tell Us* (Simon and Schuster, Inc., New York: 1959).
2. Ibid.
3. Robert Paul Smith, *Translations from the English* (Simon and Schuster, Inc., New York: 1958).
4. W. Cleon Skousen, *So You Want to Raise a Boy* (Doubleday & Company, Garden City, N.Y.: 1962).
5. Smith, *Translations from the English.*
6. Gesell and Ilg, *The Child From Five to Ten.*
7. Ibid.
8. The *New Yorker,* September 18, 1954.
9. Gesell and Ilg, *The Child from Five to Ten.*
10. Atkinson and Darrow, *What Dr. Spock Didn't Tell Us.*
11. Gesell and Ilg, *The Child from Five to Ten.*
12. Atkinson and Darrow, *What Dr. Spock Didn't Tell Us.*
13. Gesell and Ilg, *The Child from Five to Ten.*
14. Arnold Gesell, Frances Ilg, and Louise Ames, *Youth* (Harper & Row, New York: 1956).
15. Ibid.
16. Ibid.

CHAPTER NINE
1. Benjamin Fine and Lillian Fine, *How to Get the Best Education For Your Child* (Doubleday & Company, Garden City, N.Y.: 1962).
2. Haim Ginott, *Between Parent and Child* (The Macmillan Company, New York: 1965).
3. Booth Tarkington, *Penrod: His Complete Story* (Doubleday & Company, Garden City, N.Y.: 1970).
4. John Holt, *How Children Fail* (Pitman Publishing Corp., New York: 1969).
5. Ibid.
6. Ibid.
7. Joseph Stone and Joseph Church, *Childhood and Adolescence* (Random House, Inc., New York: 1968).
8. Tarkington, *Penrod.*
9. Robert Paul Smith, *Where Did You Go? Out. What Did You Do? Nothing* (W.W. Norton & Company, New York: 1957).
10. Bentz Plagemann, *This Is Goggle* (McGraw-Hill Book Company, New York: 1955).
11. Smith, *Where Did You Go? Out.*
12. Ibid.
13. Plagemann, *This Is Goggle.*
14. Sidonie Gruenberg, *The New Encyclopedia of Child Care and Guidance* (Doubleday & Company, Garden City, N.Y.: 1968).
15. Parkington, *Penrod.*

CHAPTER TEN
1. Fritz Redl, *When We Deal with Children* (Free Press, New York: 1966).
2. Ibid.
3. Plagemann, *This Is Goggle.*
4. Gesell, Ilg, and Ames, *Youth.*
5. Plagemann, *This Is Goggle.*
6. Redl, *When We Deal with Children.*
7. Flanders Dunbar, *Your Pre-Teenager's Mind and Body* (Hawthorne Books, 1962).
8. Gesell, Ilg, and Ames, *Youth.*
9. Ibid.
10. Ibid.
11. Ibid.
12. Ibid.
13. Ibid.

14. Ibid.

15. Eric Johnson, *How To Live Through Junior High School* (J.B. Lippincott Co., Philadelphia and New York: 1959).

16. Gesell, Ilg, and Ames, *Youth.*

17. Johnson, *How to Live Through Junior High School.*

18. Gesell, Ilg, and Ames, *Youth.*

19. Ibid.

20. Ibid.

21. Ibid.

22. Redl, *When We Deal with Children.*

CHAPTER ELEVEN

1. Anna Freud, "Adolescence," in *The Psychoanalytic Study of the Child* (International Universities Press, New York: 1958).

2. Lidz, *The Person.*

3. O. Spurgeon English, *Fathers Are Parents Too* (G.P. Putnam's Sons, New York: 1951).

4. Phyllis McGinley, *The Love Letters of Phyllis McGinley* (The Viking Press, Inc., New York: 1954).

5. Gesell, Ilg, and Ames, *Youth.*

6. Ibid.

7. Ibid.

8. Ibid.

9. Ibid.

10. Ibid.

11. Ibid.

12. Ibid.

CHAPTER TWELVE

1. Anita Bell, "The Role of Parents," in *Adolescents: Psychoanalytic Approach to Problems and Therapy,* edited by Sandor Lorand and Henry Schneer (Paul Hoeber, New York: 1961).

2. Joel Fort, "The Drug Explosion," *Playboy,* September 1972.

3. Donald Louria, *Overcoming Drugs* (McGraw-Hill, 1971).

4. Betty Lukas, "The Kids from St. Peters Are Building A School!" *Palos Verdes Peninsula News,* March 17, 1971.

5. Louria, *Overcoming Drugs.*

6. Paul Goldhill, *A Parent's Guide To the Prevention And Control of Drug Abuse* (Henry Regnery Co., Chicago: 1971).

7. Ibid.

8. Louria, *Overcoming Drugs.*

9. Goldhill, *A Parent's Guide.*

CHAPTER THIRTEEN

1. Gesell, Ilg, and Ames, *Youth.*

2. Ibid.

3. Ibid.

4. Robert C. Sorensen, *The Sorensen Report: Adolescent Sexuality in Contemporary America* (World Publishing Company, New York: 1973).

5. Ibid.

CHAPTER FOURTEEN

1. Russell Ray, *Divorce: A Man's Private Hell,* Singles Register, March 6-19, 1973.

2. Richard Gardner, *The Boys and Girls Book of Divorce* (Science House, Inc., New York: 1970).

3. J. Louise Despert, *Children of Divorce* (Doubleday & Company, Garden City, N.Y.: 1953).

4. Ibid.

5. Ibid.

6. Ibid.

Index

Gardner, Richard A. 368, 507, 516
Gender identity 100-07
Gentleness 20
Gesell, Arnold 22, 80, 84, 86, 143,
148-49, 241, 246, 269, 323, 326
Gifted children
books for fathers about 509-10
Ginnot, Haim 76, 505
Girl Scouts 209, 210, 213, 241
Girls
adolescent 282-83 (See also
Adolescence)
boys and 236, 248, 263, 277 (See
also Dating; Friendships)
development of separate from boys
167-68
difference from boys: explaining
111, 113
family romance and 122-24, 288-89,
290-92 (See also Family romance)
fathers and 213-14
friendships of 271 (See also
Friendships)
gangs and clubs. See Gangs and clubs
gender identity of. See Gender
identity
physical development of 167-68,
248-49
puberty and 248-49, 260-62
sexual awareness of 248
vocational choice for 333-34
Gordon, Ira 21, 379, 504
Gordon, Sol 168, 218, 249, 512-13
Gordon, Thomas 76, 505
Grades. See Report cards and grades
Groups, organized. See Organizations,
for children
Gruenberg, Sidonie M. 115
Guilt, parental. See Parental guilt

Habits, bad. See Bad habits
Hallucinogenic drugs 309-10 (See
also LSD; Marijuana; Mescaline)
Handicapped child: books for
parents of 514-15
Hartley, Ruth 92, 141, 506-07
Heroin 295, 310, 313, 314, 316, 317
High school graduation 347
Holt, John 198
Homework
fathers and 5
grade-school 5

how to study 188-92
parental attitude toward 193, 194,
195
Horror shows 154
House
how to childproof 26, 28
walls adapted to child 88
How to Father: organization of the
book 8
How to Parent 9, 22, 48, 67, 68, 76,
126, 186, 504
Humor, sense of 247
Hunger, infant's 17-18
Hunt, Morton 356, 517
Hunter, Madeline 76, 334, 505

Idealism of adolescence 266
Imitation 64-65
Impulse control 91-93
Incense 307
Incest 290-91 (See also Family
romance)
Independence: of preadolescence
255; of adolescence 259-60, 262,
278-79, 321-22, 324
Indian Guides 209, 212, 213
Indian Princesses 209, 210, 212, 213
Individuality 155
Infancy 13-23
Instruments, musical: learning to
play 157-58
Intellectual development
at various stages: infancy 21-23; pre-
school 125-32, 444-54, 496-97;
middle childhood 394-95, 500-01;
adolescence 263, 265-66, 274
selecting tools and materials for
126-27 (See also Appendices A-D
377-501)
Intelligence testing 328-29
Interests and activities, adolescent
272
Intimacy, development of. See
Friendships
Introspection: of seven-year-old 143-
44; of adolescent 265, 269, 272

Jack and Jill 185, 486
Jobs for adolescents 321, 324
Jokes 168
Junior high school 247-48
Junkyard park 206-07

equipment of for the home 384
separation from mother and 96-98
value of 93, 125, 138
Nursery tales 426

Obnoxious behavior of preadolescence
252-55
Oedipus complex. See Family
romance
Organizations: for children 152 (See
also Boy Scouts, Cub Scouts, Girl
Scouts, Indian Guides, Indian
Princesses; Sports); for parents
519-20
Overnight visits 208

Painting 88 (See also Arts and crafts)
Paperback books 184-85, 422
Parental guilt 6, 8
Parenthood (See also How to Parent)
lack of training in 334
practical mechanics of 9
Parents (See also Fathers; Mothers)
adjustment to adolescent child
287-92
as role models 9, 11, 211-12
attitudes of absorbed in middle-
childhood years 212
books for 503-20
drugs and. See Drugs and drug
culture
importance of: to infant 20; to
adolescent 342-43
jealousy of adolescent's friendships
344
middle-age crisis of 345-46
overemotionalism of 252-55
own youth less sophisticated than
today's 177-78
preadolescent and 227, 229, 242,
252-55, 285-319
rebellion against 229, 262
school and 179-97, 200
separation from 211-12, 229, 269,
278-79, 344, 347-48, 349-52 (See
also Friendships; Gang, world of
the; Gangs and clubs; Peer group)
sexuality of adolescents and 338-44
value system of questioned 229-30
vulnerable points attacked 175-76,
231, 233, 242, 345
Parties for children: books about
511-12

Peer group (See also Friendships;
Gang, world of the; Gangs and
clubs)
at various stages: preschool 98-100;
middle childhood 141, 142, 146,
150, 152, 158-59, 171-72; preadolescence 229-31, 244-45;
adolescence 262-63, 270, 281,323
books about for children 449
sexual information and 217
Personalized books 474
Pets 167, 380
Physical skills: parental help with 207
Plagemann, Bentz 204, 208-09, 226
Plastic bottles for toys 419
Play (See also Books; Games;
Records; Toys)
at various stages: infancy 21-23; first
adolescence 52, 383; preschool 83,
89-90
equipment: for large-muscle development 379-81, 382, 385; for small-
muscle development 385
field trips 391
indoor 154, 167; equipment for 380-
82, 382-84
musical instrument 157-58
outdoor 166-67; equipment for 379-
80, 382, 412-13
Playboy 249, 263, 275, 334
Poetry books for children 459-60
Pomeroy, Wardell 168, 249, 251, 513
Pop Warner football 152, 210
Popular Mechanics 185
Praise 76 (See also Criticism)
fathers and 216-17
Preadolescence 221-55 (See also
Eleven-, Twelve-, and Thirteen-
year-olds)
Pregnancy 8-9
psychological changes of wife during
9
risk of among adolescents 339-40
Preschool stage 77-132 (See also
Three-, Four-, and Five-year-olds)
books for 104, 429-60
records for 491-98
La Primera Preschool 125
Privacy: essential to adolescent
304-05
Problems: caused by parental
pressure 92
Property, concept of 152